T0335697

Introduction to Pattern Recognition and Machine Learning

IISc Lecture Notes Series

ISSN: 2010-2402

Introduction to Pattern Recognition and Machine Learning

M Narasimha Murty
V Susheela Devi

Indian Institute of Science, India

IISc
Press

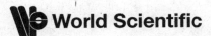

World Scientific

NEW JERSEY · LONDON · SINGAPORE · BEIJING · SHANGHAI · HONG KONG · TAIPEI · CHENNAI

Published by

World Scientific Publishing Co. Pte. Ltd.

5 Toh Tuck Link, Singapore 596224

USA office: 27 Warren Street, Suite 401-402, Hackensack, NJ 07601

UK office: 57 Shelton Street, Covent Garden, London WC2H 9HE

Library of Congress Cataloging-in-Publication Data
Murty, M. Narasimha.
   Introduction to pattern recognition and machine learning / by M Narasimha Murty &
V Susheela Devi (Indian Institute of Science, India).
      pages cm. -- (IISc lecture notes series, 2010–2402 ; vol. 5)
   ISBN 978-9814335454
   1. Pattern recognition systems. 2. Machine learning. I. Devi, V. Susheela. II. Title.
   TK7882.P3M87 2015
   006.4--dc23

2014044796

British Library Cataloguing-in-Publication Data
A catalogue record for this book is available from the British Library.

In-house Editors: Chandra Nugraha/Dipasri Sardar

Typeset by Stallion Press
Email: enquiries@stallionpress.com

Printed in Singapore

Series Preface

World Scientific Publishing Company - Indian Institute of Science Collaboration

IISc Press and WSPC are co-publishing books authored by world renowned scientists and engineers. This collaboration, started in 2008 during IISc's centenary year under a Memorandum of Understanding between IISc and WSPC, has resulted in the establishment of three Series: IISc Centenary Lectures Series (ICLS), IISc Research Monographs Series (IRMS), and IISc Lecture Notes Series (ILNS).

This pioneering collaboration will contribute significantly in disseminating current Indian scientific advancement worldwide.

The **"IISc Centenary Lectures Series"** will comprise lectures by designated Centenary Lecturers - eminent teachers and researchers from all over the world.

The **"IISc Research Monographs Series"** will comprise state-of-the-art monographs written by experts in specific areas. They will include, but not limited to, the authors' own research work.

The **"IISc Lecture Notes Series"** will consist of books that are reasonably self-contained and can be used either as textbooks or for self-study at the postgraduate level in science and engineering. The books will be based on material that has been class-tested for most part.

Editorial Board for the IISc Lecture Notes Series (ILNS):

Gadadhar Misra, Editor-in-Chief (gm@math.iisc.ernet.in)

Chandrashekar S Jog (jogc@mecheng.iisc.ernet.in)
Joy Kuri (kuri@cedt.iisc.ernet.in)
K L Sebastian (kls@ipc.iisc.ernet.in)
Diptiman Sen (diptiman@cts.iisc.ernet.in)
Sandhya Visweswariah (sandhya@mrdg.iisc.ernet.in)

Table of Contents

About the Authors

Professor M. Narasimha Murty completed his B.E., M.E., and Ph.D. at the Indian Institute of Science (IISc), Bangalore. He joined IISc as an Assistant Professor in 1984. He became a professor in 1996 and currently he is the Dean, Engineering Faculty at IISc. He has guided more than 20 doctoral students and several masters students over the past 30 years at IISc; most of these students have worked in the areas of Pattern Recognition, Machine Learning, and Data Mining. A paper co-authored by him on Pattern Clustering has around 9600 citations as reported by Google scholar. A team led by him had won the KDD Cup on the citation prediction task organized by the Cornell University in 2003. He is elected as a fellow of both the Indian National Academy of Engineering and the National Academy of Sciences.

Dr. V. Susheela Devi completed her PhD at the Indian Institute of Science in 2000. Since then she has worked as a faculty in the Department of Computer Science and Automation at the Indian Institute of Science. She works in the areas of Pattern Recognition, Data Mining, Machine Learning, and Soft Computing. She has taught the courses Data Mining, Pattern Recognition, Data Structures and Algorithms, Computational Methods of Optimization and Artificial Intelligence. She has a number of papers in international conferences and journals.

Preface

Pattern recognition (PR) is a classical area and some of the important topics covered in the books on PR include *representation of patterns*, *classification*, and *clustering*. There are different paradigms for pattern recognition including the *statistical* and *structural* paradigms. The structural or linguistic paradigm has been studied in the early days using *formal language tools*. Logic and automata have been used in this context. In linguistic PR, patterns could be represented as sentences in a logic; here, each pattern is represented using a set of primitives or sub-patterns and a set of operators. Further, a class of patterns is viewed as being generated using a grammar; in other words, a grammar is used to generate a collection of sentences or strings where each string corresponds to a pattern. So, the classification model is learnt using some grammatical inference procedure; the collection of sentences corresponding to the patterns in the class are used to learn the grammar. A major problem with the linguistic approach is that it is suited to dealing with structured patterns and the models learnt cannot tolerate noise.

On the contrary the statistical paradigm has gained a lot of momentum in the past three to four decades. Here, patterns are viewed as vectors in a multi-dimensional space and some of the optimal classifiers are based on *Bayes rule*. Vectors corresponding to patterns in a class are viewed as being generated by the underlying probability density function; Bayes rule helps in converting the *prior* probabilities of the classes into *posterior* probabilities using the likelihood values corresponding to the patterns given in each class. So, estimation schemes are used to obtain the probability density function of a class using the vectors corresponding to patterns in the class. There are several other classifiers that work with vector representation of patterns. We deal with statistical pattern recognition in this book.

Some of the simplest classification and clustering algorithms are based on matching or similarity between vectors. Typically, two patterns are similar if the distance between the corresponding vectors is lesser; Euclidean distance is popularly used. Well-known algorithms including the nearest neighbor classifier (NNC), K-nearest neighbor classifier (KNNC), and the K-Means Clustering algorithm are based on such distance computations. However, it is well understood in the literature that distance between two vectors may not be meaningful if the vectors are in large-dimensional spaces which is the case in several state-of-the-art application areas; this is because the distance between a vector and its nearest neighbor can tend to the distance between the pattern and its farthest neighbor as the dimensionality increases. This prompts the need to reduce the dimensionality of the vectors. We deal with the representation of patterns, different types of components of vectors and the associated similarity measures in Chapters 2 and 3.

Machine learning (ML) also has been around for a while; early efforts have concentrated on logic or formal language-based approaches. Bayesian methods have gained prominence in ML in the recent decade; they have been applied in both classification and clustering. Some of the simple and effective classification schemes are based on simplification of the Bayes classifier using some acceptable assumptions. Bayes classifier and its simplified version called the Naive Bayes classifier are discussed in Chapter 4. Traditionally there has been a contest between the frequentist approaches like the Maximum-likelihood approach and the Bayesian approach. In maximum-likelihood approaches the underlying density is estimated based on the assumption that the unknown parameters are deterministic; on the other hand the Bayesian schemes assume that the parameters characterizing the density are unknown random variables. In order to make the estimation schemes simpler, the notion of *conjugate pair* is exploited in the Bayesian methods. If for a given prior density, the density of a class of patterns is such that, the posterior has the same density function as the prior, then the prior and the class density form a conjugate prior. One of the most exploited in the context of clustering are the Dirichlet prior and the Multinomial class density which form a conjugate pair. For a variety of such conjugate pairs it is possible to show that when the datasets are large in size, there is no difference between the maximum-likelihood and the Bayesian estimates. So, it is important to examine the role of Bayesian methods in Big Data applications.

Some of the most popular classifiers are based on *support vector machines* (SVMs), *boosting*, and *Random Forest*. These are discussed in Chapter 5 which deals with classification. In large-scale applications like *text classification* where the dimensionality is large, linear SVMs and Random Forest-based classifiers are popularly used. These classifiers are well understood in terms of their theoretical properties. There are several applications where each pattern belongs to more than one class; soft classification schemes are required to deal with such applications. We discuss soft classification schemes in Chapter 6. Chapter 7 deals with several classical clustering algorithms including the *K-Means algorithm* and *Spectral clustering*. The so-called topic models have become popular in the context of *soft clustering*. We deal with them in Chapter 8.

Social Networks is an important application area related to PR and ML. Most of the earlier work has dealt with the structural aspects of the social networks which is based on their link structure. Currently there is interest in using the text associated with the nodes in the social networks also along with the link information. We deal with this application in Chapter 9.

This book deals with the material at an early graduate level. Beginners are encouraged to read our introductory book *Pattern recognition: An Algorithmic Approach* published by Springer in 2011 before reading this book.

M. Narasimha Murty
V. Susheela Devi
Bangalore, India

Chapter 1

Introduction

This book deals with *machine learning* (ML) and *pattern recognition* (PR). Even though humans can deal with both physical objects and abstract notions in day-to-day activities while making decisions in various situations, it is not possible for the computer to handle them directly. For example, in order to discriminate between a *chair* and a *pen*, using a machine, we cannot directly deal with the physical objects; we abstract these objects and store the corresponding representations on the machine. For example, we may represent these objects using features like *height*, *weight*, *cost*, and *color*. We will not be able to reproduce the physical objects from the respective representations. So, we deal with the representations of the patterns, not the patterns themselves. It is not uncommon to call both the patterns and their representations as patterns in the literature.

So, the input to the machine learning or pattern recognition system is abstractions of the input patterns/data. The output of the system is also one or more abstractions. We explain this process using the tasks of pattern recognition and machine learning. In pattern recognition there are two primary tasks:

1. **Classification:** This problem may be defined as follows:

   - There are C classes; these are $Class_1, Class_2, \ldots, Class_C$.
   - Given a set D_i of patterns from $Class_i$ for $i = 1, 2, \ldots, C$. $D = D_1 \cup D_2 \ldots \cup D_C$. D is called the training set and members of D are called labeled patterns because each pattern has a class label associated with it. If each pattern $X_j \in D$ is

d-dimensional, then we say that the patterns are d-dimensional or the set D is d-dimensional or equivalently the patterns lie in a d-dimensional space.

- A classification model $\mathcal{M}_c$ is *learnt* using the training patterns in D.
- Given an unlabeled pattern X, assign an appropriate class label to X with the help of $\mathcal{M}_c$.

It may be viewed as assigning a class label to an unlabeled pattern. For example, if there is a set of documents, D_p, from *politics* class and another set of documents, D_s, from *sports*, then classification involves assigning an unlabeled document d a label; equivalently assign d to one of two classes, *politics* or *sports*, using a classifier learnt from $D_p \cup D_s$.

There could be some more details associated with the definition given above. They are

- A pattern X_j may *belong to one or more classes*. For example, a document could be dealing with both *sports* and *politics*. In such a case we have multiple labels associated with each pattern. In the rest of the book we assume that a pattern has only one class label associated.
- It is possible to view the training data as a matrix D of size $n \times d$ where the number of training patterns is n and each pattern is d-dimensional. This view permits us to treat D both as a set and as a *pattern matrix*. In addition to d features used to represent each pattern, we have the class label for each pattern which could be viewed as the $(d+1)$th feature. So, a labeled set of n patterns could be viewed as $\{(X_1, C^1), (X_2, C^2), \ldots, (X_n, C^n)\}$ where $C^i \in \{Class_1, Class_2, \ldots, Class_C\}$ for $i = 1, 2, \ldots, n$. Also, the data matrix could be viewed as an $n \times (d+1)$ matrix with the $(d+1)$th column having the class labels.
- We evaluate the classifier learnt using a separate set of patterns, called *test set*. Each of the m test patterns comes with a class label called the *target label* and is labeled using the classifier learnt and this label assigned is the *obtained label*. A test pattern is correctly classified if the obtained label matches with the target

label and is *misclassified* if they mismatch. If out of m patterns, m_c are correctly classified then the % accuracy of the classifier is $\frac{100 \times m_c}{m}$.

- In order to build the classifier we use a subset of the training set, called the *validation set* which is kept aside. The classification model is learnt using the training set and the validation set is used as test set to tune the model or obtain the parameters associated with the model. Even though there are a variety of schemes for validation, K-fold cross-validation is popularly used. Here, the training set is divided into K equal parts and one of them is used as the validation set and the remaining $K-1$ parts form the training set. We repeat this process K times considering a different part as validation set each time and compute the accuracy on the validation data. So, we get K accuracies; typically we present the sample mean of these K accuracies as the overall accuracy and also show the sample standard deviation along with the mean accuracy. An extreme case of validation is to consider n-fold cross-validation where the model is built using $n-1$ patterns and is validated using the remaining pattern.

2. **Clustering:** Clustering is viewed as grouping a collection of patterns. Formally we may define the problem as follows:

   - There is a set, D, of n patterns in a d-dimensional space. A generally projected view is that these patterns are unlabeled.
   - Partition the set D into K blocks $C_1, C_2, \ldots, C_K$; C_i is called the ith cluster. This means $C_i \cap C_j = \phi$ and $C_i \neq \phi$ for $i \neq j$ and $i, j \in \{1, 2, \ldots, K\}$.
   - In classification an unlabeled pattern X is assigned to one of C classes and in clustering a pattern X is assigned to one of K clusters. A major difference is that classes have semantic class labels associated with them and clusters have syntactic labels. For example, *politics* and *sports* are *semantic labels*; we cannot arbitrarily relabel them. However, in the case of clustering we can change the labels arbitrarily, but consistently. For example, if D is partitioned into two clusters C_1 and C_2; so the clustering of D is $\pi_D = \{C_1, C_2\}$. So, we can relabel C_1

as C_2 and C_2 as C_1 consistently and have the same clustering (set $\{C_1, C_2\}$) because elements in a set are not ordered.

Some of the possible variations are as follows:

- In a partition a pattern can belong to only one cluster. However, in soft clustering a pattern may belong to more than one cluster. There are applications that require soft clustering.
- Even though clustering is viewed conventionally as partitioning a set of unlabeled patterns, there are several applications where clustering of labeled patterns is useful. One application is in efficient classification.

We illustrate the pattern recognition tasks using the two-dimensional dataset shown in Figure 1.1. There are *nine* points from class X labeled $X1, X2, \ldots, X9$ and 10 points from class O labeled $O1, O2, \ldots, O10$. It is possible to cluster patterns in each class separately. One such grouping is shown in Figure 1.1. The Xs are clustered into two groups and the Os are also clustered into two groups; there is no requirement that there be equal number of clusters in each class in general. Also we can deal with more than two classes. Different algorithms might generate different clusterings of each class. Here, we are using the class labels to cluster the patterns as we are clustering patterns in each class separately. Further we can represent

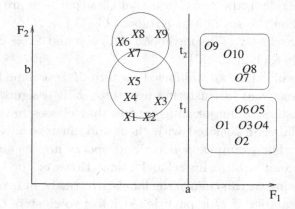

Figure 1.1.   Classification and clustering.

each cluster by its centroid, medoid, or median which helps in data compression; it is sometimes adequate to use the cluster representatives as training data so as to reduce the training effort in terms of both space and time. We discuss a variety of algorithms for clustering data in later chapters.

1. Classifiers: An Introduction

In order to get a feel for classification we use the same data points shown in Figure 1.1. We also considered two test points labeled t_1 and t_2. We briefly illustrate some of the prominent classifiers.

- **Nearest Neighbor Classifier (NNC)**: We take the nearest neighbor of the test pattern and assign the label of the neighbor to the test pattern. For the test pattern t_1, the nearest neighbor is $X3$; so, t_1 is classified as a member of X. Similarly, the nearest neighbor of t_2 is $O9$ and so t_2 is assigned to class O.
- **K-Nearest Neighbor Classifier (KNNC)**: We consider K-nearest neighbors of the test pattern and assign it to the class based on majority voting; if the number of neighbors from class X is more than that of class O, then we assign the test pattern to class X; otherwise to class O. Note that *NNC* is a special case of *KNNC* where $K = 1$.

  In the example, if we consider three nearest neighbors of t_1 then they are: X_3, X_2, and O_1. So majority are from class X and so t_1 is assigned to class X. In the case of t_2 the three nearest neighbors are: O_9, X_9, and X_8. Majority are from class X; so, t_2 is assigned to class X. Note that t_2 was assigned to class O based on *NNC* and to class X based on *KNNC*. In general different classifiers might assign the same test pattern to different classes.
- **Decision Tree Classifier (DTC)**: A DTC considers each feature in turn and identifies the best feature along with the value at which it splits the data into two (or more) parts which are as pure as possible. By purity here we mean as many patterns in the part are from the same class as possible. This process gets repeated level by level till some termination condition is satisfied; termination is affected based on whether the obtained parts at a level are totally

pure or nearly pure. Each of these splits is an *axis-parallel split* where the partitioning is done based on values of the patterns on the selected feature.

In the example shown in Figure 1.1, between features F_1 and F_2 dividing on F_1 based on value a gives two pure parts; here all the patterns having F_1 value below a and above a are put into two parts, the left and the right. This division is depicted in Figure 1.1. All the patterns in the left part are from class X and all the patterns in the right part are from class O. In this example both the parts are pure. Using this split it is easy to observe that both the test patterns t_1 and t_2 are assigned to class X.

- **Support Vector Machine (SVM)**: In a SVM, we obtain either a linear or a non-linear decision boundary between the patterns belonging to both the classes; even the nonlinear decision boundary may be viewed as a linear boundary in a high-dimensional space. The boundary is positioned such that it lies in the middle of the margin between the two classes; the SVM is learnt based on the maximization of the margin. Learning involves finding a weight vector W and a threshold b using the training patterns. Once we have them, then given a test pattern X, we assign X to the positive class if $W^t X + b > 0$ else to the negative class.

  It is possible to show that W is orthogonal to the decision boundary; so, in a sense W fixes the orientation of the decision boundary. The value of b fixes the location of the decision boundary; $b = 0$ means the decision boundary passes through the origin. In the example the decision boundary is the vertical line passing through a as shown in Figure 1.1. All the patterns labeled X may be viewed as negative class patterns and patterns labeled O are positive patterns. So, $W^t X + b < 0$ for all X and $W^t O + b > 0$ for all O. Note that both t_1 and t_2 are classified as negative class patterns.

We have briefly explained some of the popular classifiers. We can further categorize them as follows:

- **Linear and Non-linear Classifiers**: Both *NNC* and *KNNC* are non-linear classifiers as the decision boundaries are non-linear.

Similarly both *SVM* and *DTC* are linear in the example as the decision boundaries are linear. In general, *NNC* and *KNNC* are nonlinear. Even though Kernel *SVM* can be nonlinear, it may be viewed as a linear classifier in a high-dimensional space and *DTC* may be viewed as a piecewise linear classifier. There are other linear classifiers like the Naive Bayes Classifier (*NBC*) and Logistic Regression-based classifiers which are discussed in the later chapters.

- **Classification in High-dimensional Spaces:** Most of the current applications require classifiers that can deal with high-dimensional data; these applications include text classification, genetic sequence analysis, and multimedia data processing. It is difficult to get discriminative information using conventional distance based classifiers; this is because the nearest neighbor and farthest neighbors of a pattern will have the same distance values from any point in a high-dimensional space. So, *NNC* and *KNNC* are not typically used in high-dimensional spaces. Similarly, it is difficult to build a decision tree when there are a large number of features; this is because starting from the root node of a possibly tall tree we have to select a feature and its value for the best split out of a large collection of features at every internal node of the decision tree. Similarly, it becomes difficult to train a kernel *SVM* in a high-dimensional space.

    Some of the popular classifiers in high-dimensional spaces are linear *SVM*, *NBC*, and logistic regression-based classifier. Classifier based on random forest seems to be another useful classifier in high-dimensional spaces; random forest works well because each tree in the forest is built based on a low-dimensional subspace.

- **Numerical and Categorical Features:** In several practical applications we have data characterized by both numerical and categorical features. *SVM*s can handle only numerical data because they employ dot product computations. Similarly, *NNC* and *KNNC* work with numerical data where it is easy to compute neighbors based on distances. These classifiers require conversion of categorical features into numerical features appropriately before using them.

Classifiers like DTC and NBC are ideally suited to handle data described by both numerical and categorical features. In the case of DTC purity measures employed require only number of patterns from each class corresponding to the left and right parts of a split and both kinds of features can be split. In the case of NBC it is required to compute the frequency of patterns from a class corresponding to a feature value in the case of categorical features and likelihood value of the numerical features.

- **Class Imbalance:** In some of the classification problems one encounters *class imbalance*. This happens because some classes are not sufficiently represented in the training data. Consider, for example, classification of people into *normal* and *abnormal* classes based on their health status. Typically, the number of abnormal people could be much smaller than the number of normal people in a collection. In such a case, we have class imbalance. Most of the classifiers may fail to do well on such data. In the case of the abnormal (minority) class, frequency estimates go wrong because of small sample size. Also it may not be meaningful to locate the SVM decision boundary symmetrically between the two support planes; intuitively it is good to locate the decision boundary such that more patterns are accommodated in the normal (majority) class.

A preprocessing step may be carried out to balance the data that is not currently balanced. One way is to reduce the number of patterns in the majority class (undersampling). This is typically done by clustering patterns in the majority class and representing clusters by their prototypes; this step reduces a large collection of patterns in the majority class to a small number of cluster representatives. Similarly, *pattern synthesis* can be used to increase the number of patterns in the minority class (oversampling). A simple technique to achieve it is based on *bootstrapping*; here, we consider a pattern and obtain the centroid of its K nearest neighbors from the same class. This centroid forms an additional pattern; this process is repeated for all the patterns in the training dataset. So, if there are n training patterns to start with we will be able to generate additional n synthetic patterns which means bootstrapping over the entire training dataset will double the number of training patterns.

Bootstrapping may be explained using the data in Figure 1.1. Let us consider three nearest neighbors for each pattern. Let us consider $X1$; its 3 neighbors from the same class are $X2, X4$, and $X3$. Let $X1'$ be the centroid of these three points. In a similar manner we can compute bootstrapped patterns $X2', X3', \ldots, X9'$ corresponding to $X2, X3, \ldots, X9$ respectively. In a similar manner bootstrapped patterns corresponding to Os also can be computed. For example, $O2, O3, O6$ are the three neighbors of $O1$ and their centroid will give the bootstrapped pattern $O1'$. In a general setting we may have to obtain bootstrap patterns corresponding to both the classes; however to deal with the class imbalance problem, we need to bootstrap only the minority class patterns. There are several other ways to synthesize patterns in the minority class.

Preprocessing may be carried out either by decreasing the size of the training data of the majority class or by increasing the size of training data of the minority class or both.

- **Training and Classification Time:** Most of the classifiers involve a training phase; they learn a model and use it for classification. So, computation time is required to learn the model and for classification of the test patterns; these are called *training time* and *classification/test time* respectively. We give the details below:

  - **Training:** It is done only once using the training data. So, for real time classification applications classification time is more important than the training time.

    * *NNC*: There is no training done; in this sense it is the simplest model. However, in order to simplify testing/ classification a data structure is built to store the training data in a compact/compressed form.
    * *KNNC*: Here also there is no training time. However, using a part of the training data and the remaining part for validation, we need to fix a suitable value for K. Basically *KNNC* is more robust to noise compared to *NNC* as it considers more neighbors. So, smaller values of K make it noise-prone

whereas larger values of K, specifically $K = n$ makes it decide based on the *prior* probabilities of the classes or equivalently based on the frequency of patterns from each of the classes. There are variants of *KNNC* that take into account the distance between a pattern and each of the K neighbors; contribution of neighbors too far away from the pattern is ignored.

* *DTC*: The simple version of decision tree is built based on axis-parallel decisions. If there are n training patterns, each represented by a d-dimensional vector, then the effort involved in decision making at each node is of $O(d\,n\log n)$; this is because on each feature value we have to sort the n pattern values using $O(n\log n)$ time and there are d features. It gets larger as the value of d increases; further, the tree is built in a greedy manner as a feature selected leads to a split and it influences the later splits. A split made earlier cannot be redone. There are other possible ways of splitting a node; one possibility is to use an *oblique split* which could be considered as a split based on a linear combination of values of some selected features. However, oblique split based decision trees are not popular because they require time that is exponential in n.

* *SVM*: Training an SVM requires $O(n^3)$ time.

— **Testing:** Several researchers examine the testing/classification time more closely compared to the training time as training is performed only once whereas testing is carried out multiple times. The testing times for various classifiers are:

* *NNC*: It is linear in the number of patterns as for each test pattern we have to compute n distances, one for each training pattern.

* *KNNC*: It requires $O(nK)$ time for testing as it has to update the list of K neighbors.

* *DTC*: It requires $O(\log n)$ effort to classify a test pattern because it has to traverse over a path of the decision tree having at most n leaf nodes.

  * SVM: Linear SVM takes $O(d)$ time to classify a test pattern based on primarily a dot product computation.

- **Discriminative and Generative Models:** The classification model learnt is either probabilistic or deterministic. Typically deterministic models are called *discriminative* and the probabilistic models are called *generative*. Example classifiers are:

  - *Generative Models*: The Bayesian and Naive Bayes models are popular generative models. Here, we need to estimate the probability structure using the training data and use these models in classification. Because we estimate the underlying probability densities it is easy to generate patterns from the obtained probabilistic structures. Further, when using these models for classification, one can calculate the posterior probability associated with each of the classes given the test pattern. There are other generative models like the *Hidden Markov Models* and Gaussian mixture models which are used in classification.
  - *Discriminative Models*: Deterministic models including DTC, and SVM are examples of discriminative models. They typically can be used to classify a test pattern; they cannot reveal the associated probability as they are deterministic models.

- **Binary versus Multi-Class Classification:** Some of the classifiers are inherently suited to deal with two-class problems whereas the others can handle multi-class problems. For example, SVM and *AdaBoost* are ideally suited for two-class problems. Classifiers including NNC, $KNNC$, and DTC are generic enough to deal with multi-class problems. It is possible to combine binary classifier results to achieve multi-class classification. Two popular schemes for doing this are:

  1. *One versus the Rest*: If there are C classes then we build a binary classifier for each class as follows:
     - $Class_1$ versus the rest $Class_2 \cup Class_3 \cdots \cup Class_C$
     - $Class_2$ versus the rest $Class_1 \cup Class_3 \cdots \cup Class_C$
     $\vdots$
     - $Class_C$ versus the rest $Class_1 \cup Class_2 \cdots \cup Class_{C-1}$

There are a total of C binary classifiers and the test pattern is assigned a class label based on the output of these classifiers. Ideally the test pattern will belong to one class $Class_i$; so the corresponding binary classifier will assign it to $Class_i$ and the remaining $C - 1$ classifiers assign it to the rest. One problem with this approach is that each of the binary classifiers has to deal with class imbalance; this is because in each binary classification problem we have patterns of one of the classes labeled positive and the patterns of the remaining $C - 1$ classes are labeled negative. So, there could be class imbalance with the positive class being the minority class and the negative class being the majority class.

2. *One versus One:* Here out of the C classes two classes are considered at a time to form a binary classifier. There are a total of $\frac{C(C-1)}{2}$ choices and as many binary classifiers to be built. These are:

   − $Class_1$ versus $Class_2, Class_1$ versus $Class_3, \ldots, Class_1$ versus $Class_C$
   − $Class_2$ versus $Class_3, Class_2$ versus $Class_4, \ldots, Class_2$ versus $Class_C$
     $\vdots$
   − $Class_{C-1}$ versus $Class_C$

   A pattern is assigned to class C_i based on a majority voting.

- **Number of Classes:** Most of the classifiers work well when the number of classes is small. Specific possibilities are:

  − **Number of Classes C is Small:** Classifiers that work well are

    * SVM: It is inherently a binary classifier; so, it is ideally suited for dealing with a small number of classes.
    * NBC: It can estimate the associated probabilities accurately when the data is dense and it is more likely when the number of classes is small.
    * DTC: It works well when the number of features is small. In such a case we cannot have a large number of classes because if there are C leaf nodes in a binary tree then the number

of internal nodes (decision nodes) will be $C - 1$; each such node corresponds to a split on a feature. If each feature is used for splitting at m nodes on an average and there are l features then $l \times m \geq C - 1$; So, $C \leq l \times m + 1$. As a consequence Random Forest also is more suited when the number of classes is small.

* **Bayes Classifier:** For a pattern if the posterior probabilities are equal for all the classes then the probability of error is $1 - \frac{1}{C} = \frac{C-1}{C}$ and if there is one class with posterior probability 1 and the remaining $C - 1$ classes having a zero posterior probability then the probability of error is zero. So, the probability of error is bounded by $0 \leq P(error) \leq \frac{C-1}{C}$. So, if $C = 2$, then the upper bound is $\frac{1}{2}$. If $C \to \infty$ then $P(error)$ is upper bounded by 1. So, as C changes the bound gets effected.

− **Number of Classes C is Large:** Some of the classifiers that are relevant are

* *KNNC*: It can work well when the number of neighbors considered is large and the number of training patterns n is large. Theoretically it is possible to show that it can be optimal as K and n tend to ∞, K slower than n. So, it can deal with a large number of classes provided each class has a sufficient number of training patterns. However, the classification time could be large.

* *DTC*: It is inherently a multi-class classifier like the *KNNC*. So, it can work well when $n > l \times m + 1 > C$.

• **Classification of Multi-label Data:** It is possible that each pattern can have more than one class label associated with it. For example, in a collection of documents to be classified into either *sports* or *politics*, it is possible that one or more documents have both the labels associated; in such a case we have multi-label classification problem which is different from the multi-class classification discussed earlier. In a multi-class case, the number of classes is more than two but each pattern has only one class label associated with it.

One solution to the multi-label problem is to consider each subset of the set of the C classes as a label; in such a case we have again a multi-class classification problem. However, the number of possible class labels is exponential in the number of classes. For example, in the case of two class set {sports, politics}, the possible labels correspond to the subsets {sports}, {politics}, and {sports, politics}. Even though we have two classes, we can have three class labels here. In general for a C class problem, the number of class labels obtained this way is $2^C - 1$. A major problem with this process is that we need to look for a classifier that can deal with a large number of class labels.

Another solution to the multi-label problem is based on using a soft computing tool for classification; in such a case we may have the same pattern belonging to different classes with different membership values, based on using fuzzy sets.

2. An Introduction to Clustering

In clustering we group a collection, D, of patterns into some K clusters; patterns in each cluster are similar to each other. There are a variety of clustering algorithms. Broadly they may be characterized in the following ways:

- **Partitional versus Hierarchical Clustering:** In partitional clustering a partition of the dataset is obtained. In the hierarchical clustering a hierarchy of partitions is generated. Some of the specific properties of these kinds of algorithms are:

  - *Partitional Clustering:* Here, the dataset D is divided into K clusters. It is achieved such that some criterion function is optimized. If we consider the set $\{X_1, X_2, X_3\}$ then the possibilities for two clusters are:
    1. $C_1 = \{X_1, X_2\}; \ C_2 = \{X_3\}$.
    2. $C_1 = \{X_1, X_3\}; \ C_2 = \{X_2\}$.
    3. $C_1 = \{X_2, X_3\}; \ C_2 = \{X_1\}$.

    So, the number of partitions of a dataset of three patterns is 3. This number grows very fast as the set size and number of clusters increase. For example, to cluster a small dataset of 19 patterns into 4 clusters, the number of possible partitions is approximately 11,259,666,000. So, exhaustive enumeration of all possible partitions to find out the best partition is not realistic. So, each clustering algorithm is designed to ensure that only an appropriate subset of the set of all possible partitions is explored by the algorithm.

For example, one of the most popular partitional clustering algorithms is the K-means algorithm. It partitions the given dataset into K clusters or equivalently it obtains a K-partition of the dataset. It starts with an arbitrary initial K-partition and keeps on refining the partition iteratively till a convergence condition is satisfied. The K-means algorithm minimizes the *squared-error criterion*; it generates K spherical clusters which are characterized by some kind of tightness. Specifically it aims to minimize the sum over all the clusters the sum of squared distances of points in each cluster from its centroid; here each cluster is characterized and represented by its centroid. So, by its nature the algorithm is inherently restricted to generate spherical clusters. However, based on the type of the distance function used, it is possible to generate different cluster shapes. For example, it can generate the clusters depicted in Figure 1.1.

Another kind of partitional algorithm uses a threshold on the distance between a pattern and a cluster representative to see whether the pattern can be assigned to the cluster or not. If the distance is below the threshold then the pattern is assigned to the cluster; otherwise a new cluster is initiated with the pattern as its representative. The first cluster is represented by the first pattern in the collection. Here, threshold plays an important role; if it is too small then there will be a larger number of clusters and if it is large then there will be a smaller number of clusters. A simple algorithm that employs threshold as specified above is the leader algorithm; *BIRCH* is another popular clustering algorithm that employs a threshold for clustering.

 — *Hierarchical Clustering*: In hierarchical clustering we generate partitions of size 1 (one cluster) to partitions of n clusters while clustering a collection of n patterns. They are either agglomerative or divisive. In the case of agglomerative algorithms we start with each pattern in a cluster and keep merging most similar pair of clusters from $n - 1$ clusters; this process of merging the most similar pair of clusters is repeated to get $n - 2, n - 3, \ldots, 2$, and 1 clusters. In the case of divisive algorithms we start with one cluster having all the patterns and divide it into two clusters based on some notion of separation between the resulting pair of clusters; the cluster with maximum size out of these clusters is split into two clusters to realize three clusters. this splitting process goes on as we get $4, 5, \ldots, n - 1, n$ clusters.

A difficulty with these hierarchical algorithms is that they need to compute and store a proximity matrix of size $O(n^2)$. So, they may not be suited to deal with large-scale datasets.

- **Computational Requirements:** Computational requirements of the clustering algorithms include time and space requirements.

  - *Computation Time*: The conventional hierarchical algorithms require $O(n^2)$ to compute distances between pairs of points. It is possible to show that the K-means clustering algorithm requires $O(nKlm)$ where K is the number of clusters, l is the number of features, and m is the number of iterations of the algorithm. The Leader algorithm is the simplest computationally; it requires one scan of the dataset.
  - *Storage Space*: Hierarchical algorithms require $O(n^2)$ space to store the proximity matrix which is used in clustering. The K-means algorithm requires $O(Kl)$ to store the K cluster centers each in l-dimensional space; in addition we need to store the dataset which requires $O(nl)$ space. The leader algorithm has space requirements similar to the K-means algorithm.

- **Local Optimum:** Several partitional clustering algorithms including the K-means algorithm can lead to a local minimum of the associated criterion function. For example, the K-means algorithm may reach the local minimum value of the squared error criterion function if the initial partition is not properly chosen. Even though it is possible to show equivalence between the K-means type of algorithms and threshold based clustering algorithms, there may not be an explicit criterion function that is optimized by the leader like algorithms.

It is possible to show the equivalence between some of the hierarchical algorithms with their graph-theoretic counterparts. For example, the agglomerative algorithm can merge two clusters in different ways:

1. *Single-Link Algorithm (SLA)*: Here two clusters C_p and C_q are merged if the distance between a pair of points $X_i \in C_p$ and $X_j \in C_q$ is the smallest among all possible pairs of clusters. It can group points into clusters when two or more clusters have the same mean but different covariance; such clusters are called *concentric clusters*. It is more versatile than the K-means algorithm. It corresponds to the construction of the Minimal Spanning Tree of the data where an edge weight is based on the distance between the points representing the end vertices and clusters are realized by ignoring the link with the maximum weight. Here, a minimum spanning tree of the data is obtained. However, the algorithm is bound to generate a minimal spanning tree where the minimal spanning tree is a spanning tree with the sum of the edge weights being a minimum; a spanning tree is a tree that connects all the nodes.

2. *Complete-Link Algorithm (CLA)*: Here, two clusters C_p and C_q are merged if the distance between them is minimum; the distance between the two clusters is defined by the maximum of the distance between points $X_i \in C_p$ and $X_j \in C_q$ for all X_i and X_j. This algorithm corresponds to the generation of completely connected components.

3. *Average-Link Algorithm (ALA)*: Here, two clusters C_p and C_q are merged based on average distance between pairs of points where one is from C_p and the other is from C_q.

- **Representing Clusters:** The most popularly used cluster representative is the centroid or the sample mean of the points in the cluster. It may be defined as

$$\mu_C = \frac{1}{|C|} \sum_{i=1}^{|C|} X_i.$$

For example, in Figure 1.1, for the points $X6, X7, X8, X9$ in one of the clusters, the centroid is located inside the circle having these four patterns. The advantage of representing a cluster using its centroid is that it may be centrally located and it is the point from which the sum of the squared distances to all the points in the cluster is minimum. However, it is not helpful in achieving robust clustering; this is because if there is an outlier in the dataset then the centroid may be shifted away from a majority of the points in the cluster. The centroid may shift further as the outlier becomes more and more prominent. So, centroid is not a good representative in the presence of outliers. Another representative that could be used is the *medoid* of the cluster; medoid is the most centrally located point that belongs to the cluster. So, medoid cannot be significantly affected by a small number of points in the cluster whether they are outliers or not.

Another issue that emerges in this context is to decide whether each cluster has a single representative or multiple representatives.

- **Dynamic Clustering:** Here, we obtain a partition of the data using a set, D_n, of patterns. Let the partition be π_n where n is the number of patterns in D. Now we would like to add or delete a pattern from D. So, the possibilities are:
  - *Addition of a Pattern*: Now the question is whether we can reflect the addition of a pattern to D_n in the resulting clustering by updating the partition π_n to π_{n+1} without re-clustering the already clustered data. In other words, we would like to use the $n + 1$th pattern and π_n to get π_{n+1}; this means we generate π_{n+1} without reexamining the patterns in D_n. Such a clustering paradigm may be called *incremental clustering*. This paradigm is useful in stream data mining. One problem with incremental clustering is *order dependence*; for different orderings of the input patterns in D, we obtain different partitions.
  - *Deletion of a Pattern*: Even though incremental clustering where additional patterns can be used to update the current partition without re-clustering the earlier seen data is popular, deletion of patterns from the current set and its impact on the partition is not examined in a detailed manner in the literature.

By *dynamic clustering*, we mean updating the partition after either addition or deletion of patterns without re-clustering.

- **Detection of Outliers:** An outlier is a pattern that differs from the rest of the patterns significantly. It can be either an out of range or within range pattern. Outliers are typically seen as abnormal patterns which differ from the rest. Typically, they are detected based on either looking for singleton clusters or by using some density based approach. Outliers are patterns that lie in sparse regions.

  In a simplistic scenario clustering could be used to detect outliers because outliers are elements of small size clusters. Also there are density-based clustering algorithms that categorize each pattern as a core pattern or a boundary pattern and keep merging the patterns to form clusters till some boundary patterns are left out as noise or outliers. So, clustering has been a popularly used tool in outlier detection.

- **Missing Values:** It is possible that some feature values in a subset of patterns are missing. For example, in a power system it may not be possible to get current and voltage values at every node; sometimes it may not be possible to have access to a few nodes. Similarly while building a recommender system we may not have access to the reviews of each of the individuals on a subset of products being considered for possible recommendation. Also in evolving social networks we may have links between only a subset of the nodes.

  In conventional pattern recognition, missing values are estimated using a variety of schemes. Some of them are:

  - Cluster the patterns using the available feature values. If the pattern X_i has its jth feature value x_{ij} missing then

  $$x_{ij} = \sum_{p=1}^{|C|} x_{pj},$$

  where C is the cluster to which X_i belongs.
  - Find the nearest neighbor of X_i from the given dataset using the available feature values; let the nearest neighbor be X_q.

Then

$$x_{ij} = x_{qj} + \delta,$$

where δ is a small quantity used to perturb the value of x_{qj} to obtain the missing value.

In social networks we have missing links which are predicted using some link prediction algorithm. If X_i and X_j are two nodes in the network represented as a graph, then similarity between X_i and X_j is computed. Based on the similarity value, whether a link is possible or not is decided. A simple local similarity measure may be explained as follows:

- Let $NNSet(X_i) =$ Set of nodes adjacent to X_i,
- Let $NNSet(X_j) =$ Set of nodes adjacent to X_j,
- Similarity-Score $(X_i, X_j) = |NNSet(X_i) \cap NNSet(X_j)|$.

Here, the similarity between two nodes is defined as the number of neighbors common to X_i and X_j. Based on the similarity values we can rank the missing links in decreasing order of the similarity; we consider a subset of the missing links in the rank order to link the related nodes.

- **Clustering Labeled Data:** Conventionally clustering is associated with grouping of unlabeled patterns. But clustering may be viewed as data compression; so, we can group labeled patterns and represent clusters by their representatives. Such a provision helps us in realizing efficient classifiers as explained earlier using the data in Figure 1.1.

    Clustering has been effectively used in combination with a variety of classifiers. Most popularly clustering has been used along with NNC and $KNNC$ to reduce the classification time. It has been used to improve the speed of training SVM to be used in classification; clustering is used in training both linear SVM and nonlinear SVM. The most popular classifier that exploits clustering is the *Hidden Markov Model* (*HMM*).

- **Clustering Large Datasets:** Large datasets are typically encountered in several machine learning applications including *bio-informatics, software engineering, text classification, video analytics, health, education* and *agriculture*. So, the role of clustering to compress data in these applications is very natural. In data mining, one generates abstractions from data and clustering is an ideal tool for obtaining a variety of such abstractions; in fact clustering has gained prominence after the emergence of data mining.

  Some of the prominent directions for clustering large datasets are:

  — *Incremental Clustering*: Algorithms like *Leader clustering* and *BIRCH* are incremental algorithms for clustering. They require to scan the dataset only once. Sometimes additional processing is done to avoid order dependence.

  — *Divide-and-conquer Clustering*: Here, we divide the dataset of n patterns into p blocks so that each block has approximately $\frac{n}{p}$ patterns. It is possible to cluster patterns in each block separately and represent them by a small number of patterns. These clusters are merged by clustering their representatives using another clustering step and affecting the resulting cluster labels on all the patterns. It is important to observe that *Map-Reduce* is a divide-and-conquer approach that could be used to solve a variety of problems including clustering.

  — *Compress and Cluster*: It is possible to represent the data using a variety of abstraction generation schemes and then cluster the data. Some possibilities are:

    * *Hybrid clustering*: Here, using an inexpensive clustering algorithm we compress the data and cluster the representatives using an expensive algorithm. Such an approach is called hybrid clustering.

    * *Sampling*: The dataset size is reduced by selecting a sample of the large dataset and then cluster the sample but not the original dataset.

    * *Lossy and non-lossy compression*: In several applications it is adequate to deal with the compressed data. Compression may

be achieved by using a variety of lossy and non-lossy compression schemes; then clustering is performed on the compressed data. Some of the non-lossy compression schemes include run-length coding, and Huffman coding. Similarly, lossy compression schemes include representing the data using frequent itemsets, using some dimensionality reduction techniques.

* *Use a compact data structure*: Some of the data structures that are used in clustering are *Cluster Feature Tree* (*CF-Tree*), *Frequent Pattern Tree* (*FP-Tree*), and *Inverted Files*. BIRCH constructs *CF*-tree using a single dataset scan and uses it to reflect the clustering. *FP*-tree is constructed using two dataset scans and implicitly stores all the frequent itemsets. The inverted file structure is very popular in information retrieval.

- **Soft Clustering:** Most of the current day applications require soft clustering where a pattern belongs to more than one cluster. There are a variety of soft clustering approaches; these include:

1. *Fuzzy clustering*: Here, a pattern is assigned to different clusters with different membership values. It is originally designed to deal with linguistic uncertainty. If the sum of the membership values of a pattern to different clusters adds up to 1, then it is fuzzy-set theoretic clustering; otherwise we have possibilistic clustering. Fuzzy K-means is one of the most popular soft clustering algorithms.

2. *Rough clustering*: Here, patterns are divided into equivalence classes based on the notion of discernibility; if two or more patterns are not discernible then they belong to the same equivalence class. Each cluster is described using a lower and an upper approximation. All the equivalence classes that form subsets of the cluster form the *lower approximation* and all the equivalence classes that overlap with the cluster form the *upper approximation*. A pattern definitely belongs to a cluster if the pattern is in the lower approximation of the cluster and a pattern may belong to two or more clusters if it is in the upper approximation of a cluster.

3. *Neural networks*: In a neural network used for clustering each output node indicates a cluster to which a pattern belongs. Typically, we employ a soft output function in the interval $[0, 1]$; so, each output node might indicate some degree to which the input pattern might belong to the corresponding cluster. Using such an output structure it is possible to realize some kind of soft clustering.

4. *Evolutionary algorithms*: In clustering using the evolutionary algorithms, each element of the population corresponds to a clustering. If each string/element of the population is interpreted as corresponding to K cluster centroids/representatives, then each pattern may belong to more than one cluster based on its closeness (similarity) to the centroids of various clusters.

- **Topic Models:** Topic is defined as a probability distribution over words/terms in a collection. For example, in a small collection of short documents let the terms and corresponding probability of occurrence be as shown in Table 1.1. This may be viewed as a topic *cricket* where the terms shown in the table have occurred. Note that if we use it in an unsupervised setting, then we have to provide the topic its name manually. For example, we cannot automatically assign the label *cricket* to the probability mass function shown in Table 1.1. Also, topic as we understand it intuitively corresponds to some semantic label. So, it may be good to use the name *probability distribution* instead of *topic*.

Table 1.1.   A probability distribution.

Term	Probability
Cricket	0.4
Ball	0.2
Bat	0.15
Umpire	0.12
Wicket	0.08
Run	0.05

Another notion that could be used to describe a cluster is *concept*. Typically, concept is a logical description; a popular usage is conjunction of disjunctions. For example, $\left(f_1 = v_1^1 \vee v_1^3\right) \wedge \left(f_2 = v_2^2 \vee v_2^4 \vee v_2^5\right) \cdots \wedge \left(f_l = v_l^1\right)$ may be viewed as a concept; here f_i is the ith feature and the value v_i^j corresponds to jth element of the domain of feature f_i. We have assumed that the domain has a finite set of values for the sake of simplicity.

There are topic models that are popularly used in document clustering and *Latent Dirichlet Allocation* (*LDA*) is one of the recent models.

— *LDA*: It is a model where each document is made up of at most K clusters/topics. Each topic is an assignment of probabilities to words in the collection. Given the document collection or the words in the collection, the problem is to obtain the latent clusters/topics and use them to describe the documents. Each topic is viewed as a multinomial distribution and by using the conjugate prior in the form of a Dirichlet, we get the posterior also to be Dirichlet. It is possible to view this process as factorizing the document matrix. There are some simpler models like *Probabilistic Latent Semantic Indexing* (*PLSI*) that can be used as modeling the collection of documents. It is possible to show equivalence between *PLSI* and Non-negative matrix factorization (*NMF*).
— *NMF*: Here, the problem is to factorize the document-term matrix A into 2 factors $B(>0)$ and $C(>0)$ such that

$$\|A - BC\|_F^2 \text{ is minimized.}$$

It is possible to view these models as performing soft clustering; this is because a document may belong to more than one topic.

• **Knowledge-based clustering:** Even though clustering is viewed as an *unsupervised learning paradigm*, there is a well-known theorem called the *theorem of the ugly duckling* which shows that we need to use extra-logical information to discriminate a pair of patterns from another pair based on the similarity between the pairs. In short, it is not possible to have unsupervised classification; it is essential to use knowledge in the process of clustering.

There are knowledge-based clustering schemes that are based on the notion of concept; specifically they are called conceptual clustering methods. Also Wikipedia knowledge is used in clustering documents semantically to get more meaningful clusters. In the conceptual clustering framework we get both the clusters and their descriptions using concepts. Note that clustering based on topic models also generates cluster descriptions in the form of topics.

- **Cluster Validity:** One of the evasive features of clustering is the notion of *cluster validity*. If we get a clustering of the given dataset then we would like to know whether the resultant clustering and the number of clusters is acceptable. A host of cluster validity indices are proposed and used to measure the quality of clustering. However, there is a strong opinion that these measures are monotonic. That means as the number of clusters is increased the validity measure will monotonically increase or decrease. For example, if we consider the squared error criterion then when the number of clusters is 1 the value of the squared error is maximum and when the number of clusters is n then the squared error is minimum (zero). Further, an index suitable for one type of clusters may not be good to deal with other type of clusters. For example, the squared error is good for evaluating spherical clusters.

3. Machine Learning

We have seen the two important pattern recognition tasks which are classification and clustering. Another task is *dimensionality reduction* which is required in both classification and clustering. Some of the other tasks in machine learning are *regression* or curve fitting, *ranking*, and *summarization*. We deal with them in this section.

- **Dimensionality reduction**

Feature extraction/selection is almost an integral part of both classification and clustering. In classification we need to reduce the dimensionality to ensure that the classifiers work well and in clustering also we need to reduce the dimensionality to reduce the clustering time and space requirements of the algorithms. So, typically a preprocessing step is carried out to reduce the dimensionality. Some of the associated issues are:

- *Distance between patterns*: In both classification and clustering we need to compute distance between pairs of patterns. For example, in *NNC* the test pattern is classified based on the class label of its nearest neighbor which is obtained based on some type of distance. Similarly, clustering using the K-means algorithm requires distance between a pattern and each of the K centroids. These distances may not be meaningful if the patterns are represented in a high-dimensional space. So, we need to reduce the dimensionality.
- *Feature selection*: Typically, a data matrix of size $n \times l$ is used to represent n patterns in a l-dimensional space or using l features. One way of reducing the dimensionality is by selecting a subset of the given set of features or select some d out of l features. This selection is done in different ways.

  - *Filter methods*: In these methods features are evaluated based on some criterion function that is independent of the classifier. One popular function that is effectively used in text analysis is the *mutual information*. It measures some kind of information that is mutual between a class and a feature. Based on the mutual information the features are ranked and some d top ranked features out of the given l features are used to learn the classifier. So, we may use the class labels but not the classifier in selecting features here.
  - *Wrapper methods*: Here, features are selected based on the classifier used. For each subset of features one can build the classifier and it is used to evaluate the quality of the selected feature set. An example is the genetic algorithm-based feature selection; each string in a population corresponds to a subset of the features. Specifically, each string is of l bits corresponding to l given features. A 1 in the ith position corresponds to selecting the ith feature and a 0 means the ith feature is not selected. So, each string corresponds to a subset. The *fitness* of the string is

obtained by using the classifier built using the selected features; so, if the selected subset leads to a higher classification accuracy then the fitness of the corresponding string is high.

— *Embedded methods*: Here, the subset of features is obtained as a consequence of building the classifier. For example, in building a DTC, the decision tree built will have features at different internal or decision nodes of the tree. Features used at the root and other top nodes of the decision tree are relatively more important than those at the other nodes. So, selection of features can be done using the decision tree; top level features are selected. Similarly, in a linear *SVM* the learning involves obtaining a weight vector W and a threshold b. It is possible to use the entries of W to rank features; if the value is positive and large, then the presence of the feature will make the pattern move towards the positive class and a large negative value will mean that the pattern having the feature will more likely be a negative class pattern. So, one can retain features that have large corresponding components in W and ignore the remaining features. So, both *DTC* and *SVM* may be viewed as providing features in an embedded manner for selection.

• *Feature extraction*: Here, we extract new features that are either linear or nonlinear combinations of the given features and the extracted features are used in Pattern recognition. Some of the extraction schemes are:

— *Principal components*: Principal components are vectors in the directions of maximum variance. They are computed by using the *eigenvectors of the data covariance* matrix. If there are l features then the covariance matrix is of size $l \times l$ and is a symmetric matrix. So, the eigenvalues are real and eigenvectors are orthogonal to each other. The first principal component is the eigenvector corresponding to the maximum eigenvalue. The next principal component is the eigenvector of the covariance matrix corresponding to the next largest eigenvalue and so on. This is an unsupervised learning scheme and so can be used both in classification and clustering. In text mining it is popularly used under the name *latent semantic analysis.*

— *Random projections*: Here, the rows of $n \times l$ data matrix are projected to a d-dimensional space by multiplying the data matrix with a matrix of size $l \times d$ where $d << l$. The entries of the $l \times d$ matrix are randomly selected based on some distributional assumptions. It is possible to show that the projection to the lower dimensional space will protect the distance and dot product between a pair of patterns.

— *Clustering and feature extraction*: Because we know that the row-rank of a matrix is equal to its column-rank, there is an implicit relation between clustering and feature extraction. If we consider the soft clustering schemes based on matrix factorization including *latent semantic indexing* (*LSI*), *probabilistic latent semantic indexing* (*PLSI*), *LDA* and *NMF*, then there is linear feature extraction scheme corresponding to each of them. For example, consider the factorization of matrix A of size $n \times l$ into matrices B of size $n \times d$ and C of size $d \times l$; the B matrix describes d topics/clusters. Equivalently we can view them as d features and the B matrix gives the description of the n patterns in the d or extracted feature space. So, implicitly we have feature extraction in these cases; each factorization is based on a different optimization problem and so can give rise to extracting different types of features.

● **Function learning:** In classification, we assign a pattern to one of a finite number of classes. However, in function learning, we may need to assign real values to patterns. For example, the value of a share of a company could be given as a positive real number; the predicted temperature on a day in the summer at a geographical location or the predicted intensity of earthquake are all positive real numbers. In such cases we learn functions using the training data and use the function to predict values in the future. Learning classification function or a classifier may be viewed as a special case of function learning. So, there are a host of techniques that are used both in classification and general function learning. For example, decision trees, *SVM*s, and AdaBoost-based schemes have been successfully used in both classification and regression (general function learning).

- **Ranking:** Here, instead of classifying we would like to get some kind of probability with which we can assign a pattern to a class. For example, a search engine provides as a output ranked set of snippets corresponding to a query entered by the user. Here, the relevant documents based on some similarity measure are shown in a ranked fashion; top ones are more relevant to the query.

- **Summarization:** When the data is large we would like to have a summary or abstraction of the data instead of all the details. Different abstractions possible are: cluster representatives, decision tree, set of rules, and a concise abstract of one or more documents.

In this book we deal with the following topics:

1. **Types of Data:** We consider both the categorical and numerical features and their characterization along with some of the associated proximity measures.
2. **Feature Extraction and Feature Selection:** Dimensionality reduction is an important and integral part of pattern recognition and machine learning tasks. Here, we discuss some of the important schemes for feature selection and extraction.
3. **Bayesian Learning:** Bayesian approaches were popular in pattern recognition. In machine learning, Bayesian approaches are gaining prominence in both classification and clustering. We discuss *Naive Bayes classifier* and the notion of *conjugate prior* and its role in estimation of densities.
4. **Classification:** We consider some of the important classifiers including *KNNC*, *SVM*, *logistic regression*, *random forests*, and *classification in high-dimensional spaces*. We also discuss some of the modifications to these classifiers.
5. **Soft Classification:** Soft classification techniques such as fuzzy classifiers, rough classifiers, classification using evolutionary strategies and neural networks are discussed.
6. **Data Clustering:** Clustering is a compression tool; it is used as a preprocessor to handle efficient classification. We consider algorithms for both partitional and hierarchical clustering. We also

discuss incremental algorithms like Leader and BIRCH. We consider clustering algorithms that are used on graph datasets. We deal with the role of frequent itemsets in clustering and combinations of outputs generated by clustering algorithms. The role of knowledge-based clustering, labeled clustering, and divide-and-conquer clustering are discussed.

7. **Soft Clustering:** Soft clustering has become an important area of research in machine learning. In addition to the conventional paradigms, the role of topic models in realizing soft clusters and their descriptions is examined.

8. **Social and Information Networks:** We consider the application of various techniques discussed in *social networks*. Specifically, we consider some of the important concepts in analyzing social networks including *community detection, modularity, link prediction*, and *topic models*.

Research Ideas

1. What are the primary differences between *pattern recognition, machine learning*, and *data mining*. Which tasks are important in each of these areas?

Relevant References

(a) J. Han, M. Kamber and J. Pei, *Data Mining*: *Concepts and Techniques*, Third Edition. New York: Morgan Kauffmann, 2011.

(b) K. Murphy, *Machine Learning: A Probabilistic Perspective*. Cambridge, MA: MIT Press, 2012.

(c) M. N. Murty and V. Susheela Devi, *Pattern Recognition*: *An Algorithmic Approach*. London: Springer, 2011.

2. How do we evaluate classifiers performance? What is the best validation scheme? How to deal with class imbalance?

Relevant References

(a) V. Lopez, A. Fernandez and F. Herrera, On the importance of the validation technique for classification with imbalanced datasets: Addressing covariate shift when data is skewed. *Information Sciences*, 257:1–13, 2014.

(b) Q.-Y. Yin, J.-S. Zhang, C.-X. Zhang and N.-N. Ji, A novel selective ensemble algorithm for imbalanced data classification based on exploratory under-sampling. *Mathematical Problems in Engineering*, 2014.

(c) Y. Sun, A. K. C. Wong and M. S. Kamel, Classification of imbalanced data: A review. *International Journal of Pattern Recognition and Artificial Intelligence*, 23:687–719, 2009.

3. How do we represent clusters? Is it essential that there should be one representative per cluster? Is it possible to solve it using an optimization scheme?

Relevant References

(a) D. Bhattacharya, S. Seth and T.-H. Kim, Social network analysis to detect inherent communities based on constraints. *Applied Mathematics and Information Sciences*, 8:1–12, 2014.

(b) W. Hamalainen, V. Kumpulainen and M. Mozgovoy, Evaluation of clustering methods for adaptive learning systems. In *Artificial Intelligence in Distance Education*, U. Kose and D. Koc (eds.). Hershey, PA: IGI Global, 2014, pp. 237–260.

(c) P. Franti, M. Rezaei and Q. Zhao, Centroid index: Cluster level similarity measure. *Pattern Recognition*, 47:3034–3045, 2014.

4. How do we compute similarity between a pair of patterns that employ both numerical and categorical features? Can distance/dot product based methods work well with such patterns?

Relevant References

(a) Y.-M. Cheung and H. Jia, Categorical-and-numerical-attribute data clustering based on a unified similarity metric without knowing cluster number. *Pattern Recognition*, 46:2228–2238, 2013.

(b) I. W. Tsang, J. T. Kwok and P.-M. Cheung, Core vector machines: Fast SVM training on very large data sets. *JMLR*, 6:363–392, 2005.

(c) A. Ahmad and G. Brown, Random projection random discretization ensembles — ensembles of linear multivariate decision trees. *IEEE Transactions on Knowledge Data and Engineering*, 26:1225–1239, 2014.

5. In the context of so-called generative models, why should one synthesize patterns? Which classifiers exploit the synthetic patterns better?

Relevant References

(a) L. Plonsky, J. Egbert and G. T. Laflair, Bootstrapping in applied linguistics: Assessing its potential using shared data. *Applied Linguistics*, 2014.

(b) P. S. Gromski, Y. Xu, E. Correa, D. I. Ellis, M. L. Turner and R. Goodacre, A comparative investigation of modern feature selection and classification approaches for the analysis of mass spectrometry data. *Analytica Chimica Acta*, 829:1–8, 2014.

(c) H. Seetha, R. Saravanan and M. N. Murty, Pattern synthesis using multiple Kernel learning for efficient SVM classification. *Cybernetics and Information Technologies*, 12:77–94, 2012.

6. Is it meaningful to combine several binary classifiers to realize multi-class classification?

Relevant References

(a) V. Sazonova and S. Matwin, Combining binary classifiers for a multi-class problem with differential privacy. *Transactions on Data Privacy*, 7:51–70, 2014.

(b) A. Kontorovich and R. Weiss, Maximum margin multiclass nearest neighbors, arXiv:1401.7898, 2014.

(c) T. Takenouchi and S. Ishii, A unified framework of binary classifiers ensemble for multi-class classification. *Proceedings of ICONIP*, 2012.

(d) K. Hwang, K. Lee, C. Lee and S. Park, Multi-class classification using a signomial function. *Journal of the Operational Research Society*, doi:10.105.7/jors.2013.180, Published online on 5 March 2014.

7. Which classifier is ideally suited to deal with a large number, say 1000, classes? Can one design one?

Relevant References

(a) K. Mei, P. Dong, H. Lei and J. Fan, A distributed approach for large-scale classifier training and image classification. *Neurocomputing*, 144:304–317, 2014.

(b) P. Sermanet, D. Eigen, X. Zhang, M. Mathieu, R. Fergus and Y. LeCun, OverFeat: Integrated recognition, localization and detection using convolutional networks, arXiv:1312.6229, 2014.

(c) T.-N. Doan, T.-N. Do and F. Poulet, Large scale visual classification with many classes. *Proceedings of MLDM*, 2013.

(d) M. Ristin, M. Guillaumin, J. Gall and L. van Gool, Incremental learning of NCM forests for large-scale image classification. *Proceedings of CVPR*, 2014.

8. How do we classify patterns that have multiple labels?

Relevant References

(a) B. Akhand and V. S. Devi, Multi-label classification of discrete data, IEEE International conference on fuzzy systems. *FUZZ-'13*, 2013.

(b) J. Xu, Fast multi-label core vector machine. *Pattern Recognition*, 46:885–898, 2013.

(c) J. Read, L. Martino and D. Luengo, Efficient Monte Carlo methods for multi-dimensional learning with classifier chains. *Pattern Recognition*, 47:1535–1546, 2014.

(d) J. Lee and D.-W. Kim, Feature selection for multi-label classification using multivariate mutual information. *Pattern Recognition Letters*, 34:349–357, 2013.

9. It is possible to show equivalence between threshold based algorithms like leader and number of clusters based algorithms like the K-means algorithm. Is it possible to axiomatize clustering to derive such equivalences?

Relevant References

(a) R. Chitta and M. N. Murty, Two-level k-means clustering algorithm for k-tau relationship establishment and linear-time classification. *Pattern Recognition*, 43:796–804, 2010.

(b) M. Ackerman, S. Ben-David and D. Loker, Towards property-based classification of clustering paradigms. *Proceedings of NIPS*, 2010.

(c) M. Meila, Comparing clusterings — An axiomatic view. *Proceedings of ICML*, 2005.

10. In social networks that evolve over time the notion of *outlier* may have to be redefined. How do we achieve it?

Relevant References

(a) N. N. R. R. Suri, M. N. Murty and G. Athithan, Characterizing temporal anomalies in evolving networks. *Proceedings of PAKDD*, 2014.

    (b) M. Gupta, J. Gao, C. Aggawal and J. Han, *Outlier Detection for Temporal Data*. San Rafael: Morgan and Claypool Publishers, 2014.

    (c) L. Peel and A. Clauset, Detecting change points in the large-scale structure of evolving networks, arXiv:1403.0989, 2014.

11. What is the most appropriate scheme for clustering labeled data?

Relevant References

    (a) V. Sridhar and M. N. Murty, Clustering algorithms for library comparison. *Pattern Recognition*, 24:815–823, 1991.

    (b) Q. Qiu and G. Sapiro, Learning transformations for clustering and classification, arXiv:1309.2074, 2014.

    (c) A. Kyriakopoulou, Theodore Kalamboukis: Using clustering to enhance text classification. *Proceedings of SIGIR*, 2007.

12. How do we exploit *Map-Reduce* framework to design efficient clustering schemes?

Relevant References

    (a) A. Ene, S. Im and B. Moseley, Fast clustering using MapReduce. *Proceedings of KDD*, 2011.

    (b) R. L. F. Cordeiro, C. Traina Jr., A. J. M. Traina, J. Lopez, U. Kang and C. Faloutsos, Clustering very large multi-dimensional datasets with MapReduce. *Proceedings of KDD*, 2011.

    (c) S. Fries, S. Wels and T. Seidl, Projected clustering for huge data sets in MapReduce. *Proceedings of EDBT*, 2014.

13. What is the best way to exploit knowledge in clustering? Which components of the clustering system are more sensitive to the usage of knowledge?

Relevant References

    (a) A. Srivastava and M. N. Murty, A comparison between conceptual clustering and conventional clustering. *Pattern Recognition*, 23:975–981, 1990.

    (b) X. Hu, X. Zhang, C. Lu, E. K. Park and X. Zhou, Exploiting Wikipedia as external knowledge for document clustering. *Proceedings of KDD*, 2009.

    (c) W. Pedrycz, *Knowledge-Based Clustering: From Data to Information Granules*. New Jersey: John Wiley & Sons, 2005.

14. How do we generate a formal framework that can be used to summarize documents?

Relevant References

(a) N. Karthik and M. N. Murty, Obtaining single document summaries using latent Dirichlet allocation. *Proceedings of ICONIP*, 2012.

(b) B. Piwowarski, M. R. Amini and M. Lalmas, On using a quantum physics formalism for multi-document summarization. *Journal of the American Society for Information Science and Technology*, 63:865–888, 2012.

Chapter 2

Types of Data

In statistical machine learning, pattern recognition and data mining, data is represented as a *pattern matrix* or *data matrix*. We illustrate it using the data in Figure 2.1 which is represented using the matrix shown in Table 2.1. Note that in Table 2.1, there are eight patterns which are represented using *height in feet* and *weight in Kilograms*. There are two classes labeled *chair* and *human* corresponding to a possible collection of chairs and humans; each class has four patterns in this example collection. Each pattern is represented as a point in the two-dimensional space, where *weight* is the first (X_1) feature and *height* is the second (X_2) feature.

1. Features and Patterns

Typically, columns of the data matrix correspond to features. A feature is a property or characteristic of a pattern. For example, *weight* and *height* are the two different features characterizing the chairs and humans in the collection and *class label* is the dependent feature that provides the semantic labels of the objects considered in Table 2.1. In social sciences, the terms *variable* and *characteristic* are used in the place of feature and in data mining area *field* and *attribute* are popularly used instead of feature.

The rows of the data matrix correspond to patterns in the collection. A pattern is also called *point*, *vector*, and *sample* in pattern recognition, and corresponds to *record*, *transaction*, and *instance* in data mining. So, a pattern is described by a collection of

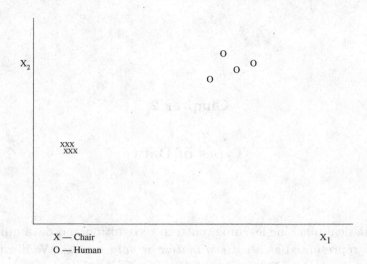

X — Chair
O — Human

Figure 2.1.   Example set of patterns.

Table 2.1.   An example pattern matrix of eight patterns.

Pattern number	Weight (in kgs)	Height (in feet)	Class label
1	10	3.5	Chair
2	63	5.4	Human
3	10.4	3.45	Chair
4	10.3	3.3	Chair
5	73.5	5.8	Human
6	81	6.1	Human
7	10.4	3.35	Chair
8	71	6.4	Human

feature values. In general, for machine-based pattern recognition and machine learning, we deal with the pattern representations rather than the patterns themselves. For example, on a computer, we represent the chairs and humans based on their weight and height.

This amounts to two levels of lossy compression. Observe that we cannot reproduce either a chair or a human from their respective representations based on height and weight alone; this corresponds to one level of abstraction. Further, the exact values of *height* and *weight* cannot be measured in practice; we use values obtained using instruments that measure these quantities with a finite precision. For example, when we say that a person's height is $5'10''$, it is not the exact value of height; it is an abstraction based on the precision of the measuring device employed.

2. Domain of a Variable

Typically, each feature is assigned a *number* or a *symbol* as its value. For example, the weight of the chair shown in the first row of Table 2.1 is 3.5 kgs where 3.5 is a real number; weight of other objects in the Table are all numbers. However, *color* of a chair could be black, red, or green which we are not using in the representation used in Table 2.1. So, color assumes *symbolic* values. It is possible for the features to assume values that could be trees or graphs and other structures. Specifically, a document collection is popularly represented as a document–term matrix, where each document (pattern) corresponds to a row and each term in the collection corresponds to a column. It is also possible to represent a document collection using an inverted index as is done by search engines for information retrieval. In the inverted index, a list of the documents in which a term occurs is stored for each term in the collection. Even though such an index is primarily used for information retrieval, it is possible to use the index structure in other machine learning tasks like classification, clustering, ranking and prediction in general.

A feature assumes values from a set: For example, the feature *weight* has its values from the set of positive reals in general and an appropriate subset in particular. Such a set is called the *domain* of the feature. It is possible that weight can be measured in terms of either kilograms or pounds. In both the cases, the domain of weight is the set of positive reals. Also, it is possible that different features can use the same domain of values. For example, a feature like *height* also has set of positive reals as its domain. For some features, these assignments are *artificial* or man-made; for others they are *natural*. For example, it is possible to use either a number or a symbol as the value of the feature *ID or Identification* of a person; the only requirement here is being able to discriminate between two individuals based on their ID values. Typically, we assign a positive integer as the ID value; this is an artificial assignment. Instead of a positive integer, we could have assigned a negative integer, a string of alphanumeric characters as the value of ID or even a real number to stand for the value of ID. However, it is natural to assign a non-negative integer value to the feature *number of dependents* of any individual. Note that number of dependents cannot be negative.

In pattern recognition (PR), it is possible to use an appropriate abstraction and still achieve an acceptable recognition accuracy. Most of the PR systems use compressed data for both training and classification. It is possible that the values used to represent a variable may not satisfy one or more properties of the variable. For example, consider the four objects shown in Table 2.2.

We may classify an object as *light* if its weight is less than 40 kgs, otherwise we classify it as *heavy*. Note that the first two patterns are *light* and the remaining two are *heavy*. The weight of the third pattern is four times that of the second pattern. Consider a transformed set of values for the four objects as shown in the third column of the table. So, the transform captures the order of the values, but not the ratio property. For example, the *light* objects have their transformed weight values below a threshold value of 70 and if the value is above 70, then the object is *heavy*. So, the first two objects are *light* and the remaining two objects are *heavy* based on the transformed values also. The transform is based on a monotonic function, which is a function $f : \Re \to \Re$ such that for $x, y \in \Re$, $x \leq y \Rightarrow f(x) \leq f(y)$, where $\Re$ is the set of real numbers. However, the ratio property is not preserved by the transformation; ratio of weights (second column) of third and second objects is 4, where the ratio of the transformed

Table 2.2.   Classification based on weight values.

Pattern number	Weight (in kgs)	Transformed weight	Class label
1	10	12.5	*light*
2	15	47	*light*
3	60	93	*heavy*
4	85	120	*heavy*

values of these two objects is 1.98 $\left(\frac{93}{47}\right)$. So, such a transformed data may be adequate for pattern classification based on choosing or learning the appropriate threshold value either in the input or in the transformed domain. This example illustrates the property that the way we measure and represent an attribute may not match its properties. However, classification is still possible. We discuss properties associated with different types of variables in the next section.

3. Types of Features

There are different types of features or variables. We may categorize them as follows:

1. **Nominal variable:** The simplest variable where the domain has distinct values.
2. **Ordinal variable:** The domain of this variable is an ordered set; so, the values are ordered.
3. **Interval variable:** The domain is an ordered set where the differences between values have a meaningful interpretation.
4. **Ratio variable:** The domain is similar to that of the interval variable where not only differences, but ratios are also meaningful.

In addition, we have temporal data, that is data which varies with time and spatial data that varies spatially. Next, we examine different types of data in detail.

3.1. Nominal data

A nominal feature f_N assumes values from a set, that is the domain of f_N denoted by $D(f_N)$. So, distinct objects can have different values that are drawn from the set $D(f_N)$. Here, different elements of $D(f_N)$ are distinct and they are not ordered as $D(f_N)$ is a set. Some examples of nominal features are:

- *Type of Curve*: A possible domain of this feature is {line, parabola, circle, ellipse}.
- *Type of Publication*: The domain of this variable will include technical report, journal paper, conference paper, and book.

- *TV Manufacturer*: The domain of this attribute could be {Sony, Philips, Samsung, LG, Videocon, Onida}.

It is possible that a nominal variable is either binary or non-binary. A binary feature has a domain with two elements. Some examples of binary nominal variables are:

- *Gender*: domain = {male, female}.
- *Beverage available*: domain = {tea, coffee}.

The most popular application area where nominal data is routinely encountered is *information retrieval*. Here, a document is typically viewed as a *bag of words*; so, it is a multiset without any ordering on the values or elements of the set. We illustrate it with an example.

Example 1. Let us consider the following *two* documents.

- D_1: The good old teacher teaches several courses
- D_2: In the big old college

We represent the *documents* as multisets given by:

$R_1 = \{$ *The, good, old, teacher, teaches, several, courses* $\}$ and
$R_2 = \{$ *In, the, big, old, college* $\}$,

where R_1 and R_2 are representations of the documents D_1 and D_2 respectively. Typically, several simple operations are performed to reduce the total number of terms. For example, converting uppercase characters to lowercase gives us the following representations:

$R_1 = \{$ *the, good, old, teacher, teaches, several, courses* $\}$ and
$R_2 = \{$ *in, the, big, old, college* $\}$.

Note that "The" is converted to "the" and "In" is transformed to "in". Further, by stemming, that is by transforming the words to their stemmed forms, we can replace "teacher" and "teaches" by "teach" and "courses" by "course" to get

$R_1 = \{$ *the, good, old, teach, teach, several, course* $\}$ and
$R_2 = \{$ *in, the, big, old, college* $\}$.

It is possible to represent a collection of documents by the union of their multisets. In the current example, the collection of the two documents may be equivalently represented by using a set of term frequency pairs.

$R = \{(\textit{the}, 2), (\textit{good}, 1), (\textit{old}, 2), (\textit{teach}, 2), (\textit{several}, 1), (\textit{course}, 1), (\textit{in}, 2), (\textit{big}, 1), (\textit{college}, 1)\}$

In R, the elements are ordered pairs of the form (*term, frequency*), where the first entry in the tuple is the term and the second entry is its cumulative frequency. For example, the pair (the, 2) indicates that the term "the" has occurred twice in the collection; note that "the" has occurred once in each of the two documents. So, its cumulative frequency is 2 (1+1). Similarly, "good" has occurred once in D_1 and it is absent in D_2; so, its cumulative frequency is 1. Such a set of term frequency pairs, or the histogram is shown in Figure 2.2. Here, terms are shown on the horizontal axis and corresponding cumulative frequencies are shown on the vertical axis.

Note it is possible to view each document also as a histogram of term frequency values. For example, the histograms corresponding to documents D_1 and D_2, after casefolding and stemming are given by

Histogram(D_1): {(the, 1), (good, 1), (old, 1), (teach, 2), (several, 1), (course, 1)}.
Histogram(D_2): {(in, 1), (the, 1), (big, 1), (old, 1), (college, 1)}.

Let us consider, in general, a collection $\mathcal{D}$ of n documents, given by

$\mathcal{D} = \{D_1, D_2, \ldots, D_n\}$.

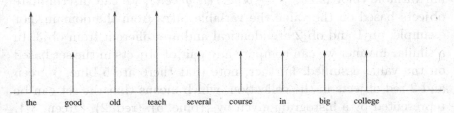

Figure 2.2.   Histogram of term frequencies.

In summary, each document is a *bag of words*. Equivalently, it may be viewed as a histogram of term-frequency values. Note that mapping the document to a histogram this way is equivalent to converting the underlying multiset into a set of ordered pairs (or tuples), where for each term that occurs in the document we include a tuple of (term, frequency). For example, in D_1 (teach, 2) and in D_2 (big, 1) are such tuples. Here, *document* is a nominal variable and its value is a specific document that may be viewed as a *bag of words* or as a *histogram* or equivalently as a set of term-frequency tuples. There is no order among the documents (histograms); so, the variable *document* is nominal. More fundamentally, the terms which are elements of the domain of the variable *term* are not ordered. So, the variable term is nominal.

3.1.1. *Operations on nominal variables*

On such nominal variables, one can perform some operations; these include *comparison, mode and entropy*. We illustrate this with an example.

Example 2. Consider a dataset of 10 objects which are characterized by only one nominal variable; let the nominal variable be *color*. The objects and their colors are given in the following set, where obj$i$ stands for object i.

{(obj1, blue), (obj2, blue), (obj3, red), (obj4, green), (obj5, blue), (obj6, green), (obj7, blue), (obj8, red), (obj9, blue), (obj10, green)}

Considering the set, we can say that the domain of the nominal variable color is $D_{\text{color}} = \{blue, red, green\}$; we can discriminate objects based on the value the variable takes from the domain. For example, obj1 and obj2 are identical and are different from obj3. In a similar manner we can compare any pair of objects in the set based on the value assumed. Further, note that there are 5 blue, 3 green and 2 red objects in the collection, which means that the set can be represented by a histogram given by {(blue, 5), (red, 2), (green, 3)}. Once we have the histogram, we can obtain the mode and entropy as follows:

- **Mode:** *Mode* is the most frequent value of the variable. In the example, we can observe from the histogram that *blue* has the highest frequency and so the mode is blue.
- **Entropy:** *Entropy* is a function of the frequencies of values. It characterizes in some sense *impurity* of the dataset; if the variable assumes only one value in the whole dataset, then the dataset is pure and the entropy is zero. On the contrary, if the variable assumes all the values with almost equal frequency in the set, then the entropy is maximum. Shannon's entropy is the most popular characterization of entropy. It is given, for the dataset $\mathcal{D}$ by

$$Entropy(\mathcal{D}) = - \sum_{i=1}^{d} p_i \log p_i,$$

where p_i is the probability of value i and d is the size of the domain of the variable under consideration.

So, for the data shown in Example 2, the values of probabilities obtained based on their frequencies of occurrence are:

$$P(blue) = \frac{5}{10} = 0.5; \quad P(green) = \frac{3}{10} = 0.3; \quad P(red) = \frac{2}{10} = 0.2.$$

For these probability values, the entropy is 0.4472 (using logarithm to the base 10).

3.2. Ordinal data

In the case of ordinal data, the elements of the domain of the variable are ordered, in addition to being distinct. Note that nominal variables satisfy only the property of their values being distinct. Some examples of ordinal features are:

- *Height* of an object: domain = {very tall, tall, medium, short, very short}.
- *Ranking* of documents. For example, quality of a document based on a scale from 1–9; typically, reviewers are asked to rank a paper

submitted for possible publication. Also, search engines provide an output of ranked documents against a query posed by a user.

- *Sentiment* mined from a collection of documents (perhaps tweets) on a product: domain = {very negative, negative, neutral, positive, very positive}.

3.2.1. *Operations possible on ordinal variables*

As an ordinal variable has domain whose elements are distinct, all the operations on nominal variables are possible on ordinal variables also. So, comparison, mode, and entropy are possible. In addition, ordering among the values permits operations like *median* and *percentile*.

- *Median* is the most centrally located value in the domain. For example, *medium* value of variable *Height*; *neutral* for variable *sentiment*; and value 5 for the variable *ranking based on a scale from 1 to 9* may be viewed as the median values in each case.
- *Percentile* makes sense when the values of the variable are ordered. Top ten percentile indicates the value below which 90% of the values are located.

It is possible to convert a nominal variable into an ordinal variable by imposing some meaningful ordering. For example, even though values of ordinal variable *color* are not ordered, it is possible to impose an order on the values based on the requirements of the application considered. For example, the values of *color* can be ordered as Violet, Indigo, Blue, Green, Yellow, Orange, and Red based on their wavelengths. We can illustrate this notion using the document data in the next example.

Example 3. Consider the two documents and their representations shown in Example 1. Observe the corresponding frequency details shown in Figure 2.2. In this figure, the terms are ordered based on the order in which they appeared in the documents and the sequence in which the documents are processed. Each term may be viewed as the value of a nominal variable; it is nominal because the ordering employed has no ordinal flavor.

An important ordering that has a great potential in *Information Retrieval* is based on the frequency of the terms in the collection. Note that there are nine terms in the collection as shown in Figure 2.2. It is possible to order these terms based on their frequency of occurrence in the collection. Further, if two or more terms have same frequency of occurrence, then corresponding terms are arranged in lexicographic order. Such a histogram is characterized by

$Histogram(\mathcal{D}) = \{(in, 2), (old, 2), (teach, 2), (the, 2), (big, 1), (college, 1), (course, 1), (good, 1), (several, 1)\}.$

The corresponding histogram is shown in Figure 2.3. Such a frequency ordered representation gives us an ordinal variable based on the frequency of terms. Note that *big* (the fifth term) is viewed as the median value among the nine terms. Another possibility is the lexicographic ordering.

In this context, it is important to note that the fundamental law in information retrieval is the *Zipf's law*; it is an empirical law. If we rank the terms based on their frequency of occurrence in a large collection of documents, with the most frequent term having the least (first) rank and the least frequent term having the largest (last) rank, then the frequency and rank of terms are related by

$$f(t_i) = \frac{C}{i},$$

where $f(t_i)$ is the frequency of the ith term t_i, C is the total number of terms in the collection, and i is the rank of t_i. This means the frequency of the first term is twice that of the second term in the collection. This law holds for large size collections.

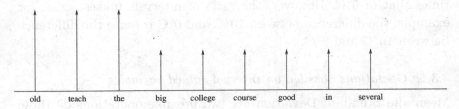

Figure 2.3.   Histogram of ordered term frequencies.

Table 2.3.   Representation of two documents in a binary form.

	Big	College	Course	Good	In	Old	Several	Teach	The
D_1	0	0	1	1	0	1	1	1	1
D_2	1	1	0	0	1	1	0	0	1

3.2.2. *Binary variables*

It is possible that a nominal or an ordinal variable could be binary. For example, consider D_1 and D_2. We can represent them as binary strings of fixed length based on the presence or absence, in a document, of each term in the collection. There are nine distinct terms in these two documents. They are: *big, college, course, good, in, old, several, teach, the* in the lexicographically sorted order. Using these nine terms, the two documents can be represented as binary strings as shown in Table 2.3.

3.3. Interval-valued variables

For interval-valued variables, the differences between values are meaningful. This is in addition to the properties satisfied by an ordinal variable. However, zero value is not properly defined. Also, products and ratios are well defined here. An example is: *Temperature in Celcius and Fahrenheit*:

Here, zero degrees Celcius or Fahrenheit do not mean no heat. However, $10°C$ is five degrees more than $5°C$; specifically the difference between $10°C$ and $5°C$ is the same as the difference between $5°C$ and $0°C$. In a sense, *interval* carries the meaning in the case of these variables and permits a variety of operations. Here, $10°C$ is not two times that of $5°C$. However, the ratio of intervals makes sense; for example, the difference between $10°C$ and $0°C$ is twice the difference between $10°C$ and $5°C$.

3.3.1. *Operations possible on interval-valued variables*

Mean and Standard Deviation are two possible operations on these variables. For example, mean or average temperature is a popularly used statistic. Here, (sample) mean and (sample) standard deviation of a collection of values, $x_1, x_2, \ldots, x_n$, of the variable are given by

$$Mean = \frac{1}{n} \sum_{i=1}^{n} x_i,$$

$$Standard\ Deviation = \frac{1}{n-1} \left(\sum_{i=1}^{n} (x_i - Mean)^2 \right)^{\frac{1}{2}}.$$

Example 4. Let us consider temperature over 5 consecutive days in summer in Bengaluru to be 35°C, 36°C, 36°C, 37°C, 36°C. Then the mean value is 36°C and the variance is 0.4. Another example of the interval-valued type is *calender dates*. Here, also differences make sense, but not ratios.

3.4. Ratio variables

A ratio variable, in addition to properties like distinctness, order, addition and subtraction, permits usage of multiplication and division. Ratio variables are the most popular in Data Mining, Pattern Recognition, and Machine Learning. A popular dichotomy of variables which is of recent origin, is to classify a variable as *categorical* or *numerical*. Nominal and ordinal variables make up for the categorical data whereas numerical variables are typically of ratio type. Interval-valued variables are so rare that all the numerical data is tacitly assumed to be of ratio type. Examples of ratio variables include weight and height of physical objects.

3.5. Spatio-temporal data

There are several applications where the data is not static or fixed; it is dynamic. Dynamic data is routinely understood as time varying. However, in a more generic way spatial variations can also be considered as dynamic. There are several applications where the data is spatio-temporal (variations in space or time or both). We consider some details next. In such dynamic datasets, we have the data to be one of the following:

1. **Spatial Data:** In some applications, learning the predictive models is influenced by the spatial information of the data. For example, in predicting earthquakes, it is possible that for all other conditions being equal, an area in some geographical location has a higher probability of being earthquake prone whereas some other area in a different geographical location may have a lower probability. Also, a search engine might retrieve different sets of results for queries posed from different geographical locations. For example, for a query posed from outside India to a search engine on "Center for Artificial Intelligence", "Centre for Artificial Intelligence and Robotics at www.utm.my/cairo" may be ranked higher; however, for the same query posed from Bengaluru, India it is highly likely that "Center for Artificial Intelligence and Robotics, Bangalore" will show up earlier. There are several other applications where spatial variations are important.

2. **Temporal Data:** Data that varies with time is called temporal data. Time series data is popular and here the successive time intervals are equally spaced or regular. Speech signal is a popular example of time series data. Another example of temporal data is encountered in web clicks; such a data is an example of stream data where the clicks can be made at irregular intervals of time.

3. **Spatio-temporal Data:** In some applications, data varies both with space and time. For example a search engine provides ranked results to a query. These results might change with time and also based on geographical location from which the user queried the search engine. Another important application area is earth sciences; for example, climatic conditions might change with time and space.

4. Proximity measures

Matching is of paramount importance in several areas of computer science and engineering. Matching trees, graphs, sequences, strings, and vectors is routinely handled by a variety of algorithms. Matching is either exact or approximate. Exact matching is popular in editors, databases, compilers and in operating system tools like *grep*. However, approximate matching is popular in pattern recognition and machine learning. A popular representation of patterns is by using vectors of feature values. Proximity between vectors is characterized by Similarity and Distance (Dissimilarity). Typically, similarity between two patterns is a numerical value in the range $[0, 1]$; similarity is higher when the matching between the objects is higher. Popularly distance functions are used to characterize dissimilarity. Similarity is captured by using a monotonically decreasing function of distance; larger the distance between a pair of patterns lower the similarity and smaller the distance, higher the similarity.

It is tacitly assumed that the distance function, $d(x, y)$ where x and y are patterns, is a *metric* which satisfies the following properties:

1. *Positive Reflexivity*

$$d(x, y) > 0 \text{ if } x \neq y \quad and \quad d(x, y) = 0 \text{ if } x = y.$$

This property has an intuitive appeal. Distance between a pair of objects is never negative. Further, if two objects (or more appropriately their representations) are identical, then they are highly similar and so the distance between them is minimum which is 0.

2. *Symmetry*

$$d(x, y) = d(y, x) \text{ for all } x \text{ and } y.$$

This property has practical implications which may be explained as follows. Consider a dataset $\mathcal{X}$ given by

$$\mathcal{X} = \{X_1, X_2, \ldots, X_n\}.$$

The corresponding distance/dissimilarity matrix is shown in Table 2.4. Here, $d(X_i, X_j)$ which corresponds to the distance between patterns X_i and X_j is represented as $d(i, j)$ for the sake of simplicity. By observing that each of the diagonal entries in the matrix is of the form $d(i, i)$ with a value 0 as specified by Property 1 and because of symmetry $d(i, j) = d(j, i)$ for $1 < i$,

Table 2.4.   Distance/dissimilarity matrix.

$$
\begin{vmatrix}
d(1,1) & d(1,2) & d(1,3) & \cdots & d(1,n) \\
d(2,1) & d(2,2) & d(2,3) & \cdots & d(2,n) \\
d(3,1) & d(3,2) & d(3,3) & \cdots & d(3,n) \\
\vdots & \vdots & \vdots & \cdots & \vdots \\
d(n,1) & d(n,2) & & \cdots & d(n,n)
\end{vmatrix}
$$

Table 2.5.   Symmetric distance matrix.

$$
\begin{vmatrix}
0 & & & & \\
d(2,1) & 0 & & & \\
d(3,1) & d(3,2) & 0 & & \\
\vdots & \vdots & \vdots & \cdots & \vdots \\
d(n,1) & d(n,2) & & \cdots & 0
\end{vmatrix}
$$

$j < n$, we can simplify the matrix in Table 2.4 to the lower-triangular matrix given in Table 2.5. Note that the value of any entry, $d(i,j)$, in the upper-triangular portion can be obtained by looking at the corresponding entry $d(j,i)$, which has the same value as $d(i,j)$, in the lower-triangular portion. This means that we can achieve reduction in both the time required to compute the distances and the space required to store the corresponding values. For n patterns, we need to compute $\frac{n(n-1)}{2}$ distances to specify the lower-triangular matrix rather than n^2 distances required to characterize the entire matrix shown in Table 2.4. This means that there is a reduction by more than a factor of 2. In a similar sense, one can analyze to show that the space required to store the possible entries in the lower-triangular matrix shown in Table 2.5 also reduces by a factor of 2. This is an advantage in using a distance function that is symmetric. Note that such a property is intrinsic to a pair of nodes in a friendship network. If we interpret such a network as a graph, then the graph is undirected.

3. *Triangular Inequality*

$$d(x,z) \le d(x,y) + d(y,z) \text{ for all } x, y, \text{ and } z.$$

This inequality is so-called because any' three patterns (or equivalently points) X_i, X_j, and X_k could be viewed as three vertices of a triangle and it is well-known that length of any side of a triangle is bounded by the sum of the lengths of the remaining two sides of the triangle. Note that length of the side (edge) uv corresponding to vertices u and v is characterized by the distance between points u and v.

Triangle inequality is exploited in pattern recognition in deriving a variety of properties associated with pattern classifiers including the Nearest Neighbor classifier, and divide-and-conquer clustering.

A distance function that satisfies the above three properties is a metric. Such a function is called *distance measure*.

(i) *Distance measures*

Various distance functions are defined and used on data represented using a collection of features. It is convenient to start with distances between binary vectors.

(ii) *Distance between binary vectors*

Let us consider two binary strings x $(= (x_1, x_2, \ldots, x_d))$ and y $(= (y_1, y_2, \ldots, y_d))$. The distance between such a pair of strings is obtained by matching x_i and y_i for all i and considering the corresponding numbers which are given by:

n_{11} = Number of times $x_i = y_i = 1$ for $i = 1, 2, \ldots, d$
n_{00} = Number of times $x_i = y_i = 0$ for $i = 1, 2, \ldots, d$
n_{10} = Number of times $x_i = 1$ and $y_i = 0$ for $i = 1, 2, \ldots, d$
n_{01} = Number of times $x_i = 0$ and $y_i = 1$ for $i = 1, 2, \ldots, d$

Using these matching counts, we can define the distance between x and y as

$$d(x, y) = \frac{n_{10} + n_{01}}{n_{11} + n_{10} + n_{01} + n_{00}}.$$

Example 5. We illustrate it using the binary representation of the documents shown in Table 2.3. Here, $n_{11} = 2$, $n_{10} = 4$, $n_{01} = 3$, and $n_{00} = 0$. So, distance between D_1 and D_2 is given by

$$d(D_1, D_2) = \frac{7}{9}.$$

(iii) *Similarity between binary strings*

Typically, similarity, $s(x, y)$, between a pair of vectors x and y ranges between 0 and 1.

$$s(x, y) = 1 - d(x, y).$$

This means that in the example above

$$s(D_1, D_2) = \frac{2}{9}, \quad as \ d(D_1, D_2) = \frac{7}{9}.$$

Note that

$$
\begin{aligned}
s(x, y) &= 1 - \frac{n_{10} + n_{01}}{n_{11} + n_{10} + n_{01} + n_{00}} \\
&= \frac{n_{11} + n_{00}}{n_{11} + n_{10} + n_{01} + n_{00}}.
\end{aligned}
$$

A more popular measure of similarity is the Jaccard coefficient, $J(x, y)$ which ignores n_{00} and is given by

$$J(x, y) = \frac{n_{11}}{n_{11} + n_{10} + n_{01}}.$$

Note that $J(D_1, D_2) = \frac{2}{9}$. Also, $s(x, y)$ and $J(x, y)$ need not be same. For example, if there are two 5 bit binary strings x and y given by

$x = 1\,0\,0\,0\,1$ and
$y = 0\,1\,0\,0\,1$
then $s(x, y) = \frac{3}{5} = 0.6$ and $J(x, y) = \frac{1}{3} = 0.33$.

(iv) *Minkowski distance*

A family of distance measures is the Minkowski measure and between a pair of patterns x and y it is given by

$$d_q(x, y) = \left[\sum_{i=1}^{p} |x_i - y_i|^q \right]^{\frac{1}{q}}.$$

1. The simplest distance in this case is the one with $q = 1$; the corresponding distance is called the L_1-*norm* (because $q = 1$) or *city-block distance* (because it is the sum of the absolute differences across the variables; it is similar to the distance traveled to reach a house from another in a city block). It is specified by

$$d_1(x, y) = \sum_{i=1}^{p} |x_i - y_i|.$$

2. *Euclidean distance* or L_2-*norm* (because $q = 2$) is the most popular among the dissimilarity measures used in pattern recognition. Euclidean distance between two patterns x and y in a p-dimensional space is given by

$$d_2(x, y) = \left[\sum_{i=1}^{p} (x_i - y_i)^2 \right]^{\frac{1}{2}}.$$

Euclidean distance is popular because:

- It is easy for human comprehension and visualization as it characterizes the *crow-flying distance*.
- It is *translation invariant*. This may be explained using two patterns x and y in a p-dimensional space represented by $x = (x_1, x_2, \ldots, x_p)$ and $y = (y_1, y_2, \ldots, y_p)$. The translated versions of x and y are x' and y' given, in general, by $x' = (x_1 + h_1, x_2 + h_2, \ldots, x_p + h_p)$ and $y' = (y_1 + h_1, y_2 + h_2, \ldots, y_p + h_p)$ where $h_1, h_2, \ldots, h_p$ are real numbers. Note that the euclidean distance between x and y is the same as that between x' and y'. In other words, $d_2(x, y) = d_2(x', y')$ which shows that euclidean distance does not change with translation.

- It is *rotation invariant*. For example, let $x = (x_1, x_2)$ and $y = (y_1, y_2)$ be two points in a two-dimensional space. It is possible to view them as two diagonally opposite vertices of a rectangle so that the line xy is a diagonal. By *rotating the line* around its midpoint by $90°$, we get the line $x'y'$ where $x' = (x_1, y_2)$ and $y' = (y_1, x_2)$. Note that this forms the other diagonal. So, the euclidean distances are equal as the diagonals in the rectangles are of equal length. That is $d_2(x, y) = d_2(x', y')$.
- However, a weakness is that it is *not scale-invariant*. For example, let us consider two two-dimensional patterns $x = (x_1, x_2)$ and $y = (y_1, y_2)$, $x \neq y$. If "x" and "y" are scaled versions of x and y by a factor α, such that $x" = (\alpha x_1, \alpha x_2)$ and $y" = (\alpha y_1, \alpha y_2)$, then we can observe that $d(x, y) \neq d(x", y")$, in general, where d(.,.) is the euclidean distance; they are equal if and only if $\alpha = 1$.

3. Another popular distance measure is the *Max distance* or L_∞-*norm*: It is the maximum of the absolute differences among all the features. Given two patterns x and y, the max distance is defined as:

$$d_\infty(x, y) = \max_i |x_i - y_i|.$$

This simplification is possible because as $q \to \infty$ the qth power of $\max_i |x_i - y_i|$ is larger than the qth power of any of the other $p-1$ components. This means that the sum over the qth powers of all the p terms can be approximated by the qth power of $\max_i |x_i - y_i|$ as the other $p - 1$ terms are negligible. So, the $\frac{1}{q}$th power of the sum can be approximated by $\max_i |x_i - y_i|$.

4.1. Fractional norms

In applications involving high-dimensional patterns, it is observed that Minkowski distances between patterns do not give a meaningful characterization of dissimilarity. One class of distance measures is based on fractional norm. Here in the norm given by

$$d_q(x, y) = [\Sigma_{i=1}^p |x_i - y_i|^q]^{\frac{1}{q}}$$

the value of q is a fraction. We consider a simple example to illustrate.

Example 6. Consider two four-dimensional patterns X_1 and X_2 given by

$$X_1 = (1, 1.16, 1, 0) \quad \text{and} \quad X_2 = (1.36, 1, 1, 0).$$

Then $d_{0.5}(X_1, X_2) = [0.6 + 0.4 + 0 + 0]^{\frac{1}{0.5}} = 1^2 = 1.$
It is not difficult to see that

$$d_1(X_1, X_2) = 0.36 + 0.16 = 0.52 \quad \text{and}$$
$$d_2(X_1, X_2) = [0.36^2 + 0.16^2]^{0.5} = 0.39.$$

To illustrate it further let us consider another pair of patterns X_3 and X_4 given by

$$X_3 = (1, 2, 1, 0) \quad \text{and} \quad X_4 = (3, 0, 1, 0).$$

The corresponding distances are

$$d_{0.5}(X_3, X_4) = [2^{0.5} + 2^{0.5}]^{\frac{1}{0.5}} = [\sqrt{8}]^2 = 8.$$

Further, observe that

$$d_1(X_3, X_4) = 2 + 2 = 4 \quad \text{and}$$
$$d_2(X_3, X_4) = [2^2 + 2^2]^{0.5} = \sqrt{8} = 2.828.$$

4.2. Are metrics essential?

There are a variety of distance functions that are not metrics; they violate one or more of the properties of metric distances. Such non-metric distance functions have been popularly used in pattern recognition and machine learning. We will examine some of these distance functions. Specifically, we will see how each of the three properties of a metric get violated by distance functions. Let us consider examples for each.

1. *Violation of Positive Reflexivity:* Let us consider a distance function that returns negative values. Specifically, consider a two-class problem in a one-dimensional space.

Example 7. Let the training data consisting of one-dimensional patterns be

Class 1: 1, 3, 8, 12   Class 2: 57, 63, 44

Let the distance function be given by

$$d(x, y) = \begin{cases} - \mid x - y \mid & \text{if } \mid x - y \mid < T \\ (x - y)^2 & \text{Otherwise} \end{cases}.$$

Now consider a test pattern with value 40 and let T be 20; the distances between the test pattern and the training patterns respectively are:

Class 1: 1521, 1369, 1024, 784   Class 2: −17, 529, −4

Now consider k nearest neighbors based on the distances; so, the $3(k = 3)$ nearest neighbors are 57, 44, and 63 respectively. All the three are from Class 2. Hence by using the class label of the majority class, we classify the test pattern to Class 2. This illustrates that distances can act meaningfully even if positive reflexivity is violated. However, in practice violation of positive reflexivity is not common.

2. *Violation of Symmetry:* The most popularly used distance function that violates symmetry is the Kullback–Leibler distance (or KL divergence) defined between two probability distributions. If p and q are discrete distributions over the same variable such that $p = \{p_1, p_2, \ldots, p_l\}$ and $q = \{q_1, q_2, \ldots, q_l\}$, then the KL distance between p and q is

$$KL(p, q) = - \sum_{i=1}^{l} p_i \log_2 \left(\frac{q_i}{p_i} \right).$$

Even though $KL(p, q)$ is non-negative and is equal to 0 when $p = q$, $KL(p, q) \neq KL(q, p)$ in general; so, KL divergence does not satisfy symmetry.

3. *Violation of Triangular Inequality:* Even though euclidean distance is a metric, the squared euclidean distance is not a metric; it violates the triangular inequality. We illustrate it with an example.

Example 8. Consider three points x, y, and z. Let the euclidean distances between pairs of points be

$$d_2(x, y) = 2; \quad d_2(y, z) = 3; \quad d_2(x, z) = 4.$$

Consider the squared euclidean distances between the corresponding pairs of points; they are given by

$$d_2^2(x, y) = 4; \quad d_2^2(y, z) = 9; \quad d_2^2(x, z) = 16.$$

Note that the squared euclidean distance does not satisfy the triangular inequality because $d_2^2(x, y) + d_2^2(y, z) = 13$ and $d_2^2(x, z) = 16$ which means sum of lengths of two sides of the triangle (13) is less than the length of the third side (16) violating the triangular inequality.

However, the squared euclidean distance is symmetric. This is because basically, euclidean distance is a metric and so it satisfies symmetry. As a consequence, for any two points u and v, $d_2(u, v) = d_2(v, u)$ which means $d_2^2(u, v) = d_2^2(v, u)$ ensuring that the squared euclidean distance is symmetric. Similarly, one can show that squared euclidean distance satisfies positive reflexivity.

4.3. Similarity between vectors

One of the most popular similarity functions between a pair of vectors x and y is the cosine of the angle between the vectors x and y and is given by

$$\cos(x, y) = \frac{(x \cdot y)}{\|x\|\|y\|},$$

where $x \cdot y$ is the dot product between x and y and $\|x\|$ is the length of x or equivalently the euclidean distance between the origin and x. This similarity function is used popularly in text mining and information retrieval.

Example 9. Consider an example where x and y are two six-dimensional vectors given by

$$x = (3, 1, 5, 1, 0, 0) \quad \text{and} \quad y = (1, 0, 1, 0, 0, 2).$$

In this case

$$x \cdot y = 3 * 1 + 1 * 0 + 5 * 1 + 1 * 0 + 0 * 0 + 0 * 2 = 8,$$

$$\|x\| = (3 * 3 + 1 * 1 + 5 * 5 + 1 * 1 + 0 * 0 + 0 * 0)^{\frac{1}{2}} = \sqrt{36} = 6,$$

$$\|y\| = (1 * 1 + 0 * 0 + 1 * 1 + 0 * 0 + 0 * 0 + 2 * 2)^{\frac{1}{2}} = \sqrt{6} = 2.245.$$

So, $\cos(x, y) = \frac{8}{6 * 2.245} = 0.594.$

Some of the issues associated with computing the cosine values are:

1. If we normalize x and y so that they are made unit norm vectors, then there is no need to divide the dot product with the norms of vectors x and y while computing the cosine value. For example, normalizing x, that is dividing each of the six components of x by $\|x\|$, we get

$$x' = \frac{1}{6}(3, 1, 5, 1, 0, 0) = (0.5, 0.166, 0.83, 0.166, 0, 0),$$

   where x' is the normalized version of x. Similarly, the normalized version y' of y is

$$y' = \frac{1}{2.245}(1, 0, 1, 0, 0, 2) = (0.445, 0, 0.445, 0, 0, 0.89).$$

   So, the dot product between x' and y' is given by

$$\cos(x', y') = (0.5 * 0.445 + 0.166 * 0 + 0.83 * 0.445$$
$$+ 0.166 * 0 + 0 * 0 + 0 * 0.89) = 0.592.$$

   So, it can simplify the cosine computation if the data are initially normalized. Data is routinely normalized when classifiers based on neural networks and support vector machines are used.

2. It is possible to approximate the cosine computation by ignoring the smaller values in a normalized vector; we replace such small

values by 0. For example, in vector x' and y' we can ignore values below 0.4. This will mean the approximate vectors x' and y' are:

$$x' = (0.5, 0, 0.83, 0, 0, 0) \quad \text{and} \quad y' = (0.445, 0, 0.445, 0, 0, 0.89).$$

In such a case, the approximate value of $\cos(x, y)$ is

$$0.5 * 0.445 + 0.83 * 0.445 = 0.592.$$

Such approximations, which can reduce the number of multiplications while computing the dot product between two normalized vectors, are not uncommon in computing the cosine of the angle between two document vectors where each vector is very high-dimensional. For example, dimensionalities in the range 50,000 to 100,000 are very common in document classification.

3. A variant of cosine similarity is the Tanimoto similarity given by

$$t(x, y) = \frac{x \cdot y}{x \cdot x + y \cdot y - x \cdot y}.$$

Note the equivalence between the Tanimoto similarity and Jaccard coefficient in the case of binary vectors by noting that

$$x \cdot y = n_{11}, \quad x \cdot x = n_{11} + n_{10}, \quad \text{and} \quad y \cdot y = n_{11} + n_{01}.$$

4.4. Proximity between spatial patterns

A simple scheme to process spatial patterns is by assuming that each pattern is represented as a vector with additional features to provide the location details. Let us consider the data given in Table 2.6 corresponding to books where copies of the same book are sold in different locations in the world. Note that based on *Location* we can get the same two groups {1, 3, 5} and {2, 4, 6}, where the first group of books are published in USA and the second group is published in India. Further, the prices of books in the first group are higher than the prices of books in the second group. In other words, the distance between any pair of books from either group 1 or group 2 is small if the location feature or price are given more importance. It is possible to assign different weightages to different

Table 2.6.   Book prices in different countries.

Title of the book	Authors	Publisher	Location	Price
1. Introduction to Data Mining	Tan, Steinbach and Vipin Kumar	Addison-Wesley	USA	US$95.12
2. Introduction to Data Mining	Tan, Steinbach and Vipin Kumar	Pearson	India	Rs. 525
3. Data Mining Concepts and Techniques	Han, Kamber	Elsevier	USA	US$59.47
4. Data Mining Concepts and Techniques	Han, Kamber	Elsevier	India	Rs. 450
5. Fundamentals of Algorithmics	Brassard, Bratley	Prentice-Hall	USA	US$51
6. Fundamentals of Algorithmics	Brassard, Bratley	Prentice-Hall	India	Rs. 225

features; perhaps a higher weight may be assigned to the *Location* feature.

4.5. Proximity between temporal patterns

One of the application areas where time varying data is popularly analyzed is speech processing. Typically speech signal is viewed as a semi-stationary time series. A time series may be represented as $\{(p_1, t_1), (p_2, t_2), \ldots, (p_m, t_m)\}$ where p_i is the value at time t_i, the values are recorded at regular intervals of time. In speech analysis and synthesis, it is assumed that the vowel sounds are periodic and consonants are generated by white noise. Some of the recognition tasks here include speaker recognition and speech recognition.

One way of carrying out classification and clustering on time series data is to find a measure of proximity between time series. Once this is taken care of, any distance-based classification or clustering technique can be used. Let us look at some proximity measures for time series data. We have already examined some of the popularly used proximity measures which are given below.

1. **Minkowski distance**
2. **Cosine similarity**
3. **KL distance:** This is an assymetric distance function. The symmetric version is:

$$D(a, b) = \frac{d(a, b) + d(b, a)}{2},$$

where $d(a, b)$ is the conventional KL distance between a and b.

4.6. Mean dissimilarity

The mean dissimilarity can be defined as a distance function

$$d_m = \frac{1}{d} \sum_{k=1}^{d} dissim(p_k, q_k),$$

where $dissim(p_k, q_k) = \frac{|p_k - q_k|}{|p_k| + |q_k|}$.

Example 10. Let us consider two time series P: $1, -3, 2, 5$ and Q: $1, 2, 3, 5$. Then the mean dissimilarity is $\frac{1}{4} \left[\frac{0}{2} + \frac{5}{5} + \frac{1}{5} + \frac{0}{10} \right] = \frac{1.2}{4} = 0.3$.

4.7. Peak dissimilarity

Peak dissimilarity between the kth values p_k and q_k is given by

$$d_p(p_k, q_k) = \frac{|p_k - q_k|}{2.max(|p_k|, |q_k|)}.$$

The peak dissimilarity between two time series P and Q will then be

$$d_p(P, Q) = \frac{1}{d} \sum_{k=1}^{d} d_p(p_k, q_k).$$

Example 11. Again considering the two time series P: $1, -3, 2, 5$ and Q: $1, 2, 3, 5$. Then the peak dissimilarity is $\frac{1}{4} \left[\frac{0}{2*1} + \frac{5}{2*3} + \frac{1}{2*3} + \frac{0}{2*5} \right] = \frac{1}{4} = 0.25$.

4.8. Correlation coefficient

If P and Q are two d-dimensional time-series, the correlation coefficient $CC(P, Q)$ is

$$CC(P, Q) = \frac{\sum_{i=1}^{d}(P_i - \mu_P)(Q_i - \mu_Q)}{s_P.s_Q},$$

where μ_P is the mean of P and is given by

$$\mu_P = \frac{1}{d}\sum_{i=1}^{d} P_i,$$

s_P is the scatter of P and is given by

$$s_P = \left[\sum_{i=1}^{d}(P_i - \mu_P)^2\right]^{0.5}.$$

Similarly, μ_Q and s_Q are the mean and scatter of Q respectively.

Based on the similarity coefficient $CC(P, Q)$, one possible distance measure is

$$d_{CC1}(P, Q) = \left(\frac{1 - CC(P, Q)}{1 + CC(P, Q)}\right)^{\beta},$$

where an appropriate value of β is to be chosen. β is a value greater than zero; typically $\beta = 2$.

Another distance measure is

$$d_{CC2}(P, Q) = 2(1 - CC(P, Q)).$$

Example 12. Considering P: $1, -3, 2, 5$ and Q: $1, 2, 3, 5$, note that $\mu_P = \frac{5}{4}$ and $\mu_Q = \frac{11}{4}$. Further, $s_P = 5.7$ and $s_Q = 2.95$. So, $d_{CC1}(P, Q) = 0.025$ and $d_{CC2}(P, Q) = 0.54$.

4.9. Dynamic Time Warping (DTW) distance

In most cases, the DTW distance is superior to Euclidean distance for classification and clustering of time series. Consider two time series P of dimension d_P and Q of dimension d_Q. The intention is to align these two time series. This is done by constructing a matrix of size $d_P \times d_Q$. The alignment between the ith value in P, P_i, and jth value in Q, Q_j, is calculated as

$$d(P_i, Q_j) = |P_i - Q_j|.$$

We have suggested the Manhattan distance or L_1 norm here; it is possible to use other distances measures like the L_2 norm.

It is necessary to find the best match between the two sequences. For this we need to find a path through the matrix that minimizes the total cumulative distance between them. A warping path through the matrix is a contiguous set of matrix elements that characterizes a mapping between P and Q. The kth element of a warping path W is $w_k = (i, j)_k$ and

$$W = w_1, w_2, \ldots, w_k, \ldots, w_m \text{ where } max(d_P, d_Q) \leq m < d_P + d_Q + 1.$$

We need to find the optimal path W^* which is the path that minimizes the warping cost. In other words

$$DTW(d_P, d_Q) = W^* = min \left(\sqrt{\sum_{i=1}^{m} (w_i)} \right).$$

Finding all paths is a time-consuming process. A dynamic programming approach is used to evaluate the cumulative distance $DST(i, j)$. This will be

$$DST(i, j) = d(p_i, q_j) + min\{DST(i - 1, j), DST(i, j - 1),$$
$$DST(i - 1, j - 1)\}.$$

This means that the cumulative distance $DST(i, j)$ is the sum of the distance in the current cell $d(i, j)$ and the minimum of the cumulative distances of the adjacent elements, $DST(i-1, j)$, $DST(i, j-1)$, and $DST(i - 1, j - 1)$.

To decrease the number of paths considered and to speed up the calculations, some constraints are considered. The paths considered should satisfy the following conditions:

1. Boundary condition: The path must start in $w_1 = (1, 1)$ and end in $w_m = (d_P, d_Q)$.
2. Continuity condition: The path must form a sequence which means that the indices i and j can only increase by 0 or 1 on each step along the path. If we are at point (i, j), the next point can only be $(i + 1, j + 1)$ or $(i + 1, j)$ or $(i, j + 1)$.
3. Monotonic condition: The path cannot go backwards in the indices. Both the i and j indices can either stay the same or increase. They can never decrease.
4. Slope constraint condition: The warping path cannot be too steep or too shallow. This means that moving for a long time along one dimension is not allowed. This is expressed as the ratio $\frac{a}{b}$ which gives the slope of the path. If we move b steps in the x direction, it is necessary to make the next step in the y direction.
5. Adjustment window condition: The warping path cannot drift very far from the diagonal. The distance the path can wander is limited to a window of size w directly above and to the right of the diagonal.

4.9.1. *Lower bounding the DTW distance*

Since DTW computation is very demanding in terms of time, it would help if we could find a lower bounding function which will prune sequences which could not possibly be the best match. The lower bounding measure should be fast to compute and should be a relatively tight lower bound. We have seen that the number of warping paths which are covered are limited by not allowing the path to stray too far away from the diagonal. The part of the matrix the warping path is allowed to visit is called the warping window or a band. Some of the warping bands used are:

1. Sakoe–Chiba Band
2. Itakura Parallelogram

They are illustrated in Figure 2.4.

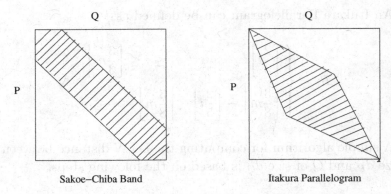

Figure 2.4. Limiting scope of the warping path.

The Sakoe–Chiba Band or the Itakura Parallelogram is used to create a bounding envelope above and below the time series P. Then the sum of the distances from every part of the time series Q not falling within the bounding envelope, to the nearest orthogonal edge of the bounding envelope, is returned as its lower bound. This helps to prune off a number of expensive DTW computations and reduce the complexity of the DTW algorithm.

We need to constrain the indices of the warping path $w_k = (i, j)_k$ such that $j - R_i \leq i \leq j + R_i$ where R_i defines the allowed range of warping for a given point in a sequence. For the Sakoe–Chiba Band, R is independent of i but for the Itakura Parallelogram, R is a function of i. R can be defined as

$$R_i = d, \quad 0 \leq d \leq m,$$

where R_i is the height above the diagonal in the y direction as well as the width to the right of the diagonal in the x direction. Any global constraint can be defined using R. For example, a Sakoe–Chiba Band of overall width 11 or a width of 5 above and to the right of the diagonal can be represented as

$$R_i = \begin{cases} 5 & \text{if } 1 \leq i \leq m - 5, \\ m - i & \text{if } m - 5 < i \leq m. \end{cases}$$

An Itukara Parallelogram can be defined as

$$
R_i = \begin{cases} \left\lfloor \dfrac{2}{3}i \right\rfloor & 1 \leq i \leq \left\lfloor \dfrac{3}{3}m \right\rfloor, \\[2em] \left\lfloor \dfrac{3}{8}m \right\rfloor - \left\lfloor \dfrac{2}{5}i \right\rfloor & \left\lfloor \dfrac{3}{8}m \right\rfloor < i \leq m. \end{cases}
$$

A simple algorithm for computing the DTW distance between P of size d_P and Q of size d_Q is based on the folowing steps.

Algorithm for Computing DTW values

- **Input** — P: $P_1, P_2, \ldots, P_{d_P}$, Q: $Q_1, Q_2, \ldots, Q_{d_Q}$, and $w(window\ size)$
- **Output** — $DTW(d_P, d_Q)$
- **Steps of the Algorithm**

  1. **Initialize** for $i = 1$ to d_P
     for $j = 1$ to d_Q DTW$(i, j) = \infty$
     DTW$(0, 0) = 0$
  2. **Update** for $i = 1$ to d_P
     for $j = max(1, i - w)$ to $min(d_Q, i + w)$
     DTW$(i, j) =\mid P_i - Q_j \mid + min(DTW(i - 1, j), DTW(i, j - 1),$
     $DTW(i - 1, j - 1))$

We illustrate it using a simple example.

Example 13. Let P: 11223 and Q: 1233. Let us look at $i = 1$ and compute the DTW values for different values of j.

1. $i = 1, j = 1$: $DTW(1, 1) = |1 - 1| + min(DTW(0, 1), DTW(1, 0) + DTW(0, 0)) = 0 + min(\infty, \infty, 0) = 0.$
2. $i = 1, j = 2$: $DTW(1, 2) = |1 - 2| + min(DTW(0, 2), DTW(1, 1) + DTW(0, 1)) = 1 + min(\infty, 0, \infty) = 1.$
3. $i = 1, j = 3$: $DTW(1, 3) = |1 - 3| + min(DTW(0, 3), DTW(1, 2), DTW(0, 2)) = 2 + min(\infty, 1, \infty) = 3.$

Table 2.7.   DTW(i, j) values for all possible i (1 to 5) and j (1 to 4).

$j \backslash i$	0	1	2	3	4	5
0	**0**	∞	∞	∞	∞	∞
1	∞	**0**	**0**	2	3	5
2	∞	1	1	**0**	**0**	1
3	∞	3	3	1	1	**0**
4	∞	5	5	2	2	**0**

Table 2.8.   DTW(i, j) values for legal values of i and j with $w = 1$.

$j \backslash i$	0	1	2	3	4	5
0	**0**	∞	∞	∞	∞	∞
1	∞	**0**	**0**	∞	∞	∞
2	∞	1	1	**0**	∞	∞
3	∞	∞	3	1	1	∞
4	∞	∞	∞	1	2	**1**

4. $i = 1, j = 4$: $DTW(1, 4) = |1 - 3| + min(DTW(0, 4), DTW(1, 3), DTW(0, 3)) = 2 + min(\infty, 3, \infty) = 5$.

By assuming a value of $w = 5$ we get the results shown in Table 2.7. Here, we give values for DTW(i, j) for all possible i and j. Note that the cumulative cost DTW$(5, 4) = 0$ and the path goes through $(1, 1)$, $(2, 1)$, $(3, 2)$, $(4, 2)$, $(5, 3)$, and $(5, 4)$. The corresponding entries (0 values) are shown in bold face.

By selecting a value of $w = 1$, we get the values shown in Table 2.8. Here, values outside the range are chosen to be ∞. All the values in the legal region are shown in boldface.

Research Ideas

1. It is pointed out in Section 1 that pattern classification can be carried out using approximate values of features. Is it possible to work out bounds on the approximation for an acceptable level of classification?

Relevant References

(a) L. E. Ghaoui, G. R. G. Lanckriet and G. Natsoulis, Robust classification with interval data. Technical Report UCB/CSD-03-1279, Computer Science Division, University of California, Berkeley, 2003.

(b) Robust Classification, www.ims.nus.edu.sg/Programs/semidefinite/files/ IMS2006_Lect2.ppt [accessed on 25 October 2014].

(c) A. Ben-Tal, S. Bhadra, C. Bhattacharyya and J. Saketha Nath, Chance constrained uncertain classification via robust optimization. *Mathematical Program*, 127(1):145–173, 2011.

(d) A. Takeda, H. Mitsugi and T. Kanamori, A unified classification model based on robust optimization. *Neural Computation*, 25:759–804, 2013.

2. Even though the domain of a variable is a large or/and possibly infinite set, it may make sense to restrict the domain size to build a variety of classifiers. For example, in document classification it is possible to ignore some terms as illustrated by stemming in Section 3.1. How to exploit such a reduction in the domain size in classification?

Relevant References

(a) A. Globerson and N. Tishby, Sufficient dimensionality reduction. *Journal of Machine Learning Research*, 3:1307–1331, 2003.

(b) C. D. Manning, P. Raghavan and H. Schutze, *Introduction to Information Retrieval*. Cambridge: Cambridge University Press, 2008.

(c) T. Berka, web.eecs.utk.edu/events/tmw11/slides/Berka.pdf, Dimensionality reduction for information retrieval using vector replacement of rare terms, 2011.

(d) D. Wang and H. Zhang, Inverse-category-frequency based supervised term weighting schemes for text categorization. *Journal of Information Science and Engineering*, 29:209–225, 2013.

3. Given the training dataset, how do we learn an appropriate distance/similarity function that could be used in classification? Is it possible to use different similarity functions in different regions of the feature space?

Relevant References

(a) M. Gonen and E. Alpaydn, Multiple Kernel learning algorithms. *Journal of Machine Learning Research*, 12:2211–2268, 2011.

(b) V. K. Garg and M. N. Murty, Feature subspace SVMs (FS-SVMs) for high dimensional handwritten digit recognition. *IJDMMM*, 1(4):411–436, 2009.

(c) D. Ramanan and S. Baker, Local distance functions: A taxonomy, new algorithms, and an evaluation. *IEEE Transactions on Pattern Analysis and Machine Intelligence*, 33:794–806, 2011.

(d) C.-M. Hsu and M.-S. Chen, On the design and applicability of distance functions in high-dimensional data space. *IEEE Transactions on TKDE*, 21:523–536, 2009.

(e) J. H. Lee, K. T. McDonnell, A. Zelenyuk, D. Imre and K. Mueller, A structure-based distance metric for high-dimensional space exploration with multidimensional scaling. *IEEE Transactions on Vizualization and Computer Graphics*, 20:351–364, 2013.

4. In the definition of Minkowski distance defined in Section 4, what is the impact on classifiers if the value of q is a negative real number. Such distances could be called negative norms.

Relevant References

(a) C.-M. Hsu and M.-S. Chen, On the design and applicability of distance functions in high-dimensional data space. *IEEE Transactions Knowledge and Data Engineering*, 21(4):523–536, 2009.

(b) C. C. Aggarwal, A. Hinneburg and D. A. Keim, On the surprising behavior of distance metrics in high dimensional spaces. *ICDT*, 420–434, 2001.

5. It is assumed that either similarity or dissimilarity between patterns is adequate; it is possible to derive one from the other. How do you characterize them as separate functions and use a linear/nonlinear combination of them in classification.

Relevant References

(a) M. Martin-Merino, Learning a combination of heterogeneous dissimilarities from incomplete knowledge. *Proceedings of ICANN*, (3), 2010.

(b) K. C. Gowda and T. V. Ravi, Divisive Clustering of symbolic clustering using the concept of both similarity and dissimilarity. *Pattern Recognition*, 28:1277–1282, 1995.

(c) Z. S. Xu and J. Chen, An overview of distance and similarity measures of intuitionistic fuzzy sets. *International Journal of Uncertainty, Fuzziness and Knowledge-Based Systems*, 16:529–555, 2008.

6. Is there an equivalence between categorical features and numerical features in terms of classification. For example, Support Vector Machines (SVMs) and Artificial Neural Networks (ANNs) are useful when the features are numerical and frequent itemset based classification algorithms are ideally suited to deal with categorical features.

Relevant References

(a) N. Lee and J. Kim, Conversion of categorical variables into numerical variables via Bayesian network classifiers for binary classifications. *Computational Statistics & Data Analysis*, 54:1247–1265, 2010.

(b) Natural Language Understanding, www.cs.stonybrook.edu/ychoi/cse507/slides/04-ml.pdf.

(c) I. W. Tsang, J. T. Kwok and P.-M. Cheung, Core vector machines: Fast SVM training on very large data sets. *JMLR*, 6:363–392, 2005.

7. In Section 4.2, a variety of distance functions that violate one or more of the metric properties have been detailed. Analyze further to rank the distance functions based on the type of property violated.

Relevant References

(a) T. Skopal and J. Bustos, On nonmetric similarity search problems in complex domains. *ACM Computing Surveys*, 43:34–50, 2011.

(b) M. Li, X. Chen, X. Li, B. Ma and P. Vitanyi, The similarity metric. *IEEE Transactions on Information Theory*, 50:3250–3264, 2004.

8. Give example algorithms where the triangular inequality satisfied by the distance measure is exploited to simplify the learning algorithm.

Relevant References

(a) S. Guha, A. Meyerson, N. Mishra, R. Motwani and L. O'Callaghan, Clustering data streams: Theory and practice. *IEEE Transactions on Knowledge Data and Engineering*, 15:515–528, 2003.

(b) D. Arthur and S. Vassilvitskii, k-means++: The advantages of careful seeding. *SODA*: 1027–1035, 2007.

9. In high-dimensional spaces it is useful to approximate the distance/similarity computation. For example, computation of the cosine of the angle between two high-dimensional document vectors is approximated by ignoring the entries that are smaller than a threshold.

Relevant References

(a) S. V. Dongen and A. J. Enright, Metric distances derived from cosine similarity and Pearson and Spearman correlations, arXiv:1208.3145v1, 2012.

(b) C. D. Manning, P. Raghavan and H. Schutze, *Introduction to Information Retrieval*. Cambridge: Cambridge University Press, 2008.

10. How do we speedup the computation of DTW values further.

Relevant References

(a) T. Giorgino, Computing and visualizing dynamic time warping alignments in R: The dtw package, cran.r-project.org/web/packages/dtw/vignettes/dtw.pdf.

(b) Y. Sakurai, M. Yoshikawa and C. Faloutsos, FTW: Fast similarity search under the time warping distance. *PODS*: 326–337, 2005.

Chapter 3

Feature Extraction and Feature Selection

Feature extraction is the process of determining the features to be used for learning. The description and properties of the patterns are known. However, for the classification task at hand, it is necessary to extract the features to be used. It may involve carrying out some arithmetic operations on the features like linear combinations of the features or finding the value of a function. **Feature selection** is the process of discarding some of the features of the patterns and using only a subset of the features.

Feature extraction and feature selection are very important problems in machine learning. To enhance the performance of the machine learning algorithm, it is necessary that the right or discriminating features are used. Use of irrelevant features may lead to unnecessary computation. In addition, due to the peaking phenomenon, as the number of features increases, a larger training dataset is required to get good classification accuracy. With a fixed dataset, the accuracy increases with the number of features upto a point, beyond which, if the number of features increases, the classification accuracy begins to drop.

Feature selection also reduces the time complexity of the training process. If the data size is very large, the training time will be very high. In some cases, the training may not be completed in an acceptable time period. If feature selection is first carried out, then the training time may come within acceptable limits.

In addition, the distances in high dimensional spaces may not capture the intended similarity appropriately. In high dimensional spaces, distances between a point X and its nearest neighbor $nn(X)$ and its furthest neighbor $fn(X)$ are shown to satisfy $d(X, nn(x)) = d(X, fn(X))$ where $d(X, nn(X))$ is the nearest neighbor distance from X and $d(X, fn(X))$ is the distance of furthest neighbor from X. If feature selection is carried out, this problem is mitigated as the dimensions are reduced.

1. Types of Feature Selection

There are three feature selection methods. They are:

1. Filter methods
2. Wrapper methods
3. Embedded methods

The filter methods compute a score for each feature and then select features according to the score. The wrapper methods score feature subsets by seeing their performance on a dataset using a classification algorithm. The embedded methods select features during the process of training.

The wrapper method finds the feature subset by the method of search. For every subset generated, its performance is evaluated on a validation dataset using a classification algorithm. The feature subset giving the best performance on the validation dataset is selected. Some of the methods used are:

1. Exhaustive enumeration
2. Branch and bound technique
3. Sequential selection

   (a) Sequential Forward Selection
   (b) Sequential Backward Selection
   (c) Sequential Floating Forward Selection
   (d) Sequential Floating Backward Selection

4. Min–max approach
5. Stochastic techniques like genetic algorithms (GA)
6. Artificial Neural Networks

This chapter explains the filter method where the interaction between the features is considered. Consider a dataset with patterns which are d-dimensional. Feature selection is the task of selecting k features where $1 \leq k < d$. So if we have a feature set $\{f_1, f_2, \ldots, f_d\}$, this entails finding the score of each feature f_i. This score represents the degree of relevance, preference or importance of the feature. The similarity between any two features f_i and f_j is then found using these scores. This is used to remove the redundancy in the selected features. In other words, the selected features should complement each other. This means that the total similarity score over all the selected features should be as small as possible.

Then an algorithm is used to maximize the total importance scores and minimize the total similarity scores of a set of features. An evaluation measure is used to find the importance score of each feature. This is discussed in the sections which follow.

The process of selecting those features with largest total importance scores can be represented as

$$\max \sum_i [w_i x_i - s_{ij} x_i x_j],$$

for $j \neq i$
s.t. $x_i \in \{0, 1\} \; i = 1, \ldots, d,$
$\sum_i x_i = k,$

where x_i is 1 if the ith feature is chosen and 0 if it is not chosen, w_i is the importance score of feature i
s_{ij} is the similarity between feature f_i and f_j,
i.e.

$$s_{ij} = \begin{cases} 1 & \text{if } x_i \text{ and } x_j \text{ are similar} \\ 0 & \text{otherwise} \end{cases}$$

d is the total number of features
and k is the number of features selected.
If x_i and x_j are similar, then the objective function will be

$$max \sum_i x_i (w_i - x_j).$$

2. Mutual Information (MI) for Feature Selection

This function is based on the information gain and takes into account how features work together. MI is used to measure the dependencies between features and classes. MI between term t and class l measures how much information the presence or absence of a term contributes to making the correct classification decision on the class l. It is computed as

$$MI = -P(u_t, u_l)\log_2\frac{P(u_t, u_l)}{P(u_t)P(u_l)} - P(\bar{u}_t, u_l)\log_2\frac{P(\bar{u}_t, u_l)}{P(\bar{u}_t)P(u_l)}$$
$$- P(u_t, \bar{u}_l)\log_2\frac{P(u_t, \bar{u}_l)}{P(u_t)P(\bar{u}_l)} - P(\bar{u}_t, \bar{u}_l)\log_2\frac{p(\bar{u}_t, \bar{u}_l)}{P(\bar{u}_t)P(\bar{u}_l)},$$

where
u_t means that the document contains the term t; and
$\bar{u}_t$ means the document does not contain the term t;
u_l means the document is in class l and;
$\bar{u}_l$ means the document is not in class l.

In other words, this can be written as

$$MI = \frac{N_{u_t u_l}}{N} \log_2 \frac{NN_{u_t u_l}}{(N_{u_t \bar{u}_l} + N_{u_t u_l})(N_{u_t u_l} + N_{\bar{u}_t u_l})}$$
$$+ \frac{N_{\bar{u}_t u_l}}{N} \log_2 \frac{NN_{\bar{u}_t u_l}}{((N_{\bar{u}_t u_l} + N_{\bar{u}_t \bar{u}_l})(N_{u_t u_l} + N_{\bar{u}_t u_l})}$$
$$+ \frac{NN_{u_t \bar{u}_l}}{N} \log_2 \frac{NN_{u_t \bar{u}_l}}{(N_{u_t u_l} + N_{u_t \bar{u}_l})(N_{u_t \bar{u}_l} + N_{\bar{u}_t \bar{u}_l})}$$
$$+ \frac{N_{\bar{u}_t \bar{u}_l}}{N} \log_2 \frac{NN_{\bar{u}_t \bar{u}_l}}{(N_{\bar{u}_t u_l} + N_{\bar{u}_t \bar{u}_l})(N_{u_t \bar{u}_l} + N_{\bar{u}_t \bar{u}_l})},$$

where
$N_{u_t u_l}$ = number of documents where the term is present which belongs to the class,
$N_{\bar{u}_t u_l}$ = number of documents belonging to the class where the term is absent,
$N_{u_t \bar{u}_l}$ = number of documents where the term is present which does not belong to the class,

$N_{\bar{u}_t \bar{u}_l}$ = number of documents where both the term and class are absent,

N = Total number of documents.

If the distribution of the term in the whole document is the same as its distribution in the class then MI = 0. If MI is large, it means the term is in a document if and only if the document is in the class. It makes sense to keep only informative terms and eliminate non-informative terms so that the performance of the classifier improves.

In the filter approach, a filter is used to discard features having a low value of MI. We can also use the *backward filter* which discards features if its value of MI with the class is less than some ϵ with probability p. The *forward filter* also can be used which includes a feature if the MI is greater than ϵ with a probability p.

3. Chi-square Statistic

The chi-square statistic is used to determine if a distribution of observed frequencies differs from the theoretical expected frequencies. This non-parametric statistical technique uses frequencies instead of using the mean and variances, since it uses categorical data.

The chi-square statistic is given by

$$\chi^2 = \sum_i |(N_i - E_i)^2 / E_i|,$$

where χ^2 is the chi-square statistic, N is the observed frequency and E is the expected frequency. The chi-square statistic sums the discrepancy of the observed number of times each outcome occurs and the expected number of times each outcome occurs for each category. The discrepancy is computed as the square of the difference between N and E divided by E.

The chi-square statistic can be computed to find the goodness of fit or to test for independence of two sets of categories.

The chi-square test for independence is used to determine if two variables are independent. The values calculated from the formula are compared with the values in the chi-square distribution table. In the chi-square distribution table, for each degree of freedom, the probability levels are given for different values of χ^2. Looking at the probability levels, if it is below 5%, it is below the significance level which implies that the two distributions are the same.

In feature selection, we test the independence between a term and a class. The following χ^2 value is calculated:

$$\chi^2(D, t, l) = \frac{(N_{u_t u_l} - E_{u_t u_l})^2}{E_{u_t u_l}} + \frac{(N_{\bar{u}_t u_l} - E_{\bar{u}_t u_l})^2}{E_{\bar{u}_t u_l}}$$
$$+ \frac{(N_{u_t \bar{u}_l} - E_{u_t \bar{u}_l})^2}{E_{u_t \bar{u}_l}} + \frac{(N_{\bar{u}_t \bar{u}_l} - E_{\bar{u}_t \bar{u}_l})^2}{E_{\bar{u}_t \bar{u}_l}},$$

where
u_t means that the document contains the term t, and
$\bar{u}_t$ means the document does not contain the term t;
u_l means the document is in class l and,
$\bar{u}_l$ means the document is not in class l;
$N =$ observed frequency and,
$E =$ expected frequency.

This means

$$\chi^2(D, t, l) = \frac{(N_{00} - E_{00})^2}{E_{00}} + \frac{(N_{01} - E_{01})^2}{E_{01}} + \frac{(N_{10} - E_{10})^2}{E_{10}}$$
$$+ \frac{(N_{11} - E_{11})^2}{E_{11}},$$

where
$N_{11} =$ number of documents which contains term t and belongs to class l;
$N_{10} =$ number of documents which contain term t and do not belong to class l;
$N_{01} =$ number of documents which do not contain term t and belong to class l;
$N_{00} =$ number of documents which do not contain term t and do not belong to class l.

If the χ^2 value is larger than the one in the table giving χ^2 distributions for the degree of freedom, then it means that we need to reject the hypothesis that they are independent. This means that since the two are dependent, the occurrence of the term makes the occurrence of the class more likely. This means the term is useful as a feature.

4. Goodman–Kruskal Measure

The Goodman–Kruskal measure λ measures the interaction between a feature and a class. If there are two classes $+$ and $-$, the measure for a feature i is

$$\lambda_i = \frac{\sum_{j=1}^{v} max(n_{j+}, n_{j-}) - max(n_+, n_-)}{n - max(n_+, n_-)},$$

where
n_{i+} = number of instances for which the value of a feature is V_i and the class is '$+$',
n_{i-} = number of instances for which the value of a feature is V_i and the class is '$-$',
v = number of discrete values taken by the feature.

Domain of the input feature $= \{V_1, V_2, \cdots, V_v\}$
n_+ = number of instances of class '$+$',
n_- = number of instances of class '$-$',
n = total number of instances.

The value of λ_i varies from 0 to 1, where $\lambda_i = 0$ means there is no predictive gain in using the feature i to predict the class. $\lambda_i = 1$ means there is perfect predictivity in using feature i.

5. Laplacian Score

The Laplacian Score measures importance of a feature by its ability for locality preserving. The features are given a score depending on their locality preserving power. The algorithm is based on finding a nearest neighbor graph for the set of nodes and finding the Laplacian of the graph. Using the Laplacian, the Laplacian score is calculated for every feature.

The algorithm is as follows:

1. Construct the nearest neighbor graph G for the set of points. For every pair of points i and j, if x_i is one of the k-nearest neighbors

of x_j or if x_j is one of the k nearest neighbors of x_i, then an edge is drawn between i and j.

2. If nodes i and j are connected, put $W_{ij} = \exp^{-\frac{\|x_i - x_j\|^2}{k}}$, where k is a user-defined constant. If i is not connected to $j, W_{ij} = 0$.

3. For a feature i, let the feature vector be
$$f_i = (f_{i1}, f_{i2}, \ldots, f_{id}).$$
The unit matrix $I = (1, \ldots, 1)^T$.

The matrix D is given by

$$D = diag(WI).$$

The Laplacian $L = D - W$.

Then $\tilde{f}_i = f_i - \frac{f_i^T DI}{I^T DI} I$.

4. The Laplacian score of the ith feature is

$$L_i = \frac{\tilde{f}_i^T L \tilde{f}_i}{\tilde{f}_i^T D \tilde{f}_i}. \tag{1}$$

The justification for Eq. (1) is as follows. Considering all pairs of points j and k, W_{jk} measures the similarity between the jth and kth node. A good feature is one on which two data points are close to each other if and only if there is an edge between the two points. The criterion for choosing a feature using the above principle can be written as:

$$L_i = \frac{\sum_{jk} (f_{ij} - f_{ik})^2 W_{jk}}{var(f_i)}, \tag{2}$$

where $var(f_i)$ is the variance of the ith feature.

The numerator of Eq. (2) can be written as

$$\sum_{jk} (f_{ij} - f_{ik})^2 W_{jk} = \sum_{jk} (f_{ij}^2 + f_{ik}^2 - 2f_{ij} f_{ik}) W_{jk}$$

$$= 2f_i^T D f_i - 2f_i^T W f_i = 2f_i^T L f_i.$$

The denominator of Eq. (2) can be written as

$$var(f_i) = \sum_j (f_{ij} - \mu_i)^2 D_{jj},$$

$$\mu_i = \sum_j \left(f_{ij} \frac{D_{jj}}{\sum_j D_{jj}} \right) = \frac{f_i^T DI}{I^T DI}.$$

Removing the mean from the samples, we get

$$\tilde{f}_i = f_i = \frac{f_i^T DI}{I^T DI} I,$$

$$var(f_i) = \sum_j \tilde{f}_{ij}^2 D_{jj} = \tilde{f}_i^T D \tilde{f}_i.$$

Putting $\tilde{f}_i^T L \tilde{f}_i = f_i^T L f_i$ and substituting in Eq. (2), we get Eq. (1).

6. Singular Value Decomposition (SVD)

SVD is the decomposition of a rectangular matrix. Given a rectangular matrix P which is $n \times m$, it can be decomposed as

$$P = A\Sigma B^T,$$

where A is a $(n \times k)$ matrix, B^T is a $k \times m$ matrix and Σ is a $k \times k$ square matrix. The rank of Σ is k and the diagonal elements have singular values and the rows can be adjusted so that $\alpha_1 \geq \alpha_2 \geq \cdots \geq \alpha_k > 0$. A column P_i of P, which is a m vector can be expressed as a linear combination of the m basis vectors of A $(A_{.1}, A_{.2}, \ldots, A_{.m})$ using the singular values in $\Sigma(\alpha_1, \alpha_2, \ldots, \alpha_m)$ and the ith column $B_{.i}^T$ of B^T.

One method of using SVD for feature selection is to approximate P by P_{k1} where $k1 < k$. In P_k, the singular values which are zero or close to zero are removed and the remaining $k1$ singular values are retained. So we get

$$P_{k1} = A_{m \times k1} \Sigma_{k1 \times k1} B_{k1 \times n}^T.$$

The $k1$ singular values which are larger are chosen. High singular values correspond to dimensions which have more variability. The dimensions with lower singular values correspond to dimensions with less variability which may not be discriminative features for learning. Classification which has to be performed on P which is an $m \times n$ matrix can now be performed on the matrix ΣB^T which is a $k1 \times n$ matrix where $k1 < m$.

It is also possible to find a basis vector A which will transform any vector from the original vector space to the new vector space. For a training dataset T, the resulting SVD $T = \tilde{A}\tilde{\Sigma}\tilde{B}^T$ will yield a set of basis vectors which can be used for the range of P. Here T is $m \times r$ where r is the number of points in the training dataset. To use the resulting SVD for T to transform P, it is necessary to project the columns of P onto a subspace spanned by the first $k1$ columns of $\tilde{A}$. A is transformed by computing $(\tilde{A}_{.1}, \tilde{A}_{.2}, \ldots, \tilde{A}_{.k1})^T A$. Hence the original patterns can be transformed using $(\tilde{A}_{.1}, \tilde{A}_{.2}, \ldots, \tilde{A}_{.k1})^T$ and classification can be carried out on the transformed patterns.

7. Non-negative Matrix Factorization (NMF)

NMF is a feature extraction algorithm that decomposes multivariate data by creating a user-defined number of extracted features which results in a reduced representation of the original data. NMF decomposes a data matrix X into the product of two lower rank matrices B and H so that X is approximately equal to BH i.e. $X \approx BH$. NMF is an iterative procedure which starts with some initial values of B and H which are modified iteratively so that the product approaches X. The procedure terminates when the approximation error converges. It can also be terminated after a specified number of iterations. The new features are a linear combination of the original features. NMF does not allow negative entries in the matrices B and H. So if X is a $n \times m$ matrix, then since finally $X = BH$, B is a $n \times r$ matrix and H is an $r \times m$ matrix. The r columns of B can be called the bases and then X will consist of original feature vectors and H is the newly learned feature vector based on the basis matrix B. If r is chosen to be smaller than n, then data compression and dimensionality reduction takes place.

An NMF factorization can be defined as the optimization problem:

$$min_{B,H} D(X\|BH),$$

such that $B, H \geq 0$.

In this formulation, B and H have to be non-negative.

$D(X\|BH)$ means the divergence of X from BH and is the cost function of the problem. If BH is actually Y, then

$$D(X\|Y) = \sum_{i,j} \left(x_{ij} \log \frac{x_{ij}}{y_{ij}} - x_{ij} + y_{ij} \right).$$

This gives a measure of the error resulting in factorizing X into BH.

The objective function can be written as

$$O = \sum_{i=1}^{n} \sum_{j=1}^{m} [X_{ij} \log(BH)_{ij} - (BH)_{ij}], \tag{3}$$

where the value X_{ij} is generated by adding Poisson noise to the product $(BH)_{ij}$. The objective function O is subject to the non-negativity constraint i.e. all the non-zero elements of B and H are positive. An iterative procedure is used to modify the initial values of B and H so that the product approaches X. This procedure terminates when the approximation error converges or after a user-defined number of iterations. The update formula for B and H is as follows:

$$B_{ik} = B_{ik} \sum_{j} \frac{X_{ij}}{(BH)_{ij}} H_{kj},$$

$$B_{ik} = \frac{B_{ik}}{\sum_{l} B_{lk}},$$

$$H_{kj} = H_{kj} \sum_{i} B_{ik} \frac{X_{ij}}{(BH)_{ij}}.$$

The learned bases using NMF are not orthonormal to each other. This is because to satisfy the non-negativity constraint the bases cannot be orthonormal. One way of handling this is to consider the learned non-orthonormal bases and orthonormalize the bases. This is found to give better results for feature extraction.

8. Random Projections (RPs) for Feature Extraction

In RP, the original high-dimensional data is projected onto a lower-dimensional subspace using a random matrix whose columns have unit lengths. The original d-dimensional data is projected to a k-dimensional subspace through the origin, using a random $k \times d$ matrix P whose columns have unit lengths. If we have n d-dimensional samples, $X_1, X_2, \ldots, X_n$, it is converted to n k-dimensional samples using a projection matrix P. This can be written as

$$Y_{k \times n} = P_{k \times d} X_{d \times n}.$$

P is not orthogonal and hence cannot be called a projection. Normally, if P is not orthogonal, it causes significant distortions in the data. But since P is sufficiently close to being orthogonal, in a high-dimensional space, the directions are almost orthogonal. The choice of P is what is to be studied.

Unlike other methods such as PCA, random projections are easier to do as they just require a matrix multiplication with a matrix that can be generated without much difficulty. In PCA, we need to compute the covariance matrix, decompose it into its singular value form and choose the top k-eigenvectors. This entire process requires a significant amount of effort.

The Euclidean distance between two points x_1 and x_2 after the random projection is approximated by the scaled Euclidean distance

$$\sqrt{\frac{d}{k}} \|Px_1 - Px_2\|.$$

The scaling fraction $\sqrt{\frac{d}{k}}$ is required due to the decrease in the dimensionality of the data. This fraction is called the Johnson–Lindenstrauss (J–L) scaling term.

In many cases where RP is used, the elements p_{ij} are Gaussian distributed. Using a simpler distribution, according to Achlioptas the elements p_{ij} can take the values

$$p_{ij} = \sqrt{s}. \begin{cases} +1 & \text{with probability } \dfrac{1}{2s} \\[2ex] 0 & \text{with probability } 1 - \dfrac{1}{s} \\[2ex] -1 & \text{with probability } \dfrac{1}{2s} \end{cases} \quad (4)$$

The value chosen for s is 1 or 3. The choice of p_{ij} as given above uses integer arithmetic and results in a sparse matrix which gives additional saving in time. The use of the J-L scaling to take into account the reduction in dimensionality ensures that the inter-pattern distances are preserved when random projections is used. The choice of k, the reduced number of dimensions needs to be selected. The L-J result gives a bound on k but it is possible to get a much tighter bound. It is also possible to find k by carrying out experiments on a validation set.

While using $s = 1$ or $s = 3$ gives sparse random projections, it is also possible to use $s >> 3$ such as $s = \sqrt{d}$ or $s = \frac{d}{\log d}$, where d is the number of dimensions, leading to very sparse random projections due to which the computation is speeded up significantly.

Some characteristics of Random Projections are now discussed. In RP, the original matrix $X \varepsilon \mathcal{R}^{n \times d}$ is multiplied with a random matrix $P \varepsilon \mathcal{R}^{d \times k}$ consisting of i.i.d $N(0,1)$ entries. Let the rows of X be denoted by $\{a_i\}_{i=1}^{n} \varepsilon \mathcal{R}^{d}$. Let $\{b_i\}_{i=1}^{n} \varepsilon \mathcal{R}^{k}$ denote the rows of the projected data. We can then write:

$$b_i = \frac{1}{\sqrt{k}} P^T a_i.$$

Considering only the first two rows, if we denote

$$m_1 = \|a_1\|^2 = \sum_{i=1}^{d} a_{1,i}^2; \quad m_2 = \|a_2\|^2 = \sum_{i=1}^{d} a_{2,i}^2, \quad (5)$$

$$u = a_1^T a_2 = \sum_{i=1}^{d} a_{1,j} a_{2,j}; \quad d = \|a_1 - a_2\|^2 = m_1 + m_2 - 2u. \quad (6)$$

Then

$$E(\|b_1\|^2) = \|a_1\|^2) = m_1; \quad var(\|b_1\|^2) = \frac{2}{k}m_1^2, \tag{7}$$

$$E(\|b_1 - b_2\|^2) = d; \quad var(\|b_1 - b_2\|^2) = \frac{2}{k}d^2, \tag{8}$$

$$E(b_1^T b_2) = u; \quad var(b_1^T b_2) = \frac{1}{k}(m_1 m_2 + u^2). \tag{9}$$

This shows that distances between two points and inner products can be computed in k dimensions. If $k \ll d$ then there is a lot of saving in time and space. Looking at $var(\|b_1\|^2), var(\|b_1 - b_2\|^2)$ and $var(b_1^T b_2)$ in Eqs. (7), (8) and (9), it can be seen that Random Projections preserve the pairwise distances in expected sense.

8.1. Advantages of random projections

Using random projections results in projecting the data onto a random lower dimensional subspace. It is found to give results comparable to other conventional dimensionality reduction methods such as Principal Component Analysis (PCA) and SVD. At the same time, use of RP is computationally less expensive. If a sparse random matrix is used, the sparseness can be used to give additional saving computationally. In additional, random projections preserves the inter-pattern distances. RP can be used in a number of different applications. Since RP preserves the distances between patterns, an application such as high dimensional clustering is highly suited to using RP.

9. Locality Sensitive Hashing (LSH)

LSH is a set of techniques for performing approximate search in high dimensions. It is used for grouping points in space into 'buckets' based on some distance metric operating on the points. Points that are close to each other under the chosen metric are mapped to the same bucket with high probability. Two points are considered to be close to each other if, after a projection of the points on to specified dimensions, the two points remain close together. In other words, if random projection operation is used to map the data points from a high-dimensional space to a low-dimensional subspace, then points which are close to each other in the low dimensional subspace are grouped together. For the purpose of grouping, the projection is put into a set of hash bins so that nearby points in the original space will fall into the same bin. The hash function for a point v is given by

$$h(v) = \left\lfloor \frac{x \cdot v + b}{w} \right\rfloor, \tag{10}$$

where w is the width of each quantization bin, b is a random variable uniformly distributed between 0 and w and x is a vector with components that are selected at random from a Gaussian distribution. The value of w influences the number of points that fall into each bucket. Increasing w will increase the number of points that fall into each bucket.

Then for any two points p and q in $\mathcal{R}^d$ that are close to each other, there is a high probability P_1 that they fall into the same bin.

$$P_H[h(p) = h(q)] \geq P_1 \quad \text{for } \|p - q\| \leq R_1.$$

For points p and q in $\mathcal{R}^d$ that are far apart, there is a low probability P_2 that they fall into the same bin. That is,

$$P_H[h(p) = h(q)] \leq P_2 \quad \text{for } \|p - q\| \geq cR_1 = R_2.$$

$\|.\|$ is the L_2 norm and $R_2 > R_1$ and $P_1 > P_2$.

Further the dot product in Eq. (10) can be done k times, thereby magnifying the difference between P_1 and P_2. The ratio of the probabilities is increased since $\left(\frac{P_1}{P_2}\right)^k > \frac{P_1}{P_2}$. The k dot products are carried out on v to transform it into k real numbers. Using Eq. (10), the k inner products are quantized into the set of hash bins. In all the k dot products, if the points and its nearest neighbor fall into the same bin, then success is achieved. This has a probability of P_1^k of occurring. It can be seen that as k increases, the probability decreases. This is repeated a number of times for different random projections so that the true nearest neighbor is found with an arbitrary high probability. So if there are k dot products and M projections, then kM neighbors are pooled to find the nearest neighbor.

Each data point is placed in a hash bucket described by k integer values using the process of projection and quantization. Hence, it can be seen that LSH performs probabilistic dimensionality reduction of high dimensional data. Similar items are mapped to the same bin and can be taken to be a single feature. One of the main applications of LSH is to provide an efficient nearest neighbor search algorithm. Depending on the metric used, items are mapped to the bins. Thus, for high-dimensional datasets, fast approximate nearest-neighbor search can be carried out using locality sensitive hashing. LSH can be viewed as random feature selection.

10. Class Separability

A measure is used for class separability for each feature. This measure is calculated by using the Kullback–Leibler (KL) distance between histograms of feature values. For each feature, for discrete valued features, each value forms a bin. In the case of numeric features, discretization is carried out using $\sqrt{n}$ equally spaced fields, where n is the size of the training data. For each bin, the bin count is divided by the total number of elements to get the probability that a feature takes a value in each of the bins. We get $p_j(b = i \mid c = c_1)$ which is the probability that the jth feature takes a value in the ith bin given a class c_1. For each feature j, the class separability is

$$CS_j = \sum_{i=1}^{c} \sum_{k=1}^{c} \delta_j(i, k),$$

where c is the number of classes and $\delta_j(i, k)$ is the KL distance between the histograms of the two classes i and k and is given by

$$\delta_j(i, k) = \sum_{k=1}^{s} p_j(b = k \mid c = i) \log \left(\frac{p_j(b = k \mid c = i)}{p_j(b = k \mid c = k)} \right),$$

where s gives the number of bins. When the CS_j values are sorted in decreasing order, if the difference between the class separability of two features differs by a very small value, say 0.001, then the feature having the smaller distance is eliminated.

11. Genetic and Evolutionary Algorithms

Genetic and evolutionary algorithms are robust algorithms based on the principles of natural selection and survival of the fittest. They are optimization techniques which find the best solution from a number of competing solutions which forms the population of candidate solutions.

The genetic algorithm (GA) consists of a population of chromosomes or strings. For feature selection, each chromosome consists of d elements where if d is the number of features. Each element is 1 if that particular feature is selected and 0 if it is not selected. For example, if $d = 6$, and a chromosome is 011001, it means that feature 2, 3 and 6 are selected. The fitness function for a chromosome is the number of correct classifications on a validation set using the features selected.

One method of feature selection using GAs is explained below. The evolutionary algorithm uses a search strategy which experiments with different combinations of features being chosen where each is a candidate solution or a string. There is a population of strings. Each such combination is evaluated. Operators are used to improve the candidate solutions over time and the candidate solution which gives the best evaluation is chosen and the feature subset pertaining to this string is selected. The population in the GA consists of strings which are binary in nature. Each string (or chromosome) is of length d, with each position i being zero or one depending on the absence or presence of feature i in the selected set. This means that each feature subset is coded as a d-element bit string or binary valued vector. Each string in the population is a feature selection vector α where each $\alpha = \alpha_1, \ldots, \alpha_d$ where α_i assumes a value 0 if the ith feature is excluded and 1 if it is present in the subset. Each chromosome is evaluated to compute its fitness by determining its performance on the training set. This is done as explained below.

The penalty function $p(e)$ is

$$p(e) = \frac{exp^{\frac{e-t}{m}} - 1}{e - 1},$$

where
$e = error\ rate$,
$t = $ feasibility threshold,
$m = $ scale factor.

This penalty function is monotonic with respect to e. If $e < t$, then $p(e)$ is negative and, as e approaches zero, $p(e)$ slowly approaches its minimal value.

If $e = t$, then $p(e) = 0$ and
if $e = t + m$, then $p(e) = 1$.

For greater values of the error rate the penalty function quickly rises towards infinity.

The score $J(a)$ is given by

$$J(a) = l(a) + p(e(a)),$$

where $a = (\alpha_1, \ldots, \alpha_d)$ is a bit string representing a feature subset. $l(a)$ is the number of features absent in the feature subset. Let $\Pi = \{a_1, \ldots, a_n\}$ denote the population of feature selection vectors. Each feature selection vector is a string in the population. Since we require a minimum of the score $J(a)$, the fitness function is

$$f(a_i) = (1 + \epsilon) \max_{a_j \in \Pi} \left[J(a_j) - J(a_i) \right],$$

where ϵ is a small positive constant.

11.1. Hybrid GA for feature selection

This algorithm uses a guided hybrid GA for feature selection which reduces the number of fitness function evaluations required. The chromosome or string consists of d bits where d is the dimensionality of the data. Each bit of the string corresponds to one feature and is 1 if the feature is included and 0 if it is excluded. The evaluation of a string s consists of two parameters $c(s)$ which is the cost function value and $f(s)$ which is based on the performance of the string on a validation set. The cost function $c(s)$ can be written as:

$$c(s) = n_{s1} + p,$$

where p is the penalty given by

$$p = 2^{\frac{max(F_A)-f(s)}{\gamma}} - 1.$$

n_{s1} gives the number of included features in s, $max(F_A)$ gives the maximum of the f value considering all chromosomes in the complete set of chromosomes A, and γ is a threshold value. The value $f(s)$ of the string s is given by

$$f(s) = 1 - \frac{var(O - O_{cv}(s))}{var(O)},$$

where O is the response variable, and $O_{cv}(s)$ gives the predicted response from a cross-validation set. In other words,

$$f(s) = 1 - \frac{m - m_c}{m},$$

where
m = number of patterns in validation set;
m_c = number of correctly classified patterns.

It can be seen that if $max(F_A) - f(s) \leq \gamma$, then $0 \leq p \leq 1$ holds. If $max(F_A) - f(s) \gg \gamma, p$ increases rapidly. A steady state GA is used. The set A is the archive which stores all the strings S_A with their modeling accuracy F_A and cost function values C_A. At each iteration, there is a subset of A which is the reproductive population R. This is the population subject to the genetic operators to produce new strings. A subset of R denoted by B forms the set of strings from which one string is selected for local feature elimination.

The algorithm can be written as:

1. Generate a number of initial random strings. Let one of the strings consist of all ones (i.e. all features are included). These strings from the archive A.
2. Evaluate A to generate F_A and C_A.

3. Set it $= 1$ and $tr = \|A\|$.
4. **While** convergence criterion is not met do.
5. Extract R from A.
6. Select two strings from R.
7. Apply crossover to get the children s_1 and s_2.
8. Apply mutation on s_1 and s_2.
9. Evaluate s_1 and s_2.
10. Add s_1 and s_2 with $f(s_1), f(s_2), c(s_1)$ and $c(s_2)$ to A.
11. **if** $it > \delta$ then.
12. **if** $(\|A\| > \beta + tr)$ then.
13. Train classifier C using A. Set $tr = \|A\|$.
14. **end if**.
15. Extract B from R.
16. Select one string s and do feature elimination on s using G.
17. Add evaluated strings to A.
18. **end if**.
19. it $=$ it $+ 1$.
20. **end while**.

In the above algorithm, upto δ iterations, the GA operates with its operations of selection, crossover, and mutation. After δ iterations, feature elimination is carried out in addition to GA operations. It can also be seen that after every β iterations, the classifier C is retrained with the A existing at that time. The convergence criterion would be either that the cost function or modeling accuracy values are not improving with iterations or that the maximum iterations have been reached.

The genetic operators, selection, crossover and mutation are explained below.

Selection involves selecting two parents from R. The first parent s_1 is chosen randomly from R. Binary tournament selection is used to select the second parent. Two strings are selected from R and the string with the smaller dissimilarity to s_1 is chosen as the second parent s_2.

The strings s_1 and s_2 are subject to subset size oriented commonality crossover (SSOCF). This type of crossover maintains, on an average, the same number of included features in the off-spring as either of the parents. The first child has features which have the set of common elements of s_1 and s_2 which are of included features. The first child also has features of $x(s_1, s_2)$ with probability $\frac{n_{c1} - n_{u1(s_1,s_2)}}{n_{x(s_1,s_2)}} \cdot x(s_1, s_2)$ are the set of elements that are not common among s_1 and s_2. $n_{u1(s_1,s_2)}$ gives the number of common elements between s_1 and s_2 which are of included features.

n_{c1} gives the number of elements of included features in the first child.

Selecting R from A is done based on properties of the strings such as whether it is inert, whether it is dominated by other strings and its crowding index.

The crowding index of string s is given by:

$$cr(s) = \frac{1}{n_{s1}} \sum_{i=1}^{|A|} n_{u1}(s, S_A(i)),$$

n_{s1} gives the number of features included in s, $n_{u1}(s, S_A(i))$ is the number of common elements that are included between s and the strings in A.

For a string s if the full set of *"leave one variable out"* S_{lo} in A is such that $n_{S_{lo}} = n_{s1}$, then s is inert.

A string s_1 is dominated i.e. $dm(s_1) = 1$ if there is at least one other string s_2 in A where $s_2^1 \subset S_1^1$ and $c(s_2) \leq c(s_1)$. This means that if $dm(s_1) = 1$, there is another string in A which has a subset of included features and of better or equal performance.

The procedure to find the subset R from A is as follows. The strings in A are arranged in decreasing order of the C_A values. The first string is then put into R. For the other strings the following procedure is used. For a string i, check if the string is dominated or inert. If not, compute the dissimilarities D_i between this string and all the strings in S_R. Also find the crowding index $Cr(i)$. $A(i)$ is selected if its crowding index $CR(i) < min(CR_R)$ and if there are less than γ strings in R with a smaller dissimilarity to $S_A(i)$. Strings are added to R till $F_A(i) < median(F_A)$.

Note that the dissimilarity between two strings s_1 and s_2 is given by

$$d(s_1, s_2) = 1 - \frac{n_{u1}(s_1, s_2)}{\sqrt{n_{s1}^1 . n_{s2}^1}},$$

where $n_{u1}(s_1, s_2)$ gives the number of common elements that are included in the feature set in s_1 and s_2, n_{s1}^1 gives the number of included features in $s1$ and n_{s2}^1 is the number of included features in s_2.

The set B contains strings which can be selected for feature elimination. The strings of R which are not inert are put into B. To select among these strings, the individuals which are most dissimilar to the inert individuals are extracted and put into B.

The individual to be selected from B for feature elimination is chosen by using tournament selection. The size of the tournament is $\left\lceil \frac{|B|}{k} \right\rceil$ where k is a constant having a default of 5.

C is a classifier trained on the dataset available in A.

12. Ranking for Feature Selection

Ranking of features entails computing a score for each of the features and sorting the features according to the scores. The order in which the features occur are considered rather than the scores themselves. Ranking of the features can be used to define a filter for feature selection. Based on the ranking, some features can be eliminated. The criteria used for ranking of the features is usually the performance of the feature subset on an input training set. The ranking method generally is a two-step process.

1. Each individual feature is used to construct a predictor of the label.
2. The features are ranked based on the errors of these predictors.

Most approaches use the same training set both for constructing the predictor and for evaluating its error.

An evaluation measure such as mean average precision (MAP) or Normalized discount cumulative gain (NDCG) is used. The features are then sorted according to the score and this ordered list of features is considered for feature selection.

Some feature ranking algorithms are discussed here.

12.1. Feature selection based on an optimization formulation

In this method, the feature selection depends on the important score of each feature f_i and the similarity between pairs of features f_i and f_j.

When the features selected are used on a validation set, the results are used to evaluate the ranking. Some measures used here are Mean Average Prediction (MAP), Normalized Discount Cumulative Gain (NDCG) and Kendal's similarity score. These are discussed below.

1. **MAP**

MAP measures the precision of the ranking results. If there are two classes, the positive and negative class, precision measures the accuracy of the top n results to a query. It is given by:

$$P(n) = \frac{no.\ of\ positive\ instances\ within\ top\ n}{n}.$$

Average precision of a query is

$$P_{\text{av}} = \sum_{n=1}^{N} \frac{P * pos(n)}{no.\ of\ positive\ instances},$$

where N is the maximum number of instances, $pos(n)$ is a binary function which indicates whether the instance at position i is positive. MAP is P_{av} averaged over all queries considered.

2. **NDCG**

NDCG measures ranking accuracy. Given a query,

$$NDCG(n) = Y_n \sum_{i=1}^{n} \frac{2^{R(i)} - 1}{\log(1 + j)},$$

where n denotes position, $R(i)$ denotes the score for rank j, Y_n is a normalization factor which ensures that a perfect ranking's NDCG at position n is 1. Finally, NDCG is averaged over all queries.

3. Similarity between Features

Similarity between two features is measured on the basis of their ranking result. The similarity between two features is represented by the similarity between the ranking results they produce. Kendall's similarity is used. The similarity between two features f_i and f_j for a query q is given by

$$K_q(f_i, f_j) = \frac{|\{(x_a, x_b) \varepsilon D | x_a \prec_{f_i} x_b \, and \, x_a \prec_{f_j} x_b\}|}{|\{(x_a, x_b) \varepsilon D\}|},$$

where D denotes all the pairs of instances (x_a, x_b) with respect to the query q, $x_a \prec_{f_i} x_b$ denotes that instance x_a is ranked ahead of instance x_b by feature f_i. The Kendall's score is averages over all queries to get $K(f_i, f_j)$. It is to be noted that $K(f_i, f_j) = K(f_j, f_i)$.

The optimization formulation can be represented as:

$$max \sum_i w_i y_i$$

$$min \sum_i \sum_{j \neq i} s(f_i, f_j) y_i y_j$$
such that $y_i \varepsilon \{0, 1\}, i = 1, \ldots, m$
$\sum_i y_i = t,$

where t is the total number of features, $y_i = 1$ indicates that the feature f_i is selected and $y_i = 0$ indicates that the feature f_i is not selected, w_i is the importance score of feature f_i and $s(f_i, f_j)$ is the similarity between features f_i and f_j. To calculate w_i, MAP or NDCG is used and for similarity, $s(f_i, f_j) = K(f_i, f_j)$.

In the above formulation, there are two objectives: To maximize the sum of the importance scores of each feature and to minimize the sum of the similarity scores between pairs of features.

Converting this multi-objective programming problem to a single-objective programming problem is done as follows:

$max \sum_i w_i y_i - K_1 \sum_i \sum_{j \neq i} s(f_i, f_j) y_i y_j$
such that $y_i \varepsilon \{0, 1\}, i = 1, \ldots, m$
$\sum_i y_i = t.$

K_1 decides the relative importance given to the first term and the second term of the objective function.

The optimization is a typical 0–1 integer programming problem. The solution using exhaustive search has high time complexity. A greedy search algorithm can be used as shown below.

The algorithm is as follows:

1. Construct an undirected graph G_0 in which each node represents a feature, the weight of node f_i is w_i and the weight of the edge between f_i and f_j is $s(f_i, f_j)$.
2. Let the set $\mathcal{F} = \Phi$.
3. For $i = 1 \ldots t$

   (a) Select node with largest weight. Let the node be f_{ki}.
   (b) A punishment term is subtracted from the weight of the other nodes which depends on their dissimilarity with f_{ki} as follows:
   $w_j = w_j - s(f_{ki}, j) * 2K_1, j \neq ki.$
   (c) Add f_{ki} to $\mathcal{F}$ and remove it from the graph G with all the edges connected to it. In other words, $\mathcal{F}_{i+1} = \mathcal{F}_i \bigcup \{f_{ki}\}$ and $G_{i+1} = G_i \backslash \{f_{ki}\}.$

4. $\mathcal{F}_i$ gives the set of features.

12.2. Feature ranking using F-score

A simple and effective way to carry out feature selection is to use the F-score. This score is based on the statistics of the patterns and does not depend on the class labels. The F-score measures the discrimination of two sets of real numbers. The F-score of every feature is computed using the information in the training data. The F-score of the jth feature $F(j)$ is

$$F(j) = \frac{\left(\overline{x}_j^{(+)} - \overline{x}_j\right)^2 + \left(\overline{x}_j^{(-)} - \overline{x}_j\right)^2}{\frac{1}{n_+-1} \sum_{i=1}^{n_+} \left(x_{i,j}^{(+)} - \overline{x}_j^{(+)}\right)^2 + \frac{1}{n_--1} \sum_{i=1}^{n_-} \left(x_{i,j}^{(-)} - (\overline{x})_j^{(-)}\right)^2},$$

(11)

where

n_+ = number of positive instances,

n_- = number of negative instances,

$\overline{x}_j$ = average of jth feature in the whole dataset,

$\overline{x}_j^{(+)}$ = average of jth feature in the positive labeled instances,

$\overline{x}_j^{(-)}$ = average of jth feature in the negative labeled instances,

$x_{i,j}^{(+)}$ = jth feature of the ith positive instance,

$x_{i,j}^{(-)}$ = jth feature of the ith negative instance.

The numerator of Eq. (11) indicates the discrimination between the positive and the negative labeled instances, and the denominator indicates the discrimination within the positive labeled set and the negative labeled set. A larger F-score is more discriminative. If $F_i > F_j$, it means that the feature i is more discriminative than feature j. The F-score considers each feature separately and therefore does not take into account the interaction between features.

12.3. Feature ranking using linear support vector machine (SVM) weight vector

This method does feature ranking using weights from linear SVM models. The SVM finds a separating hyperplane between two classes. Given a training dataset, SVM solves the following unconstrained optimization problem:

$$min_{w,b} \frac{1}{2} \mathbf{w}^t \mathbf{w} + C \sum_{i=1}^{l} \mathcal{E}(\mathbf{w}, b; X_i, y_i),$$

(12)

where $\mathcal{E}(\mathbf{w}, b; X_i, y_i)$ is a loss function, C is a penalty factor and the loss function is

$$max(1 - y_i(\mathbf{w}^t \phi(\mathbf{X}_i) + b), 0) \tag{13}$$

or

$$max(1 - y_i(\mathbf{w}^t \phi(\mathbf{X}_i) + b), 0)^2, \tag{14}$$

where ϕ is a function used when the SVM is nonlinear. If Eq. (13) is used as the loss function it is called the L1-loss SVM. If Eq. (14) is used as the loss function it is called the L2-loss SVM.

A linear SVM has $\phi(\mathbf{X}) = \mathbf{X}$. For any test pattern x, the decision function is

$$f(X) = sign(\mathbf{w}^t \phi(X) + b). \tag{15}$$

A kernel function $K(X_i, X_j) = \phi(X_i)^t \phi(X_j)$ can be used to train the SVM. In the case of linear SVM, the kernel function will be $K(X_i, X_j) = X_i^t X_j$. Another kernel is the radial basis function (RBF) which can be written as

$$K(X_i, X_j) = exp(-\alpha \|X_i - X_j\|^2), \quad \text{where } \alpha > 0.$$

Using the linear SVM, $w \in R^n$ can be used to decide the importance of each feature. If $|w_i| > |w_j|$ then ith feature is more important than the jth feature. The features can be ranked according to the values $|w_j|$. Further, training a linear SVM is simpler.

The linear SVM algorithm can be written as:

1. Use grid search to find the parameter C for Eq. (12).
2. Train a L2-loss SVM using the best value of C.
3. Sort the features according to the absolute value of the weights.

12.4. Ensemble feature ranking

A number of different approaches can be used for feature ranking. To get a better ranking of the features, the ranking obtained by different methods can be combined.

12.4.1. *Using threshold-based feature selection techniques*

Techniques based on Information Gain, Chi-square statistic, F-measure etc. can be used to find the feature ranking. Then these rankings are combined. If we have rankings $F_1, \ldots, F_T$ where T is the number of ranking methods used, to find the overall ranking of a class, the arithmetic mean is used.

12.4.2. *Evolutionary algorithm*

One technique for ensemble feature ranking extracts feature ranking using independent runs of an evolutionary learning algorithm called ROGER (ROC-based Genetic Learner). It is called ROC-based as it optimizes the Area Under the Curve (AUC) based on Receiver Operator Characteristics (ROC). An earlier technique uses GAs to find good feature subsets where the fitness function is the accuracy obtained on a validation set using kNN classifier and only the selected features. The feature subsets are then combined.

The ROGER algorithm finds a hypothesis h which measures the weighted L_1 distance to a point p in $\mathcal{R}^d$. Each string of the GA has d weights and d coordinates of the point p i.e. the string is $(w_1, w_2, \ldots, w_d, p_1, \ldots, p_d)$. This is associated with the hypothesis

$$h(X) = \sum_{i=1}^{d} w_i * |x_i - p_i|.$$

The fitness of the string is computed using Wilcoxon statistic giving the fitness of the string, $\mathcal{F} = p(h(X_i) > h(X_j) \mid y_i > y_j)$ i.e. it is the probability that the result of the hypothesis of X_i is greater than that of X_j when the class label of X_i i.e. y_i is greater than the given class label of X_j i.e. y_j. This is equivalent to the AUC criterion.

ROGER is used a number of times to get the feature rankings $F_1, \ldots, F_T$ where T is the number of times the independent runs of the GA are carried out. Then the ensemble feature ranking for the ith feature is the number of features j which are ranked before i by more than half the rankings.

12.5. Feature ranking using number of label changes

This method is a simple and fast method for ranking the features. The data is projected on to the axis being considered. It is then arranged in increasing order. Now while scanning this data, the class label of every point is noted. While scanning, the number of label changes is noted. If the number of label changes is less, the feature yields more information. The points with the same value are arranged so that all those of a single class label occur together. If the number of label changes is found for every feature, the feature which has the least number of label changes is the best attribute and so on. This method can be used to rank the features.

13. Feature Selection for Time Series Data

A good method of indexing time series is by using Spatial Access Methods (SAMs) such as R trees. Since most SAMs degrade rapidly at dimensionalities greater than 8–12, it is meaningful to carry out dimensionality reduction on the time series data. In time series data, since we consider a series of values in a sequence, the correlation between the features are very strong. While carrying out feature selection, it is necessary to maintain the existing correlation between the features while removing features.

13.1. Piecewise aggregate approximation

A very simple method of dimensionality reduction is to use piecewise aggregate approximation. If the time series has a dimensionality of d and it is required to reduce the dimensionality to k, then the data is divided into k equi-sized frames. For each of the k frames, the mean value of the data falling in the frame is taken as the data in the reduced representation. If the original time series data is $X = (x_1, \ldots, x_d)$ and the time series with the dimensionality reduced be $\bar{X} = (\bar{x}_1, \ldots, \bar{x}_k)$. Then the ith element in the k dimensional time series will be

$$\bar{x}_i = \frac{k}{d} \sum_{j=\frac{d}{k}(i-1)+1}^{\frac{d}{k}i} x_j.$$

13.2. Spectral decomposition

In spectral decomposition, the time series is represented by a super-position of a finite number of sine/cosine waves, where each wave is represented by a complex number, the Fourier coefficient. The time series is in the frequency domain. When the time series is in the frequency domain, it can be decomposed into d sine/cosine waves, i.e. d Fourier coefficients. Many of these Fourier coefficients will be of very low amplitude and can therefore be discarded without loss of much information. To carry out dimensionality reduction of a time series X of length d, the Discrete Fourier Transform (DFT) of X is calculated. The transformed vector of coefficients is truncated at $\frac{d}{2}$ as each coefficient is a complex number with real and imaginary parts to the coefficient.

13.3. Wavelet decomposition

The wavelet transform is used to transform the data to yield wavelet coefficients. The first few coefficients contain an overall, coarse approximation of the data and the later coefficients refer to specific areas of the data in high detail. To carry out dimensionality reduction of a time series X of length d, the Discrete Haar Wavelet Transform (DWT) is calculated and the first k values are chosen and the other coefficients are discarded.

13.4. Singular Value Decomposition (SVD)

Singular Value Decomposition (SVD) transforms the time series data so that the data has maximum possible variance with respect to the first axis, the second axis has the maximum possible variance orthogonal to the first, the third axis has maximum possible variance orthogonal to the first two axes and so on. To carry out dimensionality reduction of a time series X of length d, the SVD is found and the first k coefficients are chosen to represent the time series.

13.5. Common principal component loading based variable subset selection (CLeVer)

This method is based on common principal component analysis (CPCA) and retains the correlation information among the features.

The algorithm first entails finding the principal components (PCs) and the descriptive common principal components (DCPCs). Finding the PCs involves finding k out of d PCs where $k < d$. A threshold δ is used, and k is the minimum value such that the ratio of the variances determined by its first k PCs to the total variance exceeds the threshold δ. The final value of k is the maximum of these values. After this, all the time series have to be described by their first k principal components.

Research Ideas

1. It is possible to view feature selection as a specialization of either linear or nonlinear feature extraction. Under what conditions can feature extraction be preferred over feature selection? The improved performance could be in terms of space, time and/or accuracy.

   ### Relevant References

   (a) V. S. Devi and M. N. Murty, *Pattern Recognition: An Introduction*. Hyderabad, India: Universities Press, 2012.
   (b) M. N. Murty and V. S. Devi, *Pattern Recognition: An Algorithmic Approach*. New York: Springer, 2012.
   (c) Jens Kresten, Simultaneous feature selection and Gaussian mixture model estimation for supervised classification problems. *Pattern Recognition*, 47:2582–2595, 2014.
   (d) D. Zhang, J. He, Y. Zhao, Z. Luo and M. Du, Global plus local: A complete framework for feature extraction and recognition. *Pattern Recognition*, 47:1433–1442, 2014.
   (e) G. Wang, Q. Song, H. Sun, X. Zhang, B. Xu and Y. Zhou, A feature subset selection algorithm automatic recommendation method. *JAIR*, 47:1–34, 2013.

2. MI has been popularly exploited in feature selection. How can we reduce the number of features selected by such a method to get better accuracy? Will it help in improving the scalability of the feature selection scheme?

   ### Relevant References

   (a) G. Herman, B. Zhang, Y. Wang, G. Ye and F. Chen, Mutual information-based method for selecting informative feature sets. *Pattern Recognition*, 46(12):3315–3327, 2013.

(b) H. Liu, J. Sun, L. Liu and H. Zhang, Feature selection with dynamic mutual information. *Pattern Recognition*, 42:1330–1339, 2009.

(c) P. M. Chinta and M. N. Murty, Discriminative feature analysis and selection for document classification. *Proceedings of ICONIP*, 2012.

(d) J. Dai and Q. Xu, Attribute selection based on information gain ratio in fuzzy rough set theory with application to tumor classification. *Applied Soft Computing*, 13:211–221, 2013.

3. Feature selection based on MI and Chi-Square test perform reasonably well on large datasets. How do you compare them?

Relevant References

(a) C. D. Manning, P. Raghavan and H. Schutze, *Introduction to Information Retrieval*. Cambridge: Cambridge University Press, 2008.

(b) P. M. Chinta and M. N. Murty, Discriminative feature analysis and selection for document classification. *Proceedings of ICONIP*, 2012.

(c) S. R. Singh, H. A. Murthy and T. A. Gonsalves, Feature selection for text classification based on gini coefficient of inequality. *JMLR Workshop and Conference Proceedings*, 10:76–85, 2010.

4. Principal components are the eigenvectors of the covariance matrix of the data. The first principal coefficient is in the maximum variance direction; second component is orthogonal to the first and corresponds to the next variance direction and so on. Show using a simple two-dimensional example that the second principal component is better than the first principal component for discrimination. However, there are popular schemes like the latent semantic indexing which use the principal components of the high-dimensional data successfully. What could be the reason behind this?

Relevant References

(a) M. N. Murty and V. S. Devi, Pattern recognition, Web course, NPTEL, 2012, http://nptel.iitm.ac.in/courses.php [accessed on 2 November 2014].

(b) S. Deerwester, S. T. Dumais, G. W. Furnas, T. K. Landauer and R. Harshman, Indexing by latent semantic analysis. *Journal of the American Society for Information Science*, 41:391–407, 1990.

(c) M. Prakash and M. N. Murty, A genetic approach for selection of (near-) optimal subsets of principal components for discrimination. *PR Letters*, 16:781–787, 1995.

(d) S. Karamizadeh, S. M. Abdullah, A. A. Manaf, M. Zamani and A. Hooman, An overview of principal component analysis. *Journal of Signal and Information Processing*, 4:173–175, 2013.

5. In the case of NMF, we factorize a data matrix X into B and H. The associated optimization problem is not simple (not convex). If we know in addition to X either B or H, then we can have a simple optimization problem. Consider situations where B is known or H known and examine the role of NMF.

Relevant References

(a) D. D. Lee and H. S. Seung, Learning the parts of objects by non-negative matrix factorization. *Nature*, 401:788–791, 1999.

(b) D. D. Lee and H. S. Seung, Algorithms for non-negative matrix factorization. *Advances in Neural Information Processing Systems*, 13:556–562, 2001.

(c) C. C. Aggarwal and C. K. Reddy, *Data Clustering: Algorithms and Applications*. New York: CRC Press, 2014.

(d) C. Thurau, K. Kersting, M. Wahabzada and C. Bauckhage, Convex non-negative matrix factorization for massive datasets. *Knowledge and Information Systems*, 29:457–478, 2011.

6. One of the issues with *NMF* is that the resulting factorization may lead to a local minimum of the optimization function considered. What are the different ways of improving upon this?

Relevant References

(a) A. Korattikara, L. Boyles, M. Welling, J. Kim and H. Park, Statistical optimization of non-negative matrix factorization. *Proceedings of The Fourteenth International Conference on Artificial Intelligence and Statistics*, JMLR: W&CP 15, 2011.

(b) F. Pompili, N. Gillis, P.-A. Absil and F. Glineur, Two algorithms for orthogonal nonnegative matrix factorization with application to clustering. CoRR abs/1201.0901, 2014.

(c) V. Bittorf, B. Recht, C. Re and J. A. Tropp, Factoring nonnegative matrices with linear programs. CORR abs/1206.1270, 2013.

7. It is possible to project d-dimensional patterns to k-dimensional patterns using random projections where the random entries come from a Gaussian with zero

mean and unit variance. Then if X_i and X_j are a pair of patterns in the d space and the corresponding patterns after projection into the k space are X_i' and X_j', then it is possible to show that with probability greater than or equal to $1 - n^{-\beta}$

$$(1 - \epsilon)\|X_i - X_j\|^2 \leq \|X_i' - X_j'\|^2 \leq (1 + \epsilon)\|X_i - X_j\|^2$$

given positive ϵ and β and k is any number greater than $k_{min} = \frac{4+2\beta}{\frac{\epsilon^2}{2} - \frac{\epsilon^3}{3}} \log n$. How do we appreciate the role of various quantities like β, ϵ, n, and k? What can happen to the bounds when these parameters are varied within their legal ranges?

Relevant References

(a) A. K. Menon, Random projections and applications to dimensionality reduction. BS (advanced) thesis, School of Info. Tech., University of Sydney, 2007.

(b) P. Li, T. J. Hastie and K. W. Church, Very sparse random projections. *Proceedings of KDD*, 2006.

(c) R. J. Durrant and A. Kaban, Sharp generalization error bounds for randomly-projected classifiers. *Proceedings of ICML*, 2013.

8. Even though GAs have been used in feature selection and extraction, algorithms based on GAs cannot scale up well, specifically steady-state GA may be very slow in converging. How to make them scale-up well?

Relevant References

(a) I. Rejer and K. Lorenz, Genetic algorithm and forward method for feature selection in EEG feature space. *JTACS*, 7:72–82, 2013.

(b) A. Ekbal and S. Saha, Stacked ensemble coupled with feature selection for biomedical entity extraction. *Knowledge-Based Systems*, 46:22–32, 2013.

(c) D. Dohare and V. S. Devi, Combination of similarity measures for time series classification using genetic algorithms. *IEEE Congress on Evolutionary Computation*, 2011.

(d) D. Anand, Article: Improved collaborative filtering using evolutionary algorithm based feature extraction. *International Journal of Computer Applications*, 64:20–26, 2013.

(e) I. Guyon, S. Gunn, M. Nikravesh and L. A. Zadeh, *Feature Extraction*: *Foundations and Applications*. New York: Springer, 2006.

9. It is often claimed that noisy and boundary patterns qualify as support vectors. Further the weight vector W obtained by an SVM is

$$W = \sum_{X_i \in S} \alpha_i y_i X_i,$$

where S is the set of support vectors, y_i is the class label of X_i which is either $+1$ or -1, and α_i is the Lagrange variable associated with X_i. So, how can such a weight vector W be useful in ranking features?

Relevant References

(a) Y.-W. Chang and C.-J. Lin, Feature ranking using linear SVM. *JMLR Workshop and Conference Proceedings*, pp. 53–64, 2008.

(b) Y.-W. Chen and C.-J. Lin, Combining SVMs with various feature selection strategies. In *Feature Extraction, Foundations and Applications*, I. Guyon, S. Gunn, M. Nikravesh and L. Zadeh (eds.). New York: Springer, 2006.

(c) J. Wang, S. Zhou, Y. Yi and J. Kong, An improved feature selection based on effective range for classification. *The Scientific World Journal*, 1–8, 2014.

(d) H. Li, C.-J. Li, X.-J. Wu and J. Sun, Statistics-based wrapper for feature selection: An implementation on financial distress identification with support vector machine. *Applied Soft Computing*, 19:57–67, 2014.

10. Feature selection based on F-score has been effectively used in several practical applications. What is the reason for its success.

Relevant References

(a) H.-Y. Lo *et al.*, An ensemble of three classifiers for KDD cup 2009: Expanded linear model, heterogeneous boosting, and selective naive bayes. *JMLR: Workshop and Conference Proceedings*, 7:57–64, 2009.

(b) Y.-W. Chen and C.-J. Lin, Combining SVMs with Various Feature selection strategies. In *Feature Extraction, Foundations and Applications*. Berlin: Springer, 2006, pp. 315–324.

   (c) J. Xie, J. Lei, W. Xie, Y. Shi and X. Liu, Two-stage hybrid feature selection algorithms for diagnosing erythemato-squamous diseases. *Health Information Science and Systems*, 1:10, 2013.

10. Time series data can be large in several applications. How to extract features for meaningful classification?

Relevant References

   (a) P. K. Vemulapalli, V. Monga and S. N. Brennan, Robust extrema features for time–series data analysis. *IEEE Transactions on PAMI*, 35:1464–1479, 2013.

   (b) M. G. Baydogan, G. Runger and E. Tuv, A bag-of-features framework to classify time series. *IEEE Transactions on PAMI*, 35:2796–2802, 2013.

   (c) Q. Wang, X. Li and Q. Qin, Feature selection for time series modeling. *Journal of Intelligent Learning Systems and Applications*, 5:152–164, 2013.

   (d) B. D. Fulcher and N. S. Jones, Highly comparative, feature-based time-series classification, CoRR abs/1401.3531, 2014.

Chapter 4

Bayesian Learning

Bayesian approach is well established and well studied in literature. Even though it is classical, it has gained a lot of prominence more recently. An important reason for this is that domain knowledge can be suitably used to help in learning; using such prior knowledge will lead to meaningful estimation of parameters using even small size datasets. Also, when a small quantity of data is available, Bayesian approaches work better than their counterparts which are based on the data alone. Bayesian learning is used in both supervised and unsupervised settings. We consider the supervised case in this chapter and consider the unsupervised case in a later chapter.

1. Document Classification

In the Bayesian approach, typically we exploit the Bayes rule to convert the prior probabilities to posterior probabilities based on the data under consideration. For example, let us consider a collection of documents

$$\mathcal{D} = \{(d_1, C), (d_2, C), \ldots, (d_{n_1}, C), (d_{n_1+1}, \overline{C}), \ldots, (d_n, \overline{C})\},$$

where we have n_1 documents from class C and $n - n_1$ documents from class $\overline{C}$. Now a new document d can be classified using the

Bayes rule as follows:

1. Obtain the posterior probabilities $P(C|d)$ *and* $P(\overline{C}|d)$ using the Bayes rule

$$P(C|d) = \frac{P(d|C)P(C)}{P(d|C)P(C) + P(d|\overline{C})P(\overline{C})},$$

$$P(\overline{C}|d) = \frac{P(d|\overline{C})P(\overline{C})}{P(d|C)P(C) + P(d|\overline{C})P(\overline{C})}.$$

2. Assign d to class that has larger posterior probability; that is assign d to class

$$C \quad if \ P(C|d) > P(\overline{C}|d),$$
$$\overline{C} \quad if \ P(\overline{C}|d) > P(C|d).$$

Some of the important features of the classifier are:

1. It is possible to show that the Bayes classifier is optimal; it minimizes the average probability of error or error-rate.
2. Bayes classifier is basically probabilistic and theoretical; it can be made practical and useful based on statistics. In the absence of the availability of values of various probabilities required to obtain the posterior probabilities, it is not possible to use it in practice.
3. Estimation of the probabilities is achieved using the dataset $\mathcal{D}$.

A major difficulty is in using it when the data is small in size. Let us consider a simple example.

Example 1. Consider the collection of six documents shown in Table 4.1. There are six example documents shown here. There are three documents from class *sports* and two from *politics*. The sixth document d_6 is a test document; we need to find the class label to be associated with it. In order to use the Bayes classifier, here we need to know $P(Sports|d_6)$ and $P(Politics|d_6)$. Let us consider $P(Sports|d_6)$ given by

$$P(Sports|d_6) = \frac{P(d_6|Sports)P(Sports)}{P(d_6|Sports)P(Sports) + P(d_6|Politics)P(Politics)}.$$

Table 4.1. A dataset of six documents.

Document	Description	Class
d_1	Cricket Mumbai	Sports
d_2	Dravid Ball Cricket	Sports
d_3	Ball Tendulkar Pawar	Sports
d_4	Pawar Tendulkar Patil Mumbai	Politics
d_5	Sonia Singh Pawar Delhi	Politics
d_6	Tendulkar Patil Pawar Delhi	?

Noting that out of the five labeled patterns, three are from *sports*, an estimate for $P(Sports) = \frac{3}{5}$. Similarly, $P(politics) = \frac{2}{5}$. However, frequency based estimate for $P(d_6|Sports)$ is zero because none of the training documents in the class *sports* matches d_6; similarly estimate of $P(d_6|Politics)$ becomes zero. So, it becomes difficult to obtain a meaningful estimate of either $P(d_6|Sports)$ or $P(d_6|Politics)$.

2. Naive Bayes Classifier

One may argue that these probability estimates are not meaningful because the training dataset size is small. However, even when the training dataset is large in size, it is possible that a lengthy (a large number of distinct words) document can have the probability estimate to be zero. This has led to the development of the Naive Bayes Classifier where the probability estimation is simplified by assuming class-conditional independence among the words in a document. The resulting simplification may be specified as

$$P(d|C) = \prod_{w_i \in d} P(w_i|C).$$

Here, the independence of various words appearing in the document d is conditional; it depends on class C.

Finally we need to compute $P(Sports|d_6)$ and $P(Politics|d_6)$ which require

- Prior Probabilities: $P(Sports)$ and $P(Politics)$; these quantities could be estimated as explained earlier to be $P(Sports) = \frac{3}{5}$ and $P(politics) = \frac{2}{5}$.

- $P(d_6|Sports)$ and $P(d_6|Politics)$: In the current example these values are estimated by using class-conditional independence as follows:

$$P(d_6|C) = P(Tendulkar|C) \times P(Patil|C) \times P(Pawar|C)$$
$$\times P(Delhi|C).$$

In the current example, one may view C to be *Sports* and $\overline{C}$ to be *Politics*. So, the Maximum Likelihood (ML) estimates based on the frequency of occurrence are

— $P(Tendulkar|Sports) = \frac{1}{6}$. This is because out of the three documents corresponding to *Sports* there are six words totally and *Tendulkar* appeared once.

— $P(Patil|Sports) = \frac{0}{6} = 0$. Such an estimate will mean that $P(Sports|d_6)$ takes a value *zero*(0).

In order to modify such estimates which can lead to *zero* values for posterior probabilities a smoothing component is introduced to ensure that the probability estimates neither become *zero* nor *one*. This is achieved by using the following smoothed version to estimate.

$$P(w|C) = \frac{Number\ of\ occurrences\ of\ w\ in\ C + 1}{Total\ number\ of\ words\ in\ C + |V|},$$

where $|V|$ is the size of the vocabulary or the number of distinct words in the collection. In the given example the vocabulary set V is

$$V = \{Cricket, Mumbai, Dravid, Ball, Tendulkar, Pawar, Patil,$$
$$Sonia, Singh, Delhi\}.$$

So, $|V| = 10$ and the estimates of conditional probabilities are

— $P(Tendulkar|Sports) = P(Pawar|Sports) = \frac{1}{8}$,
— $P(Patil|Sports) = P(Delhi|Sports) = \frac{1}{16}$,
— $P(Tendulkar|Politics) = P(Patil|Politics) = \frac{2}{17}$,
— $P(Delhi|Politics) = \frac{2}{17}$; $P(Pawar|Politics) = \frac{3}{17}$.

Now we can use these estimates and the prior probabilities given by $P(Sports) = \frac{3}{5}$ and $P(Politics) = \frac{2}{5}$ to obtain the posterior probabilities using the following

$P(Sports|d_6)$

$$= \frac{P(d_6|Sports)P(Sports)}{P(d_6|Sports)P(Sports) + P(d_6|Politics)P(Politics)}$$

$$= 0.24,$$

$P(Politics|d_6)$

$$= \frac{P(d_6|Politics)P(Politics)}{P(d_6|Sports)P(Sports) + P(d_6|Politics)P(Politics)}$$

$$= 0.76.$$

- So we assign to d_6 class label *Politics* as the corresponding posterior probability is larger; it is 0.76.

3. Frequency-Based Estimation of Probabilities

A simple and popularly used estimate for probability of an event is based on the frequency of occurrence of the event. Let us consider a simple example of tossing a coin.

Example 2. Let a coin be tossed n times out of which let the number of times head shows up be n_h, then probability of the coin showing head, $P(h)$, is estimated using

$$P(h) = \frac{n_h}{n}.$$

Specifically let the coin be tossed six times out of which head shows up four times, so, $P(h) = \frac{4}{6} = \frac{2}{3}$. However, in another coin tossing experiment, if there are 0 (zero) heads out of five tosses of the coin, then the probability $P(h) = \frac{0}{5} = 0$. This is the problem with the frequency based estimation scheme; the estimate may not be accurate when the experiment is conducted a smaller number of times or equivalently when the dataset size is small.

One way to improve the quality of the estimate is to integrate any prior knowledge we have in the process of estimation. A simple scheme is to use some kind of uniform prior. For example, in the case of coin tossing it is safe to assume that the probability of a head or a tail is equally likely to be $\frac{1}{2}$. In such a case the estimate will be

$$P(h) = \frac{n_h + 1}{n + 2}.$$

Such an estimate will take values in the open interval $(0, 1)$. For example, if there are 0 heads out of five tosses of the coin then the estimate for $P(h)$ is $\frac{0+1}{5+2}$ which is not zero even though it could be small. In a generic setting the probability of an event $e, P(e)$ is given by

$$P(e) = \frac{n_e + 1}{n + t},$$

where n_e is the number of trails favoring event e out of a total of n trails and t is the total number of outcomes. Here, we have a uniform prior with each of the t outcomes having equal probability of $\frac{1}{t}$. In most practical applications the value of t is much smaller compared to the value of n. Also, from an asymptotic view point t is fixed, but n can keep growing. So, as $n \to \infty, P(e)$ tends to $\frac{n_e}{n}$ which is the ML estimate.

Based on the above discussion, we have the following observations:

- In frequency based estimation of probabilities, one may encounter zero probabilities. One can avoid such zero or non-discriminative estimates by softening the estimates using some prior knowledge.
- One of the simplest schemes is based on employing uniform prior; in such a case when the number of trails n is large then the resulting estimate tends to the simple frequency based estimate.
- Bayesian estimation schemes could be viewed as generalizations where the decisions are based on posterior probabilities obtained by combining knowledge in the form of priors.

We next consider the use of posterior probabilities in simple classification.

4. Posterior Probability

The most important feature of Bayesian learning is to exploit Bayes rule to convert the prior probability into the posterior probability. Specifically let C be the class label and d be the observed document. Then

- Prior probability: $P(C)$
- Posterior probability: $P(C|d)$; it is the probability of the class after observing d.
- Using Bayes rule, we have

$$P(C|d) = \frac{P(d|C) \times P(C)}{P(d|C) \times P(C) + P(d|\overline{C}) \times P(\overline{C})}.$$

Once we have the posterior probabilities, we can assign d to class C if $P(C|d) > P(\overline{C}|d)$; else assign d to $\overline{C}$. Equivalently, we assign d to class C if $\frac{P(C|d)}{P(\overline{C}|d)} > 1$. We can simplify the expressions if $P(C|d)$ and $P(\overline{C}|d)$ are exponential functions by assigning d to class C if $\log P(C|d) > \log P(\overline{C}|d)$. We consider an example involving univariate normal densities next; note that univariate normal is a member of the exponential family of distributions.

Example 3. Let us consider that the densities of classes C and $\overline{C}$ be univariate normal. Specifically let

$$P(d|C) \sim N(\mu, 1) \text{ and}$$
$$P(d|\overline{C}) \sim N(\overline{\mu}, 1).$$

Here, we consider that μ and $\overline{\mu}$ are the means of the densities of the classes C and $\overline{C}$ respectively and the variances are equal to 1. Let us assume further that the prior probabilities $P(C)$ and $P(\overline{C})$ be equal to $\frac{1}{2}$. Now $P(C|d)$ is given by

$$P(C|d) = \frac{P(d|C)}{P(d|C) + P(d|\overline{C})}$$
$$= \frac{\exp\left(-\frac{1}{2}(x - \mu)^2\right)}{\exp\left(-\frac{1}{2}(x - \mu)^2\right) + \exp\left(-\frac{1}{2}(x - \overline{\mu})^2\right)}.$$

Note that $P(\overline{C}|d)$ has the same denominator as $P(C|d)$; they differ only in their numerator values. So,

$$\frac{P(C|d)}{P(\overline{C}|d)} = \frac{\exp\left(-\frac{1}{2}(x-\mu)^2\right)}{\exp\left(-\frac{1}{2}(x-\overline{\mu})^2\right)}.$$

In this ratio we have exponentials in both the numerator and denominator; so, it is good to consider the comparison of $\log(P(C|d))$ and $\log(P(\overline{C}|d))$. We assign d to class C if

$$\log(P(C|d)) > \log(P(\overline{C}|d)).$$

Equivalently assign d to class C if

$$(x-\mu)^2 < (x-\overline{\mu})^2$$

or

$$(\mu + \overline{\mu}) < 2x \text{ assuming } \mu > \overline{\mu}.$$

So, assign d to class C if

$$x > \frac{(\mu + \overline{\mu})}{2}.$$

Similarly assign d to $\overline{C}$ if

$$x < \frac{(\mu + \overline{\mu})}{2}.$$

Decide arbitrarily if $x = \frac{\mu + \overline{\mu}}{2}$. It appears as though such a simple decision-based classifier is realized because the data distributions are univariate. However, similar decisions can be arrived at even when the distributions are multivariate. Specifically, when classes C and $\overline{C}$ are multivariate normal with means μ and $\overline{\mu}$ respectively and the covariance matrices are equal and are equal to aI where a is a non-negative real number and I is the identity matrix.

The resulting classifier is called the *Minimum Distance Classifier* (MDC). If the classes have μ and $\overline{\mu}$ as the means of the two classes C and $\overline{C}$ respectively then a pattern X is assigned to class C if

$$(X-\mu)^t\Sigma^{-1}(X-\mu) < (X-\overline{\mu})^t\Sigma^{-1}(X-\overline{\mu}).$$

If we assume in addition that $\Sigma^{-1} = \frac{1}{\sigma^2} I$, then the above inequality becomes

$$\frac{(X - \mu)^t (X - \mu)}{\sigma^2} < \frac{(X - \overline{\mu})^t (X - \overline{\mu})}{\sigma^2}.$$

This means assign X to C if the Euclidean distance between X and μ is smaller than that between X and $\overline{\mu}$; otherwise assign X to $\overline{C}$. In addition to using the Bayes rule in classification it is possible to use it in density estimation, which we consider next.

5. Density Estimation

We have noted earlier that in order to use the Bayes classifier, it is important to have the prior probabilities and the probability density function of each class. One of the simplest ways is to assume that the form of the density function is known and the parameter underlying the density function is unknown. Estimation of the density function under these conditions is called parametric estimation. In the frequentist test approach, the parameters are assumed to be unknown but deterministic. On the contrary, in the Bayesian approach the parameters are assumed to be random variables. We examine parametric estimation using these schemes in this section.

- **Bernoulli Random Variable**: Let us consider a binary random variable that can take a value of either 1 or 0. Let us assume that the probability that the random variable assumes value 1 be p_1. Let the probability of the random variable assuming value 0 be p_0. It is easy to see that $p_0 = 1 - p_1$. So, one of either p_1 or p_0 is adequate to capture the behavior. Now the probability mass function is given by

$$\text{Bernoulli}(X|p_1) = p_1^X p_0^{1-X} \quad \text{so,}$$

$$\text{Bernoulli}(X|p_1) = p_1 \quad \textit{if } X = 1 \text{ and}$$

$$\text{Bernoulli}(X|p_1) = p_0 = (1 - p_1) \quad \textit{if } X = 0.$$

It is possible to show that the expected value of X is p_1 as

$$E[X] = 1 \times p_1 + 0 \times p_0 = p_1.$$

Similarly, it is possible to show that the variance of X is $p_1 p_0$ as follows:

$$\text{Variance}[X] = E[X^2] - (E[X])^2 = (1^2 \times p_1 + 0^2 \times p_0) - p_1^2$$
$$= p_1 - p_1^2 = p_1(1 - p_1) = p_1 p_0.$$

Next we consider estimation of the parameter p_1 from the data. We consider the ML scheme for estimating the parameter p_1.

— *Maximum-likelihood estimation*: Let there be n patterns drawn independently from the unknown Bernoulli density. Let the collection of these patterns be

$$\mathcal{D} = \{X_1, X_2, \ldots, X_n\}.$$

The functional form of the density is known here; once we know the value of the parameter p_1, we know everything about the class density. Because of the independence, we have

$$P(\mathcal{D}|p_1) = \prod_{i=1}^{n} p_1^{X_i} (1 - p_1)^{1-X_i}.$$

Typically we choose the value of p_1 corresponding to the maximum value of the likelihood function $P(\mathcal{D}|p_1)$. Equivalently one can get the optimal value of p_1 by maximizing the logarithm of the likelihood function. Note that the logarithm of the likelihood function is

$$\log P(\mathcal{D}|p_1) = \sum_{i=1}^{n} [X_i \log p_1 + (1 - X_i)\log(1 - p_1)].$$

By differentiating it with respect to p_1 and equating the derivative to zero we get

$$\frac{\sum_{i=1}^{n} X_i}{p_1} - \frac{n - \sum_{i=1}^{n} X_i}{1 - p_1} = 0.$$

By simplifying the above expression we get the estimate of p_1 to be

$$p_1 = \frac{\sum_{i=1}^{n} X_i}{n}, \tag{1}$$

which is an intuitively acceptable estimate; it is the proportion of times the random variable assumes a value 1. Next we consider the Bayesian estimation scheme.

— *Bayesian estimation*: In the case of ML estimation we assume that the parameter is unknown but deterministic; once we know the parameter we have the knowledge of the entire density function. In the case of the Bayesian estimation we treat the parameter as a random variable and we assume that the prior density of the random variable is known. This is the place to use the domain knowledge; it is tacitly assumed that the domain knowledge is integrated into the model using a suitable form for the prior density. We use the Bayes rule to compute the posterior density using prior density and the likelihood function. The posterior density of the parameter p_1, after observing data $\mathcal{D}$ is given by

$$P(p_1|\mathcal{D}) = \frac{P(\mathcal{D}|p_1)P(p_1)}{\int P(\mathcal{D}|p_1)P(p_1)dp_1}$$

$$= \frac{p_1^{\sum_{i=1}^{n} X_i} \times (1-p_1)^{n-\sum_{i=1}^{n} X_i}}{\int p_1^{\sum_{i=1}^{n} X_i} \times (1-p_1)^{n-\sum_{i=1}^{n} X_i} dp_1}$$

$$\times \frac{p_1^{\sum_{i=1}^{n} X_i} \times (1-p_1)^{n-\sum_{i=1}^{n} X_i} \times (n+1)!}{\left(\sum_{i=1}^{n} X_i\right)! \times \left(n - \sum_{i=1}^{n} X_i\right)!}.$$

It is assumed that the prior density of p_1 is uniform in the range $[0, 1]$; so, $P(p_1) = 1$. In simplifying the integral in the denominator, the following identity is used:

$$\int x^p \times (1-x)^q dx = \frac{p! \times q!}{(p+q+1)!}.$$

Note that posterior density of p_1 depends both on the data $\mathcal{D}$ and also on the prior density $P(p_1)$. This is the fundamental difference between the ML estimate and the Bayesian estimate; ML estimate depends only on the data as given by (1) whereas the Bayesian estimate exploits the knowledge in the form of the prior density. One can use the posterior density in estimating $P(X|\mathcal{D})$ as shown below:

$$P(X|\mathcal{D}) = \int P(X, p_1|\mathcal{D})dp_1$$

$$= \int P(X|p_1, \mathcal{D})P(p_1|\mathcal{D})dp_1$$

$$= \int P(X|p_1)P(p_1|\mathcal{D})dp_1.$$

The last equation emerges because once p_1 is given, everything is known about the density of X; nothing else is required. In the current example of Bernoulli distribution we know the posterior density and $P(X|p_1)$ is Bernoulli in terms of the parameter p_1. Using these details and the above equality we can obtain $P(X|\mathcal{D})$ as follows:

$$P(X|\mathcal{D}) = \frac{(n+1)!}{\left(\sum_{i=1}^{n} X_i\right)! \left(n - \sum_{i=1}^{n} X_i\right)!}$$

$$\times \int p_1^X (1-p_1)^{(1-X)} \; p_1^{\left(\sum_{i=1}^{n} X_i\right)} (1-p_1)^{\left(n - \sum_{i=1}^{n} X_i\right)} dp_1$$

$$= \frac{(n+1)!}{\left(\sum_{i=1}^{n} X_i\right)! \left(n - \sum_{i=1}^{n} X_i\right)!}$$

$$\times \int p_1^{X + \sum_{i=1}^{n} X_i} (1-p_1)^{n+1 - \left(X + \sum_{i=1}^{n} X_i\right)} dp_1$$

$$= \frac{(n+1)!}{\left(\sum\limits_{i=1}^{n} X_i\right)! \left(n - \sum\limits_{i=1}^{n} X_i\right)!}$$

$$\times \frac{(X + \sum_{i=1}^{n} X_i)! \left(n + 1 - (X + \sum\limits_{i=1}^{n} X_i)\right)!}{(n+2)!}.$$

By simplifying the above expression we get

$$P(X|\mathcal{D}) = \frac{\left(X + \sum\limits_{i=1}^{n} X_i\right)!}{\left(\sum\limits_{i=1}^{n} X_i\right)!} \times \frac{\left(n + 1 - \left(X + \sum\limits_{i=1}^{n} X_i\right)\right)!}{\left(n - \sum\limits_{i=1}^{n} X_i\right)! \, (n+2)}.$$

Note that X is a Bernoulli random variable; it can take a value of either 1 or 0. When $X = 1$, we can simplify the above expression, by substituting 1 for X, to

$$P(X = 1|\mathcal{D}) = \frac{\left(1 + \sum\limits_{i=1}^{n} X_i\right)}{n+2}. \qquad (2)$$

Similarly the probability for X taking 0 is

$$P(X = 0|\mathcal{D}) = \frac{n + 1 - \sum\limits_{i=1}^{n} X_i}{n+2} = 1 - \frac{\left(1 + \sum\limits_{i=1}^{n} X_i\right)}{n+2}. \qquad (3)$$

Note the similarity between the ML estimation of p_1 as shown in (1) and the Bayesian estimate given in (2). When n is large $\sum X_i$ can be large and so the numerator in (2) may be approximated by $\sum X_i$ and $n + 2$ in the denominator tends to n. Such an approximation of (2) leads to the estimate in (1). So, when the dataset size (n) is large, there is no difference between the ML estimate and the Bayesian estimate; this is the typical behavior. So, in big data applications where the dataset size is large, ML estimate is good enough; Bayesian estimate may not reveal any additional characteristics in big data analytics.

In the above example we have assumed that the prior distribution of p_1 is uniform in the range [0, 1]. One can use other distributions for the prior distribution of the random variable p_1. Consider again the estimate shown in (2) which is

$$P(X = 1|\mathcal{D}) = \frac{\left(1 + \sum\limits_{i=1}^{n} X_i\right)}{n + 2}.$$

This estimate can still make sense when $\sum\limits_{i=1}^{n} X_i = 0$; this can happen, for example, when $n = 0$. In such a case, the probability $P(X = 1|\mathcal{D})$ is $\frac{1}{2}$; it means that *a priori* X taking a value 1 or 0 are equally likely. This is the typical behavior of the Bayes estimate; it ensures that the probabilities are in the open interval $(0, 1)$.

— *Choice of the prior density*: In the above example of Bernoulli random variable we have used uniform density for the prior. It simplified the computation of

1. Posterior density: In this case the posterior has a simple form and depends on the likelihood function.
2. Estimation of $P(X|\mathcal{D})$: It helped in obtaining a closed form expression for $P(X|\mathcal{D})$.

Even though uniform prior leads to a simple form for the resulting densities, it may not be able to capture the domain knowledge properly. For example, when we consider the frequency of each term occurring in a large collection of documents, the corresponding distribution is not uniform. It is a power law degree distribution which is characterized by Zipf's law. It was observed by Zipf that the frequency of the ith term in the collection, f_i, is given by

$$f_i = \frac{C}{r_i}, \tag{4}$$

where r_i is the rank of the ith term; most frequent term has the smallest rank of 1 and hence its frequency is the maximum given by C and the least frequent term has its rank value to be C and hence its frequency is 1 $\left(\frac{C}{C}\right)$.

Similarly in scale free networks the degree distribution is observed to be satisfying power law distribution, not uniform. Specifically it is

$$n_k = \frac{M}{k^\alpha},$$

where n_k is the number of nodes of degree k and M and α are some constants. So, using an appropriate prior density that may not be uniform may make sense based on the context. In such a case it may be difficult to get simple closed form expressions for the densities in general. However, it is theoretically possible to simplify the analysis by assuming suitable complementary or conjugate forms for the prior density. Even when closed form expression is not obtained for the density $P(X|\mathcal{D})$, it is possible to consider some simplifying scenarios where mode, mean or maximum values of the posterior densities are used. In order to explain the notion of conjugate prior we consider another popular distribution.

- *Binomial distribution*: It is one of the popularly encountered distributions. For example, consider tossing a coin n times out of which we get n_h heads and n_t tails; let the probability of head in a single toss be p_h. Then the probability of this event is given by

$$Bin(n_h \ heads \ out \ of \ n \ tosses) = \binom{n}{n_h} p_h^{n_h} (1 - p_h)^{n-n_h}.$$

More generally it is viewed as the number of successes in n trials with the probability of success being p_s and the probability of failure being $p_f = (1 - p_s)$. So, probability of k successes in n trials is given by

$$Bin(n, k) = \binom{n}{k} p_s^k (1 - p_s)^{(n-k)}.$$

It can be shown that

— Mean, $E[k] = np_s$ and
— Variance, $E[(k - E[k])^2] = np_s p_f$.

Note that both Bernoulli and binomial distributions have similar functional form in terms of the parameter given by $p_1^{\sum_{i=1}^{n} X_i} (1 - p_1)^{n - \sum_{i=1}^{n} X_i}$. This form helps in choosing an appropriate prior density; a popular notion in this context is *conjugate prior*. We have observed based on Bayes rule that the posterior density depends on the prior density and the likelihood function. For a given data distribution and correspondingly the likelihood function, a prior density is *conjugate* if resulting posterior density has the same form of the distribution as the prior.

6. Conjugate Priors

Note that both the Bernoulli and Binomial distributions have likelihood functions, based on parameter $q \in [0, 1]$, proportional to $q^a (1 - q)^b$, where a and b are constants. This suggests that we choose a prior density that is also proportional to $q^a (1 - q)^b$ so as to ensure that the posterior has a similar form; Beta density has such a form; the probability density is given by

$$Beta(q|a, b) = \frac{\Gamma(a + b)}{\Gamma(a)\Gamma(b)} q^{a-1} (1 - q)^{b-1}$$

$$where \ \Gamma(a) = \int_0^\infty v^{a-1} e^{-v} dv = (a - 1) \int_0^\infty v^{a-2} e^{-v} dv$$

$$= (a - 1)\Gamma(a - 1).$$

Note that any probability density function $p(x)$ satisfies the following properties:

1. $p(x) \geq 0$ *for all* x,
2. $\int p(x) \, dx = 1$.

So, for the Beta distribution we have

$$\int_0^1 \frac{\Gamma(a + b)}{\Gamma(a)\Gamma(b)} q^{a-1} (1 - q)^{b-1} dq = 1$$

or equivalently

$$\frac{\Gamma(a+b)}{\Gamma(a)\Gamma(b)} \int_0^1 q^{a-1}(1-q)^{b-1}dq = 1,$$

which means that

$$\int_0^1 q^{a-1}(1-q)^{b-1}dq = \frac{\Gamma(a)\Gamma(b)}{\Gamma(a+b)}. \tag{5}$$

It is possible to use this equality and the property of the Gamma distribution to show that the mean of the Beta distributed random variable is $\frac{a}{a+b}$. It may be shown as follows:

$$E[q] = \int_0^1 \frac{\Gamma(a+b)}{\Gamma(a)\Gamma(b)} q \, q^{a-1}(1-q)^{b-1}dq$$

$$= \frac{\Gamma(a+b)}{\Gamma(a)\Gamma(b)} \int_0^1 q^a(1-q)^{b-1}dq$$

$$= \frac{\Gamma(a+b)}{\Gamma(a)\Gamma(b)} \times \frac{\Gamma(a+1)\Gamma(b)}{\Gamma(a+b+1)}$$

$$= \frac{\Gamma(a+b)}{\Gamma(a)\Gamma(b)} \times \frac{a \times \Gamma(a)\Gamma(b)}{(a+b)\Gamma(a+b)}.$$

By canceling terms that are present in both the numerator and the denominator, we get

$$E[q] = \frac{a}{a+b}.$$

Similarly it is possible to show that the variance is $\frac{ab}{(a+b)^2(a+b+1)}$. Here, a and b may be viewed as hyper-parameters that characterize the distribution of q. We know that the posterior is given by

$$P(q|\mathcal{D}) = \frac{P(\mathcal{D}|q)P(q)}{\int_0^1 P(\mathcal{D}|q)P(q)dq}.$$

Noting that the denominator is independent of q it can be treated as a constant C_1. So,

$$P(q|\mathcal{D}) = C_1 P(\mathcal{D}|q) P(q).$$

Noting that $P(q)$ is Beta and the likelihood is based on Bernoulli, we can get the posterior to be

$$P(q|\mathcal{D}) = C_1 q^{\sum_{i=1}^{n} X_i} (1-q)^{n - \sum_{i=1}^{n} X_i} C_2 q^{a-1} (1-q)^{b-1},$$

where C_2 is $\frac{\Gamma(a+b)}{\Gamma(a)\Gamma(b)}$; by using C for $C_1 \times C_2$, we get

$$P(q|\mathcal{D}) = C q^{a + \sum_{i=1}^{n} X_i - 1} (1-q)^{n + b - \sum_{i=1}^{n} X_i - 1}.$$

So, the posterior is again a Beta density and the hyper-parameters are $a + \sum_{i=1}^{n} X_i$ and $b + n - \sum_{i=1}^{n} X_i$. The notion of conjugate prior is useful because it makes the posterior have a closed form expression and further it ensures that both the prior and the posterior have the same functional form for the density functions.

In the case of document collections, a frequently used assumption is that the terms occur in a document independent of each other; we are interested in the number of occurrences of the term in a document but not in the order in which terms occur in the document. *Bag of words* model is the name of such a model; it is the most popular model in *information retrieval*. In such a case if there are k distinct terms $t_1, t_2, \ldots, t_k$ in the document collection and there are m terms in a document such that term t_i occurs m_i times in the document for $i = 1, 2, \ldots, k$, then the distribution of the terms is explained by the *multinomial density*.

By assuming that p_i is the probability of term t_i occurring in the document, Multinomial may be viewed as a generalization of the Binomial distribution where $k = 2$ and the mass function of the multinomial random variable is given by

$$Mult(m_1, m_2, \ldots, m_k | p, m) = \binom{m}{m_1 m_2 \ldots m_k} \prod_{i=1}^{k} p_i^{m_i},$$

where $\binom{m}{m_1 m_2 \ldots m_k} = \frac{m!}{m_1! m_2! \cdots m_k!}$ and $p = (p_1, p_2, \ldots, p_k)^t$.

The expected value of m_i is given by

$$E[m_i] = \int \frac{m!}{m_1! m_2! \cdots m_k!} m_i \prod_{i=1}^{k} p_i^{m_i} dm_i$$

$$= mp_i \int \frac{m-1!}{m_1! m_2! \cdots (m_i-1)! m_k!} \left(\prod_{j \neq i, j=1}^{k} p_i^{m_j} dm_j \right)$$

$$\times p_i^{m_i-1} dm_i$$

$$= mp_i \times 1 = mp_i.$$

Observe that this result is similar to the estimate of mean of the binomial; similarly it is possible to show that variance of m_i is $mp_i(1-p_i)$.

We discuss next how the Dirichlet prior is the conjugate to multinomial; this result has been significantly exploited in the machine learning literature during the past decade in the form of soft clustering based on *latent Dirichlet allocation* and its variants. It is possible to show that the likelihood function corresponding to multinomial is given by

$$P(\mathcal{D}|p) \propto \prod_{j=1}^{k} p_j^{M_j},$$

where M_j is the number of times t_j occurred in the collection, $\mathcal{D}$, of documents. So, we require the prior to have a similar form which is satisfied by the Dirichlet distribution. So the prior density is given by

$$P(p) = \frac{\Gamma(a_1 + a_2 +, \ldots, + a_k)}{\Gamma(a_1), \ldots, \Gamma(a_k)} \prod_{j=1}^{k} p_j^{a_j - 1}.$$

Now the posterior $P(p|\mathcal{D})$ is given by

$$P(p|\mathcal{D}) \propto P(\mathcal{D}|p)P(p)$$

$$\propto \prod_{j=1}^{k} p_j^{M_j+a_j-1}.$$

Thus the posterior is also Dirichlet with parameters $M_j + a_j$. We will examine how this is exploited in the so-called *Topic Model* based on latent Dirichlet allocation in the chapter on Soft Clustering.

It is possible to summarize some of the important conjugate priors as shown in Table 4.2.

It is very important to note that the notion of conjugate prior helps in simplifying the process of calculating the posterior; it helps in getting a closed form expression for the posterior. It does not guarantee that the resulting expressions are practically beneficial or semantically correct. For example, it may be appropriate to use power law prior while dealing with the frequencies of terms in a collection of documents, not the Dirichlet prior.

Another issue associated with the Bayesian estimation is that there may not be any difference between the parameter estimated using the Bayesian scheme and the ML scheme when the size of the

Table 4.2.   A collection of conjugate priors.

Likelihood	Prior	Posterior
Bernoulli, Binomial $\propto p^k(1-p)^{n-k}$	Beta $\propto p^{a-1}(1-p)^{b-1}$	Beta $\propto p^{k+a-1}(1-p)^{n+a-k-1}$
Multinomial $\propto \prod_{i=1}^{k} p_i^{m_i}$	Dirichlet $\propto \prod_{i=1}^{k} p_i^{a_i-1}$	Dirichlet $\propto \prod_{i=1}^{k} p_i^{m_i+a_i-1}$
Exponential, Poisson $\propto \lambda^n e^{-\lambda \sum_{i=1}^{n} X_i}$	Gamma $\propto \lambda^{a-1}e^{-b\lambda}$	Gamma $\lambda^{n+a-1}e^{-\lambda\left(b+\sum_{i=1}^{n} X_i\right)}$
Normal $\propto \prod_{i=1}^{n} e^{-\frac{(X_i-\mu)^2}{2\sigma^2}}$	Normal $\propto e^{-\frac{(\mu-\mu_0)^2}{2\sigma_0^2}}$	Normal $\propto e^{-\frac{(\mu-\mu_n)^2}{2\sigma_n^2}}$

dataset is large. We have seen this behavior in a variety of cases when conjugate priors are used. So, in big data analysis it may make sense to use the simple scheme of ML based on frequencies first.

Another issue is that of realization. Bayesian scheme is inherently probabilistic; however, in order to obtain results in a practical setting, it requires some empirical methods.

Research Ideas

1. In Section 2, we have discussed the Naive Bayes classifier (*NBC*) which assumes that the terms are independent of each other given the class. It is not difficult to realize that this could be a gross simplification. Then why should NBC work well?

Relevant References

(a) I. Rish, An empirical study of the Naive Bayes classifier. *International Joint Conferences on Artificial Intelligence* workshop on empirical methods in artificial intelligence, 2001.

(b) L. Jiang, D. Wang and Z. Cai, Discriminatively weighted Naive Bayes and its application in text classification. *International Journal of Artificial Intelligence Tools*, 21(1), 2012.

(c) C. D. Manning, P. Raghavan and H. Schutze, *Introduction to Information Retrieval*. Cambridge: Cambridge University Press, 2008.

2. It is possible to use classifiers in feature selection. How does one use the NBC in feature selection?

Relevant References

(a) C.-H. Lee, F. Gutierrez and D. Dou, Calculating feature weights in Naive Bayes with Kullback–Leibler Measure. *IEEE International Conference on Data Mining*, 2011.

(b) J. Chen, H. Huang, S. Tian and Y. Qu, Feature selection for text classification with Naive Bayes. *Expert Systems with Applications*, 36(3):5432–5435, 2009.

(c) Z. Zeng, H. Zhang, R. Zhang and Y. Zhang, A hybrid feature selection method based on rough conditional mutual information and Naive Bayesian classifier. *ISRN Applied Mathematics*, 2014:1–11, 2014.

(d) Microsoft Naive Bayes Algorithm Technical Reference, http:// www.msdn. microsoft.com/en-us/library/cc645902.ASPX.

3. It may be meaningful to assume class-conditional independence of phrases instead of terms. This is because phrases carry more information than terms for classification. Can we use frequent itemsets or other abstractions to characterize phrases?

Relevant References

(a) S. Dey and M. N. Murty, Using discriminative phrases for text categorization. *20th International Conference on Neural Information Processing*, 2013.

(b) M. Yuan, Y. X. Ouyang and Z. Xiong, A text categorization method using extended vector space model by frequent term sets. *Journal of Information Science and Engineering*, 29:99–114, 2013.

(c) D. Gujraniya and M. N. Murty, Efficient classification using phrases generated by topic models. In *Proceedings of International Conference on Pattern Recognition*, 2012.

4. It is possible to extend the MDC discussed in Section 4 to deal with more than two classes. Specifically, if there are n classes corresponding to the n training patterns, then each class may be viewed as drawn from a normal density with mean at the point and the covariance matrix is of the form $0I$. In such a case the *MDC* converges to *Nearest Neighbor Classifier*. Is this interpretation meaningful?

Relevant References

(a) R. O. Duda, P. E. Hart and D. G. Stork, *Pattern Classification, Second Edition*. New York: Wiley Interscience, 2000.

(b) J. Ye, Multiple Closed-Form local metric learning for K-nearest neighbor classifier. CoRR abs/1311.3157, 2013.

(c) J. Liu, X. Pan, X. Zhu and W. Zhu, Using phenological metrics and the multiple classifier fusion method to map land cover types. *Journal of Applied Remote Sensing*, 8: 2014.

5. We have discussed conjugate priors in Section 6. There could be other kinds of priors that may help in getting closed form expressions. How can they be used?

Relevant References

(a) M. I. Jordan, Jeffrey's Priors and Reference Priors, Lecture 7, 2010. (www.cs.berkeley.edu/jordan/courses/260-spring10/.../lecture7.pdf)

(b) R. Yang and J. O. Berger, Estimation of a covariance matrix using the reference prior. *The Annals of Statistics*, 22(3):1195–1211, 1994.

(c) M. D. Branco, M. G. Genton and B. Liseo, Objective Bayesian analysis of skew-t distributions. *Scandinavian Journal of Statistics Theory and Applications*, 40(1):63–85, 2013.

(d) C. Hu, E. Ryu, D. Carlson, Y. Wang and L. Carin, Latent Gaussian models for topic modeling. *JMLR Workshop and Conference Proceedings*, 2014.

6. It is analytically convenient to assume that the prior is Dirichlet and the likelihood to be multinomial in finding clusters of documents. However, because we know that frequency distribution of terms satisfies power law as specified by Zipf, does it make sense to consider other forms of prior densities?

Relevant References

(a) D. M. Blei, Probabilistic topic models. *Communications of the ACM*, 55(4):77–84, 2012.

(b) C. Wang and D. M. Blei, Variational inference in non-conjugate models. *Journal of Machine Learning Research*, 14(1):1005–1031, 2013.

(c) D. Newman, E. V. Bonilla and W. Buntine, Improving topic coherence with regularized topic models. *Proceedings of Neural Information Processing Systems*, 2011.

7. Most of the times priors are selected based on analytical tractability rather than the semantic requirement. For example, Dirichlet is convenient mathematically to deal with the frequency distribution of terms in a document collection where the likelihood is characterized by multi-nomial. However, Zipf's curve based on empirical studies gives a better prior in this case. Similarly Wikipedia offers a rich semantic input to fix the prior in case of clustering and classification of documents. How does such empirical data help in arriving at more appropriate Bayesian schemes?

Relevant References

(a) C. M. Bishop, *Pattern Recognition and Machine Learning*. Singapore: Springer, 2008.

(b) X. Hu, X. Zhang, C. Lu, E. K. Park and X. Zhou, Exploiting Wikipedia as external knowledge for document clustering. *Proceedings of the 15th ACM SIG KDD*, 389–396, 2009.

(c) J. A. Hansen, E. K. Ringger and K. D. Seppi, Probabilistic explicit topic modeling using Wikipedia. *Lecture Notes in Computer Science*, 8105:69–82, 2013.

Chapter 5

Classification

Classification is the task of assigning a class label to an input pattern. The class label indicates one of a given set of classes. The classification is carried out with the help of a model obtained using a learning procedure. According to the type of learning used, there are two categories of classification, one using **supervised learning** and the other using **unsupervised learning**. **Supervised learning** makes use of a set of examples which already have the class labels assigned to them. **Unsupervised learning** attempts to find inherent structures in the data. **Semi-supervised learning** makes use of a small number of labeled data and a large number of unlabeled data to learn the classifier.

1. Classification Without Learning

A set of training patterns which are labeled is available but there is no learning procedure to generate a model of the training data. This type of classification is a non-parametric form of classification where the inbuilt distribution of the data is not explicitly used. A popular classification algorithm which carries out classification without learning is the **Nearest Neighbor (NN)** algorithm which is generally called the 1NN classifier. The pattern to be classified is compared to all the patterns in the training data and the distance between the test pattern and the other patterns is determined.

The test pattern is given a class label which is the class label of the pattern closest to it in the training data. If there are n training patterns $(X_1, w_1), (X_2, w_2), \ldots, (X_n, w_n)$, we need to classify a pattern P, and if D_{Pi} is the distance between P and pattern X_i, then if $D_{Pk} = \min D_{Pi}$ where $i = 1, 2, \ldots, n$, then P is assigned the class of pattern X_k which will be w_k.

Other algorithms based on the NN rule are the **k-nearest neighbor (kNN)** algorithm, the **modified k-nearest neighbor (mkNN)** algorithm, and the **r-nearest neighbor (rNN)** algorithm. All these algorithms do not need to develop any model for classification using the training data. Hence, no learning takes place except for fixing the parameter k. The value of k is crucial to the performance of the classifier. It can therefore be seen that these algorithms do not need any time for learning the classification model. Classification algorithms which carry out classification without going through the learning phase have no **design time** (or **training time**). These algorithms are robust. 1NN classifier has an error rate less than twice the bayes error rate which is the optimal error rate asymptotically. Similarly, the kNN classifier gives the optimal (bayes) error rate asymptotically.

Consider the set of points in Figure 5.1. It is a two-dimensional dataset with two features f_1 and f_2. The nearest neighbor or the 1NN classifier assigns the label of the closest neighbor to a test point.

Test data P will be classified as belonging to class 'square' as its closest neighbor belongs to that class. Q will be classified as belonging to the class 'circle' as it is closest to point 7. R will be classified as belonging to class 'circle' as it is closest to point 7. In the case of point P, there is no ambiguity and the 1NN classifier works well. In the case of point Q, even though it is closest to class 'circle', since it is on the boundary of the class 'cross' and class 'circle', there is some ambiguity. If kNN is used with $k = 5$, the points Q and R are labeled as belonging to class 'cross' and not class 'circle'. In the case of mkNN, the distances of the test pattern from the k neighbors is also taken into account. Out of the k neighbors, if $d_{\min}$ is the distance of the closest neighbor and $d_{\max}$ is the distance of the furthest neighbor out of the k neighbors, then the weight given to the class of neighbor

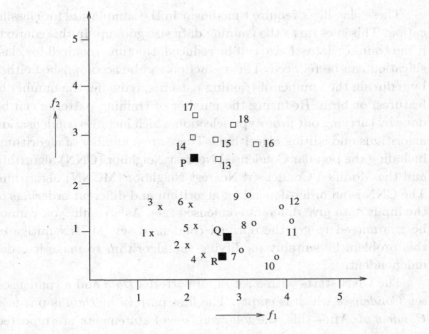

Figure 5.1.   Example dataset.

i is

$$w_i = \frac{(d_{\max} - d_i)}{(d_{\max} - d_{\min})}.$$

The NN weight w_1 is set to 1. The score of every class is initialized to 0, i.e. $\text{score}_i = 0, i = 1, \ldots, c$.

For every neighbor i out of the k neighbors, if the point belongs to class j, score_j is incremented by w_i. After doing this for the k neighbors, the test pattern belongs to the class having the largest score. In the case of pattern R, using kNN it is given the class label 'cross'. Using mkNN, since 7 is the closest neighbor, class 'circle' is given a weightage of 1. The other points 4, 2, and 5 belong to class 'cross'. The 5th neighbor is quite far away from R. If the score aggregated to class 'cross' is more than the score for class 'circle', R will be assigned to class 'cross'. It can be seen that often, using kNN may classify the test pattern differently as compared to mkNN.

These classifiers require time linear in the sample size for classification. This goes up as the training data size goes up. In this context, if the training dataset size can be reduced, the time required for classification can be reduced. This reduction can be accomplished either by reducing the number of training patterns, reducing the number of features, or both. Reducing the number of training patterns can be done by carrying out prototype selection which includes condensation algorithms and editing algorithms. There are a number of algorithms including the popular Condensed Nearest Neighbor (CNN) algorithm and the Modified Condensed Nearest Neighbor (MCNN) algorithm. The CNN is an order-dependent algorithm and different orderings of the input data give different condensed sets. As a result, you cannot be guaranteed to get the optimal condensed set. MCNN mitigates this problem by suitably modifying the algorithm to make it order independent.

The CNN starts with a set of all patterns *Data* and a condensed set *Condensed* which is empty. The first pattern in *Data* is put into *Condensed*. After this, the following set of statements are repeated till there is no change in *Condensed* in an iteration.

1. For every pattern x in *Data*, find its NN in *Condensed*.
2. If closest neighbor does not have the same class label as x, add x to *Condensed*.

It can be seen that the first pattern presented to the algorithm will be put in the condensed set. For example, in Figure 5.1, if the patterns are presented to the algorithm in the order $x_1, x_2, x_3, x_4, x_5, x_6, x_7, \ldots$, pattern x_1 belonging to class 'cross' will be first put into *Condensed*. x_2, x_3, x_4, x_5, and x_6 will be left out and x_7 which belongs to class 'circle' will be put into *Condensed*. So in the first iteration, the first pattern presented to the algorithm from each class will be included in *Condensed*, along with other patterns. Even in the subsequent iteration, the patterns included in *Condensed* will depend on the patterns already included. Hence, it is evident that the patterns put into *Condensed* depend on the order in which the patterns are presented to the algorithm. It is therefore an **order-dependent algorithm**. Obviously, when different permutations of the data give different condensed sets, the CNN algorithm does not give an optimal condensed set.

The MCNN algorithm is a modification of the CNN algorithm making it an **order-independent algorithm**. In this algorithm, in each iteration, one pattern which is a typical pattern of a class is added to *Condensed*. So in each iteration, c patterns are added to *Condensed*, one from each class. The condensed set is used to classify the training set. The misclassified patterns of each class are used to find the next typical pattern for each class which is added to *Condensed*. This is continued till there are no misclassified patterns. It is to be noted that in a particular iteration, a class which has no misclassified patterns will not have any pattern added to *Condensed*. It can be seen that in the above algorithm, all the patterns are considered. Finding the typical pattern of a class and classification of the training set using the condensed set do not depend on the order in which the patterns are presented to the algorithm. MCNN is an **order-independent** algorithm which gives better results than CNN. However, the MCNN has a higher time complexity. Since it needs to be run only once for a dataset to get the condensed set which can be used for 1NN classification, the time taken should not matter if it gives a better condensed set. It is to be noted that both CNN and MCNN work by classifying the training dataset by using the condensed dataset. Using the final **Condensed** set obtained, both the algorithms result in 100% classification accuracy on the training dataset.

2. Classification in High-Dimensional Spaces

Classification in high-dimensional spaces suffers from the problems of large data. Since the number of features is large, the space and time complexity goes up. Besides, the distance metrics generally used like the L_k metric do not work well in high-dimensional space.

One obvious solution to high-dimensional data is to reduce it to low-dimensional data by carrying out feature selection. It then becomes a problem of classification in low-dimensional spaces. It is also possible to use techniques like Fisher's linear discriminant, which reduces the problem to a linear problem with the discriminant which can be used for classification. This also helps to mitigate the curse of dimensionality problem.

Classification algorithms which use the distance metric to compare patterns have to use distance metrics which work well in high-dimensional space. The usual Minkowski's metric does not do well. Using the L_k metric, the distance to the nearest data point approaches the distance to the farthest data point. This leads to difficulty in using NN classifier since the concept of distances to different patterns does not work well. This means that the contrast in distances to different points from a particular test pattern P becomes non-existent. The difference in distance between the NN and any other points in the dataset could become very small. This means that when we consider a small value ϵ, if D_{nn} is the distance from P to the NN then most of the points in the dataset fall within a distance $(1 + \epsilon)D_{nn}$ from P. This is called the unstable phenomenon. This is shown in Figure 5.2. Since D_{max} is the distance to the furthest point, all the points in the dataset fall between the inner and the outer hyper-sphere.

Due to the unstable phenomenon which occurs in high-dimensional spaces, it is necessary to find meaningful distance

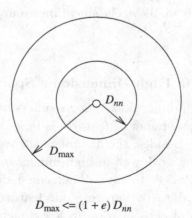

$$D_{max} <= (1 + e)\, D_{nn}$$

Figure 5.2.   Example of an unstable phenomenon.

metrics in high-dimensional spaces. The following sections discuss some distance metrics which can be used for high-dimensional space.

2.1. Fractional distance metrics

It is possible to show the following result:

$$\text{if } \lim_{d\to\infty} \text{var}\left(\frac{\|X_d\|_k}{E[\|X_d\|_k]}\right) = 0, \text{ then } \frac{D^k_{\max_d} - D^k_{nn_d}}{D^k_{nn_d}} \to_k 0, \quad (1)$$

where $E[X]$ is the expected value of a random variable X, $\text{var}[X]$ is the variance of X, $D^k_{\max_d}$ is the furthest distance of the points in the dataset from a point P when using L_k norm, $D^k_{nn_d}$ is the distance of the nearest point from the dataset when using L_k norm.

This basically says that for $X \epsilon R^d$ when using the L_k norm, as the dimensionality d increases if variance of a random variable **X** divided by its expectation tends to zero, then the difference between the maximum and minimum distance tends to zero. This shows that the difference between the maximum and minumum distances to a given test pattern does not increase as fast as the nearest distance to any point in high-dimensional space. Since the distance metric does not show enough variation in the distance to NN and furthest neighbor, it becomes meaningless to use such a distance metric as d increases. The ratio $\frac{D^k_{\max_d} - D^k_{nn_d}}{D^k_{nn_d}}$ is called the *relative contrast*.

Further, it can be proved that for a uniform distribution of n points

$$\left(\frac{C}{(k+1)^{\frac{1}{k}}}\right)\sqrt{\left(\frac{1}{2k+1}\right)} \le \lim_{d\to\infty} E\left[\frac{D^k_{\max_d} - D^k_{nn_d}}{d^{\frac{1}{k}-\frac{1}{2}}}\right]$$

$$\le \left(\frac{C(n-1)}{(k+1)^{\frac{1}{k}}}\right)\sqrt{\left(\frac{1}{2k+1}\right)}, \quad (2)$$

where C is some constant.

For an arbitrary distribution of n points, it can be shown that

$$C_k \le \lim_{d\to\infty} E\left[\frac{D^k_{\max_d} - D^k_{nn_d}}{d^{\frac{1}{k}-\frac{1}{2}}}\right] \le (n-1) \cdot C_k. \quad (3)$$

The L_k norm can be written as

$$L_k(X, Y) = [\Sigma_{i=1}^d (\|x^i - y^i\|^k)]^{\frac{1}{k}}. \tag{4}$$

In high-dimensional spaces smaller values of k do better than larger values of k. According to Eqs. (2) and (3), if we consider the difference between the maximum distance and minimum distance from a test pattern P, $|D_{\max} - D_{nn}|$, it grows as $d^{\frac{1}{k} - \frac{1}{2}}$ with increasing dimensionality d. This means that for the L_1 norm, the above expression diverges to ∞. For the L_2 norm or euclidean distance (ED), the expression is bounded by constants and for higher values of k, it converges to zero. As a result of this, only the L_1 metric among the L_k family is found to have increasing difference between the nearest and farthest neighbors of a query point as the dimensionality increases. For the L_2 metric, $|D_{\max} - D_{nn}|$ converges to a constant and for any distance metric L_i where $i \geq 3$, $|D_{\max} - D_{nn}|$ converges to zero as dimensionality d increases. Thus, for high-dimensional data, the L_1 metric is preferable to L_2 metric. Since lower values of k do better, fractional distance metrics in which k is a fraction smaller than 1 can be considered. So the fractional distance function dist_d^f can be considered where

$$\text{dist}_d^f = (\Sigma_{i=1}^d (x^i - y^i)^f)^{\frac{1}{f}}, \tag{5}$$

where $f \epsilon (0, 1)$.

It is found that fractional distance metrics show better relative contrast than integral distance metrics. Experimentation has been done with a range of values from $L_{0.1}$ to L_{10} and also for L_∞ and it is found that the classification accuracy decreases with increasing values of k in the L_k norm.

In the case of fractional metrics, for the case of uniform distribution and if $f = \frac{1}{l}$, where l is an integer, we get

$$\left(\frac{C}{(f+1)^{\frac{1}{f}}} \right) \sqrt{\left(\frac{1}{2 \cdot f + 1} \right)} \leq \lim_{d \to \infty} E \left[\frac{D_{\max_d}^f - D_{nn_d}^f}{d^{\frac{1}{f} - \frac{1}{2}}} \right]$$

$$\leq \left(\frac{C \cdot (n-1)}{(f+1)^{\frac{1}{f}}} \right) \sqrt{\left(\frac{1}{2 \cdot f + 1} \right)}. \tag{6}$$

This shows that the absolute difference between the maximum distance and minimum distance using fractional distance metric increases at the rate of $d^{\frac{1}{f}-\frac{1}{2}}$. It can be seen that the smaller the fraction, the greater is the rate of divergence between the maximum and the minimum distance.

To examine the relative contrast, we use the following equation:

$$C \cdot \sqrt{\frac{1}{2 \cdot f + 1}} \leq \lim_{d \to \infty} E\left[\frac{D^f_{\max_d} - D^f_{nn_d}}{D^f_{nn_d}}\right]$$

$$\leq C \cdot (n-1) \cdot \sqrt{\frac{1}{2 \cdot f + 1}}. \tag{7}$$

From Eqs. (1)–(3), (6), and (7), it can be seen that fractional distance metrics provide better contract than the integer valued distance metrics.

2.2. Shrinkage–divergence proximity (SDP)

The proximity between two points is computed by finding the proximity on each attribute and adding them up. SDP magnifies the variation in the distance for every attribute to avoid the unstable phenomenon. If we consider two data points P and Q whose proximity is to be found, for each attribute, the attribute's proximity is almost zero if the projected attribute values of the two data points are close to each other. To distinguish between the two points on this attribute, the projected attributes of the two data points are made more far apart to make it easy to distinguish them. In SDP, the exponential function is used to spread out the points and increase discrimination. To take care of this, SDP uses weighted attributes.

Consider a function f defined as

$$f_{p,q}(x) = \begin{cases} 0, & \text{if } 0 \leq x < p, \\ x, & \text{if } p \leq x < q, \\ e^x, & \text{otherwise.} \end{cases} \tag{8}$$

If we have two d-dimensional points $P = (p_1, p_2, \ldots, p_d)$ and $Q = (q_1, q_2, \ldots, q_d)$, then the general form of the SDP function between P and Q is defined as:

$$SDP^G(P, Q) = \Sigma_{i=1}^d w_i f_{s_{i1}, s_{i2}}(D_d(p_i, q_i)), \tag{9}$$

where w_i is the weightage given to the ith attribute and depends on the importance given to the attribute. One way of finding the values of w_i would be to give it a value of $\frac{1}{\sigma_i}$ where σ_i is the standard deviation of attribute i. Any feature weighting algorithm can be used to find the values of w_i.

The parameter s_{i1} is called the shrinkage threshold for attribute i and s_{i2} is called the divergence threshold for attribute i. The values of these two parameters are fixed empirically so that more stable performance is obtained. It is found that s_{i1} can be fixed to a very small value such as $0.005\sigma_i$ and s_{i2} is taken from the interval $[25\sigma_i, 60\sigma_i]$.

If the parameters w_i are taken to be 1, then the SDP^G will degenerate to

$$SDP_{s_1, s_2}(p, q) = \Sigma_{i=1}^d f_{s_1, s_2}(D_d(p_i, q_i)). \tag{10}$$

It is to be noted that if D_d is the L_k metric, then the SDP has the following properties:

1. SDP_{s_1, s_2} is equivalent to L_1, as $s_1 \to 0$ and $s_2 \to \infty$.
2. $SDP_{s_1, s_2}(p, q) = 0$ if and only if $0 \leq D_d(p_i, q_i) < s_1 \forall i$.
3. $SDP_{s_1, s_2}(p, q) \geq de^{s_2}$ if $D_d(p_i, q_i) \geq s_2 \forall i$.

The first property shows that SDP is a general form of the L_1 metric. The third property shows that the magnifying effect of SDP is very sharp. The SDP function is not a metric as $SDP_{s_1, s_2}(p, q) = 0$ does not mean that $p = q$ for $s_1 > 0$ and the triangular inequality does not hold in general.

3. Random Forests

Random forests or decision tree forests consist of a number of decision trees. It is an ensemble classifier. The prediction of the decision trees is combined to get the overall prediction of the decision forest. Each tree is built by considering only a random subset of the features for splitting at the nodes. Because only a subset of features is used, the decision tree forest can handle a larger number of features.

If there are N training patterns, a random sample of N is selected with replacement. Generally $\frac{2}{3}rd$ of N is chosen at random. A decision tree is built using the random sample. This decision tree is built by considering only a subset of the features for splitting at the nodes. If d is the dimensionality of the data, d_1 features are chosen at random where $d_1 < d$.

By using the above procedure, a number of decision trees are built leading to a decision tree forest. A new pattern is assigned a class label by using all the decision trees in the forest, and combined to give the final class label.

The selection of a random subset of features for each decision tree makes this a random subspace method. This prevents overfitting leading to stochastic discrimination.

One advantage of decision tree forests is that the $\frac{1}{3}rd$ patterns which are left out for building a decision tree (which are called the "out of bag" (OOB) samples) can be used as a test sample for that tree. By using the OOB samples, the error rate of prediction for each tree is computed. The average error rate for all the trees gives the generalization error of the decision tree forest.

Some of the choices to be made for building a random forest are as follows:

1. The forest size or the number of decision trees F.
2. Type of decision to be made at each node: Using a single feature at each node leads to hyper-rectangular regions. It is also possible to use oblique split (linear combinations of some features) or multivariate split (nonlinear combination of some features).
3. Parameter to be used to choose the best feature to split at a node. Generally, information gain or gini index is used. The information gain at a node N is calculated as shown further. At a node N, if we have N_i as the number of instances of class i, then the impurity

$i(N)$ is:

$$i(N) = -\sum_{i=1}^{c} f_i \log f_i,$$

where

$$f_i = \frac{N_i}{\sum_{j=1}^{c} N_j}.$$

In the case of two classes, we get

$$i(N) = -f_p \log f_p - f_n \log f_n,$$

where f_p is the fraction of positive examples given by $\frac{N_p}{N}$ and f_n is the fraction of negative examples given by $\frac{N_n}{N}$. N is the total number of instances, N_p is the number of instances of positive class, and N_n is the number of instances of negative class.

If there are s splits pertaining to a decision on an attribute a, then the impurity for split k is

$$I(ak) = -\sum_{i=1}^{c} f_{aki} \log f_{aki},$$

where f_{aki} gives the fraction of instances of attribute a in split k of class i and is given by $f_{aki} = \frac{N_{aki}}{N_{ak}}$.

N_{ak} is the total number of instances along split k and is given by $N_{ak} = \sum_{j=1}^{c} N_{akj}$ where N_{aki} gives the instances of class i with attribute a in split k.

The information gain for node N for split on attribute a is given by

$$IG(Na) = I(N) - \sum_{k=1}^{s} \frac{N_{ak}}{N} I(ak).$$

Using variance impurity, the impurity at the node N is given by

$$i(N) = \sum_{i,j,i \neq j} f_i * f_j,$$

$i = 1 \ldots c, j = 1 \ldots c.$

This can also be written as

$$i(N) = \frac{1}{2}\left[1 - \sum_{j=1}^{c} f_j^2\right].$$

This is called the Gini impurity. In the case of the two-class problem, we get

$$i(N) = f_p * f_n.$$

4. Each leaf node is associated with a predictor model. The predictor model to be used has to be chosen. It could be the conditional probability $p(c \mid \mathbf{x})$ where c refers to the class.
5. The method for injecting randomness in each tree. This is done by choosing a random subset of the dataset to be considered to build the tree and choosing only a subset of the features at random to be considered for the splitting. If there are N patterns and N_1 patterns are considered for building a tree, then the amount of randomness is controlled by the ratio $\frac{N_1}{N}$. The parameter ρ gives the number of patterns in the subset of patterns chosen. If $\rho = N$, then there is no randomness in the system. Also $\rho = 1$ gives the maximum randomness.

In view of the above, some of the key parameters of random forests are:

1. Forest size F.
2. Number of patterns considered for each tree $N1$ which gives the randomness parameter ρ.
3. Number of random features (d_1) considered for each tree.

If each leaf i gives a class conditional posterior probability $p_i(c|\mathbf{x})$, the combined output will be

$$p_i(c \mid \mathbf{x}) = \frac{1}{F}\Sigma_{i=1}^{F} p_i(c \mid \mathbf{x}). \tag{11}$$

The random forest can be used for regression when the predictor takes on numerical values instead of class labels at the leaf nodes.

This depends on the predictor model which can be constant, polynomial and linear, and probabilistic linear. For example, a polynomial model would correspond to

$$y(x) = \Sigma_{i=1}^{N_1} a_i x^i.$$

It is probabilistic linear when the output at a leaf i is of the form $p_i(\mathbf{y} \mid \mathbf{x})$.

Some of the strengths of random forests are as follows:

1. It is found to give better results than decision trees.
2. It is robust to outliers and noise.
3. A probabilistic output is provided.
4. Works well even when more than two classes are involved.
5. The overall performance of the random forest can be guaged by finding the generalization error. It is found that random forests generalize well to unseen data.
6. The algorithm can be parallelized to give improved speed.

Random forests can be used not only for supervised classification but also for clustering and semi-supervised classification.

3.1. Fuzzy random forests

In a fuzzy random forest, there is a forest of fuzzy decision trees generated randomly. To construct a fuzzy random forest, $\frac{2}{3}rd$ of the training examples are selected randomly. The other $\frac{1}{3}rd$ of the data are called OOB data. Using the selected training examples, a fuzzy tree is constructed.

Every example has a weight of 1 at the root node. At the root node, there will be a number of examples of each class. These examples are distributed to the branches. Each example is along each branch by an amount obtained as the product of its weight and the membership degree to the node. The information gain for each attribute at that node is calculated. The attribute with the highest information gain is chosen as the attribute to be split at the node. The split is made at the node. The above procedure is used at the new nodes created by the split.

To classify a new pattern, it is checked with every fuzzy tree in the forest, and the decision of each tree is taken and combined to get the final classification. Combine the information from the leaf nodes reached in each tree to get another decision forest from where the decision is taken.

For a new pattern p, each tree i gives a weight to each class c for the leaf node j reached which is $W(i, c)$. Here, the value

$$W[i, c] = \frac{E_c}{\sum_{m=1}^{C} E_m},$$

where E_j is the number of examples of class j.

The combination of these decisions can be made in a number of ways.

1. Simple majority vote: The class label which has maximum weight is assigned to the test pattern in each tree. These are combined to find the class label with the majority vote. For every tree t and for a class c, U_{tc} is 1 if weight W_{tc} is maximum in the tree otherwise U_{tc} is zero. Then we get

$$V_j = \sum_{i=1}^{i=T} U_{ij}, \quad j = 1, \ldots, c, \qquad (12)$$

where T is the number of trees and c is the number of classes. The new pattern is assigned to the class

$$c = \operatorname{argmax}_j V_j.$$

2. Weighted vote: For every class, the weights obtained from each tree are combined. The class having the maximum weight is assigned to the test pattern. We get

$$Z_j = \sum_{i=1}^{i=T} W_{ij}, \quad j = 1, \ldots, C, \qquad (13)$$

where T is the number of trees and C is the number of classes. The new pattern is assigned to the class

$$c = \operatorname{argmax}_j Z_j.$$

4. Linear Support Vector Machine (SVM)

Linear SVM is an extremely fast machine learning algorithm for very large datasets. A cutting plane algorithm is used to get an SVM which has a linear complexity. This means that it is a scalable algorithm as the model scales linearly with the size of the dataset. It is found to give superior performance when the data size is very large. Besides, it can be used for multi-class problems, whereas SVMs are suitable for two-class problems. Linear SVM is popularly used to classify high-dimensional patterns.

We explain the working and the features of the linear SVM using a simple two-dimensional example shown in Figure 5.3. There are two lines in the two-dimensional space; the points $(2,0)^t$ and $(3,1)^t$ are on one line and another point $(0,0)^t$ is on the second line. In high-dimensional spaces, we will have hyperplanes instead of lines. The first line in the example figure is given by

$$x_1 - x_2 - 1 = 1.$$

Note that both the points $(2,0)^t$ and $(3,1)^t$ satisfy this equation. Also if we consider the point $(1,-1)^t$, it satisfies the above equation as it falls on the corresponding line. The second line is characterized

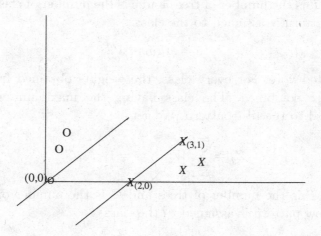

Figure 5.3.   Two-dimensional dataset.

by

$$x_1 - x_2 - 1 = -1.$$

The point $(0,0)^t$ satisfies this equation. Also, point $(1,1)^t$ satisfies this equation as it falls on this line. The first line may be represented as $W^t X + b = 1$ where W and X are vectors and b is a scalar. In the two-dimensional case

$$W = (w_1, w_2)^t; \quad X = (x_1, x_2)^t.$$

In this example, $W = (1, -1)^t$ and $b = -1$. The second line is of the form $W^t X + b = -1$. In the two-dimensional case, these lines are called *support lines*. In the high-dimensional case, we have support planes characterized by $W^t X + b = 1$ and $W^t X + b = -1$. It is possible to show that the normal distance or *margin* between these two planes is $\frac{2}{\|W\|}$. In classification based on SVM, we use the patterns from two different classes, *positive* and *negative* classes, to learn W and b.

Any point X from the positive class satisfies the property that $W^t X + b \geq 1$ with support vectors (some kind of boundary vectors) from the positive class satisfying $W^t X + b = 1$. Similarly, points from the negative class satisfy $W^t X + b \leq -1$ with support vectors from the negative class satisfying $W^t X + b = -1$. So, the margin is concerned with distance between the two support planes; we would like to *maximize the margin*. So, we would like to maximize $\frac{2}{\|W\|}$. Equivalently, we can minimize $\frac{\|W\|^2}{2}$.

By assuming a point X_i in positive class has the label $y_i = 1$ and a point X_j in the negative class has the class label $y_j = -1$. So, the optimization problem has constraints. The optimization problem is

$$\text{Minimize } \frac{\|W\|^2}{2},$$

such that $y_i(W^t X_i + b) \geq 1$ for all the patterns X_i, $i = 1, 2, \ldots, n$. The Lagrangian associated with the optimization problem is

$$L(W, b) = \frac{1}{2}\|W\|^2 - \sum_{i=1}^{n} \alpha_i [y_i(W^t X_i + b) - 1].$$

By taking the gradient of the Lagrangian with respect to W and equating to zero, we get $W = \sum_{X_i \in S} \alpha_i y_i X_i$, where α's are Lagrange variables. There are several standard methods and software packages to find the α's. Further by differentiating with respect to b and equating to zero, we get $\sum_{i+1}^{n} \alpha_i y_i = 0$.

By looking at the pattern $(3,1)^t$ on the first line and $(1,1)^t$ on the second line, we get $W = \alpha_1(3,1)^t - \alpha_2(1,1)^t$ by plugging in the values in the equation $W = \sum_{X_i \in S} \alpha_i y_i X_i$. One can find the values of α's using some standard methods. For $\alpha_1 = 1$ and $\alpha_2 = 2$, we get $W = (1,-1)^t$. Then we can use W and the points $(3,1)^t$ and $(1,1)^t$ along with the constraints, we get $b = -1$. So, in the example situation, the decision boundary between the two classes is in between the two support lines and is given by $x_1 - x_2 = 1$. It is possible to observe the following:

- W is orthogonal to the decision boundary and is directed toward the positive class. So, W decides the orientation of the decision boundary. Any point falling in the left-hand side (negative half) is labeled negative and any point falling on the right-hand side of the decision boundary is labeled as positive. For example, for the point $X = (0,1)^t$, the value of $W^t X + b$ is $-2(<-1)$ and so it is classified as a member of the negative class. The point $(3,0)^t$ has the value to be $2(>1)$ and so is classified as a member of the positive class.
- b is the threshold that decides the location of the decision boundary with respect to the origin. When b is negative as in the current two-dimensional example, then the decision boundary is below the line $x_2 = x_1$ which passes through the origin. In the current example, origin is in the negative side of the decision boundary.
- *Learning the SVM classifier* involves obtaining the weight vector W and the threshold b value from the training patterns. Typically, a subset, S, of the set of training patterns is the set of support vectors. Elements of S are adequate to obtain W and b based on $W = \sum_{X_i \in S} \alpha_i y_i X_i$. This requires learning the values of α for each element of S. The value of b is obtained from the constraints

corresponding to the elements in S; specifically we obtain b using $y_i(W^t X_i + b) = 1$ for $X_i \in S$.

- So, the whole learning boils down to learning α's for the patterns. If a pattern X_j is not a support vector, then the value of α_j is zero (0). If some $X_i \in S$, then the α_i is either positive or zero. So, typically positive α_i's identify the important support vectors which contribute to the vector W.

Most of the above observations are applicable in the high-dimensional case also. Linear SVM is adequate to deal with linearly separable classes. If there are some mis-classifications because of positive points falling in the negative half or some negative points falling in the positive half, then the optimization problem is updated to accommodate such noise.

4.1. SVM–kNN

A hybrid method is used here where SVM is not applied to the entire training data. A coarse and quick categorization is done by finding the kNN. Then SVM is performed on the smaller set of examples which are more relevant.

The algorithm is as follows:

1. Find a set of $k1$ neighbors to the query where $k1 > k$ by using a crude distance function.
2. Find k NN by using a more accurate distance function on the $k1$ samples.
3. If all the k neighbors have the same label, the query is labeled.
4. If not, find the pairwise distance of the query and the k neighbors.
5. Convert the pairwise distance matrix into a kernel matrix using the kernel trick.
6. Apply DAGSVM on the kernel matrix to label the query.

Applying DAGSVM to a large dataset is intractable. When DAGSVM is used on only the limited number of examples, the classification can be done in a reasonable time. DAGSVM can also be used for multi-class problems. It has been shown experimentally that this method when applied to very large datasets with high dimensionality gives accurate results in a reasonable time.

4.2. Adaptation of cutting plane algorithm

While SVM formulation involves a large number of examples n and a large number of features d, each example has only f features where $f << d$. The cutting-plane algorithm for training linear SVMs has a complexity of $O(fn)$. This algorithm is based on an alternative but equivalent formulation of the SVM optimization problem.

The primal form of the SVM optimization problem can be written as

$$\min_{w,\xi \geq 0} \frac{1}{2} w^T w + \frac{C}{n} \sum_{i=1}^{n} \xi_i, \tag{14}$$

s.t. $\forall i \varepsilon 1, \ldots, n : y_i(w^T x_i) \geq 1 - \xi_i$.

Another formulation of this problem uses only one slack variable ξ for all constraints. It can be written as

$$\min_{w,\xi \geq 0} \frac{1}{2} w^T w + C\xi \tag{15}$$

s.t. $\forall c \varepsilon \{0,1\}^n : \frac{1}{n} w^T \sum_{i=1}^{n} c_i y_i x_i \geq \frac{1}{n} \sum_{i=1}^{n} c_i - \xi$.

The Wolfe dual of Eq. (15) can be written as

$$\max_{\alpha} > 0 \sum_{c \varepsilon \{0,1\}^n} \frac{\|c\|_1}{n} \alpha_c - \frac{1}{2} \sum_{c \varepsilon \{0,1} \sum_{c' \varepsilon \{0,1\}^n} \alpha_c \alpha_{c'} x_c^T x_{c'} \tag{16}$$

s.t.

$$\sum_{c \varepsilon \{0,1\}^n} \alpha_c \leq C,$$

where

$$x_c = \frac{1}{n} \sum_{i=1}^{n} c_i y_i x_i.$$

Using Eq. (15), the algorithm given below can be used for training the SVM.

1. The input to the algorithm is the set of patterns $X = ((x_1, y_1), \ldots, (x_n, y_n))$, the constant C and ϵ.
2. Working set $\mathcal{WS} = \phi$
3. repeat
4. $(w, \xi) = \operatorname{argmin}_{w, \xi \geq 0} \frac{1}{2} w^T w + C\xi$

   s.t. $\forall c \varepsilon \mathcal{WS} : \frac{1}{n} w^T \sum_{i=1}^n c_i y_i x_i \geq \frac{1}{n} \sum_{i=1}^n c_i - \xi$
5. for $i = 1, \ldots, n$ do
6. $c_i = \begin{cases} 1 & y_i(w^T x_i) < 1 \\ 0 & \text{otherwise} \end{cases}$
7. end for
8. $\mathcal{WS} = \mathcal{WS} \bigcup \{c\}$
9. until $\frac{1}{n} \sum_{i=1}^n c_i y_i(w^T x_i) \leq \xi + \epsilon$
10. $\text{return}(w, \xi)$.

This algorithm has a working set $\mathcal{WS}$ which gives the constraints being considered. It starts with the working set being Φ i.e. with an empty set of constraints. In every iteration, it finds the most violated constraint for Eq. (15) and adds it to the working set $\mathcal{WS}$. The stopping criterion depends on the training loss ξ. ϵ is a small value which gives the error which can be tolerated in this value. Usually, 0.1% is an acceptable training error. The optimization problem in line 4 can be done using the Wolfe dual as given in Eq. (16). This dual requires $O(|\mathcal{WS}|^2)$ elements of the Hessian to be calculated which will take $O(|\mathcal{WS}|^2 fn)$ time. Since $d \leq fn$, the dual is independent of n and f. So, the overall time complexity per iteration is $O(\text{fn})$.

4.3. Nystrom approximated SVM

The primal form of the SVM can be written as

$$\min_{w,b} \frac{1}{2} w^T w + C \sum_{i=1}^n \eta(w; \phi(x_i), y_i). \tag{17}$$

The dual form can be written as

$$\min_\alpha \frac{1}{2}\alpha^T Q\alpha - e^T\alpha \tag{18}$$

s.t. $\alpha^T y = 0$ and $0 \le \alpha_i \le C \forall i$,

where Q is a kernel matrix such that $Q = K(X, X) = \{K[x_i, x_j]\}_{ij}$ where $K(x_i, x_j) = \phi(x_i)^T\phi(x_j)$.

The computation of Q takes $O(n^2 d)$ where n is the number of samples and d is the dimensionality. Nystrom approximation is of the form $Q = PW_d P^T$ where $P = K(X, B)\varepsilon R^{nXd}$ and $B\varepsilon R^{dXd}$ consists of $n1 \ll n$ examples which are called the projection bases. $W_d = W^{-1}$ where $W = K(B, B)$.

Finding a basis matrix for the problem is not trivial. One way of selecting the basis is to randomly sample instances from the training set to form the basis matrix. Random sampling gives the reduced support vector machine (RSVM). Generally, a stratified random sampling is carried out where equal number of patterns are selected from each class to avoid imbalance in the dataset. Another method is to find a basis set that maximizes the accuracy of the model on the dataset.

5. Logistic Regression

There are several linear models that have been successful in classifying large datasets. We have seen one such model that is the linear SVM. Another popular model that has been used on large datasets is the *logistic regression model*. Here, we model the ratio of the likelihoods. Specifically, we assume that

$$\ln\frac{P(X|C_1)}{P(X|C_2)} \text{ is linear in } X.$$

Observing that X is a vector, our assumption would result in the log-likelihood ratio being equal to some scalar of the form $W^t X + q$, where W is a vector and q is a scalar; this expression is linear in X. This may be easily achieved in the following case.

Example 1. Let the likelihood values of X be obtained based on the assumption that both the classes C_1 and C_2 are normally distributed. Further, to simplify the analysis, let us assume

- X is univariate that is X is a scalar.
- Let the standard deviation be the same for both the classes; let it be σ.
- Let the means of C_1 and C_2 be μ_1 and μ_2 respectively.

Then the likelihood ratio $\frac{P(X|C_1)}{P(X|C_2)}$ is given by

$$\frac{\exp\left[-\frac{1}{2}\frac{(X-\mu_1)^2}{\sigma^2}\right]}{\exp\left[-\frac{1}{2}\frac{(X-\mu_2)^2}{\sigma^2}\right]} = \exp\left[-\frac{1}{2\sigma^2}\{(X-\mu_1)^2 - (X-\mu_2)^2\}\right]$$

$$= \exp\left[\frac{\mu_1-\mu_2}{2\sigma^2}\{2X + (\mu_1+\mu_2)\}\right].$$

So,

$$\ln\frac{P(X|C_1)}{P(X|C_2)} = \frac{\mu_1-\mu_2}{2\sigma^2}\{2X + (\mu_1+\mu_2)\}.$$

The right-hand side of the above equation can be viewed as $WX + b$ where $W = \frac{\mu_1-\mu_2}{\sigma^2}$ and $q = \frac{\mu_1-\mu_2}{2\sigma^2}(\mu_1+\mu_2)$. In a multi-dimensional case, we will have W and X to be vectors of the same size and q to be a scalar. We can show that the logarithm of the likelihood ratio will be linear in X, specifically of the form $W^tX + q$ where W and X are d-dimensional vectors and the underlying distributions are Gaussian with different means and the same covariance matrix. This is a situation where the logistic regression is optimal for classification.

So, we have

$$\ln\frac{P(X|C_1)}{P(X|C_2)} = W^tX + q,$$

or correspondingly by considering the ratio of the posterior probabilities, with $P(C_1)$ and $P(C_2)$ as the prior probabilities

$$\ln\frac{P(C_1|X)}{P(C_2|X)} = \ln\frac{P(X|C_1)}{P(X|C_2)} + \ln\frac{P(C_1)}{P(C_2)}$$

$$= W^tX + q + \ln\frac{P(C_1)}{P(C_2)}$$

$$= W^tX + b,$$

where $b = q + \ln\frac{P(C_1)}{P(C_2)}$. This gives us a linear form for both the logarithm of the likelihood ratio and the logarithm of the ratio of the posterior probabilities. We can simplify further to write $P(C_1|X)$ in terms of $W^tX + b$ as follows. We have

$$\ln\frac{P(C_1|X)}{P(C_2|X)} = W^tX + b.$$

In a two-class problem $P(C_2|X) = 1 - P(C_1|X)$. So,

$$\ln\left(\frac{P(C_1|X)}{1 - P(C_1|X)}\right) = W^tX + b.$$

This implies, by taking exponentiation on both sides, that

$$\frac{P(C_1|X)}{1 - P(C_1|X)} = \exp(W^tX + b).$$

By simplifying further, we get

$$P(C_1|X)[1 + \exp(W^tX + b)] = \exp(W^tX + b).$$

So,

$$P(C_1|X) = \frac{\exp(W^tX + b)}{(1 + \exp(W^tX + b))}.$$

By dividing the numerator and the denominator by $\exp(W^tX + b)$, we get

$$P(C_1|X) = \frac{1}{1 + \exp[-(W^tX + b)]}.$$

The right-hand side of the above equation is the *sigmoid function*. The above equation is of the form $P(C_1|X) = \frac{1}{1+\exp(-t)}$ where $t = W^t X + b$ and $s(t) = \frac{1}{1+\exp(-t)}$ is the sigmoid function; $s(t)$ takes values in the range 0 to 1.

Given a set of n training patterns $\{X_1, X_2, \ldots, X_n\}$ where each pattern X_i is labeled using C_1 or C_2, if X_i is from class C_1, then we choose $y_i = 1$ and if X_i is from class C_2, then $y_i = 0$. Because $P(C_2|X) = 1 - P(C_1|X)$ and $P(C_1|X) = s(W^t X + b)$, we can have the following least squares learning algorithm. Obtain W and b corresponding to

$$\min \sum_{i=1}^{n} (P(C_1|X_i) - y_i)^2.$$

Because $P(C_1|X_i) = s(W^t X_i + b)$, we can write the optimization problem as find W and b that minimize

$$\frac{1}{2} \sum_{i=1}^{n} \{s(W^t X_i + b) - y_i\}^2.$$

6. Semi-supervised Classification

It is generally assumed that there is a large amount of labeled training data. In reality, this may not be true. Often, there is some labeled data and a large amount of unlabeled data. This maybe due to the fact that when preparing the training data, getting labels maybe a difficult task or the cost of obtaining labels maybe very costly. This maybe due to one of the following reasons:

1. Getting labels may require a lot of work.
2. It may require an expert to find the labels.
3. It may require some expensive device or expensive computation.

The classification of such data is called semi-supervised classification. The techniques used should take advantage of the large amount of unlabeled data but make do with just a small set of labeled data. While the unlabeled data by itself may not be sufficient to carrying out classification, they may contain discriminative information which is useful for classification. Since semi-supervised learning generally requires less human effort and helps to achieve higher classification accuracy, it is of interest to us. Generalization error is reduced by using the unlabeled data.

The problem can be described as follows. In the training data, we have l labeled data i.e.

$X_l = \{(x_1, \theta_1), (x_2, \theta_2), \ldots, (x_l, \theta_l)\}$
and the remaining data is unlabeled data

$X_u = \{x_{l+1}, \ldots, x_n\}.$

Usually the unlabeled data is very much larger than the labeled data.

i.e. $n - l >> l.$

Many of the semi-supervised learning algorithms make use of the **cluster assumption** which states that the decision boundary should not cross high density regions but should instead lie in low density regions.

Given below are some of the techniques used for semi-supervised learning.

6.1. Using clustering algorithms

This is a simple algorithm which uses existing clustering algorithms. It is as follows:

1. The clustering algorithm is run on the labeled and unlabeled data.
2. All the points in each cluster is labeled by the majority class of all the points in the cluster.
3. The newly labeled data and the labeled data are used for classification.

6.2. Using generative models

The decision boundary obtained using the labeled data and the unlabeled data is different from the decision boundary obtained by using only the labeled data. This is because we get a mixture model.

The algorithm for generative models is as follows:

1. Choose a generative model $p(x, y|\theta)$.
2. Find the maximum likelihood estimation (MLE) on labeled and unlabeled data

$$\theta^* = \text{argmax}_\theta \, p(X_l, Y_l, X_u|\theta).$$

3. Compute class distribution using Bayes' rule:

$$p(y|x, \theta^*) = \frac{p(x, y|\theta^*)}{\Sigma_{y'} p(x, y'|\theta^*)}. \tag{19}$$

One method of finding the MLE i.e. finding θ^* is by using the expectation maximization (EM) algorithm. An EM algorithm is an iterative method for finding the maximum likelihood estimate (MLE).

The steps for using EM to find θ^* are as follows:

1. Use the labeled data to find $p(y|\theta)$ which is the proportion of data with label y and $p(x|y, \theta)$ which is the mean and covariance of data with label y.
2. Repeat
   (a) Compute the expected labels $p(y|x, \theta)$ for all the unlabeled data and assign the class labels.
   (b) Update MLE θ with the labeled data and the newly labeled unlabeled data.
3. Until there is no change in θ.

6.3. Using low density separation

In this method, the **cluster assumption** is used. This states that the decision boundary should not cross high density regions, but should reside in low density regions. Graph-based distances are derived from the data points which help in identifying the low density regions between clusters. After this, an SVM is trained so that the decision boundary is placed in low density regions. To find the low density regions, a graph is drawn using the data points in the dataset. Edges are drawn between nodes which are NN. This graph is then used to identify the low density regions.

6.4. Using graph-based methods

This makes use of a graph drawn using the labeled and unlabeled training patterns as vertices and undirected edges connecting the vertices with a weight attached to it. For an edge between patterns x_i and x_j, there is an edge with a weight w_{ij} which reflects the proximity of x_i and x_j. There are a number of parameters which are used for w_{ij}.

1. **Gaussian edge weight function**:

$$w_{ij} = e^{(-\|x_i - x_j\|^2/\sigma^2)}. \tag{20}$$

The graph is fully connected but as the distance between the points increases, the weight decays.

2. **kNN edge weight function**:

In this function, w_{ij} is 1 if x_i is one of the kNN of x_j. Otherwise w_{ij} is 0.

If w_{ij} is large, it implies that $f(x_i)$ and $f(x_j)$ are likely to be the same. The graph energy of a function f is:

$$\Sigma_{i,j=1}^{l+u} w_{ij}(f(x_i) - f(x_j))^2. \tag{21}$$

Looking at the graph energy, we can order all the weight functions f. It is advantageous to use f values of top ranked functions. To find an f function which fits the data well and ranks high, we need to minimize the function:

$$\text{argmin}_f \frac{1}{f}\Sigma_{i=1}^{l} c(f(x_i), y_i) + \lambda_1 \|f\|^2 + \lambda_2 \Sigma_{i,j=1}^{l+u} w_{ij}(f(x_i) - f(x_j))^2, \tag{22}$$

where $c(f(x), y)$ is a convex loss function such as the hinge loss or the squared loss. λ_1 and λ_2 are weights assigned to the two terms. This convex optimization problem can be solved.

Some graph-based methods are described below.

1. Mincut

In the two-class problem, the positive labels act as sources and the negative labels as sinks. The minimum set of edges are found such that all flow from the source to the sink is blocked. Then all nodes connected to the source are labeled positive and those connected to the sink are labeled negative.

Another definition of mincut is the mode of a Markov random field with positive and negative labels. Mincut minimizes the function which combines the loss function and regularizer. It can be written as

$$M * \sum_{i \varepsilon L} (y_i - y_{i|L}) + \frac{1}{2} \sum_{i,j} w_{ij} (y_i - y_j)^2, \qquad (23)$$

subject to $y_i \varepsilon \{0, 1\}$.

The first term is a quadratic loss function where M is a very large constant. The second term is the regularizer.

2. Discrete Markov Random Fields

The marginal probabilities of the discrete Markov random fields are computed. A sampling technique is used.

Another approach is to use a continuous relaxation to the discrete Markov random fields by using the harmonic function method. This uses a quadratic loss function and a regularizer based on the Laplacian Δ function given by

$$M * \sum_{i \varepsilon L} (f_i - y_i)^2 + f^T \Delta f, \qquad (24)$$

Δ is the Laplacian given by $\Delta = D - W$,
D is the degree matrix and is a diagonal matrix.

$$D_{ii} = \sum_{j=1}^{n} W_{ij},$$

and W is the $n \times n$ weight matrix for both labeled and unlabeled data which is positive and symmetric.

3. The local and global consistency method uses a loss function

$$\sum_{i=1}^{n} (f_i - y_i)^2,$$

and a normalized Laplacian $D^{-\frac{1}{2}} \Delta D^{-\frac{1}{2}}$ is used in the regularizer giving the function

$$f^T D^{-\frac{1}{2}} \Delta D^{-\frac{1}{2}} f. \tag{25}$$

4. Tikhonov Regularizer

   This algorithm uses the loss function and the Tikhonov regularizer giving

$$\frac{1}{l} \sum_{i} (f_i - y_i)^2 + \beta f^T \Delta f. \tag{26}$$

   Δ can be replaced by Δ^m where m is an integer. This is the smoothness matrix. β is a parameter where $\beta \varepsilon \mathcal{R}$.

6.5. Using co-training methods

In this method, two classifiers are used. The labeled data is split into two parts and is used as labeled data for the two classifiers respectively. Each classifier adds labeled data to the other classifier.

The algorithm is as follows:

1. Split labeled dataset into two sets: $X_l^{(1)}$ and $X_l^{(2)}$. The features are split into two parts where $X_l^{(1)}$ is the labeled data using feature set 1 and $X_l^{(2)}$ is the labeled data using feature set 2.
2. Use $X_l^{(1)}$ to train classifier $\mathcal{C}^{(1)}$ and $X_l^{(2)}$ to train classifier $\mathcal{C}^{(2)}$.
3. Classify X_u separately with $\mathcal{C}^{(1)}$ and $\mathcal{C}^{(2)}$.
4. Add $\mathcal{C}^{(1)}$'s k-most confident patterns from X_u to $\mathcal{C}^{(2)}$'s labeled data.
5. Add $\mathcal{C}^{(2)}$'s k-most confident patterns from X_u to $\mathcal{C}^{(1)}$'s labeled data.
6. Repeat Steps 3, 4, and 5.

This method assumes that there is a split in the features which may not be the case. It is less susceptible to error than self-training.

Some variations of co-training are given below:

1. Co-EM:

   - For every pattern x, each classifier probabilistically gives a label.
   - Add (x, y) (where y is the label) with the weight $P(y|x)$.

2. For different feature splits

   - Create random feature splits.
   - Apply co-training.

3. Use multiple classifiers

   - Train multiple classifiers using labeled data.
   - Classify unlabeled data with all the classifiers.
   - Unlabeled data is labeled according to majority vote.

6.6. Using self-training methods

This is the simplest semi-supervised learning method. This involves using the labeled data and building a classifier. This is used to classify the unlabeled data. The sample in the unlabeled set with the highest confidence is taken and added along with its label to the labeled data. This is repeated so as to increase the size of the labeled dataset.

The algorithm is as follows:

1. Choose a classification method. Train the classifier C using X_l.
2. Use C to classify the unlabeled data $x \in X_u$.
3. Pick x^* with the highest confidence and add $(x^*, C(x^*))$ to the labeled data.
4. Repeat Steps 2 and 3 as many times as required.

This method is simple and can be used with any existing classifier but it is possible that the mistakes made in classification will keep reinforcing themselves.

6.7. SVM for semi-supervised classification

While the standard SVM maximizes the margin in the labeled data, in semi-supervised SVM, the margin is maximized for the unlabeled data. This is also called Transductive Support Vector Machine (TSVM). All the 2^u possible labelings of the unlabeled data is enumerated. For each of the labelings, a standard SVM is built. The SVM with the largest margin is picked. Finding the TSVM solution in this way is NP-hard and the algorithms cannot handle large datasets.

Another formulation of semi-supervised SVM or TSVM is as follows:

1. We have as input the kernal K, weights λ_1 and λ_2, the labeled data (X_l, Y_l) and the unlabeled data X_u.
2. Solve the optimization problem for $f(x) = h(x) + b, h(x) \in H_k$. The optimization problem can be formulated as follows:

$$\min_f \Sigma_{i=1}^l (1 - y_i f(x_i))_+ + \lambda_1 \|h\|_{H_K}^2 + \lambda_2 \Sigma_{i=l+1}^n (1 - |f(x_i)|)_+. \tag{27}$$

The last term arises from assigning the label sign $f(x)$ to the unlabeled points.
3. Classify a test pattern x by $\text{sign}(f(x))$.

6.8. Random forests for semi-supervised classification

Here the small number of labeled data and the large number of unlabeled data has to be used to build the decision trees in the forest. The features chosen at a node depends on the information gain. In the case of semi-supervised learning, the information gain at node j has two component, I_j^u and I_j^l. So we get

$$I_j = I_j^u + \beta I_j^l. \tag{28}$$

Here, I_j^l depends only on the labeled data. I_j^u depends on both the labeled and unlabeled data. β is a weighting factor.

$$I_j^l = E(Y_j) - \Sigma_{i=1,2,\ldots,s} \frac{|Y_j^i|}{|Y_j|} E(Y_j^i), \tag{29}$$

where E gives the entropy, Y_j is the subset of patterns at node j, Y_j^i is the subset of patterns at the ith split and s gives the number of branches at the node j.

$$I_j^u = \log|\mathrm{cov}(Y_j)| - \Sigma_{i=1,2,\dots,s} \frac{|Y_j^i|}{|Y_j|} \log|\mathrm{cov}(Y_j^i)|. \qquad (30)$$

Here, Y_j refers to all the labeled and unlabeled data and $\mathrm{cov}(Y_j)$ refers to the covariance matrix of the relative displacement vector for all the points belonging to Y_j.

By using this mixed information gain, it is possible to build a forest of decision trees for semi-supervised learning.

7. Classification of Time-Series Data

Time series classification is the classification of multivariate data when the values of one or more variables are in the form of a sequence. Most of the data recorded is in the form of time series, for example, electricity demand, stocks and shares prices, weather data such as rainfall and temperature, medical data such as ECG and blood pressure, etc. In fact, other forms of data can also be meaningfully converted to a time series format. These include text, DNA, video, audio, images, etc. Time series occur in medical, scientific, and business domains. Some applications of classification of time series data are

1. The electroencephalogram (EEG) signals are used to classify whether the patient is neurologically healthy or is suffering from neurological disorders such as epilepsy, etc.
2. Signature verification is used to classify whether the signature is genuine or not. This task is called anomaly detection.
3. The daily, weekly, and monthly activity of the stock prices can be used to predict future stock market prices.
4. Weather data like temperature, humidity, rainfall, etc. can be used to predict weather.

Generally, a time series $t = t_1, \dots, t_r$ is an ordered set of r data points. The data points are typically measured at successive points of time spaced at uniform time intervals. Time series classification is the task of learning a classifier $\mathcal{C}$, which is a function that maps a time series t to a class label l, i.e. $\mathcal{C}(t) = l$ where $l \in L$, the set of class labels.

The time series classification methods can be divided into three large categories:

- Distance-based classification: Distance-based methods compute the distance between pairs of time series. The method used to measure the distance is crucial to the performance of the classification algorithm.
- Feature-based classification: Feature-based methods transform the time series data into feature vectors and then apply conventional classification methods. Feature selection plays an important role in these methods as it decreases the dimensionality of the data.
- Model-based classification: Model-based methods use a model such as Hidden Markov Model (HMM), Artificial Neural Network (ANN), Recurrent Neural Network (RNN), etc. to classify time series data.

7.1. Distance-based classification

Some well-known similarity measures for time series data are Euclidean Distance (ED), dynamic time warping (DTW) distance, longest common subsequence (LCSS), etc. Once the distance computation is fixed, any of the standard classification algorithms can be used. In fact, the NN classifier is found to perform well in distance-based classification.

Some of the similarity measures used for time series data have been discussed in Chapter 2.

For symbolic sequences, such as protein sequences and DNA sequences, alignment-based distances can be adopted. An optimum alignment score can be computed between two sequences. The Needleman–Wunsch algorithm computes the optimum global alignment score between two sequences using dynamic programming. The Smith–Waterman algorithm and BLAST measure the similarity between two sequences by considering the most similar regions but not considering the alignment on the full length. These are local alignment algorithms.

7.2. Feature-based classification

The time series data is transformed into a vector of features generally using feature selection. Conventional classification methods such as decision trees, neural networks, etc. can be used on the transformed data. Some feature selection methods for time series data have been discussed in Chapter 3.

One method used for classification of time series data is the SVM. The SVM is used to map a sequence into a feature space and find the maximum-margin hyperplane to separate the two classes. Sometimes, a kernel function is found which corresponds to a high-dimension feature space. Some kernels that have been used are k-spectrum kernel or string kernel, polynomial kernel, Fisher's kernel, and diffusion kernel.

For symbolic data, each element is treated as a feature. Feature selection is carried out by selecting a short sequence segment of k consecutive symbols as a feature. These are called the k-grams. By using k-grams as features, time series data can be classified by using conventional classification methods. It is also possible to select a small informative subset of freatures from the k-grams. Another method of finding features in symbolic data is to find features which are short sequence elements which satisfy the following criteria:

1. They are frequent in at least one class.
2. They are distinctive in at least one class.
3. They are not redundant.

After finding features, a classification algorithm is used.

Another feature extraction technique is to transform the time series into the frequency domain and then carry out dimensionality reduction. Transforming the time series into frequency domain can be done using discrete fourier transform (DFT), discrete wavelet transform (DWT) or singular value decomposition (SVD).

Another method used for feature extraction is the kernel method (KM). SVM is the KM used. By calculating the inner product of the input vectors in high dimension (which represent the input time series), linear decision boundaries can be drawn between the classes.

It is possible that features are extracted from the time series. The features extracted are the mean μ, the standard deviation σ, the kurtosis ks, and the skew sk. These are given by the following equations:

$$\mu = \frac{\sum_{i=1}^{n} x(i)}{n}, \tag{31}$$

$$\sigma = \mathrm{sqrt}\frac{\sum_{i=1}^{n}(x(i) - \mu)^2}{n}, \tag{32}$$

$$sk = \frac{\sum_{i=1}^{n}(x(i) - \mu)^3}{n\sigma^3}, \tag{33}$$

$$ks = \frac{\sum_{i=1}^{n}(x(i) - \mu)^4}{n\sigma^4} - 3. \tag{34}$$

Second-order features are found by transforming the time series using a user-specified value C. The new time series is

$$\hat{x}(i) = x(i + C) - x(i), 1 \le i \le n - C.$$

The same four statistical features of Eqs. (31)–(34) are used to find the second-order features. The eight first-order features and second-order features form the feature vector and is used for classification of the time series. Multi-layered perceptron (MLP) neural network can be used for classification. Since the feature vector is of length 8, the input to the network is of size eight and will have much less neurons and weights as compared to an MLP which inputs the entire time series as the input.

7.3. Model-based classification

Model-based classification assumes that the time series are generated by an underlying model. The model finds the probability distribution of the time series. A model is defined for the time series data and the probability distributions are described by a set of parameters. In the training stage, the parameters of the model are learned. Once the parameters of the model are learned, a new time series is assigned to the class with the highest likelihood.

Some of the statistical models that can be used are Naive Bayes, Gaussian, Poisson, Markov, and hidden markov model (HMM). When using HMM, training examples are used to learn the transition probabilities between the states. An HMM consists of a set of states, an alphabet, a probability transition matrix $T = (t_{ij})$ and a probability emission matrix $M = (m_{ik})$. In state i, the system has a probability of t_{ij} of moving to state j and a probability m_{ik} of emitting symbol k. For each class, an HMM is built using the training data. A new pattern is given the class label of the model which fits the data the best.

An ANN can also be used. Two types of ANN used are MLP and RNN.

Research Ideas

1. Is it possible to design better condensation algorithms compared to CNN and MCNN in terms of space and condensation time requirements?

Relevant References

(a) V. S. Devi and M. N. Murty, An incremental prototype set building technique. *Pattern Recognition*, 35:505–513, 2002.

(b) V. S. Devi and M. N. Murty, *Pattern Recognition: An Introduction*. Hyderabad, India: Universities Press, 2012.

(c) M. N. Murty and V. S. Devi, *Pattern Recognition: An Algorithmic Approach*. London: Springer, 2012.

(d) S. Gracia, J. Derrac, J. R. Cano and F. Herrera, Prototype selection for nearest neighbor classification: Taxonomy and empirical study. *IEEE Transactions on PAMI*, 34:417–435, 2012.

2. The usual distance metrics such as ED do not work well in high-dimensional spaces. Can we find metric or non-metric distance functions such as fractional norms that work well in high-dimensional spaces?

Relevant References

(a) C. C. Aggarwal, Re-designing distance functions and distance-based applications for high dimensional data. *SIGMOD Record*, 30:13–18, 2001.

(b) K. Beyer, J. Goldstein, R. Ramakrishnan and U. Shaft, When is nearest neighbors meaningful? *Proceedings of Seventh International Conference Database Theory*, pp. 506–515, 2000.

(c) C.-M. Hsu and M.-S. Chen, On the design and applicability of distance functions in high-dimensional data space. *IEEE Transactions on Knowledge and Data Engineering*, 21:523–536, 2009.

(d) L. Chen and R. Ng, On the marriage of lp-norms and edit distance. *Proceedings of VLDB*, 2004.

3. Why should random forests exhibit superior performance over some of the other random feature selection and extraction schemes like Latent Semantic Hashing (LSH) and random projections?

Relevant References

(a) L. Breiman, Random forests. *Machine Learning*, 45(1):5–32, 2001.

(b) X. Z. Fern and C. E. Brodley, Random projection for high-dimensional data clustering: A cluster ensemble approach. *Proceedings of ICML*, 2003.

(c) A. Andoni and P. Indyk, Near-optimal hashing algorithms for approximate nearest neighbors in high dimensions. *Communications of the ACM*, 51:117–122, 2008.

(d) Y. Ye, Q. Wu, H. Z. Huang, M. K. Ng and X. Li, Stratified sampling for feature subspace selection in random forests for high dimensional data. *Pattern Recognition*, 46:769–787, 2013.

4. Bagging and boosting are two useful techniques to improve classifiers performance. How can one combine them in classification using random forests?

Relevant References

(a) L. Breiman, Bagging predictors. *Machine Learning*, 24:123–140, 1996.

(b) T. K. Ho, The random subspace method for constructing decision forests. *IEEE Transactions on PAMI*, 20:832–844, 1998.

(c) P. J. Tan and D. L. Dowe, Decision forests with oblique decision trees. *Proceedings of MICAI*, 2006.

5. Like the fuzzy random forests, is it possible to consider random forests based on other soft computing tools?

Relevant References

(a) Q.-H. Hu, D.-R. Yu and M.-Y. Wang, Constructing rough decision forests, in D. Slezak *et al.* (eds.). Berlin, Heidelberg: Springer-Verlag, 2005, pp. 147–156. LNAI 3642.

(b) H. Shen, J. Yang, S. Wang and X. Liu, Attribute weighted Mercer kernel-based fuzzy clustering algorithm for general non-spherical data sets. *Soft Computing*, 10:1061–1073, 2006.

(c) A. Verikas, A. Gelzinis and M. Bacauskiene, Mining data with random forests: A survey and results of new tests. *Pattern Recognition*, 44:2330–2349, 2011.

6. What is the reason behind the success of linear SVM classifier in dealing with classification in high-dimensional spaces?

Relevant References

(a) D. Liu, H. Qian, G. Dai and Z. Zhang, An iterative SVM approach to feature selection and classification in high-dimensional datasets. *Pattern Recognition*, 46:2531–2537, 2013.

(b) M.-H. Tsai, Y.-R. Yeh, Y.-J. Lee and Y.-C. Frank Wang, Solving nonlinear SVM in linear time? A Nystrom approximated SVM with applications to image classification. *IAPR Conference on Machine Vision Applications*, 2013.

(c) T. Joachims, Training linear SVMs in linear time. *Proceedings of KDD*, 2006.

(d) G.-X. Yuan, C.-H. Ho and C.-J. Lin, Recent advances of large-scale linear classification. *Proceedings of the IEEE*, 100:2584–2603, 2012.

7. The so-called nonlinear SVM employs the kernel trick to obtain a linear decision boundary in a higher-dimensional space, thus effectively increasing the dimensionality of the patterns. However, the random forest classifier considers a random subspace at a time to construct a decision tree which forms a part of the forest. Also, there are plenty of other dimensionality reduction techniques that perform well in classification. How can one reconcile to the fact that both increase in the dimensionality (kernel SVM) and decrease in the dimensionality (random forests and other classifiers) improve the classification performance?

Relevant References

(a) M.-H. Tsai, Y.-R. Yeh, Y.-J. Lee and Y.-C. F. Wang, Solving nonlinear SVM in linear time? A Nystrom approximated SVM with applications to image classification. *IAPR Conference on Machine Vision Applications*, 2013.

(b) S. Haykin, *Neural Networks and Learning Machines*, Vol. 3. Upper Saddle River: Pearson Education, 2009.

(c) G. Seni and J. F. Elder, Ensemble methods in data mining: Improving accuracy through combining predictions. *Synthesis Lectures on Data Mining Knowledge Discovery*, 2:1–126, 2010.

(d) X. Hu, C. Caramanis and S. Mannor, Robustness and regularization of support vector machines. *JMLR*, 10:1485–1510, 2009.

(e) N. Chen, J. Zhu, J. Chen and B. Zhang, Dropout training for support vector machines. arXiv:1404.4171v1, 16th April 2014.

8. Can we pose the semi-supervised classification problem as a simpler optimization problem?

Relevant References

(a) I. S. Reddy, S. K. Shevade and M. N. Murty, A fast quasi-Newton method for semi-supervised support vector machine. *Pattern Recognition*, 44: 2305–2313, 2011.

(b) X. Chen, S. Chen, H. Xue and X. Zhou, A unified dimensionality reduction framework for semi-paired and semi-supervised multi-view data. *Pattern Recognition*, 45:2005–2018, 2012.

(c) X. Ren, Y. Wang and X.-S. Zhang, A flexible convex optimization model for semi-supervised clustering with instance-level constraints. *Proceedings of ISORA*, 2011.

9. Is it possible to consider semi-supervised dimensionality reduction which can help in efficient and effective classification?

Relevant References

(a) K. Kim and J. Lee, Sentiment visualization and classification via semi-supervised nonlinear dimensionality reduction. *Pattern Recognition*, 47: 758–768, 2014.

(b) R. Cai, Z. Zhang and Z. Hao, BASSUM: A bayesian semi-supervised method for classification feature selection. *Pattern Recognition*, 44:811–820, 2011.

(c) X. Kong and P. S. Yu, Semi-supervised feature selection for graph classification. *Proceedings of KDD*, 2010.

(d) K. Dai, H.-Y. Yu and Q. Li, A semisupervised feature selection with support vector machine. *Journal of Applied Maths*, 2013, 2013.

10. How to scale up classification algorithms dealing with temporal data?

Relevant References

(a) S. Laxman and P. Sastry, A survey of temporal data mining. *Sadhana*, 31:173–198, 2006.

(b) Z. Xing, J. Pei and E. Keogh, A brief survey on sequence classification. *SIGKDD Explorations*, 12:40–48, 2010.

(c) N. Piatkowski, S. Lee and K. Morik, Spatio-temporal random fields: Compressible representation and distributed estimation. *Machine Learning*, 93:115–139, 2013.

11. It is possible to view patterns as transactions and use frequent itemset-based classifiers. What is the role of frequent itemsets in classification?

Relevant References

(a) H. Cheng, X. Yan, J. Han and P. S. Yu, Direct discriminative pattern mining for effective classification. *Proceedings of ICDE*, 2008.

(b) M. N. Murty and V. Susheela Devi, NPTEL Lecture Notes on Pattern Recognition, http://nptel.ac.in/courses.php [accessed on 2 November 2014].

(c) B. Fernando, E. Fromont and T. Tuytelaars, Mining mid-level features for image classification. *International Journal of Computer Vision*, 108:186–203, 2014.

12. One way to reduce space and time requirements in classification is to compress the data and design classifiers in the compressed domain. How to realize such classifiers in practice?

Relevant References

(a) D. Xin, J. Han, X. Yan and H. Cheng, Mining compressed frequent pattern ets. *Proceedings of VLDB*, 2005.

(b) T. R. Babu, M. N. Murty and S. V. Subrahmanya, *Compression Schemes for Mining Large Datasets: A Machine Learning Perspective*. New York: Springer, 2013.

(c) M. Danieletto, N. Bui and M. Zorzi, RAZOR: A compression and classification solution for the internet of things. *Sensors*, 14:68–94, 2014.

Chapter 6

Classification using Soft Computing Techniques

1. Introduction

Hard classifiers or the classical classification techniques make a hard or definite decision on the class label of the test patterns. The many classifiers we have discussed till now fall under this. However, several current day applications require each pattern to belong to one or more classes. For example, a document may belong to both *sports* and *politics*. Such applications motivate the need for soft classification. A soft classifier either gives the degree of classification of the test pattern to every class label, or may classify the test pattern as belonging to more than one class. Classifiers based on genetic algorithms (GAs) or neural networks start with some random values (for the candidate solution or the weights) and depending on the performance on training patterns, these values are adapted.

Some of these methods which we will discuss in this chapter are as follows:

1. **Fuzzy Classifier**: In this classifier, each pattern belongs to every class with a membership value. To predict the class label of a test pattern, its fuzzy membership to every class is determined and the class to which its membership is maximum is the class chosen. Further, in a multi-label scenario, classes could be ranked based on the respective membership values and more than one class label could be assigned to the test pattern based on the ranking.

2. **Rough Classifier**: Here, every pattern belongs to the lower approximation of one class or to the upper approximation of more

177

than one class. This type of classifier is suitable when the patterns in the domain can belong to more than one class.

3. **Genetic Algorithms (GAs) for Classification**: GAs work with a population of candidate solutions which are initialized randomly. Each chromosome in the population is evaluated to see how well it carries out the problem to be solved. This is called the fitness function. The advantage of GAs is that they are generally used for optimization and can handle problems which are complex, non-differentiable and are multi-modal and multi-objective. Local minima is easily avoided because of working with a population of chromosomes. GAs for classification usually attempt to find a dividing hyperplane between classes, find the set of rules for classification etc.

4. **Neural Networks**: The neural network is inspired by the neural system in human beings and the neurons in the brain. The neural network consists of the input layer, 0–2 hidden layers and an output layer. The weights in the network are adjusted so as to get the correct class label when the training patterns are input to the network.

5. **Multi-class Classification**: The patterns in this scenario belong to more than one class. If we have a label set $L = \{c_1, \ldots, c_k\}$ then each pattern belongs to a subset of L. One such application is when the news items in the newspaper have to be classified. A news item can belong to say both politics and movies if a movie star is in politics. The task is much more complex here as it is necessary to not only predict the subset of labels but also the ranking of the labels.

2. Fuzzy Classification

In the conventional classification algorithms, each pattern to be classified belongs to one class. This is a crisp classification paradigm. In fuzzy classification, each pattern belongs to each class with a membership value. If we consider a pattern P, $\mu_{P1}, \mu_{P2}, \ldots, \mu_{PC}$ are the membership values of pattern P to classes $1, 2, \ldots, C$. This can be converted into crisp classification by assigning pattern P to the class to which its membership value is highest.

2.1. Fuzzy *k*-nearest neighbor algorithm

To classify a test pattern, the *k*-nearest neighbors are found. These neighbors have a fuzzy membership degree to the class labels. A test pattern y belongs to a class C to the degree given by:

$$C(y) = \sum_{x \in N} R(x, y) C(x),$$

where $R(x, y)$ gives the similarity between x and y and is defined as:

$$R(x, y) = \frac{\|y - x\|^{-2/(m-1)}}{\sum_{j \in N} \|y - j\|^{-2/(m-1)}}.$$

2.1.1. *Fuzzy kNN classification*

This is a modification of the kNN classifier. It is used to find the membership function μ_{Pi}, which is the membership value of the pattern P to each class i. When a pattern P is to be assigned a class label, its k closest neighbors are found. If the jth nearest neighbor belongs to class i, p_{ij} is set to 1. This is done for the first k-nearest neighbors. The values for all other patterns are set to zero. Then, the membership values are calculated as follows:

$$\mu_{Pi} = \frac{\sum_{j=1}^{k} p_{ij} \left(\frac{1}{d(P, X_j)^{\frac{2}{m-1}}} \right)}{\sum_{j=1}^{k} \left(\frac{1}{d(P, X_j)^{\frac{2}{m-1}}} \right)}, \quad i = 1, \ldots, C. \tag{1}$$

The constant m generally takes the value 2. If μ_{Pl} is the largest membership value of pattern P to the classes, pattern P is assigned the class label l.

3. Rough Classification

Here, we use the notion of an upper and lower approximation of a set to define approximate classification. An approximation space A consists of $A = (U, R)$ where U is the universe and R is a binary equivalence relation over U, which is called the indiscernibility relation. If $(p, q) \varepsilon R$, then p and q are indiscernible in A. Equivalence classes of

R are called elementary sets in A. A finite union of elementary sets in A is called a definable set in A.

If we consider a set $P \subset U$, an *upper approximation* $\overline{A}P$, is the least definable set in A containing set P. A *lower approximation* of the set P is $\underline{A}P$, which is the greatest definable set in A contained in P. The *boundary set* of P in A is given by $B(X) = \overline{A}P - \underline{A}P$.

Now if we consider a family of subsets of U i.e. $C = \{P_1, P_2, \ldots, P_n\}$, $P_i \subset U$, then the lower approximation of C in A is the family

$$\underline{A}C = \{\underline{A}P_1, \underline{A}P_2, \ldots, \underline{A}P_n\}$$

and the upper approximation is the family

$$\overline{A}C = \{\overline{A}P_1, \overline{A}P_2, \ldots, \overline{A}P_n\}.$$

If C is a partition of U, then

$$P_i \bigcap P_j = \Phi \quad \text{for every } i, j, \quad 1 \leq i,\, j \leq n, \quad \bigcup_{i=1}^{n} P_i = U.$$

In this case, C is a classification of U and P_i are the classes of C.

An information system can be expressed as $I = (U, F, V, \tau)$ where U is the universe of I, F is the set of features or attributes, V gives the set of values of the attributes and τ given by $\tau\colon UXF \to V$ is a description function such that $\tau(p, f)\varepsilon V_f$ for every $f\varepsilon F$ and $p\varepsilon U$.

As an example, if we consider Table 6.1 which is an information function τ, then

$$U = \{p_1, p_2, \ldots, p_7\}, \quad F = \{a, b, c\}, \quad V_a = \{0, 1\},$$
$$V_b = \{0, 1, 2, 3, 4\}, \quad V_c = \{0, 1, 2, 3\}.$$

3.1. Rough set attribute reduction

In an information system, some attributes do not provide any additional information about the objects in U and can be removed to make the decision process simpler and more cost-effective. If a classification task maps a set of variables F to a set of labels L then a

Table 6.1. Information function τ.

U	a	b	c
p_1	0	4	1
p_2	1	2	0
p_3	1	1	3
p_4	0	0	2
p_5	1	3	2
p_6	0	4	3
p_7	0	3	0

reduct D is defined as $D \subset F$, such that $\tau(F, L) = \tau(D, L)$. A reduct set is the set $D = \{P \varepsilon PS(F) : \tau(P, L) = \tau(F, L)\}$.

A minimal reduct D_r is any reduct D such that $|D_r| \leq |P|, \forall P \varepsilon D$. It is the reduct of least cardinality.

3.2. Generating decision rules

Let the set of attributes consist of n independent attributes and one dependent attribute, i.e. $F = \{f_1, \ldots, f_n\}$ independent attributes and a dependent attribute d. Suppose we have a partition $\{P_1, \ldots, P_u\}$ induced from F and let $\{Q_1, \ldots, Q_v\}$ be a partition induced from d. With each P_i, the set $S_i = \{Q_j : P_i \bigcap Q_j \neq \phi\}$. This means that

$$\text{if } p \varepsilon P_i, \text{ then } p \varepsilon Q_{j1} \text{ or } \ldots \text{ or } p \varepsilon Q_{jv}.$$

Each class P_i corresponds to a feature vector $(a_i)_{i \leq n}$ where $p \varepsilon P_i$ only if $f_{q1} = a_1, \ldots, f_{qn} = a_n$ and $p \varepsilon Q_1$ only if $f_d = b_j$ for some $b_j \varepsilon V_d$. This means that the rule is of the form.

If $f_{q1} = a_1$ and $\ldots$ and $f_{qn} = a_n$

$$\text{then } f_d(p) = b_{j1} \text{ or } \ldots \text{ or } f_d(p) = b_{jj}. \tag{2}$$

If the pattern P_i belongs to only one partition Q_j then the value of d in the Eq. (2) is unique. Otherwise, $f_d(x)$ may belong to any class contained in S_i and there is a proper disjunction on the right-hand side of Eq. (2).

Once the decision rules in the form of Eq. (2) are generated, simplification is done so that as many of the condition attribute values are removed as possible without losing the required information. This process is called **value reduction**. All the rules are kept in a set *Rule*. One rule at a time is taken and copied to *r*. A condition is removed from *r* and rule *r* is checked for decision consistency with every rule belonging to *Rule*. If *r* is inconsistent, then the dropped condition is restored. This is repeated for every condition of the rule. The rule *r* after all these processes is the generalized rule. If *r* is included in any rule belonging to *Grule*, *r* is discarded. If any rule in *Grule* is included in *r*, these rules are removed from *Grule*. After all the rules in *Rule* is processed, we get the rules in *Grule*. This set of rules are called **maximally general** or **minimal length**.

4. GAs

GAs are a robust method of carrying out optimization based on the principles of natural selection and genetics. It is a search process where a candidate solution is used with an evaluation function. A candidate solution is a chromosome or string and there is a population of strings. These are evaluated and the next generation of strings are generated by using the operations of selection, crossover and mutation. After repeating this procedure for a number of iterations, the candidate solution generated which gives the best evaluation is the final solution.

The GA has been used for carrying out classification. The following sections discuss some algorithms using GA for classification.

4.1. Weighting of attributes using GA

This algorithm is equivalent to the weighted kNN classifier. The strings of the GA consist of *d* elements giving real valued weights. These are values between 0 and 1 which give the relative weighting to each attribute. For example, if there are 10 features then a string in the population would be of the form:

$$[0.45\ 0.20\ 0.93\ 0.11\ 0.56\ 0.77\ 0.32\ 0.45\ 0.69\ 0.85].$$

This means that the first feature is given a weight of 0.45, feature 2 is given a weight of 0.2 etc. The goal is to find the weighting which gives the optimal performance on the training data. If X_i and X_j are two d-dimensional patterns, the weighted euclidean distance is used which is:

$$D_{ij} = \sqrt{\sum_{k=1}^{k=d} w_k(X_{ik} - X_{jk})^2},$$

w_k gives the weight assigned to the kth attribute and is obtained from the string in the GA being used at that point of time.

The fitness function is calculated by using the weights and using kNN algorithm to carry out classification. The simplest fitness function would be to use the error in classification, i.e.

$$fitness = \frac{total - correct}{total},$$

where correct refers to the number of patterns correctly classified and total refers to the total number of patterns.

Another fitness function that can be used gives weights which result in the maximum class separation. This is given by:

$$fitness = a * \frac{total - correct}{total} + b * \frac{n_m/k}{total},$$

where n_m is the number of the nearest neighbors (out of the k-nearest neighbors) which are not used in any subsequent classification and is called the minority set of the nearest neighbors.

Another fitness evaluation used is to use ranking of the chromosomes. The first criterion used is the number of misclassified samples(e). If this is equal then other factors like the number of k neighbors which are of the same class (k same neighbors (ns)), the total distance to the k same neighbors (ds), the number of k neighbors which are not of the same class (k different neighbors (nd)) and the total distance to the k different neighbors (dd) are used. The criteria for chromosome A to be ranked higher than chromosome B are as follows in the order given:

$$ne_A < ne_B \text{ or;}$$

$$ne_A = ne_B \text{ and}$$
$$ns_A \geq ns_B \text{ and}$$
$$ds_A < ds_B \text{ and}$$
$$dd_A > dd_B \text{ or;}$$

$$ne_A = ne_B \text{ and}$$

$$\left(\frac{ds_A}{ns_A} + \frac{dd_A}{nd_A} \right) < \left(\frac{ds_B}{ns_B} + \frac{dd_B}{nd_B} \right).$$

Since it is necessary to work on a population of strings, the algorithm is time-consuming but parallelism can be used. A simple way of carrying out the parallelism is to use different processors to carry out the evaluation of the strings. If the evaluation process is time consuming, as usually is the case, this would help in reducing the time required for the algorithm. Parallelism can be done by distributing individuals in a landscape and the reproduction is biased according to the spatial location of individuals. **Micrograined parallelism** only carries out the fitness calculation in parallel by passing the strings to individual processors. This type of parallelism helps in speeding up the process if the fitness calculation dominates the GA calculations.

4.2. Binary pattern classification using GA

In this approach the string in the GA consists of rules of the form

$$\langle condition \rangle : \langle class - label \rangle.$$

The condition part would give values for each dimension and for each class. So the rule would be of the form

$$(y_{11}, \ldots, y_{1i}, \ldots, y_{1d}), \ldots, (y_{j1}, \ldots, y_{ji}, \ldots, y_{jd}), \ldots,$$

$$(y_{c1}, \ldots, y_{ci}, \ldots, y_{cd}) : \omega.$$

Here, $i = 1 \ldots d$, $j = 1 \ldots c$ and ω gives the class label. Since it is a binary dataset, every $y_{ji} \; \varepsilon \; 0,1^*$, where $*$ is the do not care symbol. Each string in the population refers to one rule. To evaluate the string, it is matched against the training dataset. A 0 in the string matches a 0 in the training pattern, a 1 matches a 1 and a do not care symbol * matches either a 0 or a 1. Each training pattern is matched to each of the class feature vector and is classified as belonging to the class with the largest number of matches. The class of the training pattern is compared to the class label ω given in the string. If they match then the classification is correct. The fitness function of the rule is based on the classification accuracy of the rule. The fitness function is calculated as follows:

$$fitness = \frac{correct}{total} + a * \frac{invalid}{total},$$

where invalid gives the number of attributes which have the same value in the rule for all classes, i.e. if $y_{1i} = y_{2i} \cdots = y_{ci}$, then the attribute i is invalid. After running the GA for a number of iterations, the rule which gives the best fitness is chosen.

4.3. Rule-based classification using GAs

Another formulation has each individual in the population consisting of a fixed number of rules. Each individual is a complete solution candidate. In each individual, there are a fixed number of rules. For each rule, each attribute has as many elements as the number of discrete values it takes. So for an attribute which has five discrete values, each rule in an individual has five elements corresponding to the five discrete values and each element takes the values 0 or 1. For every rule, it is said to belong to class i if

$$\frac{No.\ of\ class\ i\ matched\ by\ rule}{No.\ matched\ by\ rule} > \frac{No.\ of\ class\ i\ in\ training\ data}{No.\ of\ training\ data}.$$

The fitness function consists of four parameters. The fitness of an individual I is given by:

$$Fitness(I) = Error\ rate(I) + Entropy(I)$$
$$+ Rule\ consistency(I) + Hole(I).$$

1. Error rate: Each training pattern is classified by using all the rules in an individual and the majority class label is assigned to the pattern. This is compared with the class label given and the error rate of the individual or string is the percent of training patterns which are misclassified.

2. Entropy: In the training patterns that a rule R matches, if p_i is the percent of patterns belonging to class i, then

$$\text{Entropy}(R) = -\sum_{i=1}^{n} p_i \log_2 p_i.$$

Since an individual consists of a number of rules, the overall entropy of the individual is the average of the entropy of the individual rules.

$$\text{Entropy(individual)} = \frac{\sum_{i=1}^{L} \text{Entropy}(R_i)}{L},$$

where L is the number of rules.

3. Rule consistency: Preference is given to the individual which has the more consistent rule set.

$$\text{Rule} - \text{consistency(individual)}$$
$$= -p_{\text{corr}} \log_2 p_{\text{corr}} - (1 - p_{\text{corr}}) \log_2 (1 - p_{\text{corr}}),$$

where p_{corr} is the proportional of rules in an individual whose class label is the same as that of the training example.

4. Hole ratio: This is a measure of the coverage of the rules on the training data. The hole ratio is 1-*coverage*. In the case of the binary classification problem, it will be:

$$\text{Hole(Individual)} = 1 - \frac{No(P^+) + No(N^-)}{n},$$

where P^+ are those examples whose actual class is positive and is classified as positive by at least one rule in the individual, and N^- are those examples whose actual class is negative and is classified as negative by at least one rule in the individual and n is the total number of training patterns.

4.4. Time series classification

If the time series has a large dimension, then feature selection can be carried out. After that, when there is a reduced set of features, support vector machines (SVM) is used for classification.

One method of carrying out the feature selection is to use genetic programming. The chromosome is in the form of a tree structure which gives a feature vector. The fitness of an individual is computed as:

$$\text{Fitness} = \frac{1}{n} \sum_{i=1}^{C} n_i a_i,$$

where n is the total number of samples, n_i is the number of samples in class i, C is the total number of classes and a_i gives the accuracy for class i. These values are obtained by using an SVM and measuring the performance obtained on the training data.

Cross-validation can also be used. If we make N partitions, $P_i, i = 1, \ldots, N$, N different SVMs are trained on $\overline{P_i}$ which is the complement of partition P_i and is tested on the partition P_i. The cross-validation fitness is given by:

$$\text{fitness}_{cv} = \frac{1}{N} \sum_{i=1}^{N} a(P_i, \overline{P_i}),$$

where $a(P_i, \overline{P_i})$ is the accuracy obtained of P_i after training on $\overline{P_i}$.

4.5. Using generalized Choquet integral with signed fuzzy measure for classification using GAs

A GA is used to solve the optimization problem for a Choquet-integral classification problem. A Choquet Hyperplane H is found which separates points of the two classes.

The signed fuzzy measure μ is defined as a set function:

$$\mu: P(X) \to (-\infty, \infty),$$

where $\mu(\phi) = 0$.

The values of the set function μ on the non-empty sets in $P(X)$ are denoted by μ_i, $i = 1, \ldots, 2^n - 1$. If we have a two-class problem where the sample points belong to the same feature attributes $x_1, \ldots, x_d$, the ith sample point of the positive class denoted by r_i is:

$$r_i = (f_i(x_1), f_i(x_2), \ldots, f_i(x_d)).$$

The Choquet Hyperplane H is expressed as:

$$H \colon (c) \int (p + qf) d\mu - A = 0,$$

$p = (p_1, \ldots, p_d)$ and $q = (q_1, \ldots, q_d)$ are d-dimensional vectors where $p_i \varepsilon [0, \infty)$ with $min_i p_i = 0$, and $|q_i| \varepsilon [0, 1]$ with $max_i |q_i| = 1$. A is a real number. So all the unknown parameters can be assumed to be in $[-1, 1)$. These parameters are determined so as to maximize the total sum of signed distances of the training samples from the Choquet Hyperplane H. Samples belonging to the positive class will be on one side of H and the samples belonging to the negative class will be on the other side of H.

A Choquet integral is used to find the Choquet distance of points which can be used for classification. The distance of a point r_i which belongs to the positive class from the Choquet Hyperplane is given by:

$$d_i = \frac{(c) \int (p + qf) d\mu - A}{\sqrt{\mu_1^2 + \mu_2^2 + \cdots + \mu_{2^n-1}^2}}, \quad i_j = 1, 2, \ldots, m.$$

If r_i belongs to the negative class the distance will be given by:

$$d_i' = \frac{A - (c) \int (p + qf') d\mu}{\sqrt{\mu_1^2 + \mu_2^2 + \cdots + \mu_{2^n-1}^2}}, \quad i_j = 1, 2, \ldots, m',$$

where m is the number of instances of positive class and m' is the number of instances from the negative class.

The total signed Choquet distance is:

$$Dist = \sum_{i=1}^{m} d_i + \sum_{i'=1}^{m'} d'_i$$

$$= \frac{\sum_{i=1}^{m}((c)\int(p+qf)d\mu - A) - \sum_{i=1}^{m'}((c)\int(p+qf')d\mu - A)}{\sqrt{\sum_{i=1}^{2^n-1} \mu_i^2}}.$$

$$(3)$$

Dist has to be maximized. Misclassified samples will have a negative value in the above formula. The above formula will not work well if the dataset is unbalanced, i.e. if $m \neq m'$.

If the datasets are not of the same size, a revision has to be made in Eq. (3) where a large penalty coefficient is added for each misclassified instance. So the distance is:

$$Dist_{mod} = c_i \sum_{i=1}^{m} d_i + c'_{i'} \sum_{i'=1}^{m'} d'_i$$

$$= \frac{\sum_{i=1}^{m} c_i((c)\int(p+qf)d\mu - A) - \sum_{i=1}^{m'} c'_{i'}((c)\int(p+qf')d\mu - A)}{\sqrt{\sum_{i=1}^{2^n-1} \mu_i^2}}.$$

$$(4)$$

Here

$$c_i = \begin{cases} c & \text{if } (c)\int(p+qf)d\mu < A \\ 1 & \text{otherwise} \end{cases}$$

for $i = 1, 2, \ldots, m$ and

$$c'_{i'} = \begin{cases} c & \text{if } (c)\int(p+qf')d\mu > A \\ 1 & \text{otherwise} \end{cases}.$$

4.5.1. *Representation of chromosomes in the GA*

All the unknown parameters of the hyperplane are included in a chromosome. Each gene is a bit string. The unknown parameters are

$\mu_1, \mu_2, \ldots$, and vectors p and q and A. The population consists of a number of chromosomes (N).

4.5.2. *Fitness of the chromosomes*

To find the **fitness function**, each chromosome c has the parameters $\mu_1, \mu_2, \ldots, \mu_m, p, q$, and A which are used in Eq. (4) to find the signed Choquet distance D_c using the data samples. The fitness of a chromosome is given by

$$F_c = \frac{D_c - D_{\min}}{D_{\max} - D_{\min}},$$

where

$$D_{\min} = min_{c=1,\ldots,pop} D_c; \quad D_{\max} = max_{c=1,\ldots,pop} D_c.$$

4.5.3. *Selection of chromosomes*

Chromosomes are chosen for the next generation according to Roulette Wheel Selection where the slice of each chromosome c in the roulette wheel is the probability p_c given by:

$$p_c = \frac{F_c}{\sum_{i=1}^{N} F_i},$$

where F_c is the fitness of the cth chromosome.

4.5.4. *Generation of new chromosomes*

Two new chromosomes are generated by choosing mutation or crossover at random using a two-point probability distribution $(\alpha, 1 - \alpha)$. This is repeated $\frac{N}{2}$ times to generate N chromosomes. The fitness of the N new chromosomes are calculated and they are added to the already existing N chromosomes to form $(2N)$ chromosomes. Top N chromosomes with better fitness form the new generation.

The process of selection, generating new chromosomes and forming the next generation is repeated till there is no significant improvement in the maximum fitness. When the iterations are stopped, the chromosome with the maximum fitness in the last generation is chosen. The values of $\mu_1, \mu_2, \ldots, p, q$ and A from this chromosome are chosen to form the Choquet Hyperplane H.

4.6. Decision tree induction using Evolutionary algorithms

Decision trees have been designed using Evolutionary algorithms. These are stochastic algorithms where the solution is found by the method of search. We work on a population of chromosomes where each chromosome is a representation of the decision tree and is a candidate solution. The fitness function reflects how well the decision tree classifies patterns and generally is the classification accuracy on a validation set. In the following subsections, a number of representation schemes, various fitness functions, different types of selection, crossover and mutation have been discussed.

4.6.1. *Representation schemes*

The candidate decision tree can be encoded as a fixed length linear string or a tree-encoding scheme can be used.

The axis-parallel decision tree which is the most common type of decision tree uses a tree encoding where each node is represented by a 4-tuple

$$node = \{index, is - terminal, operator, value\}.$$

The first value is the attribute index (attribute to be represented), the second value is whether the node is a terminal or a non-terminal node, the third value is the operator to be used such as $(<, >, =)$ and the fourth is the value to be tested by the attribute (this is only in a non-terminal node). These nodes have pointers to the children nodes. For example, a node could be represented as:

$$[1 \ 0 > 5\}.$$

The above represents the rule $f_1 > 5$.

Another way of encoding also uses a tree-encoding representing each node as a 7-tuple as follows:

$$node = \{index, label, par, l, r, S\},$$

where *label* is the class label (meaningful only if the node is a terminal node), *par* is a pointer to the parent node, l and r are the pointers to the left and right children respectively. S is an array where $S[0]$ stores the attribute id and $S[1]$ stores the threshold for the feature $S[0] < S[1]$ which is boolean giving the outcomes "yes" or "no".

In another tree-based formulation, the nodes are either terminal or function nodes. Terminal nodes consist of an attribute id, attribute value or a class label. Function nodes consist of a 4-tuple given by:

$$node = \{index, value, l, r\},$$

where value gives the attribute value, l and r are children nodes.

Fixed length encoding is difficult to use for decision trees which are non-binary. Generally only binary trees are considered for this. One method, divides the genes into caltrops. Each caltrop consists of the subtree formed using the node as the root and its two children. A non-terminal node is identified by an attribute index and the terminal node is identified by the value zero.

Another method of using fixed length encoding encodes each node by two values. A node is represented by:

$$node = \{index, value\}.$$

This shows that the test performed at the node is $attribute - index \geq value$.

4.6.2. *Initialization of Population*

For fixed length encoding, a random initialization is generally used. In a tree-based encoding, attributes are chosen at random and the split values are chosen from a predefined list or range. The depth of the decision tree is chosen randomly from a range which is generally $[2, maxdepth]$ where *maxdepth* gives the maximum depth upto which a tree can grow. This is called the *full method*. Another strategy is to use varying distances from root to the leaves. This is called the *grow method*. It is also possible to use a mixture of trees generated by either the full or the grow method.

Another strategy restrains the initial population to a 2-level decision tree which has only a root and the leaves. It is assumed that the evolutionary algorithms will generate trees with greater depth. Here initialization can be done by using each of the attributes as the root and generating a number of chromosomes with different split values for the attributes. The 2-level decision trees can be combined to get trees of more depth.

The values which are chosen for the splits for the attributes is generally not chosen completely randomly but is taken from the set of values observed in the training set.

The initial population can also be generated by using a traditional decision tree algorithm on samples of the training set and using these decision trees as the initial population.

4.6.3. *Fitness value*

The most common fitness measure used is the classification accuracy η on a validation set. It is calculated as:

$$\eta = \frac{corr}{n},$$

where *corr* gives the number of correctly classified samples and n is the total number of samples. Sometimes η^2 is used.

Another fitness measure used is the **J-measure** which uses the quality of the rules that describe a class as the measure. For a k-class problem, there are k rules which are of the form (**if** Y_i **then** ω_i), where Y_i gives a set of disjunctions along the paths used to label instances belonging to class ω_i. Then the J-measure is:

$$J = \sum_{i=1}^{k} p(Y_i)p(\omega_i \mid Y_i)\log\left(\frac{p(\omega_i \mid Y_i)}{p(\omega_i)}\right),$$

where $p(Y_i)$ is the fraction of instances which satisfy condition Y_i, $p(\omega_i)$ is the fraction of instances belonging to class ω_i and $p(\omega_i|Y_i)$ is the fraction of instances that satisfy Y_i and belong to class ω_i. If the value of J is higher, it means the classification accuracy of the tree is higher.

Another measure is the distance score which can be used when the class labels are sequential integer values. The distance score D_{score} is given by:

$$D_{\text{score}} = \frac{1}{n} \sum_{i=1}^{n} 1 - \left(\frac{\omega_i - \omega_i'}{\omega_{\text{max}} - \omega_{\text{min}}} \right)^2,$$

where n is the number of instances, ω_i is the actual class of the ith instance, ω_i' is the predicted class of the ith instance, ω_{max} is the maximum value of the class labels and ω_{min} is the minimum value of the class labels.

The above measures are all single objective fitness functions. Multi-objective fitness functions try to balance the accuracy and simplicity of the decision tree. Simplicity entails finding a decision tree of less depth or smaller number of nodes. A cost-sensitive measure find a balance between sensitivity and specificity.

One such measure combines the classification accuracy and tree size as follows:

$$f(T) = w_1 * \eta_T - w_2 * size_T,$$

where w_1 and w_2 are weights. The measure $f(T)$ needs to be maximized. A cost-sensitive approach replaces the efficiency in the above formula by the misclassification cost. The size $size(T)$ could be the number of nodes in the tree or could include both tree depth and number of attributes in each path of the tree.

Another measure is the Minimum Description Length (MDL) given by:

$$MDL = ECL + TCL,$$

where ECL = Error coding length and TCL = Tree coding length. They are given by:

$$ECL = \sum_{l \in leaves} \log_2 \binom{no_l}{e_l},$$
$$TCL = (n_i + n_l) + n_i \log_2 s + n_l \log_2 k,$$

where no_l is the number of instances in leaf node l, e_l is the number of instances misclassified in leaf node l, n_i is the number of internal nodes, n_l is the number of leaf nodes, s is the number of splits and k is the number of classes.

Another multi-objective fitness function is one based on the recall and a variation of precision which penalizes false positives more severely.

4.6.4. *Genetic operators*

One of the popular methods used for selection is the tournament selection. In tournament selection, two individuals are selected and the individual with the better fitness is put into the next generation of strings. This is repeated N times where N is the size of the population. Another popular method of selection used is the roulette wheel selection. Rank-based selection is also used where the selection is based not on the actual fitness but a ranking of the individuals.

For fixed length representation, the 1-point crossover is used. For tree-based representations, nodes are selected in the two nodes to be crossed over, and the entire subtrees corresponding to these nodes are exchanged generating two children.

Some methods of *mutation* are replacing one subtree by another random subtree, replacing a subtree by a random leaf node or replacing a leaf node by a random subtree. It is also possible to replace the attribute, the test value or both of a chosen node. Another method is to replace a randomly selected node by another node which is already present in the tree and not a random subtree. One strategy uses two methods of mutation, 'switch' and 'translocation'. 'Switch' swaps children of the same parent and 'translocation' swaps children from different parents but in the same tree level. Another strategy also changes logical operations like $>$, $<$, $=$, $\neq$, etc. where one logical operator is replaced by another.

5. Neural Networks for Classification

Many artificial neural network (ANN) models have been proposed for pattern classification. The multi-layer feed forward network with back propagation is one of the popular methods. ANNs carry out classification by adjustment of the network weights using training data. ANN classification is a model which exhibits learning by example. It can thus be seen that classification using ANN requires a large training time or design time for large datasets. Once a trained network is available, the classification time for new patterns is very small. Another feature of neural network learning is that the learnt neural network acts like a black box. The new pattern is input and the class label is output. This basically means that there is no explanation ability in the classifier.

Neural networks work on the principle of the nervous system in the human brain. It basically consists of nodes which are like the neurons in the human brain and edges between nodes. The way the network is formed and the connections between the nodes determine the behavior of the network. Figure 6.1 shows a node in the neural network. As we can see, the node has one or more edges as input to the node.

A two-step process takes place in the node. First an aggregation is made of each of the inputs along the input edges multiplied by the weight along the edges. As shown in Figure 6.1. If there are four inputs $X_1, X_2, X_3,$ and X_4 to node j and the weights along these edges are w_{1j}, w_{2j}, w_{3j} and w_{4j}, then the aggregation results in:

$$b_j = \sum_{i=1}^{4} w_{ij} * X_j.$$

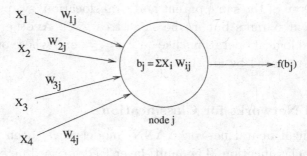

Figure 6.1.　An example of node in a neural network.

An activation function is applied to b_j giving $f(b_j)$ as the output of the neuron.

There are a number of activation functions. The unit step function is as follows:

$$f(b_j) = \begin{cases} 0 & \text{if } b_j < T \\ 1 & \text{if } b_j \geq T \end{cases}.$$

The sign function is:

$$f(b_j) = \begin{cases} -1 & \text{if } b_j < T \\ +1 & \text{if } b_j \geq T \end{cases},$$

where T is the threshold.

The sigmoidal function is:

$$f(b_j) = \frac{1}{1 + exp(-b_j)}.$$

This gives a value between 0 and 1.

5.1. Multi-layer feed forward network with backpropagation

This is the most popular method of classification. The input layer consists of d neurons where d is the dimensionality or the number of features. There are one or two hidden layers and the output layer. The nodes in a layer are connected to all the nodes in the next layer. The number of output neurons depend on the number of class labels. If there are C classes, it should be able to represent C distinct outputs. Figure 6.2 shows a multi-layer feed-forward neural network with one hidden layer.

$I_1, \ldots, I_d$ are the d input units, $H_1, \ldots, H_h$ are the h hidden units and $O_1, \ldots, O_o$ are the o output units. All the input units are connected to all the hidden units and these edges are initialized to random weights between 0 and 1. So we have weights $u_{ij}, i = 1, \ldots, d$ and $j = 1, \ldots, h$. All the hidden units are connected to the output units with the weights given by $v_{ij}, i = 1, \ldots, h$ and $j = 1, \ldots, o$. The input to a unit is the aggregate of the input along each input edge times the weight on the edge. An activation function is applied to this

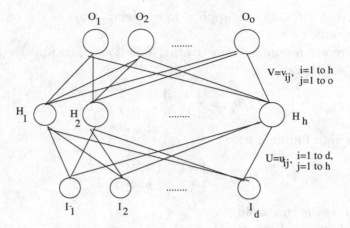

Figure 6.2. Architecture of multi-layer feed forward neural network.

total input to get the output of a unit. Popular activation functions are the sigmoidal function which give a value between 0 and 1, the unit step function which gives the output as either 0 or 1 and the sign function which gives the output as -1 or $+1$. The training data is fed into the network one by one. Since we know the class label of the instance, if the predicted class label does not match the actual class label, then the backpropagation algorithm is used to update the weights in the network. The weight between the hidden layer and output layer is updated as follows:

$$\Delta v_{ij} = \alpha * \delta_j * H_i$$

$$\text{and} \quad v_{ij} = v_{ij} + \Delta v_{ij},$$

where

$$\delta_j = (E_j - O_j) f'_j(a_j).$$

α is the learning rate and is in the range (0,1). H_i is the output of the hidden unit i, E_j is the actual output which is the actual class label of the instance. O_j is the output which gives the predicted class label of the instance. a_j is the input of the output unit j and $f'_j(a_j)$ gives the integration of the activation function on a_j.

The weights between the input layer and the hidden layer is updated as follows:

$$\Delta u_{ij} = \alpha * \delta_j * I_i$$
$$\text{and} \quad u_{ij} = u_{ij} + \Delta u_{ij},$$

where

$$\Delta u_{ij} = f_j'(a_j) \sum_{k=1}^{K} \delta_k v_{jk}.$$

I_i is the ith input; a_j is the input of the hidden unit j; $f_j'(a_j)$ gives the integration of the activation function applied to a_j; K is the number of neurons in the next layer.

The learning rate α plays a critical role in the training. If α is too low, the convergence of the weights to the optimum is very slow and if α is too high, the weight values oscillate or get stuck in a local minimum. To tackle this problem, a momentum term β can be added to make the updation equation as:

$$\Delta v_{ij}^t = \alpha * \delta_j * H_i + \beta * \Delta v_{ij}^{t-1},$$

where Δv_{ij}^{t-1} is the incremental change in v_{ij} done in the previous iteration. α and β are values between 0 and 1. Usually α is a small value like say 0.01 and β will have a larger value like 0.7 or 0.8. Looking at the error in classification, the two values can be adjusted.

As mentioned earlier, the number of inputs to the input layer is equal to the number of features and the output is the number of classes. For example, in a digit recognition problem, there are 10 classes which consist of the digits 0–9. If the digits are represented as an image with 8×8 pixels, then there are 64 features being input to the neural network, the number of inputs being 64.

5.2. Training a feedforward neural network using GAs

A feedforward neural network is generally trained using the back-propagation algorithm. The neural network is initialized by taking random weights along all the edges in the network. When a training pattern is input to the network, if the predicted class label does not match the actual class label, the weights in the network are updated using the backpropagation algorithm. Instead of using the backpropagation algorithm, a GA is used to find the best weights which fit the network.

5.2.1. *Representation and initialization*

The network design is first done and the weights in the network are encoded as a list of real numbers in the chromosome. The number of elements in the string depends on the number of inputs, number of outputs, the number of hidden layers and the number of hidden nodes. For example, if there are 5 input units, 10 hidden units and 2 output units, the number of values will be:

$$N = (5 + 1) * 10 + (10 + 1) * 2 = 82.$$

The initial weights are chosen at random, uniformly distributed in the interval $+/-$ the inverse of the square root of the fan-in (number of input edges) to the neuron. If the neuron has a fan-in of 7, then the weight is chosen to be in $\left[-\frac{1}{\sqrt{7}}; \frac{1}{\sqrt{7}}\right]$. The fitness function is determined by running the training dataset through the network, determining the predicted class labels and finding the sum of squares of the errors in classification.

5.2.2. *Operators used*

Three operators are used, mutation, crossover, and gradient. But mutation takes a chromosome and randomly changes some of the elements in the chromosome. The **crossover** operator takes two chromosomes and creates two children by exchanging some of the genetic material in the two parents. The **gradient** operator adds a multiple of the gradient with respect to the evaluation function to all the elements of a chromosome.

1. Mutation:
    (a) Unbiased mutation: For a particular chromosome, with a probability $p = 0.1$, this operator replaces each entry with a random value chosen from the initialization probability distribution.

(b) Biased mutation: For a particular chromosome, with a probability of $p = 0.1$, this operator adds a random value chosen from the initialization probability distribution.

(c) Node-based mutation: A number of nodes n which are not input nodes are selected in the network and for each of these nodes, ingoing links are taken and this operator adds to these link weights, a random value from the initialization probability distribution. Generally, n is a small number like say 2.

(d) Mutation of weakest nodes: A node has zero error if its output links are all zero and since this does not contribute anything to the network, it is a weak node. The strength of a hidden node is the difference between the evaluation of the network as it is and its evaluation with the output of this node set to zero. After calculating the strength of the hidden nodes, this operator chooses m weakest nodes and performs mutation of the ingoing and outgoing links of the node.

2. Crossover:

(a) Crossover of two chromosomes: This operator takes a child chromosome and for each position, picks one of the values from the two parent chromosomes and uses this value.

(b) Node-based Crossover: For each node encoded by the child chromosome, this operator finds the corresponding node in one of the two parents' networks. The weight of each ingoing link to the parent's node is put as the weight in the corresponding link of the child's network.

(c) Layer-wise crossover: This operator exchanges the weights on links connected to two nodes in the same layer. If we consider two nodes P and Q in the same layer, if node R is connected to node P by an ingoing or outgoing link, node R is also connected to node Q. The weight on the link between R and P is exchanged with the weight on the link between node R and node Q.

3. Gradient Operator:

The gradient for every instance in the training set is calculated and summed up to get the total gradient. The total gradient is divided by the magnitude to get the normalized gradient. The chromosome chosen is changed in the direction of the normalized gradient by an amount Δs. This value is adapted according to the performance. If the evaluation of the child is worse than the parent, then we take $\Delta s = \Delta s * 0.4$. If the child is better than the parent then $\Delta s = \Delta s * 1.4$.

When the algorithm is started, all the above operators are given equal probabilities. In the course of a run, the performance of the operators is observed and the probability of these operators being selected is increased if the operator is doing well and decreased if the operator is doing poorly.

6. Multi-label Classification

In this type of problem, each instance is associated with a set of labels. It is necessary to predict the set of labels of a test pattern using the training instances with known label sets. For example, when we are classifying the newsitems in a newspaper, the same article may belong to Politics and Entertainment say if a filmstar is standing for election. When classifying a scene, the same image may have a set of labels say hill, river, tree etc. When carrying out sentiment analysis of a document, the same document may express the sentiment sadness, anger and interest. There are a number of applications such as annotation of images and video, text classification, functional genomics and music categorization into emotions.

Let $\mathcal{X} \varepsilon R_d$ be the d-dimensional instance domain and let $L = \{l_1, \ldots, l_q\}$ be the set of labels or classes. Multi-label learning entails learning a function $h : \mathcal{X} \rightarrow 2^L$ which maps each instance $x \varepsilon \mathcal{X}$ to a set of labels. This is called multi-label ranking since the order of the labels is important. In other words, we need to predict the labels with their ranking.

Given in Table 6.2 is an example dataset where each pattern can belong to more than one class. The dataset has four features $f_i, i = 1, \ldots, 4$ and labels $l_j, 1 \leq j \leq 5$. The features have normalized values. The labels for each instance gives the subset of classes to which the instance belongs. The ranking of the class labels is also

Table 6.2.   An example multi-label dataset.

f_1	f_2	f_3	f_4	1	2	3	4	5
0.98	0.43	0.23	0.12	2	1			
0.78	0.55	0.31	0.88	5	2	1	4	
0.69	0.43	0.29	0.41	4				
0.71	0.33	0.19	0.53	3	4	1		
0.89	0.29	0.10	0.73	2	5	4	1	3
0.83	0.37	0.37	0.36	1	3			

taken into account. This means that for the first pattern, the first label is 2 and the second label is 1. For a new instance, it is necessary to predict the subset of class labels to which the instance belongs ranked in the correct order.

6.1. Multi-label kNN (mL-kNN)

mL-kNN is a multi-label lazy learning approach which is derived from the k-nearest neighbor algorithm. For a test instance, first the k-nearest neighbors are found. Then according to the number of neighboring instances belonging to each class, maximum *a posteriori* (MAP) principle is used to determine the set of labels for the test instances.

For a test instance p, the k nearest neighbors are considered. Let $N(p)$ denote the set of the k-nearest neighbors. If l_p is the category vector for p, $l_p(c)$ ($c \varepsilon L$) takes the value 1 if c is in the label set for p and 0 otherwise. Based on the label sets of the neighbors, we calculate:

$$C_p(c) = \sum_{i \in N(p)} l_i(c), \quad for\ c = l_1, \ldots, l_q,$$

where $C_p(c)$ counts the number of neighbors of p belonging to the cth class. Let E_1^c be the event that p has label c and E_0^c be the event that p does not have label c. Also let I_j^c denote the event that among the kNN's of p, there are exactly j instances having label c. Then

$$l_p(c) = argmax_{b \epsilon \{0,1\}} P(E_b^c | I_{C_p(c)}^c), \quad c = l_1, \ldots, l_q.$$

This is determined using MAP principle.

This equation can be rewritten using Bayes rule as

$$l_p(c) = argmax_{b \in \{0,1\}} \frac{P(E_b^c) P(I_{C_p(c)}^c | E_b^c)}{P(I_{C_p(c)}^c)}$$

$$= argmax_{b \in \{0,1\}} P(E_b^c) P(I_{C_p(c)}^c | E_b^c).$$

So the category vector l_p can be determined using the prior probabilities $P(E_b^c)$ where c is the label and $b = \{0,1\}$ and the posterior probability $P(I_j^c | E_b^c)$ for $j = 0, 1, \ldots, k$. These values can be directly estimated from the training set.

6.2. Probabilistic classifier chains (PCC)

This method uses the principle of the classifier chain (CC). In CC, a classifier h_i is trained for each label and assigns a scoring function f_i. For a new instance p to be classified, h_1 predicts ω_1, h_2 predicts ω_2 taking the instance p and the predicted value ω_1. We go on in this way and h_i predicts ω_i using $\omega_1, \ldots, \omega_{i-1}$.

In PCC, given a query p, the probability of a label combination $\omega = (\omega_1, \ldots, \omega_m)$ is computed using the product rule:

$$P_p(\omega) = P_p(\omega_1). \prod_{i=2}^{m} P_p(\omega_i | \omega_1, \ldots, \omega_{i-1}). \tag{5}$$

To find the joint distribution of labels, the m functions $f_i(\cdot)$ is learnt on an augmented input space $\mathcal{P}X\{0,1\}^{i-1}$, using $\omega_1, \ldots, \omega_{i-1}$ as additional features, i.e.

$$f_i : \mathcal{P}X\{0,1\}^{i-1} \rightarrow [0,1]$$

$$(\mathbf{p}, \omega_1, \ldots, \omega_{i-1}) \rightarrow P(\omega_i = 1 | \mathbf{p}, \omega_1, \ldots, \omega_{i-1}).$$

This makes Eq. (5)

$$P_p(\omega) = f_1(p). \prod_{i=2}^{m} f_i(p, \omega_1, \ldots, \omega_{i-1}).$$

Given P_p an optimal prediction can be derived.

6.3. Binary relevance (BR)

BR learns L classifiers, one for each of the class labels. The original dataset is transformed into L datasets. Each dataset contains all the instances in the original dataset with the label for each instance being either positive or negative. In the ith dataset, if the label set for a instance contains the ith label it is labeled positively; otherwise it is labeled negatively. To classify a new pattern, it is assigned a class label by all the L datasets and the union of these labels is the labelset predicted.

6.4. Using label powersets (LP)

In multi-label learning, one of the methods uses LP where every distinct combination of labels that exist in the training set is treated as a different class and single-label classification task is carried out. Though this makes the task of classification simpler, if the number of classes is large, the number of labelsets appearing in the training set maybe very large. This increases the computational cost and makes the learning difficult as the number of training examples of each labelset will be very small. To take care of this problem, the initial set of labels is broken up into small random subsets called labelsets and then LP is used on these labelsets. This method is called $RAkEL$ (Random k labelsets). The size of the labelsets is specified using k.

Consider the finite set of classes to be $C = \{\omega_i: i = 1, \ldots, L\}$. Each instance x_i is associated with a set of labels Y_i where $Y_i \subseteq C$. A labelset $S \subseteq C$ where $k = |S|$ is called the k-labelset. Two types of labelsets can be used: (a) Disjoint labelsets and (b) overlapping labelsets.

In the disjoint version, each labelset is of size k. The class labelset C is randomly divided into $l = \lceil \frac{L}{k} \rceil$ disjoint labelsets, S_i, $i = 1, \ldots, l$. Since the labelsets are disjoint, $\bigcap_{i=1}^{l} S_i = \phi$. Then, l multi-label classifiers h_i, $i = 1, \ldots, l$ are learnt using LP. Each classifier h_i is a single-label classification task having as class labels all the subsets of S_i that are in the training set.

For the classifier h_i, the dataset D_i contains all the training instances in the original set but the labels will be the intersection of the given labels and S_i. So $D_i = \{(x_j, Y_j \bigcap S_i), \, j = 1, \ldots, n\}$ where n is the total number of patterns. Some patterns may have the empty set as the label set. Given a new multi-label instance p, the binary prediction h_i of all classifiers for all labels $w_j \varepsilon S_i$ are found and used to find the multi-class classification vector.

In the case of overlapping labelsets, C^k is the set of all distinct k-labelsets of C. The size of C^k is $|C^k| = \binom{L}{k}$. If we require l classifiers and the label set size is k, we need to first select l l-labelsets $S_i, i = 1, \ldots, l$ from the set C^k via random sampling without replacement. Here the labelsets may overlap. Then l multi-label classifiers $h_i, i = 1, \ldots, l$ are learnt using LP. To classify a new instance p, every classifier h_i gives a binary prediction for each label in the corresponding labelset S_i. Taking all the decisions for the l models, the mean of the predictions is found for each label $w_j \varepsilon C$ and decides on the label if the value is greater than 0.5.

6.5. Neural networks for Multi-label classification

The multi-layer feedforward neural network which is used for single-label instances is adapted to handle multi-label classification. The neural network algorithm used is called Backpropagation for Multi-Label Learning (BP-MLL). If there are instances $\mathcal{X}$ such that $\mathcal{X} \varepsilon \nabla^d$. Let there be n training patterns $\{(x_1, Y_1), (x_2 y_2), \ldots, (x_n, Y_n)\}$. If we have a set of labels $C = \{w_i, i = 1, \ldots, l\}$, then $Y_i \subseteq C$. The architecture of BP-MLL is shown in Figure 6.3. The neural network

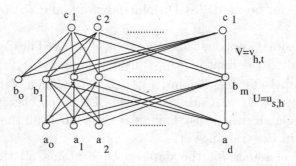

Figure 6.3.   Architecture of BP-MLL neural network.

has d input units each pertaining to one dimension of the feature vector and there are l output units, each corresponding to one class label. The hidden layer has m nodes. The input layer is completely connected to the hidden layer where the weight is u_{sg} where $1 \leq s \leq d$ and $1 \leq g \leq m$. The weights between the hidden units and the output is v_{gt} where $1 \leq t \leq l$. The bias for the hidden units γ_g is shown as an extra input unit a_0 with a fixed value of 1. The bias parameter β_l for the output units is shown as an extra hidden unit b_0 with a fixed value of 1.

The goal of learning of the labels is to minimize the error on all the n training patterns. If e_i is the error on x_i, then the overall error is:

$$E = \sum_{i=1}^{n} e_i.$$

Here, $e_i = \sum_{j=1}^{l} \left(o_j^i - d_j^i \right)^2$, where o_j^i is the actual output of the network on pattern x_i on the jth class and d_j^i is the desired output on pattern x_i on the jth class. The desired output is either $+1$(if $j\varepsilon Y_i$) or -1(if $j \notin Y_i$).

Another formulation for the overall error is:

$$E = \sum_{i=1}^{n} e_i = \sum_{i=1}^{n} \frac{1}{|Y_i||\bar{Y}_i|} \sum_{(p,q)\epsilon Y_i X \bar{Y}_i} exp\left(-\left(o_p^i - o_q^i\right)\right).$$

This equation adds up the error on each training instance (x_i, Y_i). $\bar{Y}_i$ is the complementary set of Y_i. $\left(o_p^i - o_q^i\right)$ is the difference between the actual output of the network on a label belonging to Y_i and one label not belonging to it. The bigger this difference, the better is the performance of the network. The term $\frac{1}{|Y_i||\bar{Y}_i|}$ normalizes the summation of the differences in the output.

The actual output of the jth output unit is

$$o_j = f\left(\sum_{g=1}^{m} b_g v_{gj} + \beta_j \right).$$

The activation function is the "tanh" function:

$$f(x) = \frac{e^x - e^{-x}}{e^x + e^{-x}}.$$

b_g is the output of the gth hidden unit and is given by

$$b_g = f\left(\sum_{s=1}^{d} a_s u_{sg} + \gamma_s\right).$$

The change to be made in the weights Δv and Δu is given by:

$$\Delta v_{gt} = -\alpha \frac{\partial E_i}{\partial v_{gt}} = \alpha d_t b_g, \tag{6}$$

$$\Delta u_{sg} = -\alpha \frac{\partial E_i}{\partial u_{sg}} = \alpha e_g a_s. \tag{7}$$

The change in biases is

$$\Delta \beta_t = \alpha d_t \quad and \quad \Delta \gamma_g = \alpha e_g. \tag{8}$$

e_g is the error of the gth hidden unit and is given by

$$e_g = -\frac{\partial E_i}{\partial\left(\sum_{s=1}^{d} a_s v_{sg}\right)}$$

$$= \sum_{t=1}^{l} (d_t v_{gt})(1 + b_g)(1 - b_g)$$

and α is the learning rate and the value is (0.0,1.0).

For training, the training instances are fed to the network one at a time and for each instance, Eqs. (6)–(8) are updated. Feeding the training instances once through the neural network is called a training epoch. The training epoch is repeated a number of times. The training process is repeated till the global error E does not increase or for a fixed number of training epochs.

When a new pattern is fed into the network after training, we get the outputs $c_t, t = 1, \ldots, l$. A threshold is used and if c_t is greater than the threshold, then the label is included in the labelset for the instance i.e. $Y = \{t | c_t > threshold, t\varepsilon C\}$. The total number of weights and biases in the network is given by:

$$N = (d + 1) * g + (g + 1) * C.$$

Overall time for training is $O(N \cdot n \cdot e)$ where n is the number of training examples and e is the number of training epochs.

6.6. Evaluation of multi-label classification

The performance evaluation of multi-label classification is completely different from single-label classification. In both cases, classification on a validation set is carried out and this is used to evaluate the classifier. It is also possible to carry out cross-validation on the training data. The measures used for single-label classification is error and classification accuracy. The classification accuracy η is given by:

$$\eta = \frac{N_1}{N} * 100,$$

where N_1 is the number of correct classifications and N is the total number of patterns. A classifier giving high η value is preferred. The error in classification E is given by:

$$E - \frac{N - N_1}{N} * 100.$$

In the case of multi-label classification, the evaluation metrics should depend on factors like number of labels, the ranking of the labels, the first label, etc. Consider a validation set $\{(X_1, Y_1), \ldots, (X_v, Y_v)\}$. Here, $h(X_i)$ returns a set of proper labels of X_i; $h(X_i, y)$ returns a real value which gives the confidence for y to be a proper label of X_i; rank $h(X_i, y)$ returns the rank of y derived from $h(X_i, y)$. Given below are some of the metrics used for multi-label classification.

1. *Hamming loss*: This evaluates how many times an instance-label pair is misclassified. This means that the number of times a label which is not in the label set for an instance is predicted or the number of times a label which belongs to a label set of an instance

is not predicted is counted. Hamming loss H_L is given by:

$$H_L = \frac{1}{i|v|} \sum_{i=1}^{v} \frac{1}{|y|} |h(X_i) \Delta Y_i,$$

Δ denotes the symmetric difference between the actual labels of X_i (i.e. Y_i) and the predicted set of labels ($h(X_i)$). The best performance of the algorithm is when $H_L = 0$. The lower the value of H_L, the better is the performance of h.

2. *One Error*: One Error E_{one} evaluates how many times there is an error in predicting the top ranked label. It counts the number of times the top ranked label is misclassified. It is given by:

$$E_{one} = \frac{1}{p} \sum_{i=1}^{v} \|[argmax_{y \epsilon Y} h(X_i, y) \notin Y_i]\|.$$

The smaller the value of E_{one} the better is the performance of h.

3. *Coverage*: Coverage C evaluates how far we need to go down the list of labels in order to cover the proper labels of the instance. It is given by:

$$C = \frac{1}{v} \sum_{i=1}^{v} max_{y \epsilon Y_i} rank^h(X_i, y) - 1.$$

The performance is perfect when $C = 0$ and the smaller the value of C, better is the performance.

4. *Ranking Loss*: Ranking loss R_L evaluates the average fraction of label pairs which are not in the right order for every instance.

$$R_L = \frac{1}{v} \sum_{i=1}^{v} \frac{1}{|Y_i||\bar{Y}_i|} \{(y_1, y_2)|h(X_i, y_1)$$

$$\leq h(X_i, y_2), \quad (y_1, y_2) \epsilon Y_i \times Y_i\}|.$$

$\bar{Y}_i$ is the complementary set of Y_i.

If $R_L = 0$, the performance is perfect. The smaller the value of R_L, the better is the performance of h.

5. *Average Precision*: The average precision P evaluates the average fraction of proper labels ranked above a particular label $y \epsilon Y_i$ and

is given by:

$$P = \frac{1}{v} \sum_{i=1}^{v} \frac{1}{|Y_i|} \sum_{y \in Y_i} \frac{\left|\{y' | rank^h(X_i, y') \leq rank^h(X_i, y), y' \in Y_i\}\right|}{rank^h(X_i, y)}.$$

If $P = 1$, the performance is perfect and the larger the value of P, the better is the performance of h.

Research Ideas

1. Can we apply rough-fuzzy approach and the fuzzy-rough approach to pattern classification?

Relevant References

(a) N. Verbiest, C. Cornelis and F. Herrera, FRPS: A rough-fuzzy approach for generating classification rules. *Pattern Recognition*, 46(10):2770–2782, 2013.

(b) S. K. Pal, S. K. Meher and S. Dutta, Class-dependent rough-fuzzy granular space, dispersion index and classification. *Pattern Recognition*, 45(7):2690–2707, 2012.

(c) R. Jensen and C. Cornelis, Fuzzy-rough nearest neighbor classification. *Transactions on Rough Sets*, LNCS, 6499:56–72, 2011.

(d) Y. Qu *et al.*, Kernal-based fuzzy-rough nearest neighbor classification. *International Conference on Fuzzy Systems*, FUZZ:1523–1529, 2011.

2. A neuro-fuzzy system (or a fuzzy neural network) is a fuzzy system which uses the neural network to learn the parameters of the fuzzy system. How do we use the neuro-fuzzy system for classification?

Relevant References

(a) A. Ghosh, B. U. Shankar and S. K. Meher, A novel approach to neuro-fuzzy classification. *Neural Networks*, 22:100–109, 2009.

(b) R.-P. Li, M. Mukaidono and I. B. Turksen, A fuzzy neural network for pattern classification and feature selection. *Fuzzy Sets and Systems*, 130:101–108, 2002.

3. Instead of GAs, other stochastic search techniques such as simulated annealing or Tabu search can be used. How do these techniques compare with the GA?

Relevant References

(a) D. Glez-Pena, M. Reboiro-Jato, F. Fdez-Riverola and F. Diaz, A simulated annealing-based algorithm for iterative class discovery using fuzzy logic for informative gene selection. *Journal of Integrated Omics*, 1:66–77, 2011.

(b) J. Pacheco, S. Casado and L. Nunez, A variable selection method based in Tabu search for logistic regression models. *European Journal of Operations Research*, 199:506–511, 2009.

4. Hybrid GAs combine GAs with operators from other search algorithms like simulated annealing, local search etc. Can we improve the performance of GAs by hybridizing them?

Relevant References

(a) W. Wan and J. B. Birch, An improved hybrid GAs with a new local search procedure. *Journal of Applied Mathematics*, 2013.

(b) D. Molina, M. Lozano and F. Herrera, MA-SW-Chains: Memetic algorithm based on local search chains for large scale continuous global optimization. *Proceedings of the 6th IEEE World Congress on Computational Intelligence* (WCCI'10), 2010.

(c) C. Grosan and A. Abraham, Hybrid evolutionary algorithms: Methodologies, architectures, and reviews. *Studies in Computational Intelligence* (SCI), 75:1–17, 2007.

5. A number of algorithms exist which mimic the behavior of a swarm of animals such as Particle Swarm Optimization, Ant Colony Optimization etc. How do we adapt these algorithms for pattern classification?

Relevant References

(a) B. Xue, M. Zhang and W. N. Browne, Particle swarm optimization for feature selection in classification: A multi-objective approach. *IEEE Transactions on Cybernetics*, 43(6):1656–1671, 2013.

(b) H. Dewan and V. S. Devi, A peer-peer particle swarm optimizer. *6th International Conference on Genetic and Evolutionary Computing*, pp. 140–144, 2012.

(c) D. Martens, M. De Backer, R. Haesen, J. Vanthienen, M. Snoeck and B. Baesens, Classification with ant colony optimization. *IEEE Transactions on Evolutionary Computation*, 11(5):651–665, 2007.

(d) S. Hodnefjell and I. C. Junior, Classification rule discovery with ant colony optimization algorithm. *Intelligent Data Engineering and Automated Learning-IDEAL 2012, LNCS*, 7435:678–687, 2012.

6. When the number of attributes and instances are large, the time and space complexity of multi-label classification could go up. Can we use feature selection to reduce the space and time complexity?

Relevant References

(a) N. Spolaor, E. A. Cherman, M. C. Monard and H. D. Lee, A comparison of multi-label feature selection methods using the problem transformation approach. *Electronic Notes in Theoretical Computer Science*, 292:135–151, 2013.

(b) X. Kong, N. Ng and Z. Zhou, Multi-label feature selection for graph classification. *IEEE 10th International Conference on Data Mining* (ICDM), pp. 274–283, 2010.

(c) M. L. Zhang, J. M. Pena and V. Robles, Feature selection for multi-label naive Bayes classification. *Information Sciences*, 179(19):3218–3229, 2009.

Chapter 7

Data Clustering

Clustering deals with grouping of data where a pair of similar data points are placed in the same cluster or group. So, the notion of similarity or matching between data points plays an important role in clustering. Clustering is either hard or soft. A K-partition, $\mathcal{C}$, of a set $\mathcal{X}$ of n data points is $\{C_1, C_2, \ldots, C_K\}$, where

$$\bigcup_{i=1}^{K} C_i = \mathcal{X}, \quad C_i \bigcap C_j = \phi, \ i \neq j \quad \text{and} \quad C_i \neq \phi \ for \ 1 \leq i, j \leq K.$$

The number of K-partitions of the n element set, $\mathcal{X}$, is

$$\frac{1}{K!} \sum_{i=1}^{K} (-1)^{K-i} \binom{K}{i} (i)^n. \tag{1}$$

For example, partitioning a set of three data points $\{X_1, X_2, X_3)$ into two clusters will lead to the following possible 2-partitions:

$\{\{X_1\}, \{X_2, X_3\}\}$; $\{\{X_2\}, \{X_1, X_3\}\}$; $\{\{X_3\}, \{X_1, X_2\}\}$; note that $n = 3$ and $K = 2$ here and hence there are three hard partitions each having two clusters which agrees with (1).

1. Number of Partitions

It is possible to depict onto functions from the set of data points $\mathcal{X}$ to the set of clusters $\mathcal{C}$ as shown in Figure 7.1 where $|\mathcal{X}| \geq |\mathcal{C}|$. Onto functions are important in the context of counting the number of partitions of a dataset.

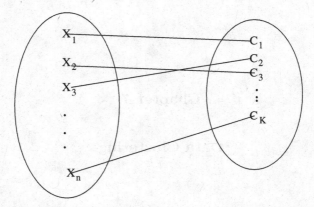

Figure 7.1.   Onto function with $|\mathcal{X}| = n \geq K = |\mathcal{C}|$.

The result in (1) may be derived by using the relation between onto functions and partitions. Specifically, if $N_{onto}(n, K)$ is the number of onto functions from the set of n patterns to the set of K clusters, then the number of K-partitions, Π_K^n is given by

$$\Pi_K^n = \frac{1}{K!} N_{onto}(n, K).$$

In order to estimate the value of $N_{onto}(n, K)$, we can start with the total number of functions from $\mathcal{X}$ to $\mathcal{C}$; it is K^n and is larger than the required number. Among these functions, every element of $\mathcal{X}$ is assigned to exactly one cluster. However, it is possible that none of the elements is assigned to one or more clusters in $\mathcal{C}$ which corresponds to having one or more empty clusters. Because we are interested in counting the number of K-partitions we need to ensure that none of the clusters is empty; this means that we need to consider the number of onto functions from $\mathcal{X}$ to $\mathcal{C}$. Specifically, we need to subtract the count of the number of functions violating the onto property from the total number of functions given by K^n. So, from K^n we need to subtract the number of functions that have one or more of $C_1, C_2, \ldots, C_K$ missing in their range leading to the violation of the onto (*surjective*) property.

Let $N(C_i)$ be the number of functions in which no element of $\mathcal{X}$ is assigned to cluster C_i which means C_i is not in the range of these functions. So, these functions assign each element of $\mathcal{X}$ to one of the remaining $K - 1$ clusters. So, this count is given by

$$N(C_i) = (K - 1)^n \quad \text{for all } 1 \le i \le K. \tag{2}$$

If N_v is the number of functions violating the onto property, then

$$N_v = N(C_1) + N(C_2) + \cdots + N(C_K) - N(C_1, C_2) - N(C_1, C_3)$$
$$- \cdots - N(C_{K-1}, C_K) + \cdots + (-1)^{K-1} N(C_2, \ldots, C_K)$$

by the principle of inclusion and exclusion where $N(C_i, C_j)$ is the number of functions with C_i and C_j, $1 \le i, j \le K$, $i \ne j$, being empty or equivalently missing in the range of the respective functions. Note that

$$N(C_i, C_j) = (K - 2)^n \quad \text{for all } 1 \le i, \ j \le K. \tag{3}$$

So, the value of N_v can be written in a compact form using (2) and (3) as

$$N_v = \binom{K}{1}(K-1)^n - \binom{K}{2}(K-2)^n + \cdots + (-1)^{K-1}\binom{K}{K-1} 1^n.$$

So, the number of onto functions is

$$N_{onto}(n, K) = K^n - N_v$$
$$= K^n - \binom{K}{1}(K-1)^n - \binom{K}{2}(K-2)^n$$
$$+ \cdots + (-1)^{K-1}\binom{K}{K-1} 1^n$$
$$= \sum_{i=1}^{K} (-1)^{K-i} \binom{K}{i} (i)^n.$$

Note that unlike in the case of onto functions, ordering of clusters is not important in partitioning as a K-partition is a *set* of K clusters. So, we get the number of K-partitions by dividing the number of onto functions, $N_{onto}(n, K)$, by $K!$ giving us the result in (1).

This result means that exhaustive enumeration of all possible partitions of a dataset could be prohibitively expensive. For example, even for a small dataset of 19 patterns to be partitioned into 4 groups, we may have to consider around 11,259,666,000 partitions. So, typically each of the clustering algorithms restricts these possibilities by selecting an appropriate subset of the set of all possible K-partitions characterized by (1).

2. Clustering Algorithms

Conventionally clustering algorithms are either partitional or hierarchical. Partitional algorithms generate a partition of the set of data points and represent or abstract each cluster using one or more patterns or representatives of the cluster. Consider the data points shown in Figure 7.2. There is a singleton cluster and two other dense clusters. Here, centroid of a cluster of patterns is used to represent the cluster as depicted in the figure.

On the other hand, hierarchical clustering algorithms generate a hierarchy of partitions. Such a hierarchy is typically generated by either splitting bigger clusters into smaller ones (divisive clustering) or by merging smaller clusters to form bigger clusters (agglomerative clustering). Figure 7.3 shows a hierarchy which is also called as *dendrogram*. There are two clusters at the top level; these are

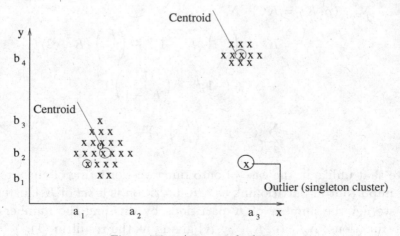

Figure 7.2.   An example dataset.

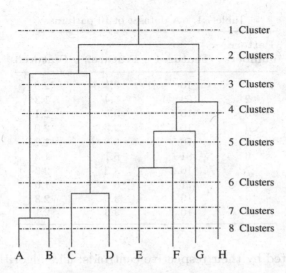

Figure 7.3.   Hierarchical clustering.

given by $\{A, B, C, D\}$ and $\{E, F, G, H\}$. The cluster $\{E, F, G, H\}$ is split into two clusters $\{E, F, G\}$ and $\{H\}$ and $\{E, F, G\}$ is further divided into $\{E, F\}$ and $\{G\}$. Similarly, the cluster $\{A, B, C, D\}$ is divided into $\{A, B\}$ and $\{C, D\}$ and so on.

A hierarchy of partitions of sizes varying from one to eight is depicted in Figure 7.3. Further, the same hierarchy depicts both the agglomerative (bottom up) and divisive (top down) clustering. In the agglomerative case, we start with eight singleton clusters and keep merging clusters successively based on similarity between clusters till finally all the patterns are put in a single cluster. The divisive algorithms start with a single cluster and keep splitting clusters successively; a cluster is selected for splitting based on the spread of points in the cluster.

We consider some variants of an important algorithm and its behavior using the dataset shown in Table 7.1.

2.1. *K*-means algorithm

K-means algorithm is the most popular partitional clustering algorithm. It generates a *K*-partition of the dataset and the clusters

Table 7.1.   A dataset of 10 patterns.

Pattern numbers	Feature1	Feature2	Feature3
1	10	3.5	2.0
2	63	5.4	1.3
3	10.4	3.5	2.1
4	10.3	3.3	2.0
5	73.5	5.8	1.2
6	81	6.1	1.3
7	10.4	3.3	2.3
8	71	6.4	1.0
9	10.4	3.5	2.3
10	10.5	3.3	2.1

are represented by their respective centroids. The algorithm is given below:

K-means Algorithm

Input: Dataset, $\mathcal{X}$; Number of Clusters, K
Output: A K-partition of $\mathcal{X}$, Π_K^n
1. Select K initial centroids corresponding to the K clusters.
2. Assign each of the n points in $\mathcal{X}$ to the cluster whose centroid is closest to the data point. Update the centroids of the clusters based on the current assignment of points to the clusters.
3. Stop if there is no change in the cluster assignments during two successive iterations. Otherwise goto 2.

Some of the important features of K-means algorithm are:

- **Optimization of Squared Error:**

  Squared error or the within-group-error-sum-of squares is the criterion function associated with the K-means algorithm. The basic idea behind K-means algorithm is to minimize this criterion function. Formally, the function may be specified as

$$\sum_{i=1}^{K} \sum_{X \in C_i} \|X - \text{centroid}_i\|^2. \tag{4}$$

Note that the squared error will be maximum when $K = 1$ and is minimum (zero) when $K = n$. So, we consider the minimization of the criterion function for a given K. The K-means algorithm does not guarantee global minimum value of the squared error criterion shown in (4). Further, the squared error minimization corresponds to minimizing the variance of points in each cluster. So, naturally this algorithm has a tendency to generate spherical clusters.

- **Selection of initial centroids:**

  1. Select K out of the n data points as the initial centroids. Various options are:

     (a) Select the first K out of n data points as the initial centroids.

     Considering the first three ($K = 3$) patterns $(10, 3.5, 2.0)$, $(63, 5.4, 1.3)$, $(10.4, 3.5, 2.1)$ in Table 7.1 as the centroids of three clusters respectively, the algorithm stops after two iterations. The three clusters obtained and their centroids respectively are:

     *Cluster*1: $\{(10, 3.5, 2.0)\}$
     *Cluster*2: $\{(63, 5.4, 1.3), (73.5, 5.8, 1.2), (81, 6.1, 1.3), (71, 6.4, 1.0)\}$
     *Cluster*3: $\{(10.4, 3.5, 2.1), (10.3, 3.3, 2.0), (10.4, 3.3, 2.3), (10.4, 3.5, 2.3), (10.5, 3.3, 2.1)\}$
     Cluster Centroids: $(10, 3.5, 2.0)$, $(72.1, 5.9, 1.2)$, $(10.4, 3.4, 2.2)$

     (b) Select K out of n data points randomly as the initial centroids.

     Selecting the points $(10.4, 3.5, 2.3)$, $(10.3, 3.3, 2.0)$, $(10, 3.5, 2.0)$ as the randomly selected initial centroids, the algorithm stops after three iterations. The three clusters and their centroids respectively are:

     *Cluster*1: $\{(63, 5.4, 1.3), (73.5, 5.8, 1.2), (81, 6.1, 1.3), (71, 6.4, 1.0)\}$
     *Cluster*2: $\{(10.4, 3.5, 2.1), (10.3, 3.3, 2.0), (10.4, 3.3, 2.3), (10.4, 3.5, 2.3), (10.5, 3.3, 2.1)\}$

     Cluster3: {(10, 3.5, 2.0)}
     Cluster Centroids: (72.1, 5.9, 1.2), (10.2, 3.4, 2.2), (10, 3.5, 2.0)

(c) Select K out of n points as initial centroids such that the K points selected are as far away from each other as possible. This scheme has a better chance of reaching the globally optimal solution of the criterion function in (4). Selection of the K initial centroids based on this scheme could be achieved as follows:

  (i) Select the most dissimilar points in $\mathcal{X}$ as two centroids. Let them be X^1 and X^2. Set $q = 2$.

  (ii) If $q = K$ stop. Otherwise select X^{q+1}, the $q + 1$th centroid from the remaining $n - q$ points, where

$$X^{q+1} = \underset{X}{argmax}\,(d(X^1, X) + \cdots + d(X^q, X))$$

$$X \in \mathcal{X} - \{X^1, X^2, \ldots, X^q\}.$$

Repeat this step till K centroids are selected.

In the dataset shown in Table 7.1 the two extreme points are $(10, 3.5, 2.0)$ and $(81, 6.1, 1.3)$; these are selected as the first two centroids. The third centroid is $(63, 5.4, 1.3)$ as it is away from the already selected centroids significantly. Using these three initial centroids, we get the three clusters and their respective centroids, in two iterations, as:

     Cluster1: {(10, 3.5, 2.0), (10.4, 3.5, 2.1), (10.3, 3.3, 2.0), (10.4, 3.3, 2.3), (10.4, 3.5, 2.3), (10.5, 3.3, 2.1)}.
     Cluster2: {(73.5, 5.8, 1.2), (81, 6.1, 1.3)}.
     Cluster3: {(63, 5.4, 1.3), (71, 6.4, 1.0)}.
     Cluster Centroids: (10.3, 3.4, 2.1), (77.3, 6, 1.2), (67, 5.9, 1.2).

Note that option 1(c) gives the minimum squared error.

2. Select K random points in the pattern space as the initial centroids. These points need not be elements of $\mathcal{X}$. Some of the practical implementations of K-means algorithm use this

scheme for initial centroid selection. One problem with this initialization is that it can lead to empty clusters. For example, consider the dataset shown in Table 7.1. Let the three initial centroids be $(10, 3.5, 2.0)$, $(81, 6.1, 1.3)$, and $(40, 4.8, 1.7)$ where the first two are the two extreme points in the dataset and the third one is approximately at the middle of the line joining the other two.

Using these three centroids, the clusters obtained are:

*Cluster*1: $\{(10, 3.5, 2.0), (10.4, 3.5, 2.1), (10.3, 3.3, 2.0),$
$(10.4, 3.3, 2.3), (10.4, 3.5, 2.3), (10.5, 3.3, 2.1)\}$
*Cluster*2: $\{(63, 5.4, 1.3), (71, 6.4, 1.0), (73.5, 5.8, 1.2),$
$(81, 6.1, 1.3)\}$
*Cluster*3: $\{\ \}$

Note that based on the patterns, the minimum and maximum values of feature1 are 10 and 81. So, the range is $10 \cdots 81$. Similarly, for feature2 the range is $3.3 \cdots 6.1$ and for feature3 it is $1.0 \cdots 2.3$. The range box in this example is a hypercube based on these three range values. So, even though all the three initial centroids are legal and fall in the range box, one of the clusters obtained using the K-means algorithms is empty in this example. In general, one or more clusters could be empty when such a scheme is used.

- **Time and Space Requirements:**

  Each iteration of the K-means algorithm requires computation of distance between every data point and each of the K centroids. So, the number of distance computations per iteration is $O(nK)$. If the algorithm takes l iterations to converge then it is $O(nKl)$. Further if each data point and the centroid are p-dimensional, then it is $O(nklp)$. Also, it needs to store the K centroids in the memory; so, the space requirement is of $O(Kp)$.

2.2. Leader algorithm

Leader is the simplest of the clustering algorithms in terms of time and space complexity. It is the earliest reported incremental algorithm in the literature on clustering. So, it can be naturally used in stream data mining. It is also a partitional clustering algorithm.

Leader Algorithm

Input: Dataset, $\mathcal{X}$; Distance threshold, T
Output: A Partition of $\mathcal{X}$, Π_K^n
1. Select the first point as the leader of the first cluster. Set $K = 1$.
2. Consider the next point in $\mathcal{X}$ and assign it to the cluster whose leader has a distance less than the user specified threshold T. Else increment the value of K and start the Kth cluster with the current point as its leader.
3. Repeat step 2 till all the points in $\mathcal{X}$ are considered for clustering.

Note that

- **Threshold Size:** The value of T decides the number of clusters generated; for a given $\mathcal{X}$ and a small value of T the algorithm generates a large number of small size clusters and for a larger value of T, the algorithm generates a small number of large size clusters.
- **Order Dependence:** The order in which points in $\mathcal{X}$ are considered plays an important role; for different orders the resulting partitions could be different.

We illustrate with a two-dimensional example using the dataset shown in Table 7.2.

Table 7.2.   A two-dimensional dataset.

Pattern number	Feature1	Feature2
1	1	1
2	2	1
3	2	2
4	3	3
5	6	6
6	7	6
7	7	7
8	8	8

Now consider a value of 0 for the threshold T. Then we get eight clusters with each cluster having one point; each point in the table is assigned to a cluster. On the other hand if the threshold value is 4, then we get two clusters; where

- the first cluster is $\{(1,1)^t, (2,1)^t, (2,2)^t, (3,3)^t\}$ and
- the second cluster is $\{(6,6)^t, (7,6)^t, (7,7)^t, (8,8)^t\}$.

In order to consider the effect of the order in which the patterns are processed, let us consider patterns in the order in which they are present in the table. Further, let us assume that the threshold value T is 2. Then we get 4 clusters where:

- the leaders are: $(1,1)^t, (3,3)^t, (6,6)^t, (8,8)^t$ and
- the clusters are: $\{(1,1)^t, (2,1)^t, (2,2)^t\}$; $\{(3,3)^t\}$; $\{(6,6)^t, (7,6)^t, (7,7)^t\}$; $\{(8,8)^t\}$.

2.3. BIRCH: Balanced Iterative Reducing and Clustering using Hierarchies

BIRCH offers a hierarchical clustering framework. It constructs a data structure called Clustering Feature tree (CF tree) which represents each cluster as a vector called CF vector.

- **CF:** Let us consider a cluster of n points, in a d-dimensional space given by, $\{(x_{11}, x_{12}, \ldots, x_{1d})^t, (x_{21}, x_{22}, \ldots, x_{2d})^t, \ldots, (x_{n1}, x_{n2}, \ldots, x_{nd})^t\}$. The CF vector is three-dimensional and is

$$\left\langle n, \left(\sum_{j=1}^{n} x_{j1}, \sum_{j=1}^{n} x_{j2}, \ldots, \sum_{j=1}^{n} x_{jd} \right), \right.$$
$$\left. \left(\sum_{j=1}^{n} x_{j1}^2, \sum_{j=1}^{n} x_{j2}^2, \ldots, \sum_{j=1}^{n} x_{jd}^2 \right) \right\rangle,$$

where the three components of the vector are:

1. The first component is the number of elements in the cluster which is n here,
2. The second component is the linear sum of all the points (vectors) in the cluster which is ls which is l-dimensional here, and

3. The third component, squared sum, another d-dimensional vector, is sum of squares of the components of the points in the cluster; here it is $(9, 6)$ $(=(1^2 + 2^2 + 2^2, 1^2 + 1^2 + 2^2))$.

- **Merging Clusters:** A major flexibility offered by representing clusters using CF vectors is that it is very easy to merge two or more clusters. For example, if n_i is the number of elements in C_i, ls_i is the linear sum and ss_i is the squared sum then

CF vector of cluster C_i is $\langle n_i, ls_i, ss_i \rangle$ and
CF vector of cluster C_j is $\langle n_j, ls_j, ss_j \rangle$, then
CF vector of the cluster obtained by merging C_i and C_j is

$$\langle n_i + n_j, ls_i + ls_j, ss_i + ss_j \rangle.$$

- **Computing Cluster Parameters:** Another important property of the CF representation is that several statistics associated with the corresponding cluster can be obtained easily using it. A *statistic* is a function of the samples in the cluster. For example, if a cluster

$C = \{X_1, X_2, \ldots, X_p\}$, then

$$\text{Centroid of } C = \text{Centroid}_C = \frac{\sum_{j=1}^{p} X_j}{p} = \frac{ls}{p},$$

$$\text{Radius of } C = R = \left[\frac{\sum_{i=1}^{p} (X_i - \text{Centroid}_C)^2}{p} \right]^{\frac{1}{2}}$$

$$= \left[\frac{ss_i - 2\frac{ls_i^2}{p} + \frac{ls_i^2}{p^2}}{p} \right]^{\frac{1}{2}},$$

$$\text{Diameter of } C = D = \left(\frac{\sum_{i=1}^{n} \sum_{j=1}^{n} (X_i - X_j)^2}{n(n-1)} \right)^{\frac{1}{2}}.$$

- **Construction of the CF-tree**

  The CF-tree may be viewed as a kind of B Tree. Some of its important features are:

  – Each leaf node has at most L entries where each entry is a CF-vector and corresponds to a cluster. Each cluster at the leaf node has a collection of points such that each of the points is within a user specified threshold distance T from the center of the cluster. This view means
    * Each leaf-level cluster may be viewed as a sphere of radius T.
    * The data points are all numerical vectors.
  – Each non-leaf node has upto B children. B is large in most of the applications where BIRCH is used. Each non-leaf node is represented by a CF-vector that is the sum of the CF-vectors of all its child nodes.
  – It is possible to insert the data points incrementally into the tree; so, it requires a single dataset scan to construct the CF-tree.

  We illustrate the construction of the CF-tree using a two-dimensional example.

  Example 1. Consider the following collection of two-dimensional patterns: $\{(2,2), (6,3), (1,2), (2,1), (6,4), (7,3), (1,1), (14,2), (14,3), (2,2)\}$. By default each pattern is a two-dimensional column vector; however, we have not explicitly shown the transpose symbol for the sake of simplicity. These vectors should be treated as column vectors. The corresponding CF-tree is shown in Figure 7.4;

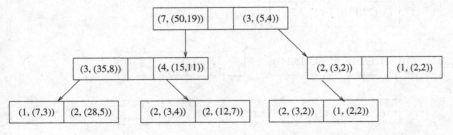

Figure 7.4. CF-tree for the two-dimensional data.

this is based on a value of 1 for T and $B = L = 2$. In the figure only a part of the CF-vector for each cluster is shown. Observe that only the number of elements in the cluster (first component) and the linear sum of the elements in the cluster (second component) are shown. The squared sum (third component) is not shown for the sake of making the figure simple. These details are adequate to explain the CF-tree construction.

The incremental construction of the CF-tree may be explained using the details shown in Figure 7.5. Figure 7.5(a) is obtained after inserting the first pattern; similarly Figures 7.5(b) and 7.5(c) are obtained after inserting the second and third points respectively. Figure 7.5(d) is obtained after inserting the first seven patterns. In order to insert a point, we need to find the nearest child of each non-leaf node including the root node. Ultimately, at the leaf node we either insert the new pattern into one of the clusters at the leaf node if the distance between the point and the CF-vector of the cluster is less than T or start a new cluster. We explain insertion of each point into the CF-tree, in the example, using

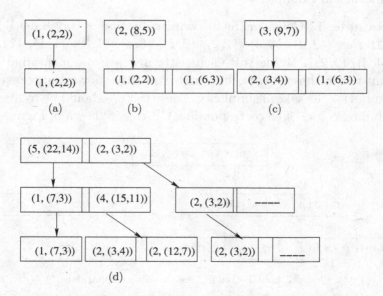

Figure 7.5.   Incremental construction of CF-tree for the data.

the following:

1. We consider the first data point $(2, 2)$. It forms a cluster and the corresponding part of the CF-vector is $(1, (2, 2))$ as shown in Figure 7.5(a).

2. Now we consider the next pattern $(6, 3)$; the only neighbor is $(2, 2)$ (centroid of the cluster represented by $(1, (2, 2))$ at a distance of approximately 4.1 units which is greater than $T(=1)$. So, a new cluster has to be initiated; further, the leaf node can accommodate one more CF entry (cluster) as $L = 2$. So, we create a new cluster and the corresponding partial CF-vector $(1, (6, 3))$ is inserted into the leaf node as shown in Figure 7.5(b).

3. Now we consider the point $(1, 2)$; the nearest centroid $(2, 2)$ is at a distance of 1 unit. So, we insert $(1, 2)$ into the cluster with the centroid $(2, 2)$; the updated part of the CF-vector is $(2, (3, 4))$ as shown in Figure 7.5(c). Note that after the updation, the current centroid is $(1.5, 2)$.

4. We consider the pattern $(2, 1)$ next; it is at a distance of approximately 1.1 units from $(1.5, 2)$ (one centroid) and at a distance of 4.5 units from the other centroid, $(6, 3)$. So, we need to start a new cluster; it cannot be accommodated in the existing leaf as $L = 2$ and already 2 CF entries (clusters) are present in the leaf node. So, a new leaf node is added. Next, we consider $(6, 4)$ which is inserted into the same cluster as $(6, 3)$ leading to the updated CF-vector $(2, (12, 7))$ as shown in Figure 7.5(d). Next insert $(7, 3)$ into a new cluster as none of the three existing centroids is at a distance of less than or equal to T from $(7, 3)$; the new CF-vector is $(1, (7, 3))$ which is shown in Figure 7.5(d). Next, we consider $(1, 1)$ which is assigned to the same cluster as $(2, 1)$ and the corresponding CF-vector becomes $(2, (3, 2))$; this is also depicted in Figure 7.5(d).

5. Now by adding the remaining three points in the order $(14, 2)$, $(14, 3)$, $(2, 2)$, we get the final tree shown in Figure 7.4.

- **Order Dependence**

Like the Leader algorithm, BIRCH also suffers from order dependence. Note that two copies of the point $(2, 2)$ are assigned to different clusters as shown in Figure 7.4. This problem is typically associated with a majority of the incremental algorithms.

2.4. Clustering based on graphs

There are several applications where the data is available in the form of a graph. Even when the data is in the form of a matrix of size $n \times d$ where there are n patterns each described by d features, it is possible to convert this data matrix into a similarity graph. In this section, we deal with algorithms that work on such graph data. First, we examine an algorithm that works on the conventional data, that is data represented in the form of $n \times d$ matrix.

2.4.1. *Single-link Algorithm (SLA)*

A graph-based method of clustering is to use the Minimal Spanning Tree (MST) corresponding to the data. In such a tree each node corresponds to a data point; so there are n nodes or vertices. In order to realize it the distance, d_{ij}, between the pair of nodes X_i, and X_j is calculated; typically Euclidean distance is used. This computation is performed between all possible pairs of patterns. This leads to the formation of a complete dissimilarity graph $G = \langle V, E, D \rangle$ where V is the set of n nodes; E is the set of edges; and D is the associated set of distances.

There are several well-known algorithms to compute the MST of the data from G. An MST is a tree that spans all the n nodes with the sum of the weights (distances) of the $n - 1$ edges in the spanning tree is the minimum. We show in Figure 7.6 the MST of eight two-dimensional points. Note that there are seven edges and one can use these edges to obtain the clusters. One can obtain two clusters by breaking the edge with the maximum weight (distance). In this case edge BF will be removed to produce two clusters $\{A, B, C, D\}$ and $\{E, F, G, H\}$. Further breaking can be done to produce more number of clusters as exemplified in Figure 7.3.

Typically, SLA is used to generate the clusters based on given data points. It is an agglomerative algorithm. It starts with n singleton clusters if there are n data points to be clustered. It uses

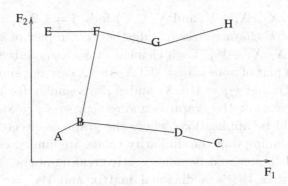

Figure 7.6.   MST of eight points in a two-dimensional space.

the interpoint distance set D to merge two clusters if the distance between them is less than or equal to the distance between any other pair of clusters. Here, distance between a pair of clusters C_i and C_j is the minimum over all possible pairs of points X and Y where $X \in C_i$ and $Y \in C_j$. A major difficulty with the usage of SLA is that it requires the dissimilarity set D to be computed and stored which requires $O(n^2)$ time and space.

2.4.2. *Spectral clustering*

Partitional clustering algorithms like the K-means produce good clusters when the data has isotropic or spherical clusters. K-means algorithm is not suited when the clusters are non-isotropic; specifically when the clusters are chain-like (elongated in a direction) or concentric (where the clusters have roughly the same centroid; imagine two circles or spheres with the same center and different radii and the points in each cluster on the respective circle or sphere). Spectral clustering algorithms are well suited to deal with such datasets.

Spectral clustering algorithms work on datasets represented in the form of a graph. Here, a graph is viewed as a triple $\langle V, E, S \rangle$ where S is the matrix of similarity values between pairs of nodes in the graph. Here, the sets V, E, and S are:

- $V = \{X_1, X_2, \ldots, X_n\}$. Each node/vertex in V corresponds to a data point in the collection.

- $E = \{\langle X_i, X_j \rangle : X_i \in V, \text{ and } X_j \in V\}$ for $i, j = 1, 2, \ldots, n$. So, each element of E characterizes an edge between a pair of vertices.
- $S = \{s_{ij} : X_i, X_j \in V\}$. Each element of S characterizes similarity between a pair of nodes. $s_{ij} = 0$ if X_i and X_j are not similar (or not connected); and $s_{ij} = 1$ if X_i and X_j are similar (or connected). In our treatment the graph is undirected; so $s_{ij} = s_{ji}$. However, there could be applications where the graph is directed. Further, we are assuming that the similarity values are binary, either 0 or 1; in general these could be non-negative real numbers.
- *Weightmatrix*, W: is a diagonal matrix and $W_{ii} = \sum_{j \in V} s_{ij}$ and $W_{ij} = 0$ if $i \neq j$. That is ith diagonal element in W is the sum of the elements in the ith row of S. This could be called the *degree matrix* when s_{ij}'s are binary as the entry W_{ii} corresponds to the degree of node X_i.

We illustrate these ideas using the graph shown in Figure 7.7. The corresponding S matrix is given by

$$
S = \begin{bmatrix}
1 & 1 & 1 & 0 & 0 & 0 \\
1 & 1 & 1 & 1 & 0 & 0 \\
1 & 1 & 1 & 0 & 0 & 0 \\
0 & 1 & 0 & 1 & 1 & 1 \\
0 & 0 & 0 & 1 & 1 & 1 \\
0 & 0 & 0 & 1 & 1 & 1
\end{bmatrix},
$$

where we are assuming that a node is similar to itself and so the diagonal entries are all 1. The weight matrix W (or degree matrix in

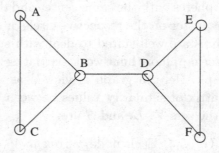

Figure 7.7.   A graph with six vertices.

this case) is

$$W = \begin{bmatrix} 3 & 0 & 0 & 0 & 0 & 0 \\ 0 & 4 & 0 & 0 & 0 & 0 \\ 0 & 0 & 3 & 0 & 0 & 0 \\ 0 & 0 & 0 & 4 & 0 & 0 \\ 0 & 0 & 0 & 0 & 3 & 0 \\ 0 & 0 & 0 & 0 & 0 & 3 \end{bmatrix}.$$

Let C_1 be a subset of V and C_2, the complement of C_1, be $V - C_1$. Based on this notation we can generate a two-partition of V using the notion of *mincut*.

$$\text{cut}(C_1, C_2) = \sum_{X_i \in C_1, X_j \in C_2} s_{ij} \tag{5}$$

and mincut is defined as

$$\text{mincut}(C_1^*, C_2^*) = \text{minimum}_{C_1, C_2} \ \text{cut}(C_1, C_2), \tag{6}$$

where C_1^* and $C_2^* (= V - C_1^*)$ are the optimal values of C_1 and C_2. Such a C_1^* and its complement C_2^* correspond to the two required clusters of the partition.

It is possible to abstract the mincut expression in a form suitable for optimization by considering the following.

- Let C_1 and C_2 be the two possible clusters being considered. Let these two clusters be viewed as negative (C_1) and positive (C_2) clusters. Based on this one can abstract the index vector I of size n where there are n vertices in the graph; let I_i be -1 if $X_i \in C_1$ and $+1$ if $X_i \in C_2$ for $i = 1, 2, \ldots, n$.
- Note that $(I_i - I_j)$ is 0 if both X_i and X_j are either in C_1 or in C_2. Further, $(I_i - I_j)^2$ is 1 if X_i belongs to one cluster and X_j is in the other cluster.
- Note that $Cut(C_1, C_2)$ considers addition of similarities s_{ij} where $X_i \in C_1$ and $X_j \in C_2$. We can select such s_{ij}'s by considering $s_{ij}(I_i - I_j)^2$ in the place of s_{ij} in the summation (5). So,

$\text{Cut}(C_1, C_2)$ can be equivalently written as

$$\text{Cut}(C_1, C_2) = \sum_{X_i \in C_1, \, X_j \in C_2} s_{ij}(I_i - I_j)^2 \qquad (7)$$

$$= \frac{1}{2} \sum_{I_i \neq I_j} s_{ij}(I_i - I_j)^2. \qquad (8)$$

- It is possible to simplify equation in (8) to show that

$$\text{Cut}(C_1, C_2) = I^t W I - I^t S I = I^t D I, \qquad (9)$$

where $D = W - S$. So, minimizing the *Cut* amounts to finding the index vector I such that $I^t D I$ is minimized; once I is known it is possible to obtain the clusters based on the polarity of the entries in I.
- So, the problem of obtaining the *mincut* amounts to

$$min_I \ I^t D I \ such \ that \ I_i \in \{-1, 1\} \ for \ all \ i \in \{1, 2, \ldots, n\}.$$

Because this is a combinatorially difficult problem to solve, we relax the selection of elements in I to real numbers which leads to

$$min_I \ I^t D I \ such \ that \ I^t I = n. \qquad (10)$$

- It is possible to see that D is symmetric as S and W are symmetric. The smallest eigenvalue of D is 0 and the corresponding eigenvector is $\mathbf{1} = (1, 1, \ldots, 1)^t$ because $D\mathbf{1} = 0 = 0\mathbf{1}$. By choosing the value of I as the eigenvector $\mathbf{1}$, it is possible to show that $I^t D I$ is equal to 0 as $DI = D\mathbf{1} = 0$. This value of I does not generate a two-partition as there is only a positive cluster.
- Instead of the smallest eigenvalue, select the next smallest eigenvalue so that $I^t D I$ is still small where I is the eigenvector corresponding to the second smallest eigenvalue. Further, because D is symmetric eigenvectors of D are orthogonal and the eigenvalues are all real. So, by choosing I to be the eigenvector corresponding to the second smallest eigenvalue, we get an I that is orthogonal to $\mathbf{1}$; this means that there will be both negative and positive entries in I. So, I is chosen to be the eigenvector corresponding to the second smallest eigenvalue.

We illustrate this algorithm using the example shown in Figure 7.7. The matrix D is given by

$$D = \begin{bmatrix} 2 & -1 & -1 & 0 & 0 & 0 \\ -1 & 3 & -1 & -1 & 0 & 0 \\ -1 & -1 & 2 & 0 & 0 & 0 \\ 0 & -1 & 0 & 3 & -1 & -1 \\ 0 & 0 & 0 & -1 & 2 & -1 \\ 0 & 0 & 0 & -1 & -1 & 2 \end{bmatrix}.$$

The eigenvalues of D are $0, \frac{5-\sqrt{17}}{2}, 3, 3, 3, \frac{5+\sqrt{17}}{2}$. The first two eigenvectors are $\mathbf{1}$ and $\left(1, \frac{-3+\sqrt{17}}{2}, 1, \frac{3-\sqrt{17}}{2}, \frac{-7+\sqrt{17}}{4}, \frac{3-\sqrt{17}}{2}\right)^t$. Note that in the second eigenvector, the first three entries are positive and the remaining three are negative. So, the clusters are $C_1 = \{D, E, F\}$ and $C_2 = \{A, B, C\}$ where C_1 is the negative cluster and C_2 is the positive cluster. Also note that this clustering is intuitively appealing as points in each cluster are completely connected.

In the example shown in Figure 7.7, we have considered the possibility of a two-partition. It is possible in general that the number of clusters K is greater than 2. In such a case we consider the K eigenvectors corresponding to the K smallest eigenvalues. Note that each eigenvector is n-dimensional. So, the K eigenvectors provide a K-dimensional representation of the n patterns by viewing the K eigenvectors as K columns in a matrix. This matrix will be of size $n \times K$. Also these K eigenvectors are orthogonal to each other. So, we can cluster the n rows (data points) into K clusters. In the above example, by considering the first two eigenvectors as two columns in a matrix we get the n two-dimensional patterns shown in Table 7.3. By employing K-means algorithm on this data with a value of 2 for K will give us the same clusters as we got earlier using only the polarity of entries in the second eigenvector.

Spectral clustering gets its name from the word spectrum. The set of all eigenvalues of a matrix is called its *spectrum*. The magnitude of the maximum eigenvalue of the matrix is called the *spectral radius*. Here, we have examined how clustering can be performed by using the eigenvalues and eigenvectors of the matrix D which is obtained

Table 7.3.   Two-dimensional representation of the six points.

$(1,\ 1)$

$\left(1,\ \dfrac{-3+\sqrt{17}}{2}\right)$

$(1,\ 1)$

$\left(1,\ \dfrac{3-\sqrt{17}}{2}\right)$

$\left(1,\ \dfrac{-7-\sqrt{17}}{2}\right)$

$\left(1,\ \dfrac{3-\sqrt{17}}{2}\right)$

---

from the weight matrix W and the similarity matrix S. It is possible to consider other variants of D to realize several other spectral clustering algorithms.

2.4.3. *Clustering based on frequent itemsets*

Another recently studied direction for clustering is based on frequent itemsets. The viability of this paradigm is because of efficient algorithms available for mining frequent itemsets. Specifically we discuss in this section a data structure called Frequent Pattern Tree (FP-tree) which can be built using two dataset scans and this framework is ideally suited for clustering large datasets. Further, frequencies of different itemsets naturally link with the probability estimates based on the popular maximum likelihood approach.

Typically frequent itemset mining is associated with transaction datasets. It is possible to view binary patterns routinely as transactions. For example, consider the dataset shown in Table 7.4. There are six binary patterns labeled P_1 to P_6; each pattern is of size 3×3 and is an example of character one. Some of them are affected by noise in one out of nine bits. In a more practical setting such characters will

Table 7.4.   Six examples of character 1.

0 0 1	0 0 1	0 0 1
0 0 1	1 0 1	0 0 1
0 0 1	0 0 1	1 0 1
P_1	P_2	P_3
1 0 1	0 0 1	0 0 1
0 0 1	0 1 1	0 0 1
0 0 1	0 0 1	0 1 1
P_4	P_5	P_6

Table 7.5.   Transactions corresponding to the six patterns.

TID	i_1	i_2	i_3	i_4	i_5	i_6	i_7	i_8	i_9
T_1	0	0	1	0	0	1	0	0	1
T_2	0	0	1	1	0	1	0	0	1
T_3	0	0	1	0	0	1	1	0	1
T_4	1	0	1	0	0	1	0	0	1
T_5	0	0	1	0	1	1	0	0	1
T_6	0	0	1	0	0	1	0	1	1

be of bigger sizes; they could be matrices of size 64×64 or 200×200. Here, 3×3 size characters are used for illustrating the idea. Each 3×3 character may be viewed as a transaction based on 9 items by considering row-major order; for example pattern P_1 is represented by the transaction: 0 0 1 0 0 1 0 0 1. It is possible to set up a correspondence between the location of an element in the ith row and jth column of the 3×3 matrix and the item number m_{ij} using the row-major order as

$$m_{ij} = (i - 1) * 3 + j \quad \text{for } i, j = 1, 2, 3.$$

The corresponding representation of the six patterns as transactions is given in Table 7.5. Here, TID stands for Transaction Identifier and i_1 to i_9 stand for the nine items. Note that pattern P_i is represented as transaction T_i for $i = 1, \ldots, 6$. By scanning the dataset once we can observe that the frequencies of the nine items in the collection of patterns are

$$f(i_1) = 1; \ f(i_2) = 0; \ f(i_3) = 6; \ f(i_4) = 1; \ f(i_5) = 1; \ f(i_6) = 6;$$
$$f(i_7) = 1; \ f(i_8) = 1; \ f(i_9) = 6.$$

If we consider items which have frequency more than 2, then we get the items

$$i_3 \ (f(i_3) = 6); \ i_6 \ (f(i_6) = 6); \ i_9 \ (f(i_9) = 6);$$

so these are the frequent itemsets.

In order to see how the frequent itemsets are useful in clustering we consider another character set shown in Table 7.6 corresponding to character 7. Representing these six patterns in the form of transactions we have the data shown in Table 7.7. The frequencies of the

Table 7.6. Six examples of character 7.

1 1 1	1 1 1	1 1 1
0 0 1	1 0 1	0 0 1
0 0 1	0 0 1	1 0 1
P_7	P_8	P_9
1 1 1	1 1 1	1 1 1
1 0 1	0 1 1	0 0 1
0 1 1	0 0 1	0 1 1
P_{10}	P_{11}	P_{12}

Table 7.7. Transactions corresponding to the six patterns of 7.

TID	i_1	i_2	i_3	i_4	i_5	i_6	i_7	i_8	i_9
T_7	1	1	1	0	0	1	0	0	1
T_8	1	1	1	1	0	1	0	0	1
T_9	1	1	1	0	0	1	1	0	1
T_{10}	1	1	1	1	0	1	0	1	1
T_{11}	1	1	1	0	1	1	0	0	1
T_{12}	1	1	1	0	0	1	0	1	1

items corresponding to the transactions in Table 7.7 are given by:

$$f(i_1) = 6; \; f(i_2) = 6; \; f(i_3) = 6; \; f(i_4) = 2; \; f(i_5) = 1; \; f(i_6) = 6;$$
$$f(i_7) = 1; \; f(i_8) = 2; \; f(i_9) = 6.$$

So, the frequent itemsets, based on a threshold of more than 2, are

$$i_1 \; (f(i_1) = 6); \; i_2 \; (f(i_2) = 6); \; i_3 \; (f(i_3) = 6); \; i_6 \; (f(i_6) = 6);$$
$$i_9 \; (f(i_9) = 6).$$

Using these frequent 1-*itemsets* which are obtained using a dataset scan we can build the *FP-tree* shown in Figure 7.8. Note that in Figure 7.8 the items are arranged in non-decreasing order; if two or more items have the same frequency, then such items are placed in a lexicographic order.

The *FP*-tree is constructed as follows:

- Scan the dataset once to obtain the frequent 1-*itemsets*. For example, from the set of transactions shown in Table 7.5 the frequent 1-*itemsets* are $\{i_3\}$, $\{i_6\}$, $\{i_9\}$ and similarly in case of the

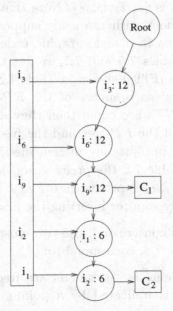

Figure 7.8. FP-tree for the 12 transactions.

Table 7.8.   Transactions based on frequent items.

FTID	Frequent itemset
FIT_1	$\langle i_3, i_6, i_9 \rangle$
FIT_2	$\langle i_3, i_6, i_9 \rangle$
FIT_3	$\langle i_3, i_6, i_9 \rangle$
FIT_4	$\langle i_3, i_6, i_9 \rangle$
FIT_5	$\langle i_3, i_6, i_9 \rangle$
FIT_6	$\langle i_3, i_6, i_9 \rangle$
FIT_7	$\langle i_3, i_6, i_9, i_1, i_2 \rangle$
FIT_8	$\langle i_3, i_6, i_9, i_1, i_2 \rangle$
FIT_9	$\langle i_3, i_6, i_9, i_1, i_2 \rangle$
FIT_{10}	$\langle i_3, i_6, i_9, i_1, i_2 \rangle$
FIT_{11}	$\langle i_3, i_6, i_9, i_1, i_2 \rangle$
FIT_{12}	$\langle i_3, i_6, i_9, i_1, i_2 \rangle$

transactions in Table 7.7 the frequent 1-*itemsets* are $\{i_3\}$, $\{i_6\}$, $\{i_9\}$, $\{i_1\}$, $\{i_2\}$.

- Arrange each transaction in the frequency order of the items in it; ignore any infrequent items. For example, consider transaction T_4 in Table 7.5; it is $\{i_1, i_3, i_6, i_9\}$. Note that i_1 is infrequent and i_3, i_6, i_9 are frequent with the same support value of 6; so, we arrange these items in a lexicographic order. So, arranging the transactions in Tables 7.5 and 7.7 we get the frequent itemset-based transactions (FITs) shown in Table 7.8.

- The FITs are used as branches of the FP-tree. If the prefixes of two or more FITs are equal then they are used to represent the same branch of the FP-tree and the frequencies of the items in the prefix are appropriately incremented. For example in the FITs shown in Table 7.8 the prefix i_3, i_6, i_9 has a frequency of 12 and the suffix i_1, i_2 is present in 6 FITs. Figure 7.9 shows the intermediate FP-trees after inserting the first 6 FITs.

Once the FP-tree is constructed, the two clusters, for the example data shown in Figure 7.8, correspond to:

1. *Cluster*$_1$ (C_1): Items i_3, i_6, and i_9 are frequent in patterns of this cluster; this is indicated by a pointer from i_9 to C_1 in a rectangular box.

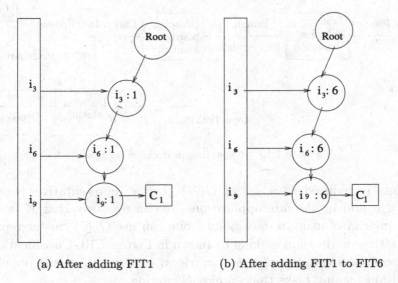

(a) After adding FIT1   (b) After adding FIT1 to FIT6

Figure 7.9. FP-trees after adding 1 and 6 transactions.

2. *Cluster$_2$ (C_2)*: Items i_3, i_6, i_9, i_1, i_2 are frequent in the transactions corresponding to this cluster; it is indicated by a pointer from item i_2 to C_2 in a rectangular box.

Note that in this example C_1 corresponds to class of *ones* and C_2 corresponds to class of *sevens*.

3. Why Clustering?

Clustering is useful in several machine learning and data mining tasks including **data compression**, **outlier detection**, and **pattern synthesis**.

3.1. Data compression

In most of the real-world applications, clustering does not produce the end product. Clustering may be viewed as a data compression tool that generates a partition of the dataset and represents the clusters using appropriate representatives/descriptions leading to data compression. Compression is achieved because the set $\mathcal{X}$ of n data

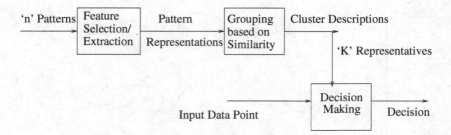

Figure 7.10.   Clustering in decision making.

points is reduced to a set of $O(K)$ cluster representatives where $K < n$ and in *big data* applications we can even say that $K \ll n$. So, instead of using n data points, one can use $O(K)$ cluster representatives in decision making as shown in Figure 7.10. Classification, regression, summarization and retrieval of documents are popular decision making tasks that employ clustering.

3.2. Outlier detection

An outlier is a data point or a pattern that differs from a majority of the patterns in the collection. For example, consider the set of two-dimensional points shown in Figure 7.2. One of the points is away from the rest; it has a value of a_3 on the x coordinate and b_2 on the y coordinate. Even though it matches with several points in the collection in terms of x or y values, it differs from the rest due to its specific location in terms of the combination of its x and y values. In general, an outlier can differ from each of the other points in one or more feature values significantly. Density around a point is useful to classify whether a point is an outlier or not; typically an outlier is located in a sparse/low-density region.

Outliers could be either out-of-range or with-in range. In the out-of-range case, the outlier will have value outside the legal domain of one or more of the variables. Identifying out-of-range outliers could be achieved easily by checking whether a feature value falls within the range of the domain of the feature or not. On the contrary, outliers falling within the range are not easily detected as they vary relative to the other values in the respective group or cluster. For example, the outlier shown in Figure 7.2 is within the range. Typical data mining schemes for outlier detection are based on clustering or density of the data in the vicinity. Once the data is clustered, one needs to examine small size clusters for possible outliers; typically singleton clusters are highly likely to be containing outliers.

3.3. Pattern synthesis

One of the important problems in machine learning is to deal with missing data. For example, consider the data shown in Table 7.1. There are 10 patterns and each pattern is described using three features. Note that the value of feature2 of pattern number 3 is 3.5. Let us assume that this value is missing and we need to estimate the missing value. We can use clustering to solve this problem as follows. Cluster the 10 points using the remaining two features, that is, feature1 and feature3 with the help of K-means algorithm.

In order to visualize the clusters, consider Figure 7.11 which shows the 10 points in the two-dimensional space corresponding to feature1 and feature3. By selecting patterns 1 and 2 in the two-dimensional space, that is $(10.0, 2.0)^t$ and $(63, 1.3)^t$, as the initial centroids, K-means algorithm gives two clusters as shown in Figure 7.11

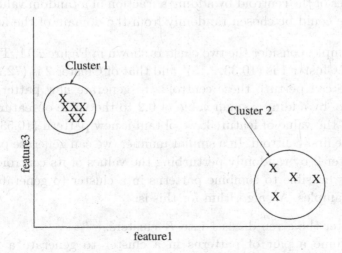

Figure 7.11. Clustering points in the two-dimensional space.

with $(10.3, 2.1)^t$ and $(72.1, 1.2)^t$ as the centroids. One can see two clusters in the collection: Cluster 1 and Cluster 2. Note that pattern 3 is in Cluster 1. Now a simple and good estimate for the missing value of feature2 of pattern 3 is the sample mean of the values of feature2 of the remaining patterns in Cluster 1. The values of feature2 of patterns falling in Cluster 1 are: 3.5, 3.3, 3.3, 3.5, 3.3; the average value is approximately 3.4. Even though the value of 3.4 is different from the actual value 3.5; the mean value is closer to 3.5 and so this simple scheme gives acceptable estimates.

In the case of missing values, we are synthesizing a part or estimating the feature value of a pattern. However, there could be applications where the entire pattern has to be synthesized. Classification based on a small set of training patterns requires such synthesis. This is because the number of training patterns required increases with the dimensionality of the dataset for a good classification.

Clustering could be used to synthesize; specifically cluster representatives could be used to synthesize patterns as follows:

1. Obtain the clusters and their representatives; let the centroids of the clusters be representatives as a special case.
2. Generate new patterns by perturbing one or more of the feature values of the centroid by adding a fraction of a random value. This value could be chosen randomly from the domain of the feature.

For example, consider the two clusters shown in Figure 7.11. The centroid of Cluster 1 is $(10.33, 2.15)^t$ and that of Cluster 2 is $(72.1, 1.2)^t$. Now we can perturb these centroids to generate new patterns. For example, by adding a small value of 0.2 to the value of feature1 and -0.1 to the value of feature3, we obtain a new pattern $(10.53, 2.05)^t$ from the first centroid. In a similar manner, we can generate patterns of Cluster 2 by randomly perturbing the values of its centroid.

It is possible to combine patterns in a cluster to generate additional samples. An algorithm for this is:

1. Cluster the given dataset into K clusters.
2. Combine a pair of patterns in a cluster to generate a pair of possible novel patterns; this combination could be done using

crossover like operator. A simple crossover operator is the single-point crossover. It may be explained as follows:

Let the crossover be applied on two vectors $U = (u_1, u_2, \ldots, u_d)^t$ and $V = (v_1, v_2, \ldots, v_d)^t$. We partition each vector into two parts; the prefix part corresponding to the first p components and the suffix part corresponding to the remaining $d - p$ components. We combine U and V to generate two possibly novel patterns X and Y, where X is the d-dimensional vector obtained by concatenating the prefix of U with the suffix of V. Similarly Y is obtained by concatenating the prefix of V with the suffix of U.

We illustrate the pattern synthesis process using the following example. Consider the patterns $(10.0, 2.0)^t$ and $(10.4, 2.1)^t$ from Cluster 1 shown in Figure 7.11. Here, the value of d is 2. We can generate possible novel patterns as follows: take the value of feature1, that is 10.0 (prefix) of the first pattern and the value of feature3, that is 2.1 (suffix) of the second pattern to form a new pattern $(10.0, 2.1)^t$ and similarly by taking the value of feature1 in the second pattern and value of feature3 of the first pattern give us another novel pattern $(10.4, 2.0)^t$. A more illustrative example is provided using the data given in Table 7.9. Let patterns numbered 1, 2, 3, 4 be given and let patterns 1 and 2 belong to Cluster 1 and patterns 3 and 4 belong to Cluster 2. Now by combining patterns 1 and 2 using features 1 and 2 to form the prefix and features 3 and 4 as the suffix, we get two more

Table 7.9.   Pattern synthesis based on clustering.

Pattern number	Feature1	Feature2	Feature3	Feature4	Cluster number
1	1	1	1	1	1
2	2	2	2	2	1
3	6	6	6	6	2
4	7	7	7	7	2
5	1	1	2	2	1
6	2	2	1	1	1
7	6	6	7	7	2
8	7	7	6	6	2

patterns in Cluster 1 which are shown in the table as patterns 5 and 6. Similarly patterns 7 and 8 belonging to Cluster 2 are obtained by combining patterns 3 and 4, in Cluster 2, as shown in the table.

4. Clustering Labeled Data

Clustering is typically associated with grouping unlabeled patterns. However, it is more practical to consider partitioning sets of labeled samples. Also, typically clustering is not an end product in itself. Clusters and their representatives are useful in further decision making as depicted in Figure 7.10. Specifically labels associated with the data points are useful in **clustering for classification** or in **knowledge-based clustering**.

4.1. Clustering for classification

Classification is an important decision making activity that can benefit from clustering. Specifically, clustering the training dataset can improve the efficiency of classification algorithms.

4.1.1. *Efficient nearest neighbor classifier*

We illustrate how the NNC can be made more efficient by using the cluster representatives rather than the original data using an example. For this we consider a modified version of the dataset shown in Table 7.1; the modification is in terms of providing the class label of each pattern. The modified dataset is shown in Table 7.10. Note that there are six patterns from one class (labeled 1) and four from the other (labeled 2).

Let us consider a test pattern $T = (70, 6.5, 1)^t$. Using the NNC we need to compute the distance between T and each of the 10 training patterns given in Table 7.10; so, we need to compute 10 distances and find the nearest neighbor of T by locating the training pattern that has the least distance value. In this example, pattern numbered 8 is the nearest neighbor with a squared Euclidean distance of 1.01. So, T is assigned to class 2 as the class label of pattern 8 is 2. In this almost trivial example, we require to compute 10 distances; however, in large-scale applications involving billions or trillions of training

Table 7.10. A training dataset.

Pattern number	feature1	feature2	feature3	Class label
1	10	3.5	2.0	1
2	63	5.4	1.3	2
3	10.4	3.5	2.1	1
4	10.3	3.3	2.0	1
5	73.5	5.8	1.2	2
6	81	6.1	1.3	2
7	10.4	3.3	2.3	1
8	71	6.4	1.0	2
9	10.4	3.5	2.3	1
10	10.5	3.3	2.1	1

patterns, the time taken to compute all the distances will be large. We can reduce this effort by clustering the datasets of each class separately and use the prototypes or representatives of clusters instead of the entire training data.

In this example, by clustering patterns in each class separately using the K-means algorithm with $K = 2$, we get the following clusters:

- Class 1:
    - Cluster11 = {1}; Centroid11 = $(10, 3.5, 2.0)^t$
    - Cluster12 = {3, 4, 7, 9, 10}; Centroid12 = $(10.4, 3.4, 2.2)^t$
- Class 2:
    - Cluster1 = {2, 8}; Centroid21 = $(67, 5.9, 1.2)^t$
    - Cluster2 = {5, 6}; Centroid22 = $(77.2, 6, 1.2)^t$

Now the cluster centroid nearest to T is Centroid21 which is at a squared Euclidean distance of 9.4. So, we assign T to Class 2 as the nearest cluster centroid is from class 2. Here, we need to compute only four distances from the test pattern T as there are only four centroids. Note that clustering of the training data needs to be done only once and it can be done beforehand (offline). Also note that clustering is done once and centroids of the clusters are obtained. The same centroids could be used to classify any number of test patterns.

4.1.2. *Cluster-based support vector machine*

Clustering is useful not only in building efficient nearest neighbor classifiers, but also in building efficient algorithms using a variety of classifiers. Here, we consider how clustering can be useful in building an efficient support vector machine based classifier; we consider a two-class classification problem for the sake of simplicity. The specific scheme employed is given below:

- **Input:** Set of positive examples, $\mathcal{X}_+$ and set of negative examples, $\mathcal{X}_-$.
- Construct CF-trees CF_+ from $\mathcal{X}_+$ and CF_- from $\mathcal{X}_-$.
- Use the centroids in the root nodes of the CF-trees to train an SVM. Obtain the **Support Centroids** of this SVM.
- Expand these support centroids; expansion implies considering all the patterns in the corresponding clusters. Add to this set patterns obtained by expanding **low margin clusters**. By low margin cluster C_i we mean a cluster which satisfies the following:

$$D_i - R_i < D_s, \tag{11}$$

where
D_i = Distance from the centroid of C_i to the boundary of the SVM obtained,
R_i = Radius of cluster C_i,
D_s = Distance from support centroid to the boundary of the SVM.

- Obtain the SVM using these patterns that are accumulated.
- Repeat this expansion and obtaining SVM till no additional patterns are accumulated.

We illustrate the role of clustering in training Linear SVM classifier using the 11 two-dimensional patterns shown in Table 7.11.
The data is processed as follows:

- Patterns in each class are clustered separately. The clusters are:

Negative $(-ve)$ *Class*: $C_{1-} = \{(-1,3)^t, (1,3)^t\}$; $C_{2-} = \{(2,1)^t\}$; $C_{3-} = \{(-3,-2)^t, (-1,-2)^t\}$.

Table 7.11. Patterns from negative and positive classes.

Pattern no.	*Feature*1	*Feature*2	Class
1	−1	3	−
2	1	3	−
3	2	1	−
4	4	8	+
5	4	10	+
6	5	5	+
7	6	3	+
8	−3	−2	−
9	−1	−2	−
10	10	4	+
11	10	6	+

The centroids of these clusters are: $(0,3)^t$, $(2,1)^t$, and $(-2,-2)^t$ respectively.

Positive (+ve) Class: $C_{1+} = \{(4,8)^t, (4,10)^t\}$; $C_{2+} = \{(5,5)^t$; $C_{3+} = \{(6,3)^t\}$; $C_{4+} = \{(10,4)^t, (10,6)^t\}$.

The corresponding centroids respectively are: $(4,9)^t$, $(5,5)^t$, $(6,3)^t$; and $(10,5)^t$.

- Obtain the *Linear* SVM using the seven centroids. The support centroids are $(2,1)^t$, $(5,5)^t$, $(6,3)^t$. Expanding them will not add any more patterns as in this simple case each of these clusters is a singleton cluster. The corresponding W and b of the SVM are:

$$W = \left(\frac{2}{5}, \frac{1}{5}\right)^t \quad \text{and} \quad b = -2.$$

- The distance of a point $X = (x_1, x_2)^t$ from the decision boundary is given by $\frac{W^t X + b}{\|W\|}$. So, the distance of support centroids $(2,1)^t$ from the decision boundary is $\sqrt{5}$ and similarly for the remaining two support centroids also the distances are $\sqrt{5}$ each.
- For the remaining cluster centroids the distances are:

1. $(0,3)^t$: Distance is $\frac{7}{\sqrt{5}}$
2. $(4,9)^t$: Distance is $\frac{7}{\sqrt{5}}$

3. $(-2, -2)^t$: Distance is $\frac{16}{\sqrt{5}}$

4. $(10, 5)^t$: Distance is $3\sqrt{5}$.

Also note that the radius of each of these clusters is 1. By noting that in the first and second cases the inequality in (11) is satisfied as $\frac{7}{\sqrt{5}} - 1 < \sqrt{5}$, we need to expand both the clusters and add the corresponding patterns to the expanded set of patterns. In the remaining two cases (3 and 4) the inequality (11) is not satisfied. So, these clusters are ignored.

- Now using the SVM on all these expanded set of patterns, that is patterns numbered 1 to 7, we get the same W and b as obtained earlier.

In this example there is no significant reduction in computation; however in large-scale datasets several clusters that do not satisfy the inequality (11) are typically present. Presence of a large number of such clusters means a large number of patterns will be ignored in obtaining the SVM and as a consequence there will be reduction in the time required to train a linear SVM.

4.2. Knowledge-based clustering

One of the important results in clustering is that *Unsupervised learning is not possible*; it is argued through the *Theorem of the ugly duckling*. It is based on the observation that the number of predicates (features in binary form) shared by any two patterns is the same. So, any two patterns are equally similar. So, similarity between a *duckling* and a *swan* is the same as the similarity between a pair of swans.

The theorem of the ugly duckling may be illustrated using the two-dimensional dataset shown in Table 7.12. Here, we considered a two-dimensional binary data; so there are four possible object types as shown in the table. The two binary features (or equivalently predicates) are f_1 and f_2. Note that any data can be represented in a binary form; in fact a digital computer processes data in a binary form at the basic hardware level.

Table 7.12.   Four object types in two-dimensional space.

Pattern	f_1	f_2
P_1	0	0
P_2	0	1
P_3	1	1
P_4	1	0

Table 7.13.   Four objects using eight boolean functions.

Pattern	f_1	f_2	$f_1 \wedge \overline{f_2}$	$\overline{f_2}$	$\overline{f_1} \wedge f_2$ (g_2)	$\overline{f_1}$ (g_1)	$f_1 \vee \overline{f_2}$	$\overline{f_1} \vee f_2$
P_1	0	0	0	1	0	1	1	1
P_2	0	1	0	0	1	1	0	1
P_3	1	1	0	0	0	0	1	1

For the sake of simplicity we consider the first three object types. Now considering all possible boolean functions we have the data shown in Table 7.13. If we had considered all the four object types we would have got 16 boolean functions; instead we considered only three types to have only eight boolean functions. We have chosen the first three types; it will lead to a similar argument ultimately even if we consider any other three types.

In Table 7.13, we have considered all possible boolean functions which are eight in this case. In this representation, between any pair of patterns exactly four predicates (boolean functions) differ. So, distance or similarity based on this matching between any pair of patterns is the same. One may argue that f_1 and f_2 are primitive because they are *given*; others are *derived*. However, it is possible to argue that $g_1 = \overline{f_1}$ (where $\overline{f_1}$ is the negation of f_1) and $g_2 = \overline{f_1} \wedge f_2$ can be considered as primitive and $f_1 = \overline{g_1}$ and $f_2 = \overline{g_1} \vee g_2$ means we can derive f_1 and f_2 from g_1 and g_2. So, it is not possible to fix some as more primitive than others. Further, for the machine it does not matter which is more primitive. This means we need to consider all possible predicates (boolean functions) and the discrimination is lost. Such an argument leads to the conclusion that it requires extra-logical evidence (or knowledge) to prioritize two or more predicates over the others.

So, it can be that clustering cannot be done without using some knowledge. Such knowledge can be used in one or more of (a) Representation, (b) Similarity computation, or (c) Grouping phases. We consider each of these below:

- **Representation:** If labeled data is clustered, then the class labels of the patterns can be used to select a subset of features for representation using *mutual information*. For example if the class labels are *tall* and *short* then *height* is more important than *weight*. So, height will have a higher mutual information with the class labels. Similarly when the patterns are not labeled, then it is possible to represent them based on the *domain knowledge*. For example, *Yahoo!* uses ontologies built either manually or automatically to group documents. Similarly documents can be represented using *Wikipedia* article titles and categories. Specifically knowledge from large document collections is used to select appropriate terms in representing the documents.

  For example by ranking terms based on their frequency of occurrence in the collection it is observed that

  $$f_i = \frac{C}{r_i}, \qquad (12)$$

  where f_i is the frequency of a term in the collection; C is a constant and r_i is the rank of the term. Note that high frequency terms have low ranks. Typically terms that are either too frequent or too infrequent are not good for discrimination. So, terms are weighed based on $tf - idf$ values. A term like *the* or *is* occurs in almost every document in the collection which makes the inverse document frequency (idf) very small or close to zero. On the other hand terms that are infrequent (or have term frequency (tf) close to zero) will also have a low $tf - idf$ value. In some sense this amounts to representing documents using terms that are neither frequent nor rare.

- **Similarity Computation:** Conventionally proximity between two patterns X_i and X_j is defined as

$$\text{Proximity}(X_i, X_j) = f(X_i, X_j),$$

where f is a function of the two patterns X_i and X_j. Popular distance measures like Euclidean distance, City-block distance and similarity functions like the cosine of the angle between X_i and X_j are examples of this kind of functions. A more generic class of functions is the contextual similarity functions given by

$$\text{Contextual} - \text{Proximity}(X_i, X_j) = g(X_i, X_j, K_{\text{context}}).$$

Here, the similarity/distance between X_i *and* X_j is not only a function of these two patterns but it depends on the contextual knowledge K_{context}. Such contextual knowledge could be expressed in terms of other points in the vicinity of X_i and X_j. Let us consider the following example using the terms:

- $N(X_i)$ = Set of neighbors of $X_i = \{X_i^1, X_i^2, \ldots, X_i^{l_i}\}$. Neighborhood here could be characterized in different ways. For example,

  1. We may have $l_i = K$ for all i which means the K nearest neighbors are considered.
  2. We may consider neighbors of X_i falling within a sphere of radius r_i around X_i.
  3. In a graph or a social network $N(X_i)$ could be the set of all the nodes connected to node X_i.

- $CN(X_i, X_j) = |N(X_i) \cap N(X_j)|$ where CN indicates Common Neighbors. This is a similarity value and it is used in *link prediction* in social networks.

One of the most generalized similarity functions is based on both the context and also domain knowledge. An instantiation of this kind of similarity is *Knowledge-Based Proximity* (*KB* Proximity) given by

$$KB - \text{Proximity}(X_i, X_j) = h(X_i, X_j, K_{\text{context}}, K_{\text{domain}}),$$

where K_{domain} is the *domain knowledge*. We can illustrate such a similarity function using a simple example using common salt (sodium chloride), pepper, and potassium cyanide. For these three objects:

– In a restaurant we group these objects into two clusters:

$$C_1 = \{salt,\ pepper\}, \quad C_2 = \{potassium\ cyanide\}.$$

Such a partitioning is based on using knowledge in the form of concepts *edible* (C_1) and *inedible* (C_2) which are relevant in the context of a restaurant.

– In a chemistry laboratory the partitioning will be:

$$C_1 = \{salt, potassium\ cyanide\}, \quad C_2 = \{pepper\}.$$

This partitioning is based on using concepts *inorganic* (C_1) and *organic* (C_2).

One of the applications in which such knowledge, both contextual and domain knowledge, is used is text mining. For example, in finding similarity between two books the *context* might be provided by *Amazon* in terms of a set of books bought along with the given books. In addition domain knowledge in the form of *Dewey Decimal Classification* or *Wikipedia* is useful in estimating the similarity better by looking at the semantic or topic matching between books.

- **Grouping Phase:** Knowledge can be used in the grouping phase in different ways. Some of them are:

1. It is possible to fix the number of clusters K in the K-means type of algorithms.

2. It is possible to fix a threshold value to examine whether a pattern belongs to a cluster or not based on domain knowledge; this scheme is useful in algorithms like Leader and BIRCH.

3. In the single link algorithm a MST of the data is formed and edges with large weights are deleted from the MST to from clusters. Here also one can use the knowledge in terms of the edge weights to automatically stop partitioning further or equivalently in deleting edges further.

4. It is possible to use knowledge in a variety of forms: in fixing the prior probabilities; in characterizing entropy, etc.

5. Combination of Clusterings

One of the more recent trends in clustering is to obtain a single partition by using multiple partitions of the data. Here, a generic framework is:

1. Obtain $l(>1)$ partitions of the dataset $\mathcal{X}$ by using different algorithms; it may be possible to run the same algorithm with different parameter/initial partition settings. Let these partitions be $\pi_1, \pi_2, \ldots, \pi_l$.
2. For each pair of patterns X_i and X_j in $\mathcal{X}$ count in how many, of the l partitions, this pair is assigned to the same cluster; let this count be s_{ij} standing for the similarity between X_i and X_j. Store the similarity values, for all possible pairs, in a matrix of size $n \times n$ where the n is the size of $\mathcal{X}$ and s_{ij} is the ijth entry in the matrix S.
3. Use the SLA along with the similarity matrix S to cluster the n points into the required number of clusters.

We illustrate this approach using a two-dimensional dataset. Consider the dataset shown in Table 7.14 and in Figure 7.12.

Table 7.14. Two chain-like clusters.

Pattern	f_1	f_2
P_1	1	1
P_2	2	2
P_3	3	3
P_4	4	4
P_5	5	5
P_6	5	1
P_7	6	2
P_8	7	3
P_9	8	4
P_{10}	9	5

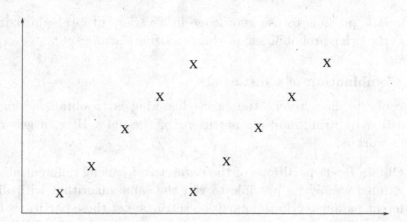

Figure 7.12.   An example dataset having two clusters.

Table 7.15.   Seven partitions of the dataset.

K	Initial centroids	Partition
2	(1,1),(9,5)	{{(1,1),(2,2),(3,3),(4,4),(5,1)} {(5,5),(6,2),(7,3),(8,4),(9,5)}}
2	(3,3),(7,3)	{{(1,1),(2,2),(3,3),(4,4),(5,5)} {(5,1),(6,2),(7,3),(8,4),(9,5)}}
2	(4,4),(6,2)	{{(1,1),(2,2),(3,3),(4,4),(5,5)} {(5,1),(6,2),(7,3),(8,4),(9,5)}}
2	(1,1),(5,1)	{{(1,1),(2,2),(3,3)}, {(4,4),(5,5),(5,1),(6,2),(7,3),(8,4),(9,5)}}
4	(1,1),(5,1),(5,5),(9,5)	{{(1,1),(2,2),(3,3)},{(4,4),(5,5)} {(5,1),(6,2),(7,3)},{(8,4),(9,5)}}
3	(1,1),(6,2),(9,5)	{{(1,1),(2,2),(3,3)},{(5,1),(6,2),(4,4),(5,5),(7,3)}, {(8,4),(9,5)}}
3	(3,3),(6,2),(9,5)	{{(1,1),(2,2),(3,3),(4,4),(5,5)},{(5,1),(6,2),(7,3)}, {(8,4),(9,5)}}

Let us consider K-means algorithm with different values of K and different initial centroids for the same value of K. We consider seven such partitions shown in Table 7.15. Once we have obtained these partitions we can form the similarity matrix based on the number of times a pair of patterns are in the same cluster in these partitions. Note that (1,1) and (2,2) are in the same cluster in all the seven partitions; however (1,1) and (5,5) are in the same cluster in only

Table 7.16. The similarity matrix.

Pattern	(1,1)	(2,2)	(3,3)	(4,4)	(5,5)	(5,1)	(6,2)	(7,3)	(8,4)	(9,5)
(1,1)	7	7	7	4	3	1	0	0	0	0
(2,2)	7	7	7	4	3	1	0	0	0	0
(3,3)	7	7	7	4	3	1	0	0	0	0
(4,4)	4	4	4	7	6	3	2	2	1	1
(5,5)	3	3	3	6	7	2	2	2	1	1
(5,1)	1	1	1	3	2	7	6	6	4	4
(6,2)	0	0	0	2	2	6	7	7	5	5
(7,3)	0	0	0	2	2	6	7	7	4	4
(8,4)	0	0	0	1	1	4	5	4	7	7
(9,5)	0	0	0	1	1	4	5	4	7	7

three out of the seven partitions. Using these counts we compute S_{ij} for all possible pairs and show the resultant matrix S in Table 7.16. Using the SLA we get a two-partition based on the following steps:

- Merge pairs of points and form clusters based on the largest similarity value of 7 between each pair of points. The clusters are:

$$\{(1,1),(2,2),(3,3)\}, \ \{(6,2),(7,3)\}, \ \{(8,4),(9,5)\}, \ \{(5,1)\},$$
$$\{(4,4)\}, \ \{(5,5)\}.$$

- Now merge pairs of clusters based on the next largest similarity value which is 6 here. The clusters are:

$$\{(1,1),(2,2),(3,3)\}, \ \{(5,1),(6,2),(7,3)\}, \ \{(8,4),(9,5)\},$$
$$\{(4,4),(5,5)\}.$$

- Now consider the similarity value of 5 to merge clusters further. The resulting clusters are:

$$\{(1,1),(2,2),(3,3)\}, \ \{(5,1),(6,2),(7,3),(8,4),(9,5)\},$$
$$\{(4,4),(5,5)\}.$$

- Finally by considering the similarity value of 4 to merge clusters we get:

$$\{(1,1),(2,2),(3,3),(4,4),(5,5)\}, \ \{(5,1),(6,2),(7,3),(8,4),(9,5)\}.$$

Now we have two clusters. So, we stop here. Note that the base algorithm used here in the form of K-means cannot generate the resulting clusters using a single application because clusters in Figure 7.12 are chain like clusters.

Research Ideas

1. In Section 1, the number of hard partitions of a set of n patterns into K clusters is discussed. How do we control the number of such partitions? Do divide-and-conquer based algorithms help?

Relevant References

(a) M. R. Anderberg, *Cluster Analysis for Applications*. New York: Academic Press, 1973.

(b) M. N. Murty and G. Krishna, A computationally efficient technique for data-clustering. *Pattern Recognition*, 12(3):153–158, 1980.

(c) S. Guha, A. Meyerson, N. Mishra, R. Motwani and L. O. Callaghan, Clustering data streams: Theory and practice. *IEEE Transactions on Knowledge and Data Engineering*, 15(3):515–528, 2003.

(d) C.-J. Hseieh, S. Si and I. Dhillon, A divide-and-conquer solver for Kernel support vector machines. In *Proceedings of ICML*, 2014.

2. In addition to divide-and-conquer which other approaches help in reducing the number of partitions being considered? Is it good to consider incremental algorithms?

Relevant References

(a) H. Spath, *Cluster Analysis Algorithms for Data Reduction and Classification of Objects*. London: E. Horwood, 1980.

(b) T. Zhang, R. Ramakrishnan and M. Livny, BIRCH: An efficient data clustering method for very large databases. *Proceedings of SIGMOD*, 1996.

(c) V. Garg, Y. Narahari and M. N. Murty, Novel biobjective clustering (BIGC) based on cooperative game theory. *IEEE Transactions on Knowledge and Data Engineering*, 25(5):1070–1082, 2013.

3. Incremental algorithms are order-dependent. Which properties does an incremental algorithm needs to satisfy so as to be order-independent?

Relevant References

(a) B. Shekar, M. N. Murty and G. Krishna, Structural aspects of semantic-directed clusters. *Pattern Recognition*, 22(1):65–74, 1989.

(b) L. Rokach and O. Maimon, Clustering methods. In *Data Mining and Knowledge Discovery Handbook*, O. Z. Maimon and L. Rokach (eds.). New York: Springer, 2006.

4. Is it possible to characterize the order-dependence property of the Leader algorithm as follows?

Conjecture 1. *The Leader algorithm is order-dependent if and only if there exist three points X_i, X_j, and X_k such that $d(X_i, X_j) < T$, $d(X_j, X_k) < T$, and $d(X_i, X_k) > T$ where T is the distance threshold specified.*

5. By specifying an axiomatic framework there are results on impossibility of clustering. How do we suitably modify such axiomatic frameworks to make clustering possible but by considering a small number of partitions?

Relevant References

(a) B. Shekar, M. N. Murty and G. Krishna, A knowledge-based clustering scheme. *Pattern Recognition Letters*, 5(4):253–259, 1987.

(b) J. Kleinberg, An impossibility theorem for clustering. *Proceedings of NIPS*, 2002.

(c) S. Ben-David and M. Ackerman, Measures of clustering quality: A working set of axioms for clustering. *Proceedings of NIPS*, 2008.

6. In Section 2, both partitional and hierarchical clustering algorithms are considered. How does one hybridize these approaches?

Relevant References

(a) M. N. Murty and G. Krishna, A hybrid clustering procedure for concentric and chain-like clusters. *International Journal of Parallel Programming*, 10(6):397–412, 1981.

(b) S. Zhong and J. Ghosh, A unified framework for model-based clustering. *Journal of Machine Learning Research*, 4:1001–1037, 2003.

(c) L. Kankanala and M. N. Murty, Hybrid approaches for clustering. *Proceedings of PREMI*, LNCS 4815:25–32, 2007.

7. In spectral clustering it is assumed that the data is presented in the form of a graph. Is there a major difference between converting high-dimensional datasets into similarity/distance weighted graphs and using graphs like the Facebook social network or www?

Relevant References

(a) N. Mishra, R. Schreiber, I. Stanton and R. E. Tarjan, Clustering social networks. *Proceedings of WAW*, LNCS 4863:56–67, 2007.

(b) U. Luxburg, A tutorial on spectral clustering. *Statistics and Computing*, 17(4):395–416, 2007.

(c) M. C. V. Nascimento and A. C. P. L. F. de Carvalho, Spectral methods for graph clustering A survey. *European Journal of Operations Research*, 211:221–231, 2011.

8. Frequent itemsets have been used successfully in both classification and clustering. What is the reason for frequent itemsets to be useful in clustering?

Relevant References

(a) S. Mimaroglu and D. A. Simovic, Clustering and approximate identification of frequent item sets. *Proceedings of FLAIRS*, 2007.

(b) H. Cheng, X. Yan, J. Han and P. S. Yu, Direct discriminative pattern mining for effective classification. *Proceedings of ICDE*, 2008.

(c) G. V. R. Kiran and V. Pudi, Frequent itemset based hierarchical document clustering using Wikipedia as external knowledge. *LNCS*, 6277:11–20, 2010.

(d) A. Kiraly, A. Gyenesei and J. Abonyi, Bit-table based biclustering and frequent closed itemset mining in high-dimensional binary data. *The Scientific World Journal*, 2014. http://dx.doi.org/10.1155/2014/870406.

9. Clustering is a data compression tool. How to exploit this feature? Are there better schemes for compression? Can we cluster compressed data?

Relevant References

(a) R. Cilibrasi and P. M. B. Vitányi, Clustering by compression. *IEEE Trans. on Information Theory*, 51(4):1523–1545, 2005.

(b) T. R. Babu, M. N. Murty and S. V. Subrahmanya, *Compression Schemes for Mining Large Datasets: A Machine Learning Perspective*. New York: Springer, 2013.

(c) A. Schmieder, H. Cheng and X. Li, A study of clustering algorithms and validity for lossy image set compression. *Proceedings of IPCV*, 2009.

(d) J. Han, M. Kamber and J. Pei, *Data Mining: Concepts and Techniques*. New York: Morgan Kaufmann, 2011.

10. How do we use clustering in synthesizing patterns?

Relevant References

(a) P. Viswanath, M. N. Murty and S. Bhatnagar, Pattern synthesis for non-parametric pattern recognition. *Encyclopedia of Data Warehousing and Mining*: 1511–1516, 2009.

(b) M. Agrawal, N. Gupta, R. Shreelekshmi and M. N. Murty, Efficient pattern synthesis for nearest neighbour classifier. *Pattern Recognition*, 38(11):2200–2203, 2005.

(c) H. Seetha, R. Saravanan and M. N. Murty, Pattern synthesis using multiple Kernel learning for efficient SVM classification. *Cybernetics and Information Technologies*, 12:77–94, 2012.

11. Clustering is usually associated with grouping unlabeled patterns. What is the advantage in clustering labeled patterns?

Relevant References

(a) V. Sridhar and M. N. Murty, A knowledge-based clustering algorithm. *Pattern Recognition Letters*, 12(8):511–517, 1991.

(b) M. Grbovic, N. Djuric, S. Guo and S. Vucetic, Supervised clustering of label ranking data using label preference information. *Machine Learning*, 93(2–3):191–225, 2013.

12. How to incorporate knowledge from multiple sources to perform clustering better?

Relevant References

(a) M. N. Murty and A. K. Jain, Knowledge-based clustering scheme for collection management and retrieval of library books. *Pattern Recognition*, 28(8):949–963, 1995.

(b) X. Hu, X. Zhang, C. Lu, E. K. Park and X. Zhou, Exploiting Wikipedia as external knowledge for document clustering. *Proceedings of KDD*, 2009.

13. How do you perform ensemble clustering in an optimal way?

Relevant References

(a) A. K. Jain, Data clustering: 50 years beyond K-means. *Pattern recognition Letters*, 31(8):651–666, 2010.

(b) S. Vega-Pons and J. Ruiz-Shulcloper, A survey of clustering ensemble algorithms. *International Journal of Pattern Recognition and Artificial Intelligence*, 25(3):337–372, 2011.

(c) T. R. Babu, M. N. Murty and V. K. Agrawal, Adaptive boosting with leader based learners for classification of large handwritten data. *Proceedings of HIS*, 2004.

Chapter 8

Soft Clustering

Clustering has been one of the most popular tools in data mining. Even though hard clustering has been popularly studied and traditionally used, there are several important applications where soft partitioning is essential. Some of these applications include *text mining* and *social networks*. Soft partitioning is concerned with assigning a document in text mining or a person in a social network to more than one cluster. For example, the same document may belong to both *sports* and *politics*. In several cases softness has to be appropriately interpreted to make a hard decision; such a process permits us to delay the decision making. So, one of the major characteristics of softness is in delaying decision making as far as possible. Another notion is to acknowledge the assignment of a pattern to more than one category.

We can work out the number of soft partitions of n patterns into K clusters as follows:

- Let $X_1, X_2, \ldots, X_n$ be the n patterns and $C_1, C_2, \ldots, C_K$ be the K clusters. In soft clustering, a pattern may belong to one or more clusters. So, if pattern X_i belongs to cluster C_j then we record a 1 as the ijth element of cluster indicator matrix (CIM) otherwise we store a 0.
- Note that the number of 1s in the ith row of CIM can vary between 1 to K. This can be chosen in $2^K - 1$ ways by ruling out the all zero vector because X_i has to be assigned to at least one of the K clusters.

- So for each row in CIM we have $2^K - 1$ choices; for all the n rows the number of possibilities is $(2^K - 1)^n$ which is of $O(2^{Kn})$. This is an upper bound because no column in CIM can be empty.
- Instead of storing a 1 or a 0 if we store one of P possible values to indicate the extent to which X_i belongs to C_j, then the number of possibilities is bounded by $(P^K - 1)^n$ as the number of distinct values each entry in CIM can assume is P. In some of the soft clustering algorithms the value of P could be very large; theoretically it could be infinite.

1. Soft Clustering Paradigms

There are a variety of soft clustering paradigms. Each of them has a distinct flavor. Some of the important ones are:

1. **Fuzzy Clustering:** Fuzzy clustering and related possibilistic clustering is the most popularly established and studied soft clustering paradigm. It is so popular that routinely soft clustering is interpreted as fuzzy clustering; again fuzzy c-means clustering algorithm is the most frequently considered algorithm here. Each pattern X_i may be assigned to a cluster C_j with a membership value μ_{ij} which indicates the degree to which X_i belongs to C_j. It is assumed that $\mu_{ij} \in [0, 1]$ and $\sum_{j=1}^{K} \mu_{ij} = 1$.

2. **Rough Clustering:** When there is uncertainty in assigning patterns to clusters which means it is difficult to specify clusters as sets, then we can use *rough sets* to characterize the uncertainty. There could be patterns that clearly belong to only one cluster; other patterns may belong to two or more clusters. This is abstracted by a rough set which is represented using two sets; these sets are called *lower approximation* and *upper approximation*. A pattern can belong to at most one lower approximation. If a pattern does not belong to any lower approximation then it belongs to two or more upper approximations.

3. **Evolutionary Algorithms for Clustering:** Evolutionary approaches including *genetic algorithms* (GAs), *evolutionary schemes*, and *evolutionary programming* are three popular tools

used in both hard and soft clusterings. Unlike the other approaches, here a collection of possible solutions (*population*) is simultaneously processed leading to a more effective scheme for pursuing important solution directions. GAs have been shown to lead to optimal hard clustering based on squared error criterion under some acceptable conditions.

4. **Statistical Clustering:** Here each pattern is viewed as a vector in the multi-dimensional space. So clusters are viewed as regions of points in the space. Hence, this approach is also based on *geometric* or *vector space* models. Typically geometric models are popular in *computational geometry, graphics and visualization*. Similarly vector space model is the most popular in *information retrieval*. Because regions can overlap or vectors can be associated with multiple regions, statistical models can be potentially soft.

Popular hard clustering algorithms like the K-means algorithm can be modified to be soft. There are several soft versions of the K-means algorithm which will be discussed in later sections. Leader algorithm is one of the most efficient hard clustering algorithms and it can be modified to perform soft clustering. Because of the similarity between leader and BIRCH it is possible to have a soft version BIRCH also.

5. **Neural Networks for Clustering:** artificial neural networks (ANNs) have been popularly used in clustering; self organizing map (SOM) is the most popular of them. Typically ANNs employ sigmoid type of activation functions which return positive real values in the range 0 to 1. So, based on the output values returned ANNs also can be used for soft clustering. ANNs may be viewed as statistical clustering tools. A major restriction of the ANNs is that they can deal with only numerical vectors. It is possible to view support vector machine (SVM) as the most popular and state-of-the-art ANN.

6. **Probabilistic Clustering:** Conventionally vector space models and probabilistic models are treated as different in the area of information retrieval. Further, probabilistic models are typically viewed as *generative models*; once we have the model

we can generate patterns of the corresponding cluster. In fact probabilistic models may be viewed as theoretical and their implementations are based on statistics. For example, the Bayesian models are inherently probabilistic and without knowing the prior probabilities and likelihood values it is not possible to use them in practice; here statistics provides appropriate implementable approximations. This is achieved by employing estimation schemes. Probabilistic models are inherently soft. For example, while using a Bayesian model in a two class problem, it is possible that none of the two posterior probabilities is zero; in such a case the pattern belongs to both the classes but to different degrees based on the posteriors.

Expectation maximization (EM) is a well-known probabilistic clustering algorithm. It may be viewed as a probabilistic variant of the K-means algorithm. It is the most popular soft clustering algorithm in the history of pattern recognition and machine learning. Some of the other examples include *probabilistic latent semantic indexing (PLSI)* and *latent dirichlet allocation (LDA)* which are popular in document clustering.

Among these, clustering based on *fuzzy sets, rough sets, evolutionary algorithms,* and *neural networks* are traditionally identified with the soft computing paradigm. Even though there is a significant amount of work done in these areas and reported in a variety of important journals and conference proceedings, statistical and probabilistic paradigms have gained a lot of prominence recently; they are fashionable currently. Because of the increasing interest in statistical learning theory, soft clustering based on EM and its variants is arguably the most popular now. We discuss each of the soft clustering paradigms in detail in the upcoming sections.

2. Fuzzy Clustering

Typically each cluster is abstracted using one or more representative patterns. For example, centroid and leader are popularly used representatives of a cluster. Let R_i be the set of representatives of a cluster C_i. Then a pattern X is assigned to one or more clusters based on the following:

- In hard clustering we assign X to cluster C_i if $Similarity(X, R_i) > Similarity(X, R_j)$ for all $j \neq i$ or equivalently $distance(X, R_i) < distance(X, R_j)$ for all $j \neq i$. It requires some appropriate definition of similarity and distance. In case of having a single representative for each cluster, for example the centroid of the cluster, Euclidean distance between X and R_i is popularly used to characterize proximity where R_i is the centroid of the ith cluster. Here the *winner-take-all* strategy is used to realize the hard clustering; this is based on assigning X to only one cluster (winner cluster gets the pattern) based on minimum distance or maximum similarity between X and the cluster representative.
- An alternative to winner-take-all is to assign X to more than one cluster based on the proximity between X and each R_i. Similarity between X and R_i is used to characterize the membership of X in C_i. This is typically used in *possibilistic clustering*; the similarity values are suitably normalized so that they add up to one in the case of *fuzzy clustering*.

Both hard K-means and Leader clustering algorithms can be suitably modified to realize their fuzzy counterparts; among them the Fuzzy K-means algorithm is more popular which we describe next.

2.1. Fuzzy K-means algorithm

It goes through an iterative scheme like the K-means algorithm. Starting with some initial assignment of points, it goes through the following steps:

1. **Obtain Membership Values:**

$$\mu_{ij} = \frac{\|X_j - R_i\|^{-2/(M-1)}}{\sum_{l=1}^{K} (\|X_j - R_l\|)^{-2/(M-1)}}.$$

2. **Compute the Fuzzy Cluster Centroids:**

$$\text{Centroid}_i = R_i = \frac{\sum_{j=1}^{n}(\mu_{ij})^M X_j}{\sum_{j=1}^{n}(\mu_{ij})^M},$$

where

- μ_{ij} = Membership value of pattern X_j in cluster C_i for $j = 1, 2, \ldots, n$ and $i = 1, 2, \ldots, K$.
- $\|X_j - R_i\|$ typically is the Euclidean distance between X_j and R_i.
- R_i = Centroid of the ith cluster.
- M is the fuzzifying constant. If $M = 1$ then the Fuzzy algorithm works like the hard K-means algorithm. This is because $\mu_{ij} = 1$ when X_j is assigned to C_i; note that in the expression for μ_{ij}, the exponent of the distance between X_j and R_l in the denominator will be tending to $-\infty$ for each l. So, the smallest of them will be selected which is equal to the numerator $(\|X_j - R_i\|^{-2/(M-1)})$ and hence $\mu_{ij} = 1$. If the value of M is large or tends to ∞ then $\mu_{ij} = \frac{1}{K}$ as the exponents in both the numerator and denominator tend to 0.

3. The above two terms are updated iteratively by the Fuzzy K-means algorithm; assign each pattern to its nearest fuzzy centroid and update the μ_{ij} and R_i values. The algorithm stops when there is no significant change in these values computed over two successive iterations.

It is possible to show that the Fuzzy K-means algorithm minimizes a variant of the squared error given by

$$\sum_{i=1}^{K} \sum_{i=1}^{n} (\mu_{ij})^M \|X_j - R_i\|^2.$$

Both the hard and fuzzy K-means algorithms can be guaranteed to reach the locally optimal solution of their respective objective functions. A similar form of softness can be extended to realize fuzzy versions of other hard clustering algorithms.

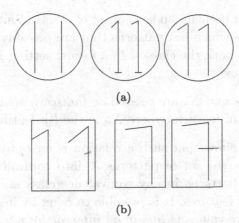

(a)

(b)

Figure 8.1. Examples of patterns from two classes. (a) A Collection of Ones. (b) A Collection of Sevens.

3. Rough Clustering

A rough set is characterized using the notion of the *indiscernability relation* that is defined based on equivalence classes of objects. Here, some patterns are known to definitely belong to a cluster. For example consider the patterns shown in Figure 8.1. There are two classes of character patterns in the figure; some are of character 1 (shown in Figure 8.1(a)) and others are of character 7 (shown in Figure 8.1(b)). There are four patterns that definitely belong to 1 and 4 patterns that definitely belong to 7. In the case of ones there are three equivalence classes bounded by circles; characters in each circle are similar to each other. Elements in the first two equivalence classes (considered from left to right) shown in Figure 8.1(a) definitely belong to class of 1 s. Similarly in Figure 8.1(b) there are three equivalence classes of sevens and these are bounded by rectangles in the figure; all of them definitely belong to class of 7 s. However, there is one equivalence class (third) in Figure 8.1(a) where the patterns are either ones or sevens; these two patterns are possibly ones or sevens.

Patterns in these equivalence classes are *indiscernible*; note that 1 s class consists of union of the two indiscernible equivalence classes and similarly all the three equivalence classes in Figure 8.1(b) are also indiscernible and their union is a subset of class of 7 s. The remaining equivalence class which has patterns that are possibly ones or sevens can be subset of both the classes. In a formal setting *indiscernability* is defined as follows:

Two patterns X_i and X_j are related or *indiscernible* if $X_{il} = X_{jl}$ for all l in a subset of features where X_{il} is the lth feature value of X_i.

It is possible to show that such a relation is an *equivalence relation* and it partitions the set of patterns $\mathcal{X}$ into equivalence classes. In this set up two patterns in any equivalence class are *identical* on a chosen subset of features. It is possible to relax by insisting that the two patterns have values *falling in an interval*, for a feature, than the values being identical. In this setting the notion of similarity based on overlapping intervals instead of values could be exploited to form the equivalence classes.

Once we have the equivalence classes based on similarity on the set of features F we can define rough set using the *lower approximation* $(\underline{F}S)$ and the *upper approximation* $(\overline{F}S)$ where $S \subseteq \mathcal{X}$ as follows:

$$\underline{F}S = \cup_i E_i, \quad \text{where } E_i \subseteq S, \tag{1}$$

$$\overline{F}S = \cup_i E_i, \quad \text{where } E_i \cap S \neq \phi. \tag{2}$$

Note that in the lower approximation we insist that each equivalence be completely (or definitely) in S whereas in the upper approximation we consider equivalence classes that partially overlap with S. Hence, the lower approximation contains patterns that definitely belong to S and the upper approximation has patterns that may possibly belong to S. Additionally, we have:

- *Boundary Region of S* is given by $\overline{F}S - \underline{F}S$. If the boundary region has no elements then there is no roughness in S with respect to F.
- Lower approximation may be viewed as the core part of a cluster. Lower approximations of two clusters do not overlap. So, if a pattern X (definitely) belongs to the lower approximation of a rough cluster then it will not be present in any other cluster.

- A lower approximation of a cluster is a subset of its upper approximation.
- If a pattern X belongs to the boundary region of a cluster, then it belongs to at least one more upper approximations.

We use these properties in designing rough clustering algorithms; a popular algorithm for rough clustering is the Rough K-means algorithm which we discuss in the next subsection.

3.1. Rough K-means algorithm

Rough K-means algorithm is the most popular among the rough clustering algorithms. Basically we have to characterize assignment of a pattern to a rough cluster and computation of the centroid of a rough cluster. We discuss these steps below:

1. **Assigning a Pattern:** A pattern X is assigned to one or more clusters. This may be done as follows:

   (a) **Initialize:** Let $C_1, C_2, \ldots, C_K$ be the K clusters with centroids $R_1, R_2, \ldots, R_K$ respectively. These centroids are obtained based on some initial assignment of patterns to clusters.

   (b) **Obtain the Nearest Centroid:** Obtain the nearest centroid R_j of pattern X based on

   $$d(X, R_j) = \frac{min}{1 \leq i \leq K} d(X, R_i).$$

   (c) **Obtain Other Nearer Centroids:** Choose an ϵ and obtain all the clusters $i \, (\neq j)$ such that $d(X, R_i) \leq (1 + \epsilon)d(X, R_j)$.

   (d) **Assign to Multiple Clusters:** If there are $q(2 \leq q \leq K - 1)$ such i's given by $i_1, i_2, \ldots, i_q$, then assign X to $\overline{F}C_{i_1}, \overline{F}C_{i_2}, \ldots, \overline{F}C_{i_q}$.

   (e) **Assign to a Single Cluster j:** If there is no such i then assign X to the lower approximation of the rough cluster C_j, that is $\underline{F}C_j$. Note that by the property of rough sets, X is also assigned automatically to $\overline{F}C_j$.

2. **Updating Centroids:** Unlike the conventional K-means algorithm, here centroids are updated by assigning different weightages to patterns based on whether they are in a lower approximation or in multiple upper approximations. Specifically centroids are updated as follows:

   (a) If $\underline{F}C_j = \overline{F}C_j$ and $\underline{F}C_j \neq \phi$ then its centroid R_j is

   $$R_j = \frac{\sum_{X \in \underline{F}C_j} X}{|\underline{F}C_j|}.$$

   (b) If $\underline{F}C_j = \phi$ and $\overline{F}C_j \neq \phi$ then $R_j = \frac{\sum_{X \in (\overline{F}C_j)} X}{|\overline{F}C_j|}$.

   (c) If $\underline{F}C_j \neq \phi$ and $\overline{F}C_j \neq \underline{F}C_j$ then

   $$R_j = w_l \frac{\sum_{X \in \underline{F}C_j} X}{|\underline{F}C_j|} + w_u \frac{\sum_{X \in (\overline{F}C_j - \underline{F}C_j)} X}{|\overline{F}C_j - \underline{F}C_j|}.$$

   Here, w_l and w_u correspond to the weightages or importance associated with the lower and upper approximations respectively. They add upto 1; that is $w_l + w_u = 1$.

The above two steps are iteratively used to realize the Rough K-means algorithm.

4. Clustering Based on Evolutionary Algorithms

Evolutionary algorithms are inspired by some of the important properties of natural evolution; *survival of the fittest* and *exchange of genetic material* using crossover or recombination are two such functions captured by evolutionary operators. An evolutionary algorithm typically has the following steps:

(1) **Initialization:** A collection of possible solutions, called *population*, is chosen.
(2) **Evaluation:** The *fitness* of each element of the population is computed based on a fitness function.
(3) **Selection:** A pair of solutions is selected at a time based on the fitness value assigned to each of the possible solutions in Step 2.

It is common to view selection as an *exploitation operator* where domain-knowledge-based fitness values are exploited to select fit individuals for further processing. Recombination and mutation are helpful in exploring the search space and are described next. Because of this judicial combination of exploitation and exploration, evolutionary algorithms may be considered as focused (exploitation) random-search (exploration) algorithms.

(4) **Recombination:** Using the recombination operation on the two selected solutions, two offspring/children are generated.

(5) **Mutation:** The two children generated using recombination are modified based on randomly chosen values in the string and by mutating these values. The resulting solutions are placed in the next population. The process of selecting a pair of strings, recombination and mutation are repeated till the required number of solutions to fill the next population is generated.

(6) **Termination:** Steps 2 to 5 are repeated till some termination condition is satisfied. Going through Steps 2 to 5 once generates from the population at the current instance ($\mathcal{P}_t$) a new population corresponding to the next time instance ($\mathcal{P}_{t+1}$). Such a process of generating $\mathcal{P}_{t+1}$ from $\mathcal{P}_t$ is called a *generation*. In a practical setting the evolutionary algorithm terminates after a specified number of generations.

We briefly explain below how various steps listed above are realized in clustering a collection of n patterns. For the sake of illustration we consider a two-dimensional dataset: $\mathcal{X} = A : (1,1)^t; B : (1,2)^t; C : (2,2)^t; D : (6,2)^t; E : (7,2)^t; F : (6,6)^t; G : (7,6)^t$.

1. Initialization:

- Let N be the size of a population; N is typically chosen to be even. The size of the population is chosen based on the size of the solution space and computational resources.
- The N initial solutions are typically randomly chosen; it is the right thing to do in the absence of any other information. If additional knowledge about the problem is available, then it can be used to choose the initial solutions.

- Each solution corresponds to a partition of the dataset and may be viewed as a string. Some of the possibilities are:

  (a) In the case of GAs, each solution string is conventionally a binary string. We can represent the partition: $C_1 = \{A, B, C\}$; $C_2 = \{D, E\}$; $C_3 = \{F, G\}$ using the binary string

  1 1 1 0 0 0 0; 0 0 0 1 1 0 0; 0 0 0 0 0 1 1

  which has 3 substrings where each cluster is represented by a substring of size 7; if a pattern is in a cluster then we place a 1 in that location, otherwise a 0. There will be K substrings if there are K clusters and each substring is of length n. This view permits soft clustering. For example, the binary string

  1 1 1 0 0 0 0; 1 0 0 1 1 0 0; 0 0 0 0 1 1 1

  indicates overlapping clusters where A belongs to both C_1 and C_2 and E is in both C_2 and C_3.

  (b) Another popular representation employs string-of-group-numbers. Each character in the string represents a cluster (or group) number. For example:

  1 1 1 2 2 3 3 represents a hard partition which indicates that A, B, and C belong to cluster 1; D and E belong to cluster 2; patterns F, G are in cluster 3. This characterizes the hard partition $C_1 = \{A, B, C\}; C_2 = \{D, E\}; C_3 = \{F, G\}$. This representation does not permit soft clustering using cluster numbers 1 to K.

  (c) String-of-centroids representation employs a real vector to represent each location in the string. Specifically each string represents K cluster centers; each cluster center is a string of size d where d is the dimensionality of the vectors. For example consider the representation:

  1.33, 1.66; 6.5, 2.0; 6.5, 6.0

which consists of three centroids each of them in a two-dimensional space which corresponds to the partition: $C_1 = \{A, B, C\}; C_2 = \{D, E\}; C_3 = \{F, G\}$ because A, B and C are closer to the centroid $(1.33, 1.66)^t$; D and E are nearer to the centroid $(6.5, 2.0)^t$; and F and G are closer to the centroid $(6.5, 6.0)^t$. Note that the string-of-centroids representation corresponds to the string-of-group-numbers representation given by 1 1 1 2 2 3 3; in fact there is a correspondence between these two representations in general. There is a bijection between sets of equivalence classes of the two types defined as follows:

— Two string-of-group-numbers S_{g_i} and S_{g_j} are related by a binary relation R_g if they both correspond to the same partition of $\mathcal{X}$. For example, consider the strings 1 1 1 2 2 3 3 and 2 2 2 1 1 3 3; both of them lead to the same partition of $\mathcal{X}$ given by $\{\{X_1, X_2, X_3\}, \{X_4, X_5\}, \{X_6, X_7\}\}$. Note that R_g is an equivalence relation on the set of string-of-group-numbers representations; R_g partitions the set into equivalence classes where all the strings in each equivalence class are related. Let EC_{R_g} be the set of equivalence classes.

— Two strings-of-centroids S_{c_i} and S_{c_j} are related by a binary relation R_c if they both correspond to the same partition of $\mathcal{X}$. For example, the strings-of-centroids $(1, 1); (1.5, 2); (6.5, 4),$ and $(1, 1); (1.5, 2); (6, 4)$ correspond to the same partition of $\mathcal{X}$ given by $\{\{(1, 1)\}, \{(1, 2), (2, 2)\}, \{(6, 2), (7, 2), (6, 6), (7, 6)\}\}$. Again note that R_c is an equivalence relation on the set of strings-of-centroids and partitions it into equivalence classes. Let EC_{R_c} be the set of these equivalence classes.

— There is a bijection between EC_{R_g} and EC_{R_c}. Associated with each partition of $\mathcal{X}$ there is an element of EC_{R_g} and an element of EC_{R_c} which map to each other by the bijection.

2. **Fitness Computation:** It is essential to associate a fitness value with each solution string; this association could be based on one or more criterion functions. This is required to select highly fit strings for further exploration. Let us consider for each type of representation how fitness value is computed.

   (a) Because there is a correspondence between string-of-group-numbers and string-of-centroids we consider them together. Consider the partition given by

   String-of-group-numbers: 1 1 1 3 3 2 2 and equivalently
   String-of-centroids: 1.33,1.66; 6.5,2.0; 6.5,6.0

   it is the optimal partition and the with-in-group-error-sum-of-squares value is

   $1.33 + 0.5 + 0.5 = 2.33$, where the left-hand side indicates the contribution of each cluster.

   Next consider the partition given by

   string-of-group-numbers: 1 2 2 3 3 3 3 and equivalently
   string-of-centroids: 1.0,1.0; 1.5,2.0; 6.5,4.0.

   Here, the squared error value given by the sum over the three clusters is

   $$0 + 0.5 + 17.0 = 17.5.$$

   (b) Consider the binary representation for a hard partition given by

   1 1 1 0 0 0 0; 0 0 0 1 1 0 0; 0 0 0 0 0 1 1.

   In this case also the squared error is given by 2.33 which corresponds to the optimal partition. It is possible to consider the soft partition given by

   1 1 1 0 0 0 0; 1 0 0 1 1 0 0; 0 0 0 0 0 1 1.

   In this case there are some patterns that belong to more than one cluster. In such a situation we can compute a modified version of the squared error. This modification is achieved by adding weighted contributions from different patterns in computing the squared error. The weight for a pattern is 1 if it belongs to a single cluster. If a pattern belongs to more than one cluster, then a suitable weight is assigned to a pattern for each cluster based on its distance to centroid of each cluster to which the pattern belongs.

For example consider the soft partition given by

$$1\ 1\ 1\ 0\ 0\ 0\ 0; 1\ 0\ 0\ 1\ 1\ 0\ 0; 0\ 0\ 0\ 0\ 1\ 1\ 1,$$

where $A \in C_1$ and C_2 and $E \in C_2$ and C_3. By noting that the cluster centers are: $(1.33,1.66)$; $(4.66,1.66)$; $(6.66,4.66)$ we can compute the distances between A $(1,1)^t$ and the centroids of C_1 and C_2; the squared distances are $\frac{5}{9}$ and $\frac{125}{9}$ which can be used to assign the weights as $\frac{125}{130}$ and $\frac{5}{130}$. In a similar manner one can compute the weights for E $(7,2)^t$ based on the ratio of squared distances to centroids of C_2 and C_3 which will be $\frac{50}{9}$ and $\frac{65}{9}$. So, the weights are $\frac{50}{115}$ and $\frac{65}{115}$. Using these weights the squared error computed is $1.3 + 5.6 + 8.5 = 15.4$. We have suggested a simple scheme here; a modified version of this scheme is used in characterizing the fuzzy criterion function.

(c) **Multi-objective Optimization Problem (MOOP):** In several real-world problems the optimization problem might involve more than one criterion function to be optimized. For example, minimizing squared error without any constraint on the number of clusters K will mean that the minimum squared error is zero when $K = n$; in this case each pattern is a cluster. However, in real-world applications, we want a much smaller K. So, we need to minimize both the squared error and the number of clusters. In addition to the objective function, we may have a set of constraints. The two directions for dealing with MOOP are:

(i) Take a weighted combination of the multiple criterion functions and treat the resulting function as a single-objective criterion function.

(ii) Treat the multi-objective criterion as a vector of individual objectives. Here we consider a feasible solution dominating another based on how the two solutions are related on each criterion function value; based on the non-dominated set of solutions we have pareto-optimal set and we consider such solutions.

3. **Selection:** Selection is carried out by using the *survival of the fittest strategy*. We have to select a solution so that the squared error is minimized. However, it is convenient to implement selection based on maximizing some criterion function. So, a simple mapping that we implement is to take the reciprocal of the squared error value and maximize it assuming that the squared error is not 0 for any solution string. Let us illustrate using the two-dimensional example considered in computing the squared error values. We use the string-of-centroids representation. We give in Table 8.1 a string-of-centroids; the squared error; its reciprocal; and the probability of selection proportional to the reciprocal. Note that selection probability shown in the last column is obtained by normalizing the reciprocal of the fitness value. For example, for string 1 the selection probability is $\frac{0.43}{(0.43+0.057+0.046)} = 0.807$. The other probability values are obtained similarly. Assuming for a while that the population has three strings shown in Table 8.1 we generate a uniformly distributed random number r in the range 0 to 1. We select the first string if $r \leq 0.807$; the second string if $0.807 < r \leq 0.914(0.807 + 0.107)$; a copy of the third string is selected if $0.914 < r \leq 1$. Note that the first string has very high

Table 8.1. Three different solution strings.

String number	Centroid1	Centroid2	Centroid3	Squared error	Fitness = 1/squared error	Selection probability
1	(1.33,1.66)	(6.5,2.0)	(6.5,6.0)	2.33	0.43	0.807
2	(1.00,1.00)	(1.5,2.0)	(6.5,4.0)	17.5	0.057	0.107
3	(1.00,1.00)	(1.0,2.0)	(5.6,3.6)	21.88	0.046	0.086

Table 8.2. Crossover on two strings.

String	Centroid1	Centroid2	Centroid3	Squared error	Fitness = 1/squared error
Parent 1	*(1.0,1.0)*	*(6.5,2.0)*	*(1.5,2.0)*	33.5	0.03
Parent 2	(1.0,1.0)	(1.0,2.0)	(6.0,6.0)	34	0.03
Child 1	*(1.0,1.0)*	*(6.5,2.0)*	(6.0,6.0)	3.5	0.29
Child 2	(1.0,1.0)	(1.0,2.0)	*(1.5,2.0)*	134	0.007

probability of selection. Selection is the popularly used term in GAs; reproduction is the term used in other evolutionary algorithms.

4. **Crossover:** Crossover is a binary operator; it takes two strings as input and combines them to output two children strings. This may be illustrated using the data in Table 8.2. By considering two parent strings that are not highly fit crossover results a child (child 1) that is highly fit (squared error = 3.5).

   - Here we have used a single-point crossover operator where the genetic material is exchanged across the crossover point.
   - The crossover point is randomly selected. In the dataset shown in Table 8.2, the crossover point is selected between centroid2 and centroid3.
   - Based on this crossover point the prefix (centroid1 and centroid2) of parent 1 is combined with the suffix (centroid3) of parent 2 to generate child 1. Similarly prefix of parent 2 and suffix of parent 1 are combined to form child 2.
   - Note that in the string-of-centroids representation considered here the crossover point can be selected between two successive centroids.
   - Typically crossover is the popularly used term in GAs whereas *recombination* is used in Evolutionary search.

5. **Mutation:** Mutation is a unary operator; it takes a string as input and outputs a string by mutating some randomly selected values. If the value at position i is v_i and $\delta \in [0,1]$. After mutation v_i

Table 8.3.   A string before and after mutation.

String	Centroid1	Centroid2	Centroid3	Squared error	Fitness = 1/squared error
Input	(1.5,1.5)	(6.5,3.0)	(6.5,6.0)	4.25	$\dfrac{4}{17}$
Output	(1.5,1.5)	(6.5,2.0)	(6.5,6.0)	2.25	$\dfrac{4}{9}$

becomes $v_i + 2\delta v_i$ or $v_i - 2\delta v_i$. We show how it works using the input and output strings shown in Table 8.3.

- By mutating the value 3.0 to 2.0 in centroid2 the reciprocal of the squared error almost doubles.
- Mutation working on a binary string randomly selects a bit position and replaces 0 by 1 and 1 by 0.
- It is possible to show that selection (or reproduction) and mutation are adequate for simulating evolution.
- *Evolutionary Programming* based algorithms use only reproduction and mutation; they do not use recombination.

6. **Steady-state genetic algorithm (SSGA):** Typically crossover and mutation are performed with probabilities P_c and P_μ respectively; further larger P_c values are common, but the value of P_μ is typically very small. Increasing the mutation rate P_μ can lead to random search. It is possible to avoid random search and still increase the value of P_μ by copying some highly fit (*elitist*) strings to the next population. This is exploited by SSGA. It can help us in exploring the search space better by using larger values for P_μ, however it requires a longer time to converge based on generation gap. *Generation gap* between two successive populations $\mathcal{P}_t$ and $\mathcal{P}_{t+1}$ is characterized by the percentage of elitist strings copied from $\mathcal{P}_t$ to $\mathcal{P}_{t+1}$.

It is possible to show that using an elitist strategy the GA converges to the globally optimal solution of the criterion function under some acceptable conditions.

5. Clustering Based on Neural Networks

Some of the important properties of neural networks are *competitive learning* and *self-organization*. Competitive learning is concerned with assigning an input pattern to one or more of the competing output neurons. Typically it is implemented using a two-layer neural network where each input node is connected to all the output nodes. Competitive learning is abstracted with the help of minimization of the error function given by:

$$\sum_{i=1}^{n} \sum_{j=1}^{K} \mu_{ij} \|X_i - R_j\|^2,$$

where μ_{ij} is the membership of X_i in C_j and R_j is the prototype from cluster j that is closer to X_i. Self organization is achieved by using lateral inhibition. The most influential network is the SOM where the output layer is typically two-dimensional. Some of the important features of SOM are:

- It can be viewed as a feature extractor; it can be viewed as representing a high-dimensional input vector as a member of a cluster present in the two-dimensional output layer.
- It is a topological map where transitions in the input patterns are captured in the output layer with topological properties preserved. For example, if we look at transitions from character 1 to character 7 as shown in Figure 8.1 it is captured in the output layer of SOM so that these transitions are captured topologically.
- It employs a strategy called *winner-take-most WTM* which is a soft version of *winner-take-all* strategy. The soft version is implemented by assigning a pattern X_i to more than one node in the output layer by using appropriate values of μ_{ij}. A neighborhood function is used to achieve it.
- Training a SOM works as follows:

  1. If the patterns are d-dimensional, then the input layer has d nodes. Each of the input nodes is connected initially using some random weights to all the nodes in the output layer. The number of nodes in the output layer is chosen based on the resolution at

which the clustering is required. So, each output node is viewed as a d-dimensional vector based on the weights with which the d input nodes are connected to it.

2. For each pattern X_i $(i = 1, 2, \ldots, n)$, the nearest output node is selected based on the Euclidean distance between the pattern and the node which are both d-dimensional vectors. The winner node and its neighbors are updated by

$$R_l(k + 1) = R_l(k) + \eta(k)g_{lm}(k)(X_i - R_l(k)),$$

where the nearest node to X_i is m. $\eta(k)$ is a monotonically decreasing learning rate. In addition to the winning node m, the other nodes (l) in its vicinity are also updated. But the extent to which a neighbor is updated is based on its distance to m and is reflected in g_{lm}. One popularly used function for g_{lm} is the Mexican hat function; another is the Gaussian function given by

$$g_{lm}(k) = c_1 \, exp^{-\frac{\|R_l - R_m\|^2}{exp^{-c_2 k}}},$$

where c_1 and c_2 are constants. Note that if we want to use winner-take-all strategy then we have to update only R_m.

3. It is possible to show that because of the WTM strategy the learning is not trapped by local minima easily and also based on the choice of values of η and other constants like c_1 and c_2 in the update equation it is possible to show some kind of probabilistic convergence to the global optimum.

6. Statistical Clustering

K-means algorithm is a well-known hard partitional clustering algorithm where we use the winner-take-all strategy. It is possible to have an overlapping version of the K-means algorithm that generates a covering instead of a partition. In a covering we have the clusters $C_1, C_2, \ldots, C_K$ of the given dataset $\mathcal{X}$ satisfying the following:

$$\cup_{i=1}^{K} C_i = \mathcal{X} \quad \text{and} \quad C_i \neq \phi \forall i$$
$$\forall X_i \in \mathcal{X} \exists C_j \quad s.t. \ X_i \in C_j.$$

The difference between a covering and a partition is that $C_i \cap C_j = \phi$ for $i \neq j$ in a partition whereas the intersection need not be empty in a covering. Next we describe the Overlapping K-means (OKM) algorithm with the help of a two-dimensional dataset.

6.1. OKM algorithm

1. Let the dataset $\mathcal{X}$ be $\{(1,1), (1,2), (2,2), (6,1), (6,3), (8,1), (8,3)\}$. Choose $K (= 3)$ clusters C_1, C_2, and C_3 with the initial centers randomly chosen from $\mathcal{X}$, say $M_1^{(0)} = (1,2)$, $M_2^{(0)} = (6,1)$, $M_3^{(0)} = (8,3)$.
2. For each $X_i \in \mathcal{X}$ obtain L_i, the list of centroids of clusters to which X_i is assigned. L_i is obtained as follows:

   (a) Compute the distance between X_i and each of the K centroids and rank them in increasing order of distance. For example, the Euclidean distances between $(1,1)$ and the centroids are $1, 5, \sqrt{53}$.

   (b) Assign the nearest centroid to L_i. So, in the example $L_1 = ((1,2)$.

   (c) Keep on including the next centroid in L_i, based on the rank order, if the error in representing X_i using the centroids in L_i is non-increasing. Let $|L_i|$ be the size of L_i; then the error is defined as

$$error(X_i, L_i) = \left\| X_i - \frac{\sum\limits_{j=1}^{|L_i|} M_j}{\sum\limits_{j=1}^{|L_i|} 1} \right\|.$$

In the case of $(1,1)$ the error in using $(1,2)$ is 1. If we consider adding the next centroid, in the rank order, $(6,1)$ then the error is $\left\| (1,1) - \frac{1}{2}[(1,2) + (6,1)] \right\| = 2.55$ which is larger than 1; so, the error increases and we do not add $(6,1)$ to $L1$. So, $L_1 = ((1,2))$.

(d) Similarly for the other patterns we have the lists as follows:

$$(1,2) : L_2 = ((1,2)); (2,2) : L_3 = ((1,2)).$$
$$(6,1) : L_4 = ((6,1)); (6,3) : L_5 = ((6,1),(8,3)).$$
$$(8,1) : L_6 = ((6,1),(8,3)); (8,3) : L_7 = ((8,3)).$$

3. Obtain the clusters based on the assignments and L_i's:

$$C_1 = \{(1,1),(1,2),(2,2)\},$$
$$C_2 = \{(6,1),(6,3),(8,3)\},$$
$$C_3 = \{(6,3),(8,1),(8,3)\}.$$

4. Update the centroids using the weighted average given below:

$$M_k^* = \frac{1}{\sum\limits_{X_i \in C_k} w_i} \sum\limits_{X_i \in C_k} w_i \cdot C_k^i,$$

where $w_i = \frac{1}{|L_i|^2}$ and $C_k^i = |L_i|X_i - \sum_{M_j \in L_i - \{M_k\}} M_j$.

5. Now the updated centroids are

$$M_1^{(1)} = \left(\frac{4}{3}, \frac{5}{3}\right), \quad M_2^{(1)} = \left(\frac{19}{3}, \frac{4}{3}\right), \quad M_3^{(1)} = \left(\frac{23}{3}, \frac{8}{3}\right).$$

6. For the other patterns we have the lists as follows:

$$(1,1) : L_1 = \left(\left(\frac{4}{3}, \frac{5}{3}\right)\right); (1,2) : L_2 = \left(\left(\frac{4}{3}, \frac{5}{3}\right)\right);$$

$$(2,2) : L_3 = \left(\left(\frac{4}{3}, \frac{5}{3}\right)\right)$$

$$(6,1) : L_4 = \left(\left(\frac{19}{3}, \frac{4}{3}\right)\right); (6,3) : L_5 = \left(\left(\frac{19}{3}, \frac{4}{3}\right), \left(\frac{23}{3}, \frac{8}{3}\right)\right)$$

$$(8,1) : L_6 = \left(\left(\frac{19}{3}, \frac{4}{3}\right), \left(\frac{23}{3}, \frac{8}{3}\right)\right); (8,3) : L_7 = \left(\left(\frac{23}{3}, \frac{8}{3}\right)\right).$$

7. Using the details given in Step 4, the updated centroids are:

$$M_1^{(1)} = \left(\frac{4}{3}, \frac{5}{3}\right), \; M_2^{(1)} = \left(\frac{19}{3}, \frac{4}{3}\right), \; M_3^{(1)} = \left(\frac{23}{3}, \frac{8}{3}\right).$$

8. There is no change in the clusters and their centroids during two successive iterations. So, the algorithm terminates and the final clusters obtained are:

$\{(1,1), (1,2), (2,2)\}; \; \{(6,1), (6,3), (8,1)\}; \; \{(8,3), (6,3), (8,1)\}.$

Note that (6,3) and (8,1) belong to two clusters leading to a soft partition.

9. However, initial centroid selection is important here. If the initial centroids chosen are $(1, 2); \; (6, 1); \; (8, 3)$ then the clusters obtained using this algorithm are:

$\{(1,1), (1,2), (2,2)\}; \; \{(6,1), (6,3)\}; \; \{(8,3), (8,1)\}$ which is a hard partition.

6.2. EM-based clustering

K-means algorithm is the most popular hard clustering algorithm in the history of clustering. However several important applications of current interest require soft clustering; these applications include document clustering, customer churn prediction, and social networks. EM algorithm plays an important role in soft clustering. Each of the clusters is viewed as being generated by a hidden or latent variable.

EM has been used in learning hidden markov models (HMMs) in the form of the well-known Baum–Welch algorithm. It is also used in learning the PLSI model. In a nutshell it has revolutionized learning based on probabilistic models including Bayes belief nets and gaussian mixture models (GMMs). It can be viewed as a soft clustering paradigm; more specifically it is a probabilistic version of the popular K-means algorithm.

From a theoretical perspective it could be viewed as data likelihood maximizer. It can effectively deal with incomplete data; such an incompleteness could result because of different reasons:

1. In supervised classification we are given training data $\mathcal{X}$ of n patterns where the ith pattern $X_i \in \mathcal{X}$, $i = 1, \ldots, n$, is a $(d + 1)$-dimensional vector. Typically the first d features are independent and the $(d + 1)$th feature is the class label of the pattern. In such a classification context, it is possible that values of one or more features are missing. Here, EM can be used to learn the parameter values using a single or a mixture of distributions to characterize each class. This is where EM is used in GMMs and HMMs.

2. In clustering, the data given has no class labels; so, each pattern is a d-dimensional vector. Here, EM could be used to obtain the clusters. Note that in this context, the actual clusters are latent or hidden. More specifically we would like each d-dimensional pattern here to be associated with an additional feature; this $(d + 1)$th feature will have as its value one or more cluster labels resulting in a soft clustering of patterns in $\mathcal{X}$. Note that one can use a mixture distribution here also; for example one can learn a mixture of Gaussians using the EM where each cluster is represented by a Gaussian component.

We concentrate on the application of EM to clustering here. We assume that the data given in the form of $\mathcal{X}$ is incomplete because the cluster labels associated with the patterns are not available. The log likelihood function is

$$l(\theta) = \ln p(\mathcal{X}|\theta), \tag{3}$$

where θ is the vector of parameters, corresponding to the distribution/s to be learnt. Let $z_1, z_2, \ldots, z_K$ be the K hidden/latent variables corresponding to the K unknown clusters. Let the joint density of $\mathcal{X}$ and z conditioned on θ be $p(\mathcal{X}, z|\theta)$. Then we can write the log likelihood as the marginal of the conditioned joint likelihood given by

$$l(\theta) = \ln \sum_z p(\mathcal{X}, z|\theta). \tag{4}$$

This equality is difficult to deal with as it involves logarithm of a sum. A form of the Jensen's inequality is useful in simplifying such an expression. We discuss this inequality next.

6.2.1. *Jensen's inequality*

It is important to examine the notion of *convex function* before we discuss Jensen's inequality.

Definition 1. A *function* $f(t)$ *is convex* if

$$f(\alpha t_0 + (1 - \alpha)t_1) \leq \alpha f(t_0) + (1 - \alpha)f(t_1) \quad \text{for } 0 \leq \alpha \leq 1. \quad (5)$$

For example, $f(t) = t^2$ is a convex function because

$$f(\alpha t_0 + (1 - \alpha)t_1) = (\alpha t_0 + (1 - \alpha)t_1)^2$$
$$= \alpha^2 t_0^2 + (1 - \alpha)^2 t_1^2 + 2\alpha(1 - \alpha)t_0 t_1 \quad (6)$$
$$\text{and } \alpha f(t_0) + (1 - \alpha)f(t_1) = \alpha t_0^2 + (1 - \alpha)t_1^2. \quad (7)$$

(7)–(6) gives us

$$\alpha(1 - \alpha)[(t_0 - t_1)^2] \quad (8)$$

which is equal to 0 if either $\alpha = 0$ or $\alpha = 1$; otherwise it is proportional to $(t_0 - t_1)^2$ which is non-negative as it is the square of a real number. So, we can infer that

left-hand side of (6) *is* $\leq$ *left-hand side of* (7) which shows that $f(t)$ is convex.

Theorem 1. If $f(t)$ is a convex function then

$$f\left(\sum_{i=1}^{K} \alpha_i t_i\right) \leq \sum_{i=1}^{K} \alpha_i f(t_i) \quad \text{where } \alpha_i \geq 0$$

$$\text{for } 1 \leq i \leq K \quad \text{and} \quad \sum_{i=1}^{K} \alpha_i = 1. \quad (9)$$

Proof. We show the result using mathematical induction.

- **Base case:** The property holds for $K = 2$ as

$$f(\alpha_1 t_1 + \alpha_2 t_2) \leq \alpha_1 f(t_1) + \alpha_2 f(t_2)$$
$$\text{for } \alpha_1, \alpha_2 \geq 0 \quad \text{and} \quad \alpha_1 + \alpha_2 = 1. \tag{10}$$

This is because f is a convex function.

- **Induction Hypothesis:** Let the property hold for $K = l$. That is

$$f\left(\sum_{i=1}^{l} \alpha_i t_i\right) \leq \sum_{i=1}^{l} \alpha_i f(t_i), \quad \text{where } \alpha_i \geq 0$$

$$\text{for } 1 \leq i \leq l \quad \text{and} \quad \sum_{i=1}^{l} \alpha_i = 1. \tag{11}$$

- **Induction Step:** Using the Induction Hypothesis (inequality in (11)) we need to show that

$$f\left(\sum_{i=1}^{l+1} \alpha_i t_i\right) \leq \sum_{i=1}^{l+1} \alpha_i f(t_i), \quad \text{where } \alpha_i \geq 0$$

$$\text{for } 1 \leq i \leq l+1 \quad \text{and} \quad \sum_{i=1}^{l+1} \alpha_i = 1. \tag{12}$$

Consider the left-hand side of the inequality (12) which could be simplified as

$$f\left(\sum_{i=1}^{l+1} \alpha_i t_i\right) = f\left(\sum_{i=1}^{l} \alpha_i t_i + \alpha_{l+1} t_{l+1}\right).$$

We can write it in the required form by multiplying and dividing by $(1 - \alpha_{l+1})$ as

$$f\left[(1 - \alpha_{l+1}) \sum_{i=1}^{l} \alpha_i \frac{t_i}{1 - \alpha_{l+1}} + \alpha_{l+1} t_{l+1}\right]. \tag{13}$$

Using the base case we can show that the expression in (13) is

$$\leq (1 - \alpha_{l+1}) f \left[\sum_{i=1}^{l} \frac{\alpha_i}{(1 - \alpha_{l+1})} t_i \right] + \alpha_{l+1} f(t_{l+1})$$

$$\leq (1 - \alpha_{l+1}) \sum_{i=1}^{l} \frac{\alpha_i}{(1 - \alpha_{l+1})} f(t_i) + \alpha_{l+1} f(t_{l+1})$$

$$= \sum_{i=1}^{l+1} \alpha_i f(t_i) = \text{right-hand side of (12) thus proving the result.}$$

We can use Jensen's inequality to simplify the expression of logarithm of the sum seen in (4); it is transformed to a sum of logarithm form which is easier to deal with. In order to achieve it we need to have appropriate αs which are non-negative and add upto 1. Probability mass function (discrete random variable) is ideally suited for this and we know from (4) that z is a discrete random variable. This prompts us to find a suitable form for the mass function on z. Further, we need to recognize that the function under consideration in (4) is natural logarithm (ln) which is a concave function or equivalently $-\ln(x)$ is convex. In order to show that ln is concave we can use the following definition.

Definition 2. A *function f is concave* on an interval if its second derivative $f''(x)$ is negative in the interval.

Note that if $f(x) = \ln(x)$ then $f''(x) = -\frac{1}{x^2}$ which is strictly decreasing if $x > 0$. So, $\ln(x)$ is concave and $-\ln(x)$ is convex.

We can rewrite Eq. (4) by multiplying and dividing by $p(z|\mathcal{X}, \theta_i)$, where θ_i is the estimate of θ at the ith step of the iterative scheme that we need to use, as

$$l(\theta) = \ln \sum_z p(z|\mathcal{X}, \theta_i) \frac{p(\mathcal{X}, z|\theta)}{p(z|\mathcal{X}, \theta_i)}. \tag{14}$$

By using the Jensen's inequality seen earlier, we can show that the above is

$$\geq \sum_{z} p(z|\mathcal{X}, \theta_i) \ln \frac{p(\mathcal{X}, z|\theta)}{p(z|\mathcal{X}, \theta_i)}. \tag{15}$$

It is possible to show that θ that maximizes the *right-hand side* of (15) is the same as the θ that maximizes (14). Further as θ appears only in the numerator of the argument of ln, the same θ that maximizes (15) also maximizes

$$\sum_{z} p(z|\mathcal{X}, \theta_i) \ln p(\mathcal{X}, z|\theta) = \text{Expectation } (\ln p(\mathcal{X}, z|\theta)), \tag{16}$$

where the expectation is over z conditioned on $\mathcal{X}$ and the value of θ in the form of θ_i. So, the two important steps in the EM algorithm are:

1. **Expectation or E Step:** Compute $E_{z|\mathcal{X}, \theta_i}(\ln p(\mathcal{X}, z|\theta))$.
2. **Maximization or M Step:**

$$\theta_{i+1} = \underset{\theta}{argmax} \quad E_{z|\mathcal{X}, \theta_i}(\ln p(\mathcal{X}, z|\theta)).$$

EM algorithm also can reach only a locally optimal solution.

6.2.2. *An example*

Let us consider a one-dimensional example with two clusters. Let the dataset be

$$\mathcal{X} = \{2.1, 5.1, 1.9, 4.9\}.$$

It is easy to see the two intuitively appealing clusters in the form of $\{2.1, 1.9\}$ $\{5.1, 4.9\}$. Now let us examine how EM can be used to cluster the set $\mathcal{X}$. Let the clusters be c_1 and c_2. Let us assume that these data points are drawn from two normals each with the same variance ($\sigma^2 = 1$) of value 1. The parameter vector $\theta = (\mu_1, \mu_2)^t$ where μ_1, μ_2 are the means of the normals is to be estimated. The log likelihood function is given by

$$\ln p(\mathcal{X}, z|\theta) = \ln \Pi_{i=1}^{4} p[X_i, P_i|\theta] = \sum_{i=1}^{4} \ln p[X_i, P_i|\theta], \tag{17}$$

where $P_i = (P_{i1}, P_{i2})$; P_{ij} = Probability that X_i belongs to cluster c_j.

$$E[\ln p(\mathcal{X}, z | \theta)] = \sum_{i=1}^{4} \left[\ln \left(\frac{1}{\sqrt{2\pi\sigma^2}} - \frac{1}{2\sigma^2} \sum_{j=1}^{2} E(P_{ij})(x_i - \mu_j)^2 \right) \right].$$
(18)

Here, $E(P_{ij}) = P_{ij}$ as i and j are fixed. Looking at the right hand side of the above equation, the first term $\ln\left(\frac{1}{\sqrt{2\pi\sigma^2}}\right)$ in the summation does not play any role as we are interested in μs only and σ is known. By equating the gradient, with respect to θ, of the resulting expression we get $\sum_{i=1}^{4} P_{ij}(X_i - \mu_j) = 0$ which implies

$$\mu_j = \frac{\sum_{i=1}^{4} P_{ij} X_i}{\sum_{i=1}^{4} P_{ij}}.$$
(19)

So, in order to estimate the parameter vector θ or equivalently, the values of μ_1, μ_2 we need to get the values of $P_{ij}s$; note that P_{ij} is the probability that X_i belongs to cluster C_j or equivalently X_i is generated by the corresponding (jth) normal density. So,

$$P_{ij} = \frac{exp\left[-\frac{1}{2\sigma^2}(X_i - \mu_j)^2\right]}{\sum_{l=1}^{2} exp\left[-\frac{1}{2\sigma^2}(X_i - \mu_l)^2\right]}.$$
(20)

So, in this case, Eqs. (20) and (19) characterize the *Expectation* and *Maximization* steps and they are repeated iteratively till convergence.

Let $\theta_0 = (2, 4)^t$ be the initial selection of the μs. Let us consider computation of P_{11}. By using (20) and $\sigma = 1$, it is given by

$$P_{11} = \frac{exp\left[-\frac{1}{2}(2.1 - 2)^2\right]}{exp\left[-\frac{1}{2}(2.1 - 2)^2\right] + exp\left[-\frac{1}{2}(2.1 - 4)^2\right]} = 0.728.$$

In a similar manner P_{21}, P_{31}, P_{41} can be computed. Once we have these values, we can estimate μ_1 using Eq. (19). In a similar manner one can estimate P_{i2}, for $i = 1, \ldots, 4$ and μ_2. These values are shown

Table 8.4.   Values during the first iteration.

j	P_{1j}	P_{2j}	P_{3j}	P_{4j}	μ_j
1	0.728	0.018	0.9	0.015	2.76
2	0.272	0.982	0.1	0.985	4.53

Table 8.5.   Values during the second iteration.

j	P_{1j}	P_{2j}	P_{3j}	P_{4j}	μ_j
1	0.94	0.09	0.96	0.1	2.26
2	0.06	0.91	0.04	0.9	4.6

Table 8.6.   Values during the third iteration.

j	P_{1j}	P_{2j}	P_{3j}	P_{4j}	μ_j
1	0.946	0.214	0.97	0.03	2.345
2	0.04	0.786	0.03	0.97	4.88

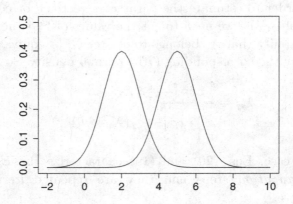

Figure 8.2.   The densities corresponding to the two clusters.

in Table 8.4. So, at the end of the first iteration we get $\mu_1 = 2.76$ and $\mu_2 = 4.53$. So, $\theta_1 = (2.76, 4.53)^t$. Using this value of θ, the corresponding values of the parameters are given in Table 8.5. Table 8.6 shows the parameters in the third iteration. After some more iterations we expect the value of $\theta = (2, 5)$ to be reached. The corresponding densities are shown in Figure 8.2.

7. Topic Models

One of the important areas of current interest is large-scale document processing. It has a variety of applications including:

- **Document retrieval:** Here, the documents in a collection are represented, typically, using the bag-of-words (BOW) model in the case of text. In the BOW model, the order of occurrence of words is not important; their frequency of occurrence is important. Here for a given input query, a collection of documents is presented in a ranked order as output. Classification, clustering and ranking of documents are important machine learning tasks that are useful in this application.
- **Spam filtering:** Spam electronic mails are unsolicited mails which can be wasting resources of the recipient. So, spam mails need to be identified and isolated appropriately. This activity requires clustering and classification of email messages.
- **Verification (biometrics):** There are several applications concerned with forensics and cyber security where biometrics plays an important role. These include identification based on biometrics like fingerprint, speech, face, and iris. So, classification and clustering are important again in this application.
- **Pin-Code recognition:** Automatic pin-code recognition is required to route surface mail to its destination mechanically. This involves recognition of handwritten numerals.
- **Multimedia and multi-lingual document classification:** Classification and summarization of reports in legal and medical domains.

It is possible to view most of the data stored and processed by a machine as comprising of documents. In this sense, the following are some of the popularly considered document categories:

- *Web pages*: These are easily the most popular type of semi-structured documents. Every search engine crawls and indexes web pages for possible information retrieval; typically search engines return, for a query input by the user, a collection of documents in a ranked manner as output. Here, in addition to the *content* of the webpages, the link structure in terms of *hyperlinks* is also exploited.

- *Academic publications*: This kind of documents are also prominent to the extent that their content and links in terms of co-citations are used by search engines in document retrieval.
- *Research grant applications*: It is typically a semi-structured text document containing charts, graphs, and some images.
- *Company reports*: It may also be semistructured text document.
- *Newspaper articles*: This could be typically a short text document and it can have images at times.
- *Bank transaction slips*: This is another semi-structured short text document.
- *Manual pages*: This is another short size text document with possible figures.
- *Tweets*: Tweets are short text documents and they may employ several non-standard words.
- *Encyclopedia*: This could be a very lengthy and comprehensive text document with figures and images combined. *Wikipedia* is a well-known example where search is facilitated.
- *Images* (*video*): It is an example of a non-textual document.
- *Speech records*: These are also examples of non-textual documents.
- *Fingerprints*: It is also a non-textual type of document used as a biometric.
- *Electronic mails*: It is one of the most popularly used type of documents for communication between two or more individuals; it is typically a short text.
- *Health records*: It could be a multimedia document. The prescription and diagnosis in handwritten textual form, ultrasound and X-rays in the form of images form a part of the document.
- *Legal records*: It is another textual document and words here may have to be precise.
- *Software code*: Analysis of software code is gaining a lot of importance to identify bugs and inefficient parts of the code.
- *Bug reports*: These are reports used to indicate various bugs encountered in the software package and how some of them are fixed periodically.

There could be several other kinds of documents. In order to analyze document collections, a variety of topic based schemes have been proposed. It is possible to view these methods to be performing factorization of the document term matrix. So, we consider these matrix factorization based methods next.

7.1. Matrix factorization-based methods

Let X be the document term matrix of size $n \times l$ which means that there are n documents and l terms. Typically l could be very large in most of the practical settings. A possible generic factorization is:

$$X_{n \times l} = B_{n \times K} \, D_{K \times K} \, C_{K \times l}. \tag{21}$$

The basic idea behind such a factorization is that it permits us to work with documents represented in a lower-dimensional (K-dimensional) space. The value of K corresponds to the number of non-zero eigenvalues of XX^t or the rank of the matrix X. In other words we can work with the B matrix instead of the X matrix. Further, it is possible to view this as working with K *topics/clusters* instead of l terms or words.

7.1.1. *Why should this work?*

It is well-known that conventional distance-based methods fail to characterize neighbors in high-dimensional spaces. This is because the ratio of $d(x, NN(x))$ and $d(x, FN(x))$ tends to 1 as the dimensionality gets larger and larger; here $d(x, NN(x))$ is the distance between a point x and its nearest neighbor, $NN(x)$, and $d(x, FN(x))$ is the distance between x and its farthest neighbor, $FN(x)$. Two different ways of solving this problem are:

1. **Explicit Dimensionality Reduction:** Here the data in the high-dimensional space is projected into a low-dimensional space by using either a linear or a nonlinear projection tool. For example Random Projections are useful in unsupervised feature extraction; similarly mutual information has been successfully used in feature selection. Once the dimensionality is reduced, it is possible

to successfully use classifiers based on matching. In such a case the data matrix X becomes a $n \times K$ matrix instead of $n \times l$ where K is the number of features extracted from the given l features.

2. **Implicit Dimensionality Reduction:** Instead of explicit selection it is possible to use matrix factorization approaches to implicitly get the features. For example, if we assume that D is an identity matrix of size $K \times K$, then the resulting equation is $X = BC$; note that even though X is a collection of n data points (rows) in a possibly high-dimensional space of l terms (columns), the resulting B matrix represents the n patterns in a reduced-dimensional (K) space. This amounts to dimensionality reduction; specifically each of the K columns of B may be viewed as a linear combination of the l columns in A. Further it is important that entries of C are well-behaved; popularly the objective function of the optimization problem deals with some error between A and its approximation in the form of BC. In addition C is constrained to be sparse, for example. We deal with different factorization approaches in this chapter.

7.2. Divide-and-conquer approach

The simplest scheme to deal with high-dimensional spaces is to partition the set of features $\mathcal{F}$ into some P blocks $F_1, F_2, \ldots, F_P$ such that $\mathcal{F} = \bigcup_{i=1}^{P} F_i$; cluster subpatterns in each of these P subspaces and use the cluster representatives to realize a compact set of prototypes. We can use them in large data classification. We illustrate it with a simple example.

Let us consider the dataset shown in Table 8.7; there are two classes and each pattern is four dimensional as indicated by the features f_1, f_2, f_3 and f_4. Now given a test pattern $(2, 2, 2, 2)$, it is classified as belonging to class 1 using the nearest neighbor classifier as its nearest neighbor is pattern number 4, given by $(1, 2, 2, 2)$, which is in class 1. Let this set of features be partitioned into $F_1 = \{f_1, f_2\}$ and $F_2 = \{f_3, f_4\}$. Now we cluster data in each class separately and while clustering we consider each subset of features

Table 8.7.   Patterns corresponding to two classes.

Pattern no.	f_1	f_2	f_3	f_4	Class
1	1	1	1	1	1
2	1	2	1	1	1
3	1	1	2	2	1
4	1	2	2	2	1
5	6	6	6	6	2
6	6	7	6	6	2
7	6	6	7	7	2
8	6	7	7	7	2

separately. We explain the specific steps as:

- Consider patterns 1 to 4 which are from class 1. Cluster these patterns based on F_1 and F_2 separately.
  - The subpatterns based on F_1 are $(1, 1)$, $(1, 2)$, $(1, 1)$, and $(1, 2)$. If we seek two clusters using any conventional algorithm, we get the two clusters: $\{(1, 1), (1, 1)\}$, and $\{(1, 2), (1, 2)\}$. The cluster centroids are $(1, 1)$ and $(1, 2)$ respectively.
  - The subpatterns based on F_2 are $(1, 1)$, $(1, 1)$, $(2, 2)$, $(2, 2)$ which form two clusters with $(1, 1)$ and $(2, 2)$ as representatives.
- Similarly consider patterns 5 to 8 that belong to class 2. Again by clustering the subpatterns based on F_1 and F_2 we have
  - Cluster representatives based on F_1 are $(6, 6)$ and $(6, 7)$.
  - Cluster representatives based on F_2 are $(6, 6)$ and $(7, 7)$.

We collect these cluster representatives corresponding to different classes based on different feature subsets. In this example, the relevant details are shown in Table 8.8. It is possible to use data in Table 8.8 to classify a test pattern. For example, consider the pattern $(2, 2, 2, 2)$; we consider its subpatterns corresponding to F_1 and F_2 which are $(2, 2)$ and $(2, 2)$. Now we obtain the nearest neighbors of these subpatterns in each class. They are given by

- The nearest subpatterns of $(2, 2)$ (based on F_1) are $(1, 2)$ from class 1 and $(6, 6)$ from class 2; of these class 1 subpattern $(1, 2)$ is nearer.

Table 8.8. Cluster representatives of the two classes.

Representative number	Based on F_1	Based on F_2	Class
1	1 1	1 1	1
2	1 2	2 2	1
1	6 6	6 6	2
2	6 7	7 7	2

- The nearest neighbors of $(2, 2)$ (based on F_2) are $(2, 2)$ from class 1 and $(6, 6)$ from class 2; of these two $(2, 2)$ is nearer.

Observing that the nearest subpatterns are from class 1 based on both F_1 and F_2, we assign $(2, 2, 2, 2)$ to class 1. If we concatenate the nearest subpatterns $(1, 2)$ and $(2, 2)$ then we get $(1, 2, 2, 2)$ as the nearest neighbor pattern. We can abstract the whole scheme using the following steps.

1. Let there be C classes with the ith class having n_i patterns. Partition patterns of the ith class into P_i subsets of features. In the above example $C = 2$ and $P_1 = P_2 = 2$ as in both the classes we have used the same F_1 and F_2.
2. For the test pattern we obtain the nearest neighbors from each of the C classes.
   - For class i consider the P_i subsets of features. Find the nearest subpattern of each test subpattern in each of the corresponding subsets from the training data.
   - Concatenate the P_i nearest subpatterns of the test subpatterns. Compute the distance between the test pattern and this concatenated pattern.
3. Assign the test pattern to class j if the nearest pattern from the jth class is nearer than the other classes.

It is possible to consider several variants of this simple divide-and-conquer approach. Some of them are:

- Instead of using a single nearest neighbor one can use K nearest neighbors from each class to realize a robust classifier.

- Instead of concatenating the P_i nearest subpatterns one can consider K nearest subpatterns based on each of the P_i feature subsets. Then generate neighbors by concatenating P_i subpatterns selecting one from each of the K subpatterns selected based on each of the P_i feature sets. This leads to selection of P_i^K concatenated patterns. Select K of these patterns based on nearness to the test pattern. If there are C classes then we get CK neighbors, K from each class. Select K nearest of these and use majority voting to decide the class label.
- Computation of distance between the test pattern and a neighbor can be obtained by summing partial distances across the P_i subpatterns in some cases. This is possible when squared Euclidean distance or city-block distance is used to compute partial distances.

7.3. Latent Semantic Analysis (LSA)

In this factorization D is a diagonal matrix. LSA employs this factorization directly. In such a case, the above factorization exploits the Singular Value Decomposition (SVD) where the diagonal entries in D are singular values and they correspond to the eigenvalues of the matrices XX^t and X^tX where X^t is the transpose of X. This may be explained as follows:

Consider XX^t; it is a square matrix of size $n \times n$. If β is an eigenvector and λ the corresponding eigenvalue then we have

$$XX^t\beta = \lambda\beta$$

by premultiplying both sides by X^t we have

$$X^t(XX^t\beta) = X^t(\lambda\beta).$$

By using the associativity of matrix multiplication and noting that λ is a scalar, we have

$$(X^tX)X^t\beta = \lambda(X^t\beta).$$

Note that X^tX is a square matrix of size $l \times l$; β is a $n \times 1$ vector and $X^t\beta$ is a $l \times 1$ vector. By assuming that $X^t\beta = \gamma$ we can write the above equation as

$$X^t X \gamma = \lambda \gamma,$$

which means that γ is the eigenvector of $X^t X$ with the associated eigenvalue being λ. This means that λ is an eigenvalue of both XX^t and $X^t X$ but with the corresponding eigenvectors being β and γ (= $X^t \beta$) respectively.

Given a matrix X of size $m \times n$ the SVD is given by

$$X = B\,D\,C,$$

where size of B is $m \times K$; D is a $K \times K$ diagonal matrix; and C is of size $K \times n$. Here, B consists of K eigenvectors of the matrix XX^t; these are eigenvectors corresponding to the K non-zero eigenvalues of the matrix XX^t. Similarly C is composed of K eigenvectors of $X^t X$ as the K rows of C. We now illustrate these ideas using an example.

7.3.1. *Illustration of SVD*

Consider a 3×2 size matrix X given by

$$X = \begin{pmatrix} 1 & -1 \\ 1 & 0 \\ 0 & 1 \end{pmatrix}.$$

Note that $X^t X$ is given by

$$X^t X = \begin{pmatrix} 2 & -1 \\ -1 & 2 \end{pmatrix}.$$

The characteristic equation of $X^t X$ is $\lambda^2 - 4\lambda + 3 = 0$ and so the roots of the equation or eigenvalues of $X^t X$ are 3 and 1.

The corresponding eigenvectors are

$$\begin{pmatrix} 1 \\ -1 \end{pmatrix}$$

and

$$\begin{pmatrix} 1 \\ 1 \end{pmatrix}.$$

The corresponding normalized vectors are:

$$\begin{pmatrix} \dfrac{1}{\sqrt{2}} \\ -\dfrac{1}{\sqrt{2}} \end{pmatrix}$$

and

$$\begin{pmatrix} \dfrac{1}{\sqrt{2}} \\ \dfrac{1}{\sqrt{2}} \end{pmatrix}.$$

In a similar manner it is possible to observe that the matrix XX^t is

$$\begin{pmatrix} 2 & 1 & -1 \\ 1 & 1 & 0 \\ -1 & 0 & 1 \end{pmatrix}.$$

The corresponding eigenvalues are 3, 1, and 0 and the eigenvectors corresponding to the non-zero eigenvalues after normalization are

$$\begin{pmatrix} \dfrac{2}{\sqrt{6}} \\ \dfrac{1}{\sqrt{6}} \\ -\dfrac{1}{\sqrt{6}} \end{pmatrix}$$

and

$$\begin{pmatrix} 0 \\ \dfrac{1}{\sqrt{2}} \\ \dfrac{1}{\sqrt{2}} \end{pmatrix}.$$

The entries of the diagonal matrix Σ are the square roots of the eigenvalues (singular values) 3 and 1. So, the various matrices are

$$B = \begin{pmatrix} \dfrac{2}{\sqrt{6}} & 0 \\[2mm] \dfrac{1}{\sqrt{6}} & \dfrac{1}{\sqrt{2}} \\[2mm] -\dfrac{1}{\sqrt{6}} & \dfrac{1}{\sqrt{2}} \end{pmatrix},$$

$$D = \begin{pmatrix} \sqrt{3} & 0 \\ 0 & 1 \end{pmatrix},$$

$$C = \begin{pmatrix} \dfrac{1}{\sqrt{2}} & -\dfrac{1}{\sqrt{2}} \\[2mm] \dfrac{1}{\sqrt{2}} & \dfrac{1}{\sqrt{2}} \end{pmatrix}.$$

So, finally we have the SVD of X given by

$$\begin{pmatrix} 1 & -1 \\ 1 & 0 \\ 0 & 1 \end{pmatrix} = \begin{pmatrix} \dfrac{2}{\sqrt{6}} & 0 \\[2mm] \dfrac{1}{\sqrt{6}} & \dfrac{1}{\sqrt{2}} \\[2mm] -\dfrac{1}{\sqrt{6}} & \dfrac{1}{\sqrt{2}} \end{pmatrix} \begin{pmatrix} \sqrt{3} & 0 \\ 0 & 1 \end{pmatrix} \begin{pmatrix} \dfrac{1}{\sqrt{2}} & -\dfrac{1}{\sqrt{2}} \\[2mm] \dfrac{1}{\sqrt{2}} & \dfrac{1}{\sqrt{2}} \end{pmatrix}.$$

7.4. SVD and PCA

Principal component analysis (PCA) is a well-known tool for dimensionality reduction. Here, linear combinations of the original features are obtained which are uncorrelated. Mathematically it amounts to computing the eigenvectors of the covariance matrix. The covariance matrix is symmetric and the entries are real numbers; so, the eigenvectors are orthogonal. The eigenvector corresponding to the largest eigenvalue is the first principal component; the one corresponding to the next largest eigenvalue is the second principal component, and so on. We illustrate the computation of PCA using a two-dimensional example.

7.4.1. *Example to illustrate PCA*

Consider the four two-dimensional patterns given by

$$\begin{pmatrix} 1 \\ 2 \end{pmatrix} \begin{pmatrix} 2 \\ 1 \end{pmatrix} \begin{pmatrix} 6 \\ 7 \end{pmatrix} \begin{pmatrix} 7 \\ 6 \end{pmatrix}.$$

The sample mean of the 4 data points is $\begin{pmatrix} 4 \\ 4 \end{pmatrix}$. The zero mean normalized set of points is

$$\begin{pmatrix} -3 \\ -2 \end{pmatrix} \begin{pmatrix} -2 \\ -3 \end{pmatrix} \begin{pmatrix} 2 \\ 3 \end{pmatrix} \begin{pmatrix} 3 \\ 2 \end{pmatrix}.$$

The sample covariance matrix of the data is given by

$$\frac{1}{4} \left[(-3, -2)^t (-3, -2) + (-2, -3)^t (-2, -3) \right.$$

$$\left. + (2, 3)^t (2, 3) + (3, 1)^t (3, 1) \right]$$

$$= \frac{1}{4} \begin{pmatrix} 26 & 24 \\ 24 & 26 \end{pmatrix} = \begin{pmatrix} 6.5 & 6 \\ 6 & 6.5 \end{pmatrix}.$$

The eigenvalues of the matrix are 12.5 and 0.5 and the respective eigenvectors are $\begin{pmatrix} 1 \\ 1 \end{pmatrix} \begin{pmatrix} 1 \\ -1 \end{pmatrix}$. After normalization we get the unit-norm orthogonal eigenvectors given by $\begin{pmatrix} \frac{1}{\sqrt{2}} \\ \frac{1}{\sqrt{2}} \end{pmatrix} \begin{pmatrix} \frac{1}{\sqrt{2}} \\ -\frac{1}{\sqrt{2}} \end{pmatrix}$. The four data points and the corresponding principal components are shown in Figure 8.3.

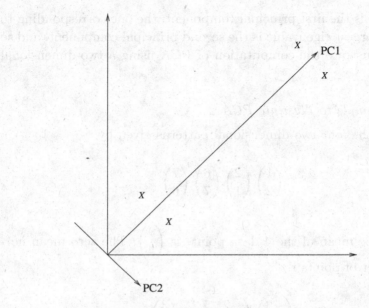

Figure 8.3.   The two principal components.

7.4.2. *Computing PCs using SVD*

Consider the four data points after zero-mean normalization. It is given by the matrix X of size 4×2:

$$X = \begin{pmatrix} -3 & -2 \\ -2 & -3 \\ 2 & 3 \\ 3 & 2 \end{pmatrix}.$$

The SVD of X is given by

$$\begin{pmatrix} -3 & -2 \\ -2 & -3 \\ 2 & 3 \\ 3 & 2 \end{pmatrix} = \begin{pmatrix} -\dfrac{1}{2} & -\dfrac{1}{2} \\ -\dfrac{1}{2} & \dfrac{1}{2} \\ \dfrac{1}{2} & -\dfrac{1}{2} \\ \dfrac{1}{2} & \dfrac{1}{2} \end{pmatrix} \begin{pmatrix} \sqrt{50} & 0 \\ 0 & \sqrt{2} \end{pmatrix} \begin{pmatrix} \dfrac{1}{\sqrt{2}} & \dfrac{1}{\sqrt{2}} \\ \dfrac{1}{\sqrt{2}} & -\dfrac{1}{\sqrt{2}} \end{pmatrix}.$$

Note that the rows of the matrix C correspond to the principal components of the data. Further, the covariance matrix is proportional to $X^t X$ given by

$$X^t X = \begin{pmatrix} \dfrac{1}{\sqrt{2}} & \dfrac{1}{\sqrt{2}} \\ \dfrac{1}{\sqrt{2}} & -\dfrac{1}{\sqrt{2}} \end{pmatrix} \begin{pmatrix} 50 & 0 \\ 0 & 2 \end{pmatrix} \begin{pmatrix} \dfrac{1}{\sqrt{2}} & \dfrac{1}{\sqrt{2}} \\ \dfrac{1}{\sqrt{2}} & -\dfrac{1}{\sqrt{2}} \end{pmatrix}.$$

In most of the document analysis applications, it is not uncommon to view a document collection as a document-term matrix, X as specified earlier. Typically such a matrix is large in size; in a majority of the practical applications the number of documents is large and the number of terms in each document is relatively small. However, such data is high-dimensional and so the matrix can be very sparse. This is because even though the number of terms in a document is small, the total number of distinct terms in the collection could be very large; out of which a small fraction of terms appear in each of the documents which leads to sparsity. This means that dimensionality reduction is essential for applying various classifiers effectively.

Observe that the eigenvectors of the covariance matrix are the principal components. Each of these is a linear combination of the terms in the given collection. So, instead of considering all possible eigenvectors, only a small number of the principal components are considered to achieve dimensionality reduction. Typically the number of terms could be varying between 10,000 to 1 million whereas the number of principal components considered could be between 10 to 100. One justification is that people use a small number of topics in a given application context; they do not use all the terms in the given collection.

Latent semantic analysis involves obtaining topics that are *latent* and possibly *semantic*. It is based on obtaining latent variables in the form of linear combinations of the original terms. Note that the terms are observed in the given documents; however the topics are *latent* which means topics are not observed. Principal components are such linear combinations. The eigenvalues of the covariance matrix represent variances in the directions of the eigenvectors. The first principal component is in the direction of maximum variance. In a general setting dimensionality reduction is achieved by considering only the top K principal components where K is smaller than the rank, r, of the matrix X. Specifically dimensionality reduction is useful when the data points in X are high-dimensional.

It is possible to use the SVD to obtain a low-rank representation X_K which is an approximation of X. This is obtained by considering the largest K singular values and forcing the remaining $r - K$ singular values in D to be zero. So, X_K is given by

$$X_K = BD_KC,$$

where D_K is a $r \times r$ diagonal matrix with the top K eigenvalues in D and the remaining $r - K$ diagonal values to be zero. Note that X_K is an approximation of X. It is an optimal approximation in the sense that among all possible K rank matrices X_K has the minimal Frobenius norm with X. It is possible to show that this Frobenius norm is

$$\|X - X_K\|_F = \lambda_{K+1},$$

where λ_{K+1} is the largest singular value ignored among the least $r - K$ singular values.

There are claims that the resulting reduced dimensional representation is *semantic* and can handle both synonymy and polysemy in information retrieval and text mining. Here, by synonymy we mean two words having the same meaning are synonymous. Similarly we have polysemy when the same word has multiple meanings. This will have impact on the similarity between two documents. Because of synonymy the similarity value computed using dot product type of functions will be less than the intended. For example, if *car* and *automobile* are used interchangeably (synonymously) in a document and only car is used in the query document then the similarity measure will fail to take into account the occurrences of automobile. In a similar manner because of polysemy it is possible that similarity between a pair of documents is larger than what it should be. For example if *tiger* is used in a document both to mean an animal and

say airlines and the query document has tiger in only one sense then
the dot product could be larger than the intended value.

An important feature of the SVD is that it is a deterministic
factorization scheme and the factorization is unique. Here each row
of the matrix C is a topic and it is an assignment of weights to each
of the terms. The entry C_{ij} is the weight or importance of the jth
term $(j = 1, \ldots, l)$ to the ith topic. The entry D_{ii} in the diagonal
matrix indicates some kind of weight assigned to the entire ith topic.

7.5. Probabilistic Latent Semantic Analysis (PLSA)

Latent semantic analysis employs a deterministic topic model that
is reasonably popular in analyzing high-dimensional text document
collections. However it does not offer a framework to synthesize or
generate documents. PLSA is a generative model; it is also a topic
model where each topic is a mapping from set of terms to $[0, 1]$.
Specifically a topic assigns a probability to each term.

It is possible to view the probability, $P(t)$, of a term t as

$$P(t) = \sum_{i=1}^{K} P(C_i)P(t|C_i) \quad \text{where} \quad \sum_{i=1}^{K} P(C_i) = 1,$$

where C_i is a soft cluster or topic. It is possible to use the Bayes rule
to write the joint probability $P(d, t_j)$ as

$$P(d, t_j) = P(d)P(t_j|d) \quad \text{where} \quad P(t_j|d) = \sum_{i=1}^{K} P(t_j|C_i)P(C_i|d).$$

It is possible to view the PLSA as a matrix factorization scheme
as follows:

$$P(d, t_j) = \sum_{i=1}^{K} P(d|C_k)P(C_k)P(t_j|C_k).$$

This can be viewed as a matrix factorization of the form $X = BD_K E$,
where the diagonal matrix D_K is made up of probabilities of the
K topics. Specifically the ith element on the diagonal is given by
$P(C_i)$. The element B_{ij} is given by $P(d_i|C_k)$ where d_i is the ith

document and C_k is the kth topic. Similarly, E_{jk} corresponds to $P(t_j|C_k)$.

Learning the model involves, given the document topic matrix X to get the B, D_K and E matrices or equivalently getting the values of $P(d_i|C_k)$, $P(C_i)$, and $P(t_j|C_k)$. Alternatively, one may consider the parameters to be $P(d_i)$, $P(t_j|C_k)$ and $P(C_k|d_i)$. These are obtained using the EM algorithm. The EM iteratively goes through the expectation and maximization steps. In the expectation step the expected value of the log-likelihood function is obtained and in the maximization step, parameter values are obtained based on the maximization of the expected value. Let us assume the following:

- Let the input X be a document collection of n documents and each is a vector in an l dimensional space; this means the vocabulary size is l.
- Let $n(d_i, t_j)$ be the number of times term t_j occurred in document d_i and $P(d_i, t_j)$ be the probability of term t_j in document d_i.
- Let us assume the *bag of terms model* which means each term occurs independent of the others and it may occur more than once in a document.
- Let θ be the parameter vector with components $P(d_i)$, $P(t_j|C_k)$ and $P(C_k|d_i)$; learning involves estimating the values of these parameters from X.

The likelihood function, $L(\theta)$, is given by

$$L(\theta) = \prod_{i=1}^{n} \prod_{j=1}^{l} P(d_i, t_j)^{n(d_i, t_j)}.$$

The log-likelihood function, $l(\theta)$ is given by

$$l(\theta) = \sum_{i=1}^{n} \sum_{j=1}^{l} n(d_i, t_j) \log P(d_i, t_j),$$

Hence, $l(\theta) = \sum_{i=1}^{n} \sum_{j=1}^{l} n(d_i, t_j) \log[P(d_i)P(t_j|C_k)P(C_k|d_i)]$.

So, expected value of $l(\theta)$ with respect to the latent cluster C_k conditioned on d_i and t_j is given by

$$E_{C_k|d_i,t_j}(l(\theta)) = \sum_{i=1}^{n}\sum_{j=1}^{l} n(d_i,t_j) \sum_{k=1}^{K} P(C_k|t_j,d_i)$$

$$\times [\log P(d_i) + \log P(t_j|C_k) + \log P(C_k|d_i)].$$

Here, $P(C_k|t_j,d_i) = \dfrac{P(t_j|C_k)P(C_k|d_i)}{\sum_{k=1}^{K} P(t_j|C_k)P(C_k|d_i)}.$

In addition to the expected value of $l(\theta)$, we need to consider the constraints on the probabilities which are

$$\sum_{i=1}^{n} P(d_i) = 1; \quad \sum_{j=1}^{l} P(t_j|C_k) = 1; \quad \sum_{j=1}^{l} P(C_k|d_i) = 1.$$

The corresponding Lagrangian is given by

$$E_{C_k|d_i,t_j}(l(\theta)) + \alpha_1\left(\sum_{i=1}^{n} P(d_i) - 1\right) + \alpha_2\sum_{k=1}^{K}\left(\sum_{j=1}^{l} P(t_j|C_k) - 1\right)$$

$$+ \alpha_3\sum_{i=1}^{n}\left(\sum_{k=1}^{K} P(C_k|d_i) - 1\right),$$

where α_1, α_2, and α_3 are the Lagrange variables.

By taking the partial derivatives of this Lagrange function with respect to the three parameters $P(d_i)$, $P(t_J|C_k)$, and $P(C_k|d_i)$ and equating them to zero we get the following estimates:

- $P(d_i) = \dfrac{\sum_{j=1}^{l}\sum_{k=1}^{K} n(d_i,t_j)P(C_k|t_j,d_i)}{\sum_{i=1}^{n}\sum_{j=1}^{l}\sum_{k=1}^{K} n(d_i,t_j)P(C_k|t_j,d_i)},$

- $P(t_j|C_k) = \dfrac{\sum_{i=1}^{n} n(d_i,t_j)P(C_k|t_j,d_i)}{\sum_{j=1}^{l}\sum_{i=1}^{n} n(d_i,t_j)P(C_k|t_j,d_i)}.$

- $P(C_k|d_i) = \dfrac{\sum_{j=1}^{l} n(d_i,t_j)P(C_k|t_j,d_i)}{\sum_{j=1}^{l}\sum_{k=1}^{K} n(d_i,t_j)P(C_k|t_j,d_i)}.$

7.6. Non-negative Matrix Factorization (NMF)

NMF is another popular soft clustering tool. Here, in the factorization shown in (21), D is the Identity matrix I of size $K \times K$ and so $X = BC$. Further, given that X has non-negative entries, we insist that B and C also have only non-negative entries. Hence this factorization is called NMF. Typically we seek an approximate factorization of X into the product BC. There are several possibilities for realizing the approximate factors B and C; some of them are:

- Obtain B and C such that $\|X - BC\|^2$ is minimized. This corresponds to the minimization of squared Euclidean distance between the matrices X and BC; such a kind of expression stands for the squared *Frobenius Norm* or element-wise distance given by

$$\|X - BC\|^2 = \sum_{ij} \left(X_{ij} - \sum_{k=1}^{K} B_{ik}C_{kj} \right)^2.$$

It is easy to observe that the minimum value of such a distance is zero when $X = BC$.
- Minimize a generalized *Kullback–Leibler divergence* between X and BC given by

$$\sum_{ij} \left[X_{ij} \log \frac{X_{ij}}{\sum_{k=1}^{K}(B_{ik}C_{kj})} - X_{ij} + \sum_{k=1}^{k}(B_{ik}C_{kj}) \right].$$

When entries of X and BC are normalized or probabilities such that $\sum_{ij} X_{ij} = \sum_{ij} \sum_{k}(B_{ik}C_{kj}) = 1$. It could be seen that the minimum value of this divergence is zero.

So, the problem of the minimization of distance is

Minimize $\|X - BC\|^2$ with respect to B and C
such that B and C have non-negative entries. Equivalently, $B, C \geq 0$.

There is no guarantee that we can get the globally optimal solution. However, it is possible to get the local optimum using the following update rules.

$$B_{ij} \leftarrow B_{ij} \frac{(XC^t)_{ij}}{(BCC^t)_{ij}},$$

$$C_{ij} \leftarrow C_{ij} \frac{(B^t X)_{ij}}{(B^t BC)_{ij}}.$$

It is possible to show some kind of equivalence between NMF and the K-means algorithm; also between NMF and PLSA.

7.7. LDA

Even though PLSA offers an excellent probabilistic model in characterizing the latent topics in a given collection of documents, it is not a fully generative model. It cannot explain documents which are not part of the given collection. Some of the important features of the PLSA are:

- A document d_i and a term t_j are assumed to be independent conditioned on a cluster C_k. Because of this we could write

$$P(d_i, t_j) = P(d_i) \sum_{k=1}^{K} P(t_j, C_k | d_i).$$

By using Bayes rule we can write $P(t_j, C_k | d_i)$ as $P(t_j, d_i | C_k) \frac{P(C_k)}{P(d_i)}$. This will mean that

$$P(d_i, t_j) = P(d_i) \sum_{k=1}^{K} P(t_j, d_i | C_k) \frac{P(C_k)}{P(d_i)}$$

$$= P(d_i) \sum_{k=1}^{K} P(t_j | C_k) P(d_i | C_k) \frac{P(C_k)}{P(d_i)}.$$

The independence between d_i and t_j is used to simplify the previous expression which leads to

$$P(d_i, t_j) = P(d_i) \sum_{k=1}^{K} P(t_j | C_k) P(C_k | d_i).$$

- A document may contain multiple topics or equivalently belong to multiple clusters; $P(C_k|d_i)$ is learnt only on those documents on which it is trained. It is not possible to make probabilistic assignment to an unseen document.
- $P(t_j|C_k)$ and $P(C_k|d_i)$ are important parameters of the model. The number of parameters is $Kl + Kn$; so there will be a linear growth with corpus size and also can overfit.
- Each cluster C_k is characterized by l probabilities $P(t_j|C_k)$ for $j = 1, 2, \ldots, l$. So, a cluster C_k associates different probabilities to different terms. Specifically, a topic or a description of the cluster is explained by the l probabilities.

A more appropriate probabilistic topic model is the LDA; it exploits the conjugate prior property between Dirichlet and multinomial distributions. LDA is a truly generative probabilistic model that can assign probabilities to documents not present in the training set unlike the PLSA. Some of the important features of the LDA are

- Each document is a random mixture over latent topics or clusters; each cluster is characterized by a distribution over terms.
- It is assumed that there are a fixed number of topics or clusters that are latent and using them one can generate documents.
- Each topic is a multinomial over the l terms.
- It is assumed that the prior density is Dirichlet which is characterized by a K-dimensional vector θ such that the ith component of θ, given by θ_i is non-negative for all j and $\sum_{k=1}^{K} \theta_k = 1$. The functional form of the density is given by

$$p(\theta|\alpha) = C(\alpha) \prod_{k=1}^{K} \theta_k^{\alpha_k - 1},$$

where

$$B(\alpha) = \frac{\Gamma\left(\sum_{i=1}^{K} \alpha_i\right)}{\prod_{i=1}^{K} \Gamma(\alpha_i)},$$

where Γ stands for the Gamma function and α is the input parameter vector.

- Here Dirichlet is chosen because it is the conjugate prior of the multinomial distribution. Multinomial is useful here because topics/clusters are drawn using the multinomial distribution. Specifically description of the cluster C_k is viewed as a multinomial based on the parameter vector θ.

- Documents are given; terms in the document collection form the observed random variables. Clusters or topics are hidden or latent. The idea of learning or inference in this model is to estimate the cluster structure latent in the collection; typically these clusters are soft.

- The hidden variables characterizing the model are α, a K-dimensional vector and β, a matrix of size $K \times l$ when there are K soft clusters/topics and l distinct terms in the entire document corpus.

- In order to generate a document having N terms, it is assumed that each term is generated based on a topic. So, in order to generate a term, a topic is sampled and using the topic and β matrix a term is generated. This procedure is repeated N times to generate the document.

- The generative process may be characterized by a joint probability distribution over both the observed and hidden random variables. The posterior distribution of the latent cluster structure conditioned on the observed distribution of the terms in the document collection is derived out of this.

- The entire document generation process is formally characterized as follows:

  — The vector ϕ is sampled from a Dirichlet distribution $p(\phi|\beta)$ where ϕ is a vector of size K where the kth component corresponds to the kth cluster in the document collection.

  — The vector θ is sampled from a Dirichlet distribution $p(\theta|\alpha)$ where θ is the vector of K cluster distributions at the document level.

  — For each term in the document, sample a topic/cluster using a multinomial distribution $p(C_k|\theta)$; use a multinomial $p(t_j|\phi_k)$ to sample a term t_j.

— So, the probability of the document with N terms drawn independently is given by

$$p(d, \theta, \mathcal{C}, \phi | \alpha, \beta) = p(d|\phi)p(\phi|\beta)p(\mathcal{C}|\theta)p(\theta|\alpha).$$

The document generation scheme is explained using this equation. It explains how a collection of documents is generated by using the parameters α and β and assuming independence between documents. However the learning or inference process works by using the documents as input and learning the parameter vector θ, ϕ and the set of clusters $\mathcal{C}$. The corresponding posterior distribution obtained using Bayes rule is given by

$$p(\theta, \phi, \mathcal{C}|d, \alpha, \beta) = \frac{p(\theta, \phi, \mathcal{C}, d|\alpha, \beta)}{p(d|\alpha, \beta)}.$$

Unfortunately exact computation of this quantity is not possible; the basic difficulty is associated with the denominator which has a coupling between θ and β. There are several approximations suggested in the literature; we consider a popular scheme based on Gibbs sampling.

7.7.1. *Gibbs Sampling-based LDA*

It is based on the observation that the complete cluster structure can be derived if one knows the assignment of a cluster/topic given a word. Specifically it needs to compute the probability of a cluster C_i being relevant for a term t_i given all other words being relevant to all other clusters. Formally, this probability is

$$p(C_i|C_{-i}, \alpha, \beta, d),$$

where C_{-i} means all cluster associations other than C_i. We can show using Bayes Rule

$$p(C_i|C_{-i}, \alpha, \beta, d) = \frac{p(C_i, C_{-i}, d|\alpha, \beta)}{p(C_{-i}, d|\alpha, \beta)},$$

where the denominator is independent of C_i; so, it can be ignored but for a scaling factor and the expression may be written as

$$p(C_i | C_{-i}, \alpha, \beta, d) \propto p(C_i, C_{-i}, d | \alpha, \beta) = p(C, d | \alpha, \beta).$$

Note that C_i and C_{-i} together correspond to C which is used in simplifying the expression to get $p(C, d | \alpha, \beta)$.

We can get the required marginal as

$$p(d, C | \alpha. \beta) = \iint p(d, C, \theta, \phi | \alpha, \beta) d\theta \, d\phi.$$

The joint distribution can be simplified as

$$p(d, C | \alpha, \beta) = \iint p(\phi | \beta) p(\theta | \alpha) p(C | \theta) p(d | \phi_C) d\theta \, d\phi.$$

We could separate terms having dependent variables to write the above equation as a product of two integrals.

$$p(d, C | \alpha, \beta) = \int p(\theta | \alpha) p(C | \theta) d\theta \int p(d | \phi_C) p(\phi | \beta) d\phi.$$

Both the integrands have Dirichlet priors in the form of $p(\theta | \alpha)$ and $p(\phi | \beta)$; also there are multinomial terms, one in each integrand. The conjugacy of Dirichlet to the multinomial helps us here to simplify the product to a Dirichlet with appropriate parameter setting. So, it is possible to get the result as

$$p(\mathcal{D}, \mathcal{C} | \alpha, \beta) = \prod_{i=1}^{n} \frac{B(\alpha)}{B(n_{d_i, \cdot} + \alpha)} \prod_{k=1}^{K} \frac{B(\beta)}{B(n_{\cdot, k} + \beta)},$$

where $n_{d_i, k}$ is the number of terms in document d_i that are associated with cluster C_k. There are n documents in the set D. A '.' indicates summing over the corresponding index; for example, $n_{d_i, \cdot}$ is the total number of terms in d_i and $n_{\cdot, k}$ is the number of terms in the entire collection that are associated with C_k. It is possible to use the above equation to get the estimate for $p(C_k|\mathcal{C}_{-k}, D, \alpha, \beta)$ as

$$p(C_m|\mathcal{C}_{-m}, D, \alpha, \beta) = \frac{p(\mathcal{D}, \mathcal{C}|\alpha, \beta)}{p(\mathcal{D}, \mathcal{C}_{-m}|\alpha, \beta)}$$

$$\propto \left(n_{d,k}^{(-m)} + \alpha_k \right) \frac{n_{t,k}^{-(m)} + \beta_t}{\sum_{t'} n_{t',k}^{(-m)} + \beta_{t'}}.$$

Here the superscript $(-m)$ corresponds to not using the mth token in counting; note that $n_{d,k}$ and $n_{t,k}$ are the counts where k is the topic, d is the document, and t and t' are terms. So, Gibbs sampling based LDA essentially maintains various counters to store these count values. Basically, it randomly initializes K clusters/topics and iterates in updating the probabilities specified by the above equation which employs various counters and also in every iteration the counters are suitably updated.

7.8. Concept and topic

Another related notion that is used in clustering is *concept*. A framework called conceptual clustering is a prominent soft clustering paradigm that employs classical logic and its variants to describe clusters. For example, a cricket ball could be described using $(color = red \lor white) \land (make = leather) \land (dia = medium) \land (shape = sphere)$ which is a conjunction of internal disjunctions (or predicates). Each of the conjuncts is viewed as a concept that describes a set of objects; for example, $(color = red)$ describes a set of red colored objects. This framework is called *conjunctive conceptual clustering*. This is also related to frequent itemset based clustering and classification.

For example, consider patterns of 7 and 1 shown in Table 8.9 wherein the left part is character 7 and in the right part character 1 is depicted; each is in the form of a 3×3 binary matrix (image). In a realistic scenario the size of the matrix could be larger and the number of 1 pixels will also be larger; possibly there could be noise affecting the pixel values mutating a zero by a one and a one by a zero. If there are n such character patterns with half of them from class 7 and the other half from class 1, then it is possible to describe

Table 8.9. Printed characters of 7 and 1.

1	1	1		1	0	0
0	0	1		1	0	0
0	0	1		1	0	0
	7				1	

Table 8.10. Description of the concepts.

Concept	i_1	i_2	i_3	i_4	i_5	i_6	i_7	i_8	i_9
Class 1	1	0	0	1	0	0	1	0	0
Class 7	1	1	1	0	0	1	0	0	1

the classes as follows. Consider the 9 pixels in the 3×3 matrix and label them as $i_1, i_2, \ldots, i_9$ in a row-major fashion. Then the frequent itemset corresponding to 7 is $i_1 \wedge i_2 \wedge i_3 \wedge i_6 \wedge i_9$ because this pattern is present in half the number of characters given and the frequent itemset in class 1 is $i_1 \wedge i_4 \wedge i_7$. So, it is possible to have the following classification rules where the antecedent of the rule is the frequent itemset and the consequent is the Class Label:

- Character 1: $i_1 \wedge i_4 \wedge i_7 \rightarrow Class1$
- Character 7: $i_1 \wedge i_2 \wedge i_3 \wedge i_6 \wedge i_9 \rightarrow Class7$

Equivalently one can describe these conjunctive concepts as shown in Table 8.10. Note the similarity between concept which describes a cluster or a class by selecting a subset of items or features and topic which assigns a probability to each item or feature; both describe clusters. In the example shown in Table 8.10 both the class descriptions (concepts) select item i_1 indicating softness.

Research Ideas

1. Derive an expression for the number of soft clusterings of n patterns into K soft clusters.

2. Discuss Rough Fuzzy Clustering in the case of leader and what can happen to other algorithms.

Relevant References

(a) S. Asharaf and M. N. Murty, An adaptive rough fuzzy single pass algorithm for clustering large data sets. *Pattern Recognition*, 36:3015–3018, 2003.

(b) V. S. Babu and P. Viswanath, Rough-fuzzy weighted k-nearest leader classifier for large data sets. *Pattern Recognition*, 42:1719–1731, 2009.

(c) P. Maji and S. Paul, Rough-fuzzy clustering for grouping functionally similar genes from microarray data. *IEEE/ACM Transactions on Computational Biology Bioinformatics*, 10:286–299, 2013.

3. A difficulty with the use of GAs is that they are not scalable. The problem gets complicated further when one considers MOOP. How to design scalable GAs?

Relevant References

(a) A. Kink, D. Coit and A. Smith, Multi-objective optimization using genetic algorithms: A tutorial. *Reliability Engineering and System Safety*, 91(9):992–1007, 2006.

(b) K. Amours, Multi-objective optimization using genetic algorithms. Master's thesis, Jinking University, 2012.

(c) D. Yumin, X. Shufen, J. Fanghua and L. Jinhai, Research and application on a novel clustering algorithm of quantum optimization in server load balancing. *Mathematical Problems in Engineering*, 2014.

4. Discuss the possibilities of abstracting soft clustering using the string-of-centroids. Can we extend the string-of-group-representation to realize a soft partition? How?

Relevant References

(a) U. Maulik and S. Bandyopadhyay: Genetic algorithm-based clustering technique: *Pattern Recognition*, 33:1455–1465, 2000.

(b) M. N. Murty, Clustering large data sets. In *Soft Computing Approach to Pattern Recognition and Image Processing*, A. Ghosh and S. K. Pal (eds.), pp. 41–63. New Jersey: World-Scientific, 2002.

(c) L. Zhu, L. Cao and J. Yang, Multiobjective evolutionary algorithm-based soft subspace clustering. *Proceedings of IEEE Congress on Evolutionary Computation*, 2012.

5. EM is a probabilistic version of the K-Means algorithm. Why did EM became so popular in Machine Learning?

Relevant References

(a) T. Hoffman, Latent semantic models for collaborative filtering. *ACM Transactions on Information Systems*, 22(1):89–115, 2004.

(b) D. Sontag and D. M. Roy, Complexity of inference in latent Dirichlet allocation. *Proceedings of NIPS*, 2011.

(c) S.-K. Ng, Recent developments in expectation-maximization methods for analyzing complex data. *Wiley Interdisciplinary Reviews: Computational Statistics*, 5:415–431, 2013.

6. Matrix factorization is useful in clustering. It is possible to show equivalence between PLSA and NMF; similarly between K-Means and NMF. Is it possible to unify clustering algorithms through matrix factorization?

Relevant References

(a) A. Roy Chaudhuri and M. N. Murty, On the relation between K-Means and PLSA. *Proceedings of ICPR*, 2012.

(b) C. Ding, T. Li and W. Peng, On the equivalence between non-negative matrix factorization and probabilistic latent semantic indexing. *Computational Statistics and Data Analysis*, 52:3913–3927, 2008.

(c) J. Kim and H. Park, Sparse nonnegative matrix factorization for clustering. Technical Report, Georgia Technical, GT-CSE-08-01.pdf, 2008.

7. Is it possible to view clustering based on frequent itemsets as a matrix factorization problem?

Relevant References

(a) B. C. M. Fung, K. Wang and M. Ester, Hierarchical document clustering using frequent itemsets. *Proceedings of SDM*, 2003.

(b) G. V. R. Kiran, R. Shankar and V. Pudi, Frequent itemset-based hierarchical document clustering using Wikipedia as external knowledge. *Proceedings* of *Knowledge-Based and Intelligent Information and Engineering Systems*, Lecture Notes in Computer Science, Vol. 6277, 2010.

(c) J. Leskovec, A. Rajaraman and J. D. Ullman, Mining massive datasets, http://infolab.stanford.edu/~ullman/mmds/book.pdf, 2014.

8. LDA employs Dirichlet and multinomial conjugate pair of distributions. Is it possible to use other distributions?

Relevant References

(a) D. M. Blei, Probabilistic topic models. *Communications of the ACM*, 55:77–84, 2012.

(b) D. Newman, E. V. Bonilla and W. L. Buntine, Improving topic coherence with regularized topic models. *Proceedings of NIPS*, 2011.

(c) H. M. Wallach, D. M. Mimno and A. McCallum: Rethinking LDA: Why priors matter. *Proceedings of NIPS*, 2009.

Chapter 9

Application — Social and Information Networks

1. Introduction

Social networks characterize different kinds of interactions among individuals. Typically, a social network is abstracted using a network/graph. The individuals are represented as nodes in a network and interaction between a pair of individuals is represented using an edge between the corresponding pair of nodes. Usually a social network is represented as a graph. The nodes represent individuals or entities with attributes such as interests, profile, etc. The interactions among the entities could be one of friendship, business relationship, communication, etc.

These graphs could be either directed or undirected. Typically friendship between two individuals is mutual; so, edges in a friendship network are undirected. However, in influence networks the relation may not be symmetric; a person A may influence B, but B may not be able to influence A. So, in influence networks, the edges could be directed. Note that author–co-author relation is symmetric and network of authors is undirected whereas the citation network/graph is directed.

Such a graphical representation can help in analyzing not only the social networks but also other kinds of networks including document/term networks. For example, in *information retrieval* typically a *bag of words* paradigm is used to represent document collections. Here, each document is viewed as a vector of terms in the collection; it only captures the frequency of occurrence of terms not the co-occurrence of terms in the document collection. It is possible to extract a collection of co-occurring terms by viewing each term as a node in a graph and co-occurrence of a pair of terms using an edge between the corresponding nodes. Typically a clique of size l in the graph characterizes a collection of l co-occurring terms; it is possible to perform clustering of nodes in the graph to obtain such co-occurring term collections. The corresponding operation is called *community detection* in social networks.

Another important problem in social networks is *link prediction*. In link prediction, a similarity function is used to predict whether two nodes which are not currently linked can have a link between them in the future. A popular subset, of such functions which compute similarity between a pair of nodes, is based on the set of adjacent nodes.

2. Patterns in Graphs

It is found that networks have some distinguishing features. The main features associated with them are

- Follow power law distributions
- Have small diameters
- Exhibit community structure

According to the power law, two variables x and y are related by a power law when

$$y(x) = Cx^{-\gamma},$$

where C and γ are constants.

A random value is distributed according to a power law when the probability distribution function is given by:

$$p(x) = Ax^{-\gamma}, \quad \gamma > 1, x \geq x_{\min}.$$

In the case of internet graphs, a number of parameters follow the power law. Firstly, if we find the degree d_i of every node i and arrange them in decreasing order of d_i, then if r_i is the index of node i when arranged in decreasing order (called the rank), then for every node i

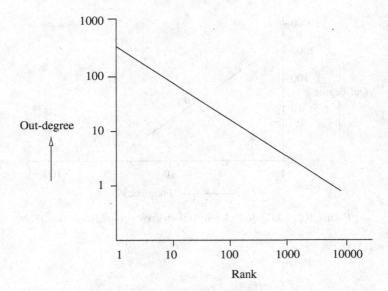

Figure 9.1.   Log–log plot of out-degree versus rank.

we get

$$d_i \propto r_i^R.$$

R is called the rank exponent and is the slope of the plot of out-degree of the nodes versus the rank drawn in log–log scale. If the nodes are sorted in decreasing order of out-degree d_i and the log–log plot of the out-degree versus the rank is plotted, the plot is as shown in Figure 9.1.

Secondly, for every out-degree d we find the number of nodes with that out-degree. This is called the frequency f_d of the degree d. If f_d versus d is plotted for every degree d, we get

$$f_d \propto d^O.$$

The constant O is the slope of the plot of frequency of the out-degree versus the out-degree drawn in the log–log scale. Figure 9.2 shows this plot.

Thirdly, if we find the eigenvalues of the adjacency matrix A and arrange them in decreasing order then an eigenvalue λ_i has an

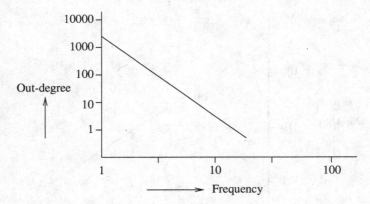

Figure 9.2.   Log–log plot of out-degree versus frequency.

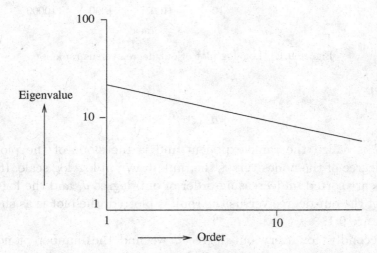

Figure 9.3.   Log–log plot of eigenvalue versus order.

order i. Then we get

$$\lambda_i \propto i^E.$$

E is called the eigenvalue exponent and is the slope of the eigenvalues versus the order in log–log scale. Figure 9.3 shows this plot.
It shows the log–log plot of the eigenvalues in decreasing order.

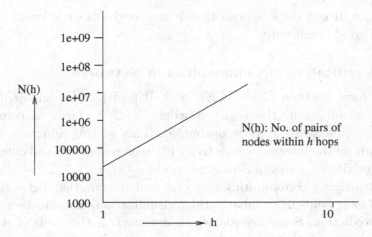

Figure 9.4. Log–log plot of number of pairs of nodes within h hops versus h.

Fourthly, the total number of pairs of nodes $N(h)$ which are within h hops is proportional to the number of hops to the power of a constant $\mathcal{H}$. It can be represented as:

$$N(h) = h^{\mathcal{H}}.$$

$\mathcal{H}$ is called the hop-plot exponent. This is shown in Figure 9.4.

The **effective diameter** of a graph is the minimum number of hops required for some fraction (say 90%) of all connected pairs of nodes to reach each other.

A social network gives more importance to the topology and ignores information pertaining to each node. Information networks give importance to this information also. It is found that a group of nodes interact strongly among themselves than with the outside world. These groups of nodes are the communities or groups in the network. It can be seen that the intra-group connectivity is much more than the inter-group connectivity. A measure commonly used for the notion of community is the conductance or the normalized cut metric. The conductance of a community is the ratio of the number of cut edges between the set of nodes in the community and its complement divided by the number of internal edges inside the set of nodes. It can thus be seen that if the conductance is small, then it is a good community.

3. Identification of Communities in Networks

If we have a graph $G = \langle V, E \rangle$, with $|V|(=n)$ nodes and $|E|(=e)$ edges, a subset of the nodes S where $S \subset V$ forms a community if some score $f(S)$ is optimized. This scoring function $f(S)$ depends on the internal connectivity between nodes in S and external connectivity of nodes in S to other nodes.

Identifying communities in social and information networks is useful as it helps in summarization, visualization, classification, and link prediction. Some criteria which are used on the basis of which the clustering is done are as follows:

Clustering Coefficient:

One of the related issues dealing with some notion of connectivity or transitivity is the *clustering coefficient*. It may be viewed as the probability that two randomly selected neighbors of a node are neighbors of each other. It is defined for node i as

$$C_i = \frac{2e_i}{k_i(k_i - 1)},$$

where e_i is the number of links among the neighbors of i, k_i is the number of neighbors of i and $\frac{k_i(k_i-1)}{2}$ is the maximum number of links possible among the k_i neighbors of i. We illustrate it with the help of the network shown in Figure 9.5. There are eight nodes in

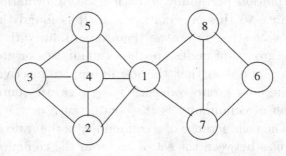

Figure 9.5.   An example network to illustrate clustering coefficient.

Table 9.1. Clustering coefficients for the nodes.

Node number	Set of neighbors	Clustering coefficient
1	{2,4,5,7,8}	0.3
2	{1,3,4}	0.66
3	{2,4,5}	0.66
4	{1,2,3,5}	0.75
5	{1,3,4}	0.66
6	{7,8}	1
7	{1,6,8}	0.66
8	{1,6,7}	0.66

the network and the clustering coefficient for each of the nodes in the network is given in Table 9.1. Note that the average clustering coefficient is 0.67; this gives a measure of how the nodes can form clusters.

Modularity:

Another important notion associated with clustering is *Modularity* of the network. A network is said to be modular if it has a higher clustering coefficient compared to any other network with the same number of nodes assuming the appropriate degree of distribution.

It is possible to define modularity using the following notation:

- Let $|E|$ be the total number of edges in the network.
- Let d_i and d_j be the degrees of the vertices i and j.
- Let A be the adjacency matrix where $A_{ij} = 1$ if there is a link between nodes i and j and $A_{ij} = 0$ otherwise.
- Let there be two communities in the network, C_1 and C_2.
- Let Q be the modularity and it is given by

$$Q = \frac{1}{2|E|} \sum_{i,j \in C_l} \left(A_{ij} - \frac{d_i d_j}{2|E|} \right).$$

In some sense it characterizes how clustered some nodes are; the summand for each ij pair consists of the difference between the A_{ij} value and the expected value based on the degrees d_i and d_j.

Graph clustering algorithms can be used to identify communities. Some approaches for graph clustering are:

1. Graph partitioning
2. Spectral clustering
3. Linkage-based clustering
4. Hierarchical clustering
5. Random walks

3.1. Graph partitioning

Partitioning of the graph into smaller components is carried out such that the number of edges connecting vertices from different components is minimized. One method for doing this is Multi-level recursive bisection where the actual graph is coarsened into a much smaller graph. The communities are computed in this smaller graph and projected back to the original graph.

Some graph partitioning algorithms which are used for community detection are flow-based methods, spectral methods and hierarchical methods.

One way of partitioning the graph is to use bisection of the graph. If more clusters are needed, bisection can be done iteratively.

One of the earlier methods starts with an initial partition which is improved over a number of iterations. The parameter to be optimized is a benefit function Q which is the difference between the number of edges in the clusters and the number of edges between the clusters. Nodes are swapped between clusters in such a way that Q increases. To avoid the local maxima of Q, swaps giving lower Q values are also accepted. Finally, the partition giving largest Q is accepted. This procedure is used to get a bisection of the graph. Then a cluster is chosen which is divided into two smaller clusters and this goes on till there are a predefined number of clusters.

According to the max-flow min-cut theorem, the minimal subset of edges whose deletion would separate two nodes s and t carries the maximum flow that can be transported from s to t across the graph. An artificial sink t is added to the graph and the maximum flow from a source vertex s to t is calculated which helps to identify the minimum cut separating the graph into communities.

Graphs can also be partitioned by minimizing the conductance. In a graph G, consider a subgraph G_1. Then the conductance C of G_1 is

$$C(G_1) = \frac{no(G_1, G \backslash G_1)}{min(d_{G1}, d_{G \backslash G_1})},$$

where $no(G_1, G \backslash G_1)$ is the cut size of G_1 and d_{G1} and $d_{G \backslash G1}$ are the total degrees of G_1 and the total degree of the rest of the graph respectively.

3.2. Spectral clustering

The similarity matrix for the graph is computed. The eigenvectors of this matrix are used to partition the graph into clusters. The unnormalized and normalized graph Laplacian is used for the partitioning.

Unnormalized graph Laplacian L is given by

$$L = D - W,$$

where W is the weight matrix such that for some i and j, $w_{ij} = w_{ji}$ gives the weight between two nodes. D is the degree matrix which is a diagonal matrix with the degrees $d_1, \ldots, d_n$ on the diagonal.

The matrix L is symmetric and positive semi-definite. L has n non-negative, real eigenvalues and the smallest eigenvalue of L is 0. This means

$$0 = \lambda_1 \leq \lambda_2 \leq \cdots \leq \lambda_n.$$

Also for any vector $v \varepsilon \mathcal{R}^n$

$$v^T L v = \frac{1}{2} \sum_{i,j=1}^{n} w_{ij}(v_i - v_j)^2.$$

Spectral clustering is carried out by finding the k eigenvectors of L where k is the number of clusters. The n data points are transformed using the k eigenvectors and clustered using the k-means algorithm.

The normalized graph Laplacian can be got in two ways. The first matrix is L_{sym} which is a symmetric matrix and L_{rw} which corresponds to a random walk. These can be computed as:

$$L_{sym} = D^{-\frac{1}{2}} L D^{-\frac{1}{2}} = I - D^{-\frac{1}{2}} W D^{-\frac{1}{2}},$$

$$L_{rw} = D^{-1} L = I - D^{-1} W.$$

Some properties of the normalized graph Laplacian are to be noted. λ is an eigenvalue of L_{rw} with eigenvector u if and only if λ is an eigenvalue of L_{sym} with eigenvector $w = D^{\frac{1}{2}} u$. Also λ is an eigenvalue of L_{rw} with eigenvector u if and only if λ and u solve $Lu = \lambda D u$.

0 is an eigenvalue of L_{rw} and L_{sym}. Both L_{rw} and L_{sym} are positive semidefinite and have n non-negative real valued eigenvalues $0 = \lambda_1 \leq \cdots \leq \lambda_n$.

Additionally, if we take a vector $v \varepsilon \mathcal{R}^n$, we get

$$v^T L_{sym} v = \frac{1}{2} \sum_{i,j=1}^{n} w_{ij} \left(\frac{v_i}{\sqrt{(d_i)}} - \frac{v_i}{\sqrt{(d_j)}} \right)^2.$$

Normalized spectral clustering is done in two ways.

Method 1:

The unnormalized Laplacian L is computed using the weight matrix W and the degree matrix D. If there are k clusters, find the first k eigenvectors of the generalized eigen problem $Lu = \lambda D u$. The n data points are transformed using the k eigenvectors and these points are clustered using k-means algorithm as discussed in the chapter on clustering.

Method 2:

The normalized Laplacian L_{sym} is computed. Using L_{sym}, the first k eigenvectors $u_1, \ldots, u_k$ are computed. If $U \varepsilon \mathcal{R}^{n \times k}$ is the matrix containing $u_1, \ldots, u_k$ as the columns, a new matrix $P \varepsilon \mathcal{R}^{n \times k}$ is formed from U by normalizing the rows, i.e. $p_{ij} = u_{ij}/(\sum_k u_{ik}^2)^{\frac{1}{2}}$. The datapoints are transformed using the P matrix. These points are clustered using k-means algorithm.

3.3. Linkage-based clustering

The similarity between two objects is recursively defined as the average similarity between objects linked with them. The links between different objects with the similarities are used for clustering the graph.

If the edges that connect vertices of different communities are identified, then by removing those edges, communities can be identified.

One of the earliest methods use the edge betweenness. This is called the Girvan–Newman algorithm. The edge centrality is measured according to some property of the graph. The edge with the largest centrality is removed. The edge centralities are again measured and the edge with the largest centrality is again removed. Edges are found which have highest "betweenness measure" for dividing the network. One measure of betweenness is the shortest-path betweenness. Here the shortest paths between all pairs of vertices is found and it is necessary to count how many run along each edge. The other measure of betweenness is the current-flow betweenness. A circuit is created by placing a unit resistance on each edge of the network and unit current source and sink at the pair of vertices being considered. The resulting current flow in the network will travel along the various paths where the edges with least resistance carry more current. The current-flow betweenness for an edge is the absolute value of the current aggregated over all source/sink pairs. After the edge with highest betweenness measure is removed, the betweenness measure is recalculated to find the next edge to remove.

3.4. Hierarchical clustering

Social networks generally have a hierarchical structure where smaller communities are embedded within larger communities. This will be reflected in the dendrogram. Depending on the level in which the dendrogram is considered, different partitions will result.

One hierarchical clustering algorithm that employs agglomerative clustering based on random walk to find the similarity measures between vertices is considered next.

3.4.1. *Random walks*

In this algorithm, a measure of similarity between vertices is found based on random walks. This measure can be used in agglomerative clustering to determine the communities. A discrete random walk process on a graph is one where at each time step a walker is on a vertex and moves to a vertex chosen randomly and uniformly among its neighbors. The sequence of vertices visited is a Markov Chain. At each step, the transition probability from vertex i to vertex j is $P_{ij} = \frac{A_{ij}}{D_{ii}}$. By doing this, we can get the transition matrix P which can be written as $P = D^{-1}A$ where A is the adjacency matrix and D is a diagonal matrix with the degree of the nodes along the diagonal.

To find the distance r between nodes, note the following:

- If two vertices i and j belong to the same community, then P_{ij}^t will be high where t gives the length of the random walk.
- P_{ij}^t is influenced by the degree D_{jj} as the walker has a higher probability to go to the node of higher degree.
- For two vertices i and j belonging to the same community, probably $\forall k, P_{ik}^t \simeq P_{jk}^t$.

The distance r_{ij} between two vertices will be

$$r_{ij} = \sqrt{\sum_{k=1}^{n} \frac{(P_{ik}^t - P_{jk}^t)^2}{D_{kk}}} = \left\| D^{-\frac{1}{2}} P_{i.}^t - D^{-\frac{1}{2}} P_{j.}^t \right\|.$$

The distance between two communities C_1 and C_2 can be defined as

$$r_{C_1 C_2} = \sqrt{\sum_{k=1}^{n} \frac{(P_{C_1 k}^t - P_{C_2 k}^t)^2}{D_{kk}}} = \left\| D^{-\frac{1}{2}} P_{C_1.}^t - D^{-\frac{1}{2}} P_{C_2.}^t \right\|.$$

The probability to go from community C to vertex j is given by

$$P_{Cj}^t = \frac{1}{|C|} \sum_{i \varepsilon C} P_{ij}^t.$$

The algorithm used is the agglomerative clustering. At first, each vertex belongs to a different clusters. At each step k two communities

C_1 and C_2 are chosen to be merged together. The two communities to be chosen has to minimize the mean σ_k of the squared distances between each vertex k and its community. This means

$$\sigma_k = \frac{1}{n} \sum_{C \varepsilon P_k} \sum_{i \varepsilon C} r_{iC}^2.$$

This is done by computing the variation $\triangle \sigma(C_1, C_2)$ for every pair of adjacent communities $\{C_1, C_2\}$. This is given by

$$\triangle \sigma(C_1, C_2) = \frac{1}{n} \left(\sum_{i \varepsilon C_3} r_{iC3}^2 - \sum_{i \varepsilon C_1} r_{iC_1}^2 - \sum_{i \varepsilon C_2} r_{iC_2}^2 \right).$$

Two communities which give the lowest value of $\triangle \sigma$ are merged at each step.

3.4.2. *Divisive hierarchical clustering*

This method finds edges which have highest "betweenness" measure for dividing the network. One measure of betweenness is the shortest-path betweenness. Here, the shortest paths between all pairs of vertices is found and it is necessary to count how many runs along each edge. The other measure of betweenness is the current-flow betweenness. A circuit is created by placing a unit resistance on each edge of the network and unit current source and sink at the pair of vertices being considered. The resulting current flow in the network will travel along the various paths where the edges with least resistance carry more current. The current-flow betweenness for an edge is the absolute value of the current aggregated over all source/sink pairs. After the edge with the highest betweenness measure is removed, the betweenness measure is recalculated to find the next edge to remove.

3.5. **Modularity optimization for partitioning graphs**

High values of modularity indicate good partitions. An optimization of the modularity Q of a graph is intractable as there are a very large number of ways in which a graph can be partitioned. Some approximation algorithms are used instead to get the partition with the maximum modularity. Some of them are:

3.5.1. *Iterative greedy methods*

In one technique, an agglomerative clustering technique is used. At first there are n clusters if there are n vertices, i.e. each cluster consists of a single vertex. First one edge is connected making the number of clusters from n to $n - 1$, giving a new partition of the graph. The edge is chosen such that the partition formed gives the maximum increase in modularity. At each iteration, an edge is added so that the modularity increase is maximum. It is to be noted that if it is an internal edge of a cluster, then the modularity does not change.

Since calculation of ΔQ for each edge requires a constant time, this calculation requires $O(m)$ where m is the number of edges. After merging the chosen communities, the matrix which indicates the fraction of edges between two clusters i and j of the running partition is updated in $O(n)$. Since the algorithm runs for $n - 1$ iterations, its complexity is $O((n + n)n)$ which is $O(n^2)$ for sparse graphs. An improvement on the time is obtained when the ΔQ values are stored in a max-heap and the matrix which expresses the fraction of edges between clusters is replaced by an array which contains the sums of the elements of each row. The complexity of the algorithm is $O(md \log n)$ where d is the depth of the dendrogram which shows the successive partitions found as the iterations progress. For graphs with a strong hierarchical structure, the complexity is $O(n \log^2 n)$.

The above algorithm tends to form large communities rather than smaller communities which leads to poor values of Q. One method to address this problem is to normalize the increase in modularity ΔQ by dividing it with the fraction of edges incident on one of the communities. Another method is to choose the communities to be merged at each step by finding the largest value of ΔQ times a factor. This factor known as the consolidation ratio is larger for communities of equal size. Another variation to take care of the problem of larger communities is to allow more than one community pair to be merged in each iteration. It also allows the movement of single nodes from a community to a neighboring community. Another method of greedy optimization is to start from some promising intermediate configuration rather than from individual nodes which is measured by the topological similarity between clusters. Using an algorithm which alternates between greedy optimization and stochastic perturbation of the partitions is known to be a good strategy.

Another greedy approach initially puts all the vertices of the graph in different communities and conducts a sequential sweep over the vertices. For a vertex i, the gain in modularity from putting i in the neighboring communities is found. The community giving largest increase in Q is selected to move i. At the end of the sweep, a first level partition is obtained. The communities are then replaced by supervertices, and supervertices are connected if there is at least an edge between the nodes of the two communities. The weight given to the edge is the sum of the weights of the edges between the communities at the lower level. The two steps of sequential sweep and forming supervertices is repeated forming new hierarchical levels and different supergraphs. When modularity does not increase any further, the iterations are stopped. This method is very fast and the time complexity is of the order of $O(m)$ where m is the number of edges.

3.5.2. *Simulated annealing (SA)*

In SA, the solution is found by the method of search. A string S_c represents the trial solution. This is called the current solution which is evaluated to get E_c. A new trial solution S_t is found which is a neighbor of the current solution. Its evaluation E_t is found. If $E_t > E_c$ then S_t is accepted as the new current solution. If $E_t \leq E_c$, S_t is accepted as the new current solution with a probability p given by

$$p = exp\left(\frac{-\Delta E}{T}\right),$$

where $\Delta E = E_c - E_t$ and T is the temperature which is high at the beginning so that p is high. As the iteration progress, T is reduced using the cooling rate α which has a typical value of 0.9 or 0.95. Every few iterations, $T = \alpha * T$ is carried out. As T reduces the probability

p of accepting a solution which is worse than the current solution decreases. The procedure is stopped when T becomes very small.

SA has been used for modularity optimization where the current solution is a clustering of the data. The moves carried out are the local moves where a single node is moved from one cluster to another and global moves which consist of mergers and splits of clusters. The evaluation of a solution is done by finding the modularity increase. It is to be noted that the method is slow and can be used only for small graphs of upto 10^4 nodes.

3.5.3. *Extremal optimization*

Extremal Optimization is a heuristic technique where the contribution of local variables to the overall modularity of the system is studied and optimized. For every vertex the local modularity is divided by the degree of the vertex to get a fitness measure. Initially the graph is randomly partitioned into two groups, each having equal number of nodes. At each iteration, the fitness measure of every node is calculated. The node with the lowest fitness is shifted to the other cluster. The local fitness values are again recalculated and new partitions are formed by moving a node. This process is repeated till there is no improvement in the global modularity Q. This process is likely to sometimes give local optima. This can be improved if probabilistic selection is carried out. The nodes are ranked according to their fitness value and the vertex of rank r is selected with probability

$$P(r) = r^{-\alpha},$$

where α is a constant. Sorting the fitness values is $O(n \log n)$. Choosing the node to be moved is $O(\log n)$. Checking whether the modularity can be improved is $O(n)$. The complexity of this method is $O(n^2 \log n)$. This method gives accurate results in reasonable time.

3.5.4. *Spectral optimization*

In this method, a modularity matrix M is formed whose elements are:

$$M_{ij} = A_{ij} - \frac{d_i d_j}{2m},$$

where A is the adjacency matrix, m is the number of edges in the graph and d_i and d_j are the degrees of the nodes i and j.

The modularity Q can be written as:

$$Q = \frac{1}{2m} \sum_{ij} \left(A_{ij} - \frac{d_i d_j}{2m} \right) \delta_{C_i, C_j}, \tag{1}$$

where δ_{C_i, C_j} is the Kronecker delta. It takes the value 1 if $C_i = C_j$ i.e. if the two points belong to the same community.

In the case of a partition of the graph into two clusters, if $u_i = +1$ when vertex i belongs to cluster C_1 and $s_i = -1$ when vertex i belongs to cluster C_2, the Eq. (1) can be written as

$$Q = \frac{1}{4m} \sum_{ij} \left(A_{ij} - \frac{d_i d_j}{2m} \right) (u_i u_j + 1)$$

$$= \frac{1}{4m} \sum_{ij} B_{ij} u_i u_j = \frac{1}{4m} \mathbf{u}^T \mathbf{B} \mathbf{u}.$$

The vector u can be expressed using the eigenvectors v_i of the modularity matrix B. We get

$$u = \sum_i (v_i^T \cdot u) v_i. \quad Q \text{ then becomes}$$

$$Q = \frac{1}{4m} \sum_i (v_i \cdot u) v_i^T B \sum_j (v_j \cdot u) u_j = \frac{1}{4m} \sum_{i=1}^{n} (v_i^T \cdot u)^2 \beta_i,$$

where β_i is the eigenvalue of B corresponding to the eigenvector v_i.

It is to be noted that B has the trivial eigenvector $(1, 1 \ldots, 1)$ with eigenvalue zero. Hence if B has no positive eigenvalues, only the trivial solution exists which consists of a single cluster with Q_0. Otherwise, the eigenvector of B corresponding to the largest positive eigenvalue, v_1 and group the nodes according to the signs of the components of v_1. This result can be further improved if nodes are shifted from one community such that modularity increases. The drawback of the spectral bisection is that it gives good results for two communities but is not so accurate for larger number of communities. To take care of this, more than one eigenvector can be used. Using the first p eigenvectors, n p-dimensional vectors can be constructed, each corresponding to a node. The components of the vector of node i is proportional to the p values of the eigenvectors in position i. Community vectors can be found by summing the vectors of the nodes in a community. Then if two community vectors form an angle larger than $\frac{\pi}{2}$, keeping the two communities separate yields larger modularity.

Spectral optimization of modularities to find communities is $O(n(m + n))$ which is $O(n^2)$ on a sparse graph.

The above methods can be extended to graphs with weighted edges where the adjacency matrix A is replaced by the weight matrix W. We get the equation:

$$Q = \frac{1}{2W} \sum_{ij} \left(W_{ij} - \frac{u_i u_j}{2W} \right) \delta(C_i, C_j).$$

It can also be extended to directed graphs where $d_i d_j$ is replaced by $d_i^{\text{out}} d_j^{\text{in}}$ where d^{in} is the indegree and d^{out} is the out-degree. The expression becomes:

$$Q = \frac{1}{m} \sum_{ij} \left(A_{ij} - \frac{d_i^{\text{out}} d_j^{\text{in}}}{m} \right) \delta(C_1, C_2).$$

Another way of spectral optimization uses the weighted adjacency matrix W and an assignment matrix X which is $n \times k$ where k is the number of clusters. In $X, x_{ij} = 1$ if node i belongs to cluster j and zero otherwise. The modularity can be written as:

$$Q \propto tr[X^T (W - D)X] = -tr[X^T L_Q X].$$

Here entries of D are $D_{ij} = d_i d_j$. $L_Q = D - W$ is called the Q-Laplacian. Setting the first derivative of Q with respect to X to zero, we get

$$L_Q X = X \cdot C, \tag{2}$$

where C is a diagonal matrix. Equation (2) uses the Q-Laplacian matrix to carry out modularity maximization. For larger graphs, the Q-Laplacian can be approximated by the transition matrix W' which is obtained by normalizing W such that the sum of the elements of each row is one. The first k eigenvectors of the transition matrix W' can be computed where k is the number of clusters. This can be used to find the co-ordinates of the graph nodes which can be clustered using k-means clustering.

3.5.5. *Mathematical programming*

Modularity optimization can be formulated as a linear or quadratic program. The linear program is defined on the links and the modularity matrix B. It can be written as:

$$Q \propto \sum_{ij} B_{ij}(1 - x_{ij}), \tag{3}$$

where $x_{ij} = 1$ if i and j belong to the cluster and zero otherwise. Equation (3) is an integer programming problem and is NP-hard. However, if x is made real-valued, it can be solved in polynomial time. Since the solution does not correspond to an actual partition as the values of x are fractional, a rounding step is required. The values of the x variables is used as a sort of distance and those close to each other in the x values are put in the same cluster.

Quadratic programming can also be used. The equation used is:

$$Q = \frac{1}{4m} \sum_{ij} B_{ij}(1 + u_i u_j),$$

where $u_i = 1$ if vertex i belongs to cluster 1 and $u_i = 0$ if vertex i belongs to cluster 2.

This problem is NP-complete, and can be solved in polynomial time only if u is allowed to be real. Each scalar u is transformed into a n-dimensional vector $\mathbf{u}$ and a product such as $u_i u_j$ is a scalar product between vectors. The vectors are normalized so that their tips are on a unit-sphere of the n-dimensional space. An $(n-1)$-dimensional hyperplane centered at the origin cuts the space in two giving two subsets for the vectors. The hyperplane which gives the highest modularity is picked.

3.5.6. *Mean field annealing*

This method is an alternative to SA. Gibbs probabilities are used to compute the conditional mean value for a node. This is the community membership of the node. Mean field approximation is made on all the nodes to find a consistent set of nonlinear equations in an iterative way. This requires a time of $O[n(m + n)]$.

3.5.7. *Genetic algorithms*

The chromosome in the genetic algorithm gives the partition to which each node belongs. At each step, a bipartition of the graph is carried out. For the original two partitions and the successive bipartitions, a genetic algorithm is applied on the graph/subgraphs formed. The fitness function of each chromosome is the modularity of the partition.

4. Link Prediction

There are several applications associated with networks/graphs where predicting whether a pair of nodes X and Y which are not currently connected will get connected (or have a *link*) in the future is important. Based on the type of objects the nodes represent in a network, we may have either a *homogeneous* or a *heterogeneous* network.

- **Homogeneous network:** Here, all the nodes represent the same type of objects. For example, in a social network each node represents an individual and the links characterize the type of interaction; so, such a network is homogeneous. Another example of a homogeneous network is the citation network where each node represents a publication and a directed link from node X to node Y indicates that publication represented by X is citing the publication corresponding to Y.
- **Heterogeneous network:** In a heterogeneous network nodes may correspond to different types of objects. For example, in an author-paper network some nodes may correspond to authors and others correspond to papers. There could be a co-author link between two

authors. Also there could be a link between an author and a paper. So, not only nodes, even the edges could be of different types.

Even though these two types could be different in terms of nodes and edges, generically a proximity function is used to predict the possibility of a link between a pair of nodes. In the current chapter we consider only homogeneous networks. Also we consider simple graphs where it is not possible to have multiple edges between a pair of nodes, even though the graphs need not be simple in general. For example, a pair of individuals could have co-authored more than one paper together; if there is one link for each co-authored paper, then the graph could be a multi-graph. Further in the discussion here we consider undirected graphs only.

Some of the specific applications of link prediction are:

- **Suggesting friends** in a social network. Two individuals have a better possibility of becoming friends even if they are not currently so provided they have a larger number of common friends.
- **Recommending collaborators:** It involves recommending a collaborator Y to an employee X where X and Y are from the same or different organizations.
- **Monitoring Terrorist Networks:** It identifies possible links between terrorists; this may involve predicting links that are not explicit currently.
- **Recommending a movie or a book** to a user based on a possible link or association between a person and a movie or a book which requires link prediction in heterogeneous networks; such a network will have as nodes people, movies, and books.

4.1. Proximity functions

Predicting the link between a pair of nodes is inherently characterized by some notion of *proximity* between them. Such proximity functions should be based on the knowledge of how the network *evolves*. By proximity we mean either similarity or distance/dissimilarity. Two currently unconnected nodes X and Y are highly likely to have a link between them if similarity between them is high or correspondingly distance/dissimilarity between them is low. Some of the popular local similarity measures, between a pair of nodes X and Y, are based on the nodes that are directly linked to both X and Y; such nodes are typically called *common neighbors* of X and Y. Another intuitively appealing proximity function is based on some weighted distance between the two nodes. We discuss below some of the popularly used proximity functions.

Two important types of functions for characterizing proximity between a pair of nodes are based on similarity or those based on distance. We explain some of these functions using the example network shown in Figure 9.6.

4.1.1. *Similarity functions*

Typically the similarity functions are based on the *common neighbors* as they depend on information corresponding to the two nodes; so, they are called local similarity functions as they use the information local to the nodes. Let X and Y be two nodes in the network. Let

- $N(X) =$ set of neighbors of $X = \{t | there\ is\ a\ link\ between\ X\ and\ t\}$.
- $Z = N(X) \cap N(Y) = \{z | z \in N(X)\ and\ z \in N(Y)\}$.

Note that Z is the set of common neighbors. The related similarity functions, where $S(X, Y)$ is the similarity between X and Y, are

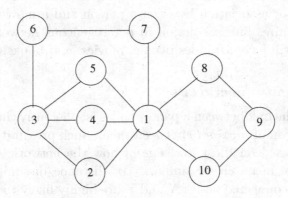

Figure 9.6.   An example network.

1. **Preferential Attachment:** Here, the similarity $S_{\text{pa}}(X, Y)$ is proportional to the product of the degrees of X and Y. It is given by

$$S_{\text{pa}}(X, Y) = |N(X)| \times |N(Y)|.$$

This function encourages links between high degree nodes. The similarity values for the missing links in the example graph are:

- $S_{\text{pa}}(1, 3) = 6 \times 4 = 24$
- $S_{\text{pa}}(1, 6) = S_{\text{pa}}(1, 9) = 12$
- $S_{\text{pa}}(3, 7) = S_{\text{pa}}(3, 8) = S_{\text{pa}}(3, 9) = S_{\text{pa}}(3, 10) = 8$
- $S_{\text{pa}}(2, 4) = S_{\text{pa}}(2, 5) = S_{\text{pa}}(4, 5) = S_{\text{pa}}(2, 6) = 4.$
- $S_{\text{pa}}(2, 7) = S_{\text{pa}}(2, 8) = S_{\text{pa}}(2, 9) = S_{\text{pa}}(2, 10) = 4$
- $S_{\text{pa}}(4, 6) = S_{\text{pa}}(4, 7) = S_{\text{pa}}(4, 8) = S_{\text{pa}}(4, 9) = S_{\text{pa}}(4, 10) = 4$
- $S_{\text{pa}}(5, 6) = S_{\text{pa}}(5, 7) = S_{\text{pa}}(5, 8) = S_{\text{pa}}(5, 9) = S_{\text{pa}}(5, 10) = 4$
- $S_{\text{pa}}(6, 8) = S_{\text{pa}}(6, 9) = S_{\text{pa}}(6, 10) = 4$
- $S_{\text{pa}}(7, 8) = S_{\text{pa}}(7, 9) = S_{\text{pa}}(7, 10) = S_{\text{pa}}(8, 10) = 4$

So, the link $(1, 3)$ has the largest similarity value; this is followed by $(1, 6)$ and $(1, 9)$. Also note that this function considers possible links between every pair of nodes that are not linked currently.

2. **Common Neighbors:** The similarity $S_{\text{cn}}(X, Y)$ is

$$S_{\text{cn}}(X, Y) = |N(X) \cap N(Y)|.$$

This captures the notion that two people will become friends if they share a large number of friends or they have a large number of common friends. Note that for the missing links (currently unconnected nodes) in the example graph

- $S_{\text{cn}}(1, 3) = |\{2, 4, 5\}| = 3$
- $S_{\text{cn}}(1, 9) = S_{\text{cn}}(2, 4) = S_{\text{cn}}(2, 5) = S_{\text{cn}}(4, 5) = S_{\text{cn}}(8, 10) = 2$
- $S_{\text{cn}}(1, 6) = S_{\text{cn}}(2, 6) = S_{\text{cn}}(2, 7) = S_{\text{cn}}(2, 8) = S_{\text{cn}}(2, 10) = S_{\text{cn}}(3, 7) = 1$

- $S_{cn}(5,8) = S_{cn}(5,10) = S_{cn}(4,6) = S_{cn}(4,7) = S_{cn}(4,8) = S_{cn}(4,10) = 1$
- $S_{cn}(5,6) = S_{cn}(5,7) = S_{cn}(5,8) = S_{cn}(5,10) = S_{cn}(7,8) = S_{cn}(7,10) = 1$

Observe that the node pairs with zero similarity value are not shown; for example, $S_{cn}(6,8) = 0$. Based on these similarity values, we can make out that the pair of nodes 1 and 3 has the largest similarity value of 3; this is followed by pairs $(1,9)$, $(2,4)$, $(2,5)$, $(2,8)$, $(2,10)$, and so on. Here, the link $(1,9)$ has a larger similarity value compared to the link $(1,6)$. Note that the similarity function is symmetric because the graph is undirected.

3. **Jaccard's Coefficient:** The similarity function S_{jc} may be viewed as a normalized version of S_{cn}. Specifically, $S_{jc}(X,Y)$ is given by

$$S_{jc}(X,Y) = \frac{|N(X) \cap N(Y)|}{|N(X) \cup N(Y)|} = \frac{S_{cn}(X,Y)}{|N(X) \cup N(Y)|}.$$

So, this similarity function gives importance to those pairs of nodes with smaller degree. If two pairs (X_1, Y_1) and (X_2, Y_2) have the same number of common neighbors but if $|N(X_1) \cup N(Y_1)| < |N(X_2) \cup N(Y_2)|$ then the pair (X_1, Y_1) has larger similarity than the pair (X_2, Y_2). Note that the scores for the missing links in the example graph are:

- $S_{jc}(8,10) = S_{jc}(2,5) = S_{jc}(2,4) = S_{jc}(4,5) = \frac{2}{2} = 1$
- $S_{jc}(1,3) = \frac{|\{2,4,5\}|}{|\{2,4,5,6,7,8,10\}|} = \frac{3}{6} = 0.5$
- $S_{jc}(1,9) = S_{jc}(2,6) = S_{jc}(2,7) = S_{jc}(2,8) = S_{jc}(2,10) = \frac{1}{3}$
- $S_{jc}(4,6) = S_{jc}(4,7) = S_{jc}(4,8) = S_{jc}(4,10) = S_{jc}(5,6) = \frac{1}{3}$
- $S_{jc}(5,7) = S_{jc}(5,8) = S_{jc}(5,10) = S_{jc}(7,10) = S_{jc}(7,8) = \frac{1}{3}$
- $S_{jc}(3,7) = \frac{1}{5}$
- $S_{jc}(1,6) = \frac{1}{7}$

Note that unlike the common neighbors function which ranks the link $(1, 3)$ above the others the Jaccard coefficient ranks the links $(2, 4)$, $(2, 5)$, $(4, 5)$, $(8, 10)$ (with similarity 1) above the pair $(1, 3)$ (similarity value is 0.5). Also links between 1 and 9 and 1 and 6 have lesser similarity values.

4. **Adamic–Adar:** This similarity function S_{aa} may be viewed as a weighted version of the common neighbors similarity function. It gives less importance to high degree common neighbors and more importance to low degree common neighbors. The similarity function is given by

$$S_{aa}(X, Y) = \sum_{z \in N(X) \cap N(Y)} \frac{1}{\log |N(z)|}.$$

For the given example graph, the similarity values are:

- $S_{aa}(1, 3) = \frac{1}{\log 2} + \frac{1}{\log 2} + \frac{1}{\log 2} = \frac{3}{0.3} = 10$
- $S_{aa}(1, 6) = 3.3$; $S_{aa}(1, 9) = 6.6$
- $S_{aa}(2, 4) = S_{aa}(2, 5) = S_{aa}(4, 5) = 2.9$; $S_{aa}(2, 6) = 1.65$
- $S_{aa}(2, 7) = S_{aa}(2, 8) = S_{aa}(2, 10) = 1.29$
- $S_{aa}(3, 7) = 3.3$; $S_{aa}(4, 6) = S_{aa}(5, 6) = 1.65$
- $S_{aa}(4, 7) = S_{aa}(4, 8) = S_{aa}(4, 10) = S_{aa}(5, 7) = 1.29$
- $S_{aa}(5, 8) = S_{aa}(5, 10) = S_{aa}(7, 8) = S_{aa}(7, 10) = 1.29$
- $S_{aa}(8, 10) = 4.59$

Note that $S_{cn}(1, 9) = S_{cn}(2, 4) = 2$ whereas $S_{aa}(1, 9) = 6.6$ and $S_{aa}(2, 4) = 2.9$. Also the similarity between 1 and 6 is 3.3. So, the similarity functions can differ; different similarity functions can give rise to different ranks.

5. **Resource Allocation Index:** This also is a weighted version of the common neighbors function; here the contribution of a common neighbor is the reciprocal of its degree. The function is

$$S_{ra}(X, Y) = \sum_{z \in N(X) \cap N(Y)} \frac{1}{|N(z)|}.$$

The similarity values of links in the example graph are:

- $S_{ra}(1,3) = \frac{1}{2} + \frac{1}{2} + \frac{1}{2} = \frac{3}{2} = 1.5$
- $S_{ra}(1,6) = 0.5$; $S_{ra}(1,9) = 1$
- $S_{ra}(2,4) = S_{ra}(2,5) = S_{ra}(4,5) = \frac{5}{12}$; $S_{ra}(2,6) = 0.25$
- $S_{ra}(2,7) = S_{ra}(2,8) = S_{ra}(2,10) = 0.17$
- $S_{ra}(3,7) = 0.5$; $S_{ra}(4,6) = S_{ra}(5,6) = 0.25$
- $S_{ra}(4,7) = S_{ra}(4,8) = S_{ra}(4,10) = S_{ra}(5,7) = 0.17$
- $S_{ra}(5,8) = S_{ra}(5,10) = S_{ra}(7,8) = S_{ra}(7,10) = 0.17$
- $S_{ra}(8,10) = 0.67$

Observe that the ranking is similar to that provided by the Adamic–Adar function in this example; the major difference is that the weights come from a larger range in the case of Adamic–Adar compared to that of Resource Allocation Index as the denominators corresponding to each common neighbor are smaller as they are compressed logarithmically in the case S_{aa}.

4.1.2. *Distance functions*

One may use some kind of distance/dissimilarity between nodes X and Y to explore the possibility of having a link between them. Based on the pair of nodes being considered it may be required to consider several nodes in the network to compute the distance; so these distance functions may be characterized as looking for some global dissimilarity. Also it is not uncommon to convert the distance values to the corresponding similarity values and use the similarity values. Larger the distance between the two nodes X and Y smaller the similarity $S(X,Y)$ and *vice versa*. Some of the distance functions that are popular are:

1. **Graph Distance:** Here the distance is the length of the shortest path between the two nodes; typically the negated value of the distance is used to characterize the similarity. Specifically,

$$S_{gd}(X,Y) = -\text{length of the shortest path}(X,Y).$$

The similarity values between some of the unconnected links in the example graph are:

- $S_{gd}(1,3) = S_{gd}(1,6) = S_{gd}(1,9) = -2$
- $S_{gd}(2,9) = S_{gd}(3,8) = S_{gd}(4,9) = S_{gd}(5,9) = -3$
- $S_{gd}(3,9) = S_{gd}(6,9) = -4$

Note that in this case all the three links $(1,3), (1,6), (1,9)$ are equally ranked unlike any of the other functions.

2. **Katz Similarity:** It accumulates all the paths of the same length between the two nodes and weighs appropriately the number of such paths to get the distance. Specifically, it is

$$S_{kd}(X,Y) = -\sum_{l=1}^{\infty} \beta^l \cdot |path_{X,Y}^{(l)}|,$$

where $path_{X,Y}^{(l)}$ is the set of all paths of length l between X and Y. The similarity for some of the pairs in the example graph are:

- $S_{ks}(1,3) = 2\beta^2 + \beta^3 = 0.02 + 0.001 = 0.021$
- $S_{ks}(1,9) = 2\beta^2 = 0.02$
- $S_{ks}(1,6) = \beta^2 + 3\beta^3 = 0.013$
- $S_{ks}(7,8) = \beta^2 + \beta^3 = 0.011$

Note that the similarity values are computed using a value of 0.1 for β; the similarity between 1 and 6 is different from that between 1 and 9.

3. **SimRank:** It may be viewed as a recursive version of simple similarity. It is given by

$$S_{sr}(X,Y) = \frac{\sum_{P \in N(X)} \sum_{Q \in N(Y)} S_{sr}(P,Q)}{|N(X)| \cdot |N(Y)|}.$$

5. Information Diffusion

Any information communicated in a social network spreads in the network. The study of how this information gets disseminated in the network is called information diffusion. The shape of the network is influenced by the way the information diffusion occurs. It is necessary to model the process of information diffusion. The movement of information from one individual to another, from one location to another, from one node in the network to another either in the same community or another community is called information diffusion or information propagation. Information diffusion helps in several areas such as marketing, security, search etc. In marketing, for example, it is useful to know in what way to advertise a product so as to have better information diffusion. In security, criminal investigators need to understand how and where the criminal information is spreading in a community. It can thus be seen that we need to answer questions such as what type of information or topics are popular and diffuse the most, which are the paths through which the diffusion is taking place and will take place in the future and which are the users of the social network who play important roles in the diffusion. It is necessary to predict the temporal dynamics of information diffusion.

In information diffusion, a **closed world assumption** is made which means that the information only propagates from node to node along the edges in the network and nodes are not influenced by external sources. This is not always true. Though most of the influence is from internal nodes, there is some influence by external nodes. Another assumption generally made is that the diffusion processes are independent. However, this may not be true and there is a model proposed where different diffusion processes interact with each other. The emphasis of information diffusion can be such that it is sender-centric or receiver-centric.

In diffusion, the **activation sequence** gives an ordered set of nodes which gives the order in which the nodes of the network adopt a piece of information. A **spreading cascade** is a directed tree with the first node of the activation sequence as the root. The tree shows the influence between nodes and captures the same order as the activation sequence.

5.1. Graph-based approaches

In the graph-based approach the topology of the process in a graph structure is used. The two models are (i) Independent Cascades (IC) and (ii) linear threshold (LT). Both these models are synchronous along the time-axis. IC is sender-centric whereas LT is receiver-centric.

5.1.1. *Independent cascade model*

In IC a directed graph is used where each node is either activated (or informed) or not. Monotonicity is assumed which means that activated nodes cannot be deactivated. Each edge in the graph is associated with a diffusion probability. The diffusion process proceeds along a discrete time-axis. In each iteration, the nodes which are newly activated try to activate their neighbors with the diffusion probability defined on the edge. The activations made are effective at the next iteration. This process is continued till there are no new nodes which can be activated.

5.1.2. *Linear threshold model*

In LT also a directed graph is used where the nodes are either activated or not. Each edge has an influence degree defined and a influence threshold for each node. At each iteration, inactive nodes are activated by their active neighbors if the sum of the influence degrees is higher than its influence threshold. The new activations are considered from the next iteration. When no new activations are possible, the process ends.

Both IC and LT proceed in a synchronous manner which is not true in a social network. Asynchronous versions of IC and LT are AsIC and AsLT; they use a continuous time line and use a time-delay parameter for each edge.

5.2. Non-graph approaches

5.2.1. *SIR and SIS*

In non-graph approaches there are two models called SIR and SIS where S stands for "susceptible", I stands for "infected" and R stands for "recovered". Nodes in S class move to I class with a fixed probability β. Then in SIS, nodes in I class move to S class with a fixed probability γ and in the case of SIR, they switch permanently to the R class. Connections are made at random as every node as the same probability to be connected to another node.

5.2.2. *Using influence of nodes*

Another approach uses the influence of nodes to control the diffusion. A time series is used to describe the rate of diffusion of a piece of information. The volume of nodes that adopt the information over time is measured. A linear influence model (LIM) is developed. The influence functions are non-parametric and a non-negative least squares problem is solved using reflective newton method to find the value of the functions.

5.2.3. *Using partial differential equation (PDE)*

The diffusion of a piece of information in the network by a node can also be modeled using a PDE. A logistic equation is used to model the density of influenced users at a given distance from the source and at a given time. The parameters of the model are estimated using the Cubic Spline Interpolation method.

Another approach is the time-based asynchronous independent cascades (T-BAsIC) model. The parameters of this model are not fixed values but functions which depend on time.

5.2.4. *A predictive model*

A predictive model for temporal dynamics of information diffusion, considers the following three types of attributes for calculating diffusion probability: (i) semantics, (ii) social and (iii) time. The propagation is modeled as an asynchronous process like the asynchronous independent cascades (AsIC). The attributes given above are used to define the diffusion probability on each edge of the graph.

The social attributes are activity (Ac), Homogeneity (H), ratio of directed tweets for each user, whether the user has had active interactions in the past, and the mention rate of the users.

The activity is the average amount of tweets emitted per hour which varies from 0 to 1. For a user u, it is given by

$$Ac(u) = \begin{cases} \dfrac{V_u}{\epsilon} & \text{if } V_u < \epsilon \\ 1 & \text{Otherwise} \end{cases},$$

where V_u is the volume of tweets of user u and $\epsilon = 30.4 \times 24$.

The Homogeneity of two users u_1 and u_2 is the overlap in the users with whom the pair of users interact with. It is given by

$$H(u_1, u_2) = \frac{|V_{u1} \bigcap V_{u2}|}{|V_{u1} \bigcup V_{u2}|}.$$

The ratio of directed tweets $T(u)$ of a user u is computed as:

$$T(u) = \begin{cases} \dfrac{|D_u|}{|V_u|} & \text{if } |V_u| > 0 \\ 0 & \text{Otherwise} \end{cases},$$

where D_u is the directed tweets including the retweets.

Between pairs of users a boolean relationship exists ($F(u1, u2)$) which shows if they have had active interaction in the past. This shows if they are "friends" of each other. It is determined by using the following equation:

$$F(u1, u2) = \begin{cases} 1 & \text{if } u2 \varepsilon V_{u1} \\ 0 & \text{Otherwise} \end{cases}.$$

The mention rate of a user u is $R(u)$ and is the volume of directed tweets received by her. It is given by

$$R(u) = \begin{cases} \dfrac{|V^u|}{k} & \text{if } |V^u| < k \\ 1 & \text{Otherwise} \end{cases}.$$

The semantic attribute $S(u, i)$ states whether a particular user u has tweeted about a topic c_i in the past and is given by:

$$S(u, i) = \begin{cases} 1 & \text{if } c_i \varepsilon K_u \\ 0 & \text{Otherwise} \end{cases},$$

where K_u is the set of keywords in the messages of u.

The temporal attribute looks at the activity of the user at different times of the day. A receptivity function $F(u, t)$ for a user u considers an interval of time $[t_1 : t_2]$ which is a 4 hour interval. This is because the day is divided into 6 intervals of 4 hours each. So $t_1 < t < t_2$. The receptivity will be:

$$P(u, t) = \frac{|V_u^t|}{|V_u|},$$

where V_u is the messages of user u and V_u^t gives the messages of user u during time t.

For every pair of nodes u and v, the above parameters are used to find 13 features. These features are $Ac(u)$, $Ac(v)$, $S(u, i)$, $S(v, i)$, $F(u, v)$, $F(v, u)$, $R(u)$, $R(v)$, $T(u)$, $T(v)$, $P(u, t)$, $P(v, t)$ and $H(u, v)$. For a month, the data of the social network is used and according to the spreading cascades available, each link with its 13 features is classified as "diffusion" or "non-diffusion". This data is then used to predict the diffusion for the next month.

5.2.5. *Using core index*

In a diffusion process, it is also critical to find the **most influential spreaders** in a network. There are a number of ways of finding the most important users in a network. However, many a time the best spreaders are not necessarily the most important users in a network. The most efficient spreaders are those located within the core of the network. A core index is assigned to each node in the network. Those nodes which have the lowest values are located at the periphery of the network and the nodes with the highest values are located in the center of the network. These nodes form the core of the network.

6. Identifying Specific Nodes in a Social Network

It is essential to identify central or important nodes in a network. It maybe necessary to find the influential users in a network. The influence measure can be used for doing this. One way of doing this is to say that the influence of a node is the number of in-network votes his posts generate. An influence model needs to be used here. The network is a graph $G(V, E)$ where there are n nodes and m edges. There is an edge between two nodes i and j, if actor i is linked to actor j. It can also be a weighted graph where the edges have a weight which reflects the strength of the link. Centrality measures help to find the important nodes. Some of the centrality measures include Closeness Centrality, Graph Centrality and Betweenness Centrality. These measures depend on network flow.

- **Closeness Centrality**

  Closeness centrality of a node i is the inverse of the shortest total distance from i to every connected node j. It can be written as:

  $$C_c(i) = \frac{1}{\sum_{j=1}^{n} d_{ij}},$$

  where d_{ij} gives the distance between nodes i and j. In case the network is not strongly connected, the closeness centrality depends also on the number of nodes, R_i, reachable from i. It can be written as:

  $$C_c(i) = \frac{\frac{R_i}{n-1}}{\frac{\sum_{j=1}^{n} d(i,j)}{R_i}}.$$

- **Graph Centrality**

  For this measure, it is necessary to find the node k which is far away in terms of distance from the node i. Graph centrality is the inverse of the distance from i to k. It can be written as

  $$C_g(i) = \frac{1}{max_{j \in V(i)} \, d(i,j)},$$

  where $V(i)$ is the set of nodes reachable from i.

- **Betweenness Centrality**

  Considering all paths between pairs of nodes in the graph G, betweenness centrality counts the number of times the path crosses the node i. It can be written as

  $$C_b(i) = \sum_{i \neq j \neq k} \frac{N_{jk}(i)}{N_{jk}},$$

  where N_{jk} is the number of paths between j and k and $N_{jk}(i)$ gives the number of shortest paths between j and k passing through i.

- **Page rank Centrality**

  The Page rank is given by

  $$C_{\mathrm{pr}}(i) = (1 - \alpha) + \alpha \sum_{j \varepsilon out(i)} \frac{C_{\mathrm{pr}}(j)}{outdeg_j}$$

  where α is the damping factor and $out(i)$ gives the out incident nodes of i. In matrix form, this can be written as

  $$C_{\mathrm{pr}} = (1 - \alpha)e + \alpha C_{\mathrm{pr}}P,$$

  where e is the $(1 \times n)$ unit vector, C_{pr} is the $(1 \times n)$ Page Rank vector and P is the $(n \times n)$ transition matrix.

- **Degree Centrality**

  This measure uses the topology of the graph. The in-degree centrality of a node i is the in-degree of node i and can be written as

  $$C_d(i) = \mathrm{indeg}_i.$$

  Similarly, the out-degree centrality of a node i is the out-degree of the node i and can be written as

  $$C_d(i) = \mathrm{outdeg}_i.$$

- **α-Centrality**

  This is a path-based measure of centrality. It can be defined as

  $$C_\alpha = v \left(\sum_{t=0}^{k \to \infty} \alpha^t A^t \right).$$

This converges only if $\alpha < \frac{1}{|\lambda_1|}$. In this method, α is called the attenuation factor.

- **Katz Score**

The α-Centrality when $v = \alpha e A$ yielding:

$$C_{\text{katz}} = \alpha \epsilon A (1 - \alpha A)^{-1}.$$

So far we have considered analysis of social networks based only on their link structure. It is possible to exploit the content associated with the nodes in the network also to understand its behavior better. Typically, content is analyzed using *Topic Models* which we discuss next.

7. Topic Models

Topic modeling is a method used to analyze large documents. A topic is a probability distribution over a collection of words and a topic model is a statistical relationship between a group of observed and unknown(latent) random variables which specifies a generative model for generating the topics. Generative models for documents are used to model topic-based content representation. Each document is modeled as a mixture of probabilistic topics.

7.1. Probabilistic latent semantic analysis (pLSA)

In pLSA, the latent or hidden variables which are the topics and are associated with the observed variables such as documents and words.

For any document, a document-term matrix can be formed which is also called the co-occurrence matrix. This co-occurrence matrix can be used to extract the topics occurring in the document.

Consider N documents $d = \{d_1, \ldots, d_N\}$ consisting of M words $w = \{w_1, \ldots, w_M\}$. The latent variables are the K topics $z = \{z_1, \ldots, z_K\}$.

A generative process is carried out for the documents as follows:

1. Select a document d_j with probability $P(d)$.
2. For each word w_i in the document d_j:

(a) Select a topic z_i from a multinomial conditioned on the given document with probability $P(z|d_j)$.
(b) Select a word w_i from a multinomial conditioned on the topic chosen in the previous step with probability $P(w|z_i)$.

The model can be specified as

$$P(d, w) = P(d)P(w|d).$$

Considering the set of topics

$$P(w|d) = \sum_{z \varepsilon Z} P(w, z|d)$$

$$= \sum_{z \varepsilon Z} P(w|d, z)P(z|d).$$

Due to conditional independence $P(w|d, z) = P(w|z)$ and we get

$$P(w|d) = \sum_{z \varepsilon Z} P(w|z)P(z|d).$$

Then

$$P(w, d) = \sum_{z \varepsilon Z} P(z)P(d|z)P(w|z).$$

Since the predictive model of the pLSA mixture model is $P(w|d)$, the objective function of the maximization is given by

$$\prod_{d,w} P(w|d) = \prod_{d \varepsilon D} \prod_{w \varepsilon W} P(w|d)^{n(d,w)}.$$

Using Expectation-Maximization (EM) algorithm, we find the log-likelihood as

$$\sum_{d \varepsilon D} \sum_{w \varepsilon W} n(d, w) \cdot \log \sum_{z \varepsilon Z} P(w|z)P(z|d).$$

It is also possible to take the document-word matrix or the co-occurrence matrix which is a sparse matrix and split it into three matrices. The document-word matrix A can be written as:

$$A = L \cdot U \cdot R.$$

Here, L and R are low ranked matrices and U is a diagonal matrix. The first matrix contains the document probabilities $P(d|z)$, the second diagonal matrix U contains the prior probabilities of the topics $P(z)$ and the third matrix R contains the word probabilities $P(w|z)$.

7.2. Latent dirichlet allocation (LDA)

Consider a dataset with a number of documents D where each document has T topics each being a multinomial containing K elements where each element is a term in the corpus. The LDA generative process randomly chooses a distribution over topics for each document, for every word in the document one of the T topics is drawn probabilistically from the distribution over topics and one of the K words is drawn probabilistically. The process is given below:

1. For each document
   (a) Draw a topic distribution, $\theta_d \sim \text{Dir}(\alpha)$ which is drawn from a uniform Dirichlet distribution with scaling parameter α.
   (b) For each word in the document
       i. Draw a specific topic $z_{d,n} \sim \text{multi}(\theta_d)$ which is a multinomial.
       ii. Draw a word $w_{d,n} \sim \beta_{z_{d,n}}$

The posterior distribution of the latent variable in a document is

$$p(\theta, z|w, \alpha, \beta) = \frac{p(\theta, z, w|\alpha, \beta)}{p(w|\alpha, \beta)}, \tag{4}$$

where w represents a word and w represents a document of N words. i.e. $w = (w_1, w_2, \ldots, w_N)$.

$\alpha = (\alpha_1, \alpha_2, \ldots, \alpha_N)$ where α is the Dirichlet distribution parameter. z is a vector of topics.

Taking the right hand side of Eq. (4), the numerator can be written as

$$p(\theta, z, w | \alpha, \beta) = \left(\frac{\Gamma(\sum_{i=1}^{k} \alpha_i)}{\prod_{i=1}^{k} \Gamma(\alpha_i)} \prod_{i=1}^{k} \theta_i^{\alpha_i - 1} \right) \prod_{n=1}^{N} \prod_{i=1}^{k} \prod_{j=1}^{V} (\theta_i \beta_{i,j})^{w_n^j z_n^i}.$$

(5)

The denominator is

$$p(w | \alpha, \beta) = \frac{\Gamma\left(\sum_{i=1}^{k} \alpha_i\right)}{\prod_{i=1}^{k} \Gamma(\alpha_i)} \int \left(\prod_{i=1}^{k} \theta_i^{\alpha_i} \right) \left(\prod_{n=1}^{N} \prod_{i=1}^{k} \prod_{j=1}^{V} (\theta_i \beta_{ij})^{w_n^j} \right) d\theta.$$

(6)

A simpler, convex distribution is used to find the lower bound on the log likelihood and are optimized. In Figure 9.7, due to the edges between θ, z and w, the coupling between θ and β makes this inference intractable. By dropping the edges between θ, z and w, we get the simplified model as shown in Figure 9.8. We get a family of distributions for ϕ and γ on the latent variables θ and z.

Using this distribution, the posterior is

$$p(\theta, z | \gamma, \phi) = p(\theta | \gamma) \prod_{n=1}^{N} p(z_n | \phi_n).$$

(7)

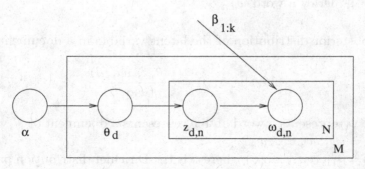

Figure 9.7.   LDA model.

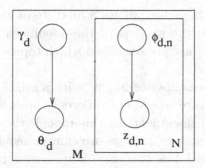

Figure 9.8. Simplified LDA model.

To find the optimal values of γ and ϕ, we need to solve the optimization problem

$$(\gamma*, \phi*) = argmin_{(\gamma,\phi)} D(p(\theta, z|\gamma, \phi) \parallel p(\theta, z|w, \alpha, \beta)). \qquad (8)$$

This is the minimization of the Kullback–Liebler divergence between the variational distribution and the actual posterior distribution. The EM algorithm can be used to estimate β and α.

In the EM algorithm, given a set of observed variables, a set of latent variables and the model parameters, the log probability of the observed data is optimized. In the E-step of the EM algorithm, the log likelihood of the data is found. In the M-step, the lower bound on the log likelihood with respect to α and β is maximized.

The algorithm is as follows:

1. E-step: Find the optimal values of γ_d^* and ϕ_d^* for every document in the corpus. This is used to compute the expectation of the log likelihood of the data.
2. M-step: Maximize the lower bound on the log likelihood of

$$\mathcal{L}(\alpha, \beta) = \sum_{d=1}^{D} \log p(w_d|\alpha, \beta).$$

7.3. Author–topic model

The author–topic model simultaneously models the contents of documents and authors. Each document is represented as a mixture of topics and author modeling allows a mixture of weights for different topics according to the authors of the document. The set of topics that are in a corpus are obtained and which topics are used by which authors is identified.

The model represents documents with a mixture of topics like in LDA and the mixture weights of different topics are determined by the authors of the document. In this model, the contents of documents and the interest of authors are simultaneously modeled.

The LDA model has two sets of unknown parameters — the document distribution and the topic distribution. Also unknown are the latent variables corresponding to the assignment of individual words to topics. For LDA, we get

$$P(z_i = j | w_i = m, z_{-i}, w_{-i}) \alpha \frac{P_{mj} + \beta}{\sum_{m'} P_{m'j} + V\beta} \frac{Q_{dj} + \alpha}{\sum_{j'} Q_{dj'} + T\alpha},$$

where $z_i = j$ represents the assignment of the ith word in the document to topic j, $w_i = m$ represents the fact that the ith word is the mth word in the lexicon, z_{-i} represents all topics not including the ith word. P_{mj} is the number of times word m is assigned to topic j, not including the current instance and Q_{dj} is the number of times topic j has occurred in document d, not including the current instance.

$$\phi_{mj} = \frac{P_{mj} + \beta}{\sum_{m'} P_{m'j} + V\beta},$$

$$\theta_{dj} = \frac{Q_{dj} + \alpha}{\sum_{j'} Q_{dj'} + T\alpha},$$

where ϕ_{mj} is the probability of using word m in topic j, and θ_{dj} is the probability of topic j in document d.

In the author–topic model,

$$P(z_i = j, x_i = k | w_i = m, z_{-i}, x_{-i} w_{-i}, a_d)$$

$$\times \alpha \frac{P_{mj} + \beta}{\sum_{m'} P_{m'j} + V\beta} \frac{R_{kj} + \alpha}{\sum_{j'} R_{kj'} + T\alpha},$$

where $z_i = j$ represents the assignment of the ith word in a document to topic j, $x_i = k$ represents the assignment of the ith word to author k, $w_i = m$ represents the fact that the ith word is the mth word in the lexicon, z_{-i}, x_{-i} represents all topics and author assignment not including the ith word. R_{kj} is the number of times author k is assigned to topic j not including the current instance. The random variables ϕ and θ are estimated as:

$$\phi_{mj} = \frac{P_{mj} + \beta}{\sum_{m'} P_{m'j} + V\beta},$$

$$\theta_{kj} = \frac{R_{kj} + \alpha}{\sum_{j'} R_{kj'} + T\alpha}.$$

Research Ideas

1. The similarity measure SimRank may be viewed as a recursive version of simple similarity. It is given by

$$S_{\text{sr}}(X, Y) = \frac{\displaystyle\sum_{P \in N(X)} \sum_{Q \in N(Y)} S_{\text{sr}}(P, Q)}{|N(X)| \cdot |N(Y)|}.$$

Note that it is a global measure of similarity. How do you justify its need against its computational cost?

Relevant References

(a) G. Jeh and J. Widom, SimRank: A measure of structural-context similarity. *Proceedings of the ACM SIGKDD International Conference* on KDD, July 2002.

(b) D. Liben-Nowell and J. Kleinberg, The link prediction problem for social networks. *Proceedings of CIKM*, 2003.

(c) L. Lu and T. Zhou, Link prediction in complex networks: A survey. *Physica A*, 390:1150–1170, 2011.

(d) M. A. Hasan and M. J. Zaki, A survey of link prediction in social networks. *Social Network Data Analysis*:243–275, 2011.

2. It was observed that Adamic–Adar and Resource Allocation Index are found to perform better among the local similarity measures. Why?

Relevant References

(a) L. Adamic, and E. Adar, Friends and neighbours on the web. *Journal of Social Networks*, 25:211–230, 2003.

(b) T. Zhou, L. Lu, and Y.-C. Zhang, Predicting missing links via local information. *Journal of European Physics B*, 71:623–630, 2009.

(c) Z. Liu, W. Dong and Y. Fu, Local degree blocking model for missing link prediction in complex networks, arXiv:1406.2203 [accessed on 29 October 2014].

(d) N. Rosenfeld, O. Meshi, D. Tarlow and A. Globerson, Learning structured models with the AUC loss and its generalizations. *Proceedings of AISTATS*, 2014.

3. What is the relevance of the power-law degree distribution in link prediction?

Relevant References

(a) Y. Dong, J. Tang, S. Wu, J. Tian, N. V. Chawla, J. Rao and H. Cao, Link prediction and recommendation across heterogeneous social networks. *Proceedings of ICDM*, 2012.

(b) S. Virinchi and P. Mitra, Similarity measures for link prediction using power law degree distribution. *Proceedings of ICONIP*, 2013.

4. How can one exploit community detection in link prediction?

Relevant References

(a) S. Soundararajan and J. E. Hopcroft, Using community information to improve the precision of link prediction methods. *Proceedings of WWW* (Companion Volume), 2012.

(b) B. Yan and S. Gregory, Detecting community structure in networks using edge prediction methods, *Journal of Statistical Mechanics: Theory and Experiment*, P09008, 2012.

5. In link prediction we deal with adding links to the existing network. However, in a dynamically changing network it makes sense to delete some of the links. How to handle such deletions?

Relevant References

(a) J. Preusse, J. Kunegis, M. Thimm, S. Staab and T. Gottron, Structural dynamics of knowledge networks. *Proceedings of ICWSM*, 2013.

(b) K. Hu, J. Xiang, W. Yang, X. Xu and Y. Tang, Link prediction in complex networks by multi degree preferential-attachment indices, CoRR abs/1211.1790 [accessed on 29 October 2014].

6. How can we link the Modularity of the network with spectral clustering?

Relevant References

(a) M. E. J. Newman, Community detection and graph partitioning. CoRR abs/1305.4974 [accessed on 29 October 2014].

(b) M. W. Mahoney, Community structure in large social and information networks. *Workshop on Algorithms for Modern Massive Data Sets* (MMDS), 2008.

(c) U. von Luxburg, A tutorial on spectral clustering. *Statistics and Computing*, 17(4):395–416, 2007.

(d) S. White and P. Smyth, A spectral clustering approach to finding communities in graph. *SDM*, 5:76–84, 2005.

(e) M. E. J. Newman and M. Girvan, Finding and evaluating community structure in networks. *Physical Review E*, 69(2):56–68, 2004.

7. Can we use the Modularity matrix to design better classifiers?

Relevant References

(a) P. Schuetz and A. Caflisch, Efficient modularity optimization: Multi-step greedy algorithm and vertex mover refinement. CoRR abs/0712.1163, 2007.

(b) P. Schuetz and A. Caflisch, Multi-step greedy algorithm identifies community structure in real-world and computer-generated networks. CoRR abs/0809.4398, 2008.

8. How does diffusion help in community detection?

Relevant References

(a) A. Guille, H. Hacid and C. Favre, Predicting the temporal dynamics of information diffusion in social networks. *Social and Information Networks*, 2013.

(b) F. Wang, H. Wang and K. Xu, Diffusive logistic model towards predicting information diffusion in online social networks. *ICDCS' Workshops*, pp. 133–139, 2012.

(c) K. Saito, M. Kimura, K. Ohara and H. Motoda, Selecting information diffusion models over social networks for behavioral analysis. *PKDD '10*, 2010.

(d) A. Guille and H. Hacid, A predictive model for the temporal dynamics of information diffusion in online social networks. *WWW 2012*, 2012.

(e) J. Yang and J. Leskovec, Modeling information diffusion in implicit networks. *ICDM '10*, pp. 599–608, 2010.

9. Most of the community detection methods are computationally expensive. How do we realize scalable versions?

Relevant References

(a) V. D. Blondel, J.-L. Guillaume, R. Lambiotte and E. Lefebvre, Fast unfolding of communities in large networks. *Journal of Statistical Mechanics*, 10:P10008, 2008.

(b) K. Wakita and T. Tsurumi, Finding community structure in mega-scale social networks, eprint arXiv:cs/070248, 2007.

(c) L. Danon, A. Diaz-Guilera and A. Arenas, The effect of size heterogeneity on community identification in complex networks. *Journal of Statistical Mechanics*, P11010, 2006.

(d) P. Pons and M. Latapy, Computing communities in large networks using random walks. *Computer and Information Sciences*, ISCIS 2005, Springer Berlin Heidelberg, pp. 284–293, 2005.

(e) F. Radicchi, C. Castellano, F. Cecconi, V. Loreto and D. Parisi, Defining and identifying communities in networks. *Proceedings of the National Academy of Science USA*, 101:2658–2663, 2004.

(f) A. Clauset, M. E. J. Newman and C. Moore, Finding community structure in very large networks. *Physical Review E*, 70:066111, 2004.

Index

Printed in the United States
By Bookmasters

Printed in the United States
By Bookmasters